PROJECT MANAGEMENT PROFESSIONAL

PMP® Project Management Professional Study Guide

PROJECT MANAGEMENT PROFESSIONAL

PMP® Project Management Professional Study Guide

Joseph Phillips

McGraw-Hill/Osborne

New York   Chicago   San Francisco   Lisbon   London   Madrid
Mexico City   Milan   New Delhi   San Juan   Seoul   Singapore   Sydney   Toronto

The McGraw·Hill Companies

McGraw-Hill/Osborne
2100 Powell Street, 10th Floor
Emeryville, California 94608
U.S.A.

To arrange bulk purchase discounts for sales promotions, premiums, or fund-raisers, please contact **McGraw-Hill**/Osborne at the above address. For information on translations or book distributors outside the U.S.A., please see the International Contact Information page immediately following the index of this book.

PMP® Project Management Professional Study Guide

234567890 CUS CUS 01987654

Book p/n 0-07-223063-0 and CD p/n 0-07-223064-9
parts of
ISBN 0-07-223062-2

Publisher
Brandon A. Nordin

**Vice President &
Associate Publisher**
Scott Rogers

Editorial Director
Gareth Hancock

Project Editors
Jody McKenzie
Julie M. Smith

Acquisitions Coordinator
Jessica Wilson

Technical Editor
Cyndi Snyder

Copy Editors
Carl Wikander
Mike McGee

Proofreaders
Carol Burbo
Linda Medoff
Paul Medoff

Indexer
Valerie Perry

Composition
Apollo Publishing Services

Series Design
Roberta Steele

Cover Series Design
Peter Grame

This book was composed with Corel VENTURA™ Publisher.

For my son, Kyle

ABOUT THE AUTHOR

Joseph Phillips, PMP, IT Project+, is the Director of Education for Project Seminars, a PMI Registered Education Provider. He has managed and consulted on projects for industries including technical, pharmaceutical, manufacturing, and architectural, among others. Phillips has served as a project management consultant for organizations creating project offices, maturity models, and best practice standardization.

As a leader in adult education, Phillips has taught organizations how to successfully implement project management methodologies, information technology project management, risk management, and other courses. Phillips has taught for Columbia College, University of Chicago, Indiana University, among others. He is a Certified Technical Trainer and has taught over 10,000 professionals. Phillips has contributed as an author or editor to more than 30 books on technology, careers, and project management.

Phillips is a member of the Project Management Institute and is active in local project management chapters. He has spoken on project management, project management certifications, and project methodologies at numerous trade shows, PMI chapter meetings, and employee conferences. When not writing, teaching, or consulting Phillips can be found behind a camera or on the working end of a fly rod. You can contact Phillips through www.projectseminars.com.

ABOUT THE TECHNICAL EDITOR

Cyndi Snyder is s a professional consultant, facilitator, instructor, author and partner in Vista Performance Group. She is an experienced leader in developing strategic and operating plans that have resulted in organizational growth and maturity. Cyndi has 10 years of experience managing a variety of projects from public sector program development to acquisitions and system implementation.

Cyndi has experience in training for the corporate, public sector and academic environment. She currently instructs for UC Irvine, CalTech, and USC. Cyndi also participates in the UC Irvine Project Management Program Advisory Committee. In addition she was a contributor to the Project Management Competency Model was published by the Project Management Institute.

Cyndi is a member of the Project Management Institute and is the Chair of the Chapter Leadership Development and Excellence Committee for 2003 – 2005. She received and award for Outstanding Chapter President of the Year for 2002. Cyndi is a certified Project Management Professional (PMP) and earned her Masters in Business Administration from Pepperdine University.

About LearnKey

LearnKey provides self-paced learning content and multimedia delivery solutions to enhance personal skills and business productivity. LearnKey claims the largest library of rich streaming-media training content that engages learners in dynamic media-rich instruction complete with video clips, audio, full motion graphics, and animated illustrations. LearnKey can be found on the Web at www.LearnKey.com.

CONTENTS AT A GLANCE

CONTENTS

xiii

Part II
PMP Exam Essentials 127

4 Implementing Project Integration Management 129

ACKNOWLEDGMENTS

Books, like projects, are never done alone.

I'd like to thank Cyndi Snyder for keeping me on track and focused on PMP requirements and test-centric ideas. A big thank you goes to Gareth Hancock for his patience, guidance, conversation, and overall support for this book. Thank you to Jody McKenzie and Julie Smith for their keen organizational skills, attention to details, and ability to keep me moving. Mike McGee and Carl Wikander—thank you for tightening my writing, clarifying my thoughts, and helping me to be a better writer. Thanks also to Jessica Wilson, Carol Burbo, Paul and Linda Medoff, and the talented people in the production department for all of their hard work.

Thank you to my friends and colleagues for their encouragement as this book was created: Linda Barron, Brad Bobich, Stacey Beheler, Scot Conrad, Kallie Cremer, Emmett Dulaney, Rick Gordon, Greg Kirkland, Don Kuhnle, Nancy Maragioglio, Deanna Moreland, Heather Rippey, Phil Stuck and my brothers Steve, Mark, Sam, and Ben.

INTRODUCTION

This book is divided into two major sections. The first section, which consists of Chapters 1, 2, and 3, discusses the broad overview of project management and how it pertains to the PMP examination. Section two contains Chapter 4 through 13, which detail each of the nine knowledge areas and the PMP Code of Professional Conduct.

If you are just beginning your PMP quest you should read the first section immediately as it'll help you build a strong foundation for the PMP exam. If you find, however, that you've already a strong foundation in project management and need specific information on the knowledge areas then move onto the second section. PMP candidates that have years of project management experience – move onto the second section.

The book is designed so you can read the chapters in any order you'd like. However, if you examine the Guide to the Project Management Body of Knowledge you'll notice that the order of information presented is the same as the order of information in this book. In other words, you can read a chapter of the PMBOK and then read a more detailed explanation in this book. We're kind of a like a guide to the guide.

Exam Readiness Checklist

Study Guide Coverage	Chapter #
Initiating the Project	
Determine project goals	1, 2, 5
Determine project deliverables	1, 2, 5
Determine process outputs	3
Document project constraints	1, 5
Document project assumptions	1, 2, 11
Define project strategy	1, 4, 5
Identify project performance requirements	1, 4, 5, 7, 8

Exam Readiness Checklist

Study Guide Coverage	Chapter #
Determine resource requirements	5, 6, 7
Define project budget	2, 7, 12
Provide comprehensive project information	5, 10
Planning the Project	
Refine project requirements	3, 4, 5
Create Work Breakdown Structure	1, 2, 4, 6, 7
Develop Resource Management Plan	9, 10
Refine project time and project cost estimates	6, 7
Establish project controls	3, 5, 6, 7, 8
Develop Project Plan	1, 2, 4, 5
Obtain Plan Approval	1, 5, 6, 7, 10
Executing the Project	
Commit project resources	9, 12
Implement Project Plan	1, 2, 3,
Manage project progress	1, 2, 3, 6, 7, 10, 12
Communicate project progress	10
Implement QA	4, 8
Controlling the Project	
Measure project performance	6, 7, 8, 10
Refine project control limits	6, 7, 8, 11
Implement corrective actions	4, 8, 10
Evaluate corrective actions' effectiveness	4, 8, 10
Ensure project plan compliance	5, 8, 10, 11
Reassess project control plans	6, 7, 8, 10
Respond to risk triggers	11
Monitor project activity	2, 3, 4, 5, 6, 7, 8, 9, 10, 11, 12

Exam Readiness Checklist

Study Guide Coverage	Chapter #
Closing the Project	
Confirm formal acceptance of project deliverables	1, 3, 5, 12
Finalize Lessons Learned documentation	1, 3, 5, 10
Facilitate project closure activities	1, 2, 3, 5, 10
Preserve product records and tools	1, 2, 3, 6, 7, 10
Release project resources	9
Professional Responsibility	
Ensure integrity and professionalism	12, 13
Contribute to project management knowledge base	10, 13
Enhance individual competence	9, 13
Manage stakeholder interests	1, 2, 4, 5, 8, 9, 10, 13
Interact with project team and stakeholders	1, 2, 3, 5, 8, 9, 10, 13

Part I

Project Initiation

I

Introducing Project Management

This chapter provides an overview of project management, exploring its five processes—memorize them. These five processes will guide you through the life of a project, and, more importantly, through the PMP examination.

We'll also examine the project framework, general management expertise, and other related areas of project management. The information you'll learn in this chapter will help you succeed in the world of PMP, so let's get started!

Defining What a Project Is—and Is Not

Meet Jane. Jane is a project manager for her organization. Vice presidents, directors, and managers with requests to investigate or to launch potential projects approach her daily—or so it seems to Jane. Just this morning the Sales Manager met with Jane because he wants to implement a new direct mail campaign to all of the customers in the sales database. He wants this direct mail campaign to invite customers to visit the company web site to see the new line of products. Part of the project also requires that the company web site be updated so it's in sync with the mailing. Sounds like a project, but is it really? Could this actually be just a facet of an on-going operation?

Projects vs. Operations

In some organizations, everything is a project. In other organizations, projects are rare exercises in change. There's a fine line between projects and operations, and often these separate entities overlap in function. Consider the following points shared by projects and operations:

- Both involve employees
- Both typically have limited resources: people, money, or both
- Both are hopefully designed, executed, and managed by someone in charge

So what *is* a project—and how do you know if you're managing one? The definitive book from the Project Management Institute, *A Guide to the Project Management Body of Knowledge* (simply referred to as the PMBOK), defines a project as "a temporary endeavor undertaken to create a unique product or service." *Temporary* means that the project, thankfully, has an end date. *Unique* means that the project's end result is different than the results of other functions of the organization.

In your organization, projects may be defined slightly different than here. Some organizations qualify every action as a project.

In the preceding example, Jane has been asked to manage a direct mail campaign to all of the customers in the sales database. Could this be a project? Sure—if this company has never completed a similar task and there are no internal departments that do this type of work as part of their regular activities. Often projects are confused with general business duties: marketing, sales, manufacturing, and so on. The tell-tale sign of a project is that is has an end date and that it's unique from other activities within the organization. Some examples of projects include

- Designing a new product or service
- Converting from one computer application to another
- Building a new warehouse
- Moving from one building to another
- Organizing a political campaign
- Designing and building a new airplane

The end results of projects can result in operations. For example, imagine a company creating a new airplane. This new airplane will be a small personal plane (like one of those bubble cars from *The Jetsons*) that would allow people to fly to different destinations with the same freedom they use in driving their car. The project team will have to design an airplane from scratch that'd be similar to a car so consumers could easily adapt and fly to Sheboygan at a moment's notice. This project, to create a personal plane, is temporary, but not necessarily short term. It may take years to go from concept to completion—but the project does have an end date. A project of this magnitude may require hundreds of prototypes before a working model is ready for the marketplace. In addition, there are countless regulations, safety issues, and quality control issues that must be pacified before completion.

Once the initial plane is designed, built, and approved, the end result of the project is business operations. As the company creates a new vehicle, it would follow through with their design by manufacturing, marketing, selling, supporting, and improving their product. The initial design of the airplane is the project—the business of manufacturing it, supporting sold units, and marketing the product constitutes the ongoing operations part of business.

Operations are the day-to-day work that goes on in the organization. A manufacturer manufactures things, scientists complete research and development, and businesses provide goods and services. Operations are the heart of organizations. Projects, on the other hand, are short-term endeavors that fall outside of the normal day-to-day operations an organization offers.

Once the project is complete, the project team moves along to other projects and activities. The people who are actually building the airplanes on the assembly line, however, have no end date in sight, and will continue to create airplanes as longs as there is a demand for the product.

Progressive Elaboration

All projects begin as a concept. A project concept, to create a new product or service, typically includes a broad vision of what the end result of the project will be. The temporary project results in the unique product or service through progressive elaboration. Progressive elaboration is the incremental design and refinement of the initial concept toward the project plan.

As a project moves closer to completion, the identified needs that launched the project are revisited and monitored. Complete understanding of the needs—and the ability to fulfill those needs—comes from progressive elaboration. Progressive elaboration is an iterative process designed to correctly and completely fulfill the project objectives. This is evident in how the planning and execution processes each contribute to one another. A similar example can be seen in the process to create a Work Breakdown Structure (WBS). The WBS begins with the project vision, which is then elaborated upon to create the project scope, and then expanded again into the WBS, and so on.

Consider a concept to build a new building that would handle the manufacturing and shipping of blue jeans. It would begin broadly, with materials delivered, the assembly equipment, and the outward-bound shipping bays. As the project team continues to research the needs and expectations of the project, the project vision would be refined, honed, and polished to a detailed outline of what the project would deliver. As you can see in Figure 1-1, through incremental steps, the project plan is developed and the unique project deliverables are created.

Defining Project Management

Project management is the supervision and control of the work required to complete the project vision. The project team carries out the work needed to complete the project, while the project manager schedules, monitors, and controls the various

FIGURE 1-1

Progressive
elaboration is
the refinement of
project concept
to project plan.

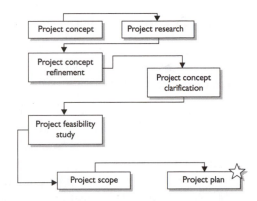

project tasks. Projects, being the temporary and unique things that they are, require the project manager to be actively involved with the project implementation. They are not self-propelled.

Project management is comprised of the following nine knowledge areas. Chapters 4 through 12 will explore the knowledge areas in detail.

- **Project Integration Management**   This knowledge area focuses on project plan develop and execution.

- **Project Scope Management**   This knowledge area deals with the planning, creation, protection, and fulfillment of the project scope.

- **Project Time Management**   Time management is crucial to project success. This knowledge area covers activities, their characteristics, and how they fit into the project schedule.

- **Project Cost Management**   Cost is always a constraint in project management. This knowledge area is concerned with the planning, estimating, budgeting, and control of costs.

- **Project Quality Management**   This knowledge area centers on quality planning, assurance, and control.

- **Project Human Resource Management**   This knowledge area focuses on organizational planning, staff acquisition, and team development.

- **Project Communications Management**   The majority of a project manager's time is spent communicating. This knowledge area details how communications can improve.

- **Project Risk Management**   Every project has risks. This knowledge area focuses on risk planning, analysis, monitoring, and control.

■ **Project Procurement Management** This knowledge area involves planning, solicitation, contract administration, and contract closeout.

Defining the Project Life Cycle

One common attribute of all projects is that they eventually end. Think back to one of your favorite projects. The project started with a desire to change something within an organization. The idea to change this "something" was mulled around, kicked around, and researched until someone with power deemed it a good idea to move forward and implement the project. As the project progressed towards completion there were some very visible phases within the project life. Each phase within the life of the project created a deliverable.

For example, consider a project to build a new warehouse. The construction company has some pretty clear phases within this project: research, blueprints, approvals and permits, breaking ground, laying the foundation, and so on. Each phase, big or small, results in some accomplishment that everyone can look to and say, "Hey! We're making progress!" Eventually the project is completed and the warehouse is put into production.

At the beginning of the project, through planning, research, experience, and expert judgment, the project manager and the project team will plot out when each phase should begin, when it should end, and the related deliverable that will come from each phase. Often, the deliverable of each phase is called a milestone. The milestone is a significant point in the schedule that allows the stakeholders to see how far the project has progressed—and how far the project has to go to reach completion.

Defining the Project Management Process

Will all projects have the same phases? Of course not! A project to create and manufacture a new pharmaceutical will not have the same phases as a project to build a skyscraper. Both projects, however, can map to the five project management processes. These processes are typical of projects, and are iterative in nature—that is, you don't finish a process never to return. Let's take a look at each process and its attributes.

Initiating

This process launches the project, or phase. The needs of the organization are identified and alternative solutions are researched. The power to launch the project or phase is given through a project charter, and when initiating the project, the wonderful project manager is selected.

Planning

Can you guess what this process is all about? The planning process requires the project manager and the project team to develop the various core and subsidiary management plans necessary for project completion. This process is one of the most important pieces of project management.

Executing

This process allows the project team and vendors to move toward completing the work outlined in the Planning process. The project team moves forward with completing the project work.

Controlling

The project manager must control the work the project team and the vendors are completing. The project manager checks that the deliverables of the phases are in alignment with the project scope, defends the scope from changes, and confirms the expected level of quality of the work being performed. This process also requires the project manager to confirm that the cost and schedule are in sync with what was planned. Finally, the project team will inform the project manager of their progress, who will, in turn, report on the project's progress to the project sponsor, to management, and perhaps even to key stakeholders in the organization.

Closing

Ah, the best process of them all. The closing process, sometimes called the project postmortem, involves closing out the project accounts, completing final acceptance of the project deliverables, filing the necessary paperwork, and assigning the project team to new projects. Oh yeah, and celebrating!

Most projects have similar characteristics, such as the following:

They Are Demanding   The stakeholders, the people with a vested interested in the project, are all going to have different expectations, needs, and requests of the project deliverables. No doubt there will be conflict between the stakeholders.

They Have Clear Requirements   Projects should have a clearly defined set of requirements. These requirements will set the bar for the actual product or service created by the project, the quality of the project, and the timeliness of the project's completion.

They Come with Assumptions   Projects also have assumptions. Assumptions are beliefs held to be true, but that haven't been proven. For example, the project may be operating under the assumption that the project team will have access to do the work at any time during the workday, rather than only in the evenings or weekends.

Constraints Are Imposed   Within every project there is a driving force for the project. You've probably experienced some force first-hand. For example, ever had a project that had to be done by an exact date or you'd face fines and fees? This is a schedule constraint. Or a project that could not go over it's set budget? This is a financial constraint. Or what about a project that had to hit an exact level of quality regardless of how long the project took? This is scope constraint. All are forces that tend to be in competition with each other.

Specifically, there are three constraints that a project manager will encounter:

- **Project Scope**   The scope of the project constitutes the parameters of what the project will, and will not, include. As the project progresses, the stakeholders may try to change the project scope to include more requirements than what was originally planned for (commonly called scope creep). Of course, if you change the project scope to include more deliverables, the project will likely need more time and/or money to be completed. We will talk about scope in Chapter 5.

- **Schedule**   This is the expected time when the project will be completed. Realistic schedules don't come easily. You'll learn all about scheduling and estimating time in Chapter 6. As you may have experienced, some projects require a definite end date rather than, or in addition to, a definite budget. For example, imagine a manufacturer creating a new product for a tradeshow. The tradeshow is not going to change the start date of the show just because the manufacturer is running late with their production schedule.

- **Cost**   Budgets, monies, greenbacks, dead presidents, whatever you want to call it—the cost of completing the project is always high on everyone's list of questions. The project manager must find a method to accurately predict the cost of completing the project within a given timeline, and then control the project to stay within the given budget. We will learn more about this in Chapter 7. Sounds easy, right? The following diagram illustrates the Iron Triangle of scope, schedule, and cost constraints.

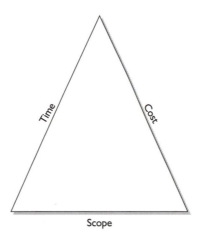

Consider the Project Risk

Do you play golf? In golf, as in project management, there is a theory called *The Risk-Reward Principle*. You're teeing off for the seventh hole. If you shoot straight, you can lay up in the fairway, shoot again, and then two-putt for par. Pretty safe and predictable. However, if you have confidence in your driver, you may choose to cut the waterway and get on the green in one. If you accept and beat that risk, you'll have a nice reward. Choke and land in the water and you're behind the game. In project management, the idea is the same. Some risks are worth taking, while others are worth the extra cost to avoid. You'll learn all about risks in Chapter 11.

Consider the Expected Quality

What good is a project if it is finished on time and on budget, but the quality of the deliverable is so poor it is unusable? Some projects have a set level of quality that allows the project team to aim for. Other projects follow the organization's Quality Assurance Program such as ISO 9000. And, unfortunately, some projects have a general, vague idea of what an acceptable level of quality is. Without a specific target for quality, trouble can ensue. The project manager and project team may spend more time and monies to hit an extremely high level of quality when a lower, expected level of quality would suffice for the project. Quality is needed, but an exact target of expected quality is demanded.

Management by Projects

In today's competitive, tight-margin business world, organizations have to move and respond quickly to opportunity. Many companies have moved from a functional environment—that is, organization by function—to an organization, or management, by projects. A company that organizes itself by job activity, such as sales, accounting, information technology, and other departmental entities is a functional environment. A company that manages itself by projects may be called a projectized company.

An organization that uses projects to move the company forward is using the *Management by Projects* approach. These project-centric entities could manage any level of their work as a project. These organizations, however, apply general business skills to each project to determine their value, efficiency, and, ultimately, their return on investment. As you can imagine, some projects are more valuable, more efficient, or more profitable than others.

There are many examples of organizations that use this approach. Consider any business that completes projects for their clients, such as architectural, graphic design, consulting, or other service industries. These service-oriented businesses typically complete projects as their business.

Here are some other examples of management by projects:

- Training employees for a new application or business method
- Marketing campaigns
- The entire sales cycle from product or service introduction, proposal, and sales close
- Work completed for a client outside of the organization
- Work completed internally for an organization

Building the Project Management Framework

Have you ever watched a house being built? Or built your own home? There's all the pre-building excitement: blueprints, permits, inspectors, approval, contracts, aspirin, and more planning. Finally, the workers come together and build a foundation and the house begins to appear. In the first few months, what do you have? You've nothing more than a skeleton of a house: the frame. If you were to look at other homes, big or small, they'd have a similar launch process—and a similar way of having the house created.

On a project, any project, there are fundamental activities that must happen before the work begins. The rules, management principles, planning, and general guidelines for a project are the project management framework. The project management framework is the skeleton of projects. And, just like a house, even though every project has a general framing, the end results are typically different.

The management of a project, the day-to-day activities, is the bones of successful project management. A project manager must monitor, maintain, and control the work of the project to ensure timeliness, accountability, quality, and success. Just as you wouldn't randomly build a home without plans and a level of control, a project requires a level of detail and management to guarantee completion and acceptability.

The five processes of a project are initiation, planning, execution, control, and closure (known as IPECC; you can remember these by thinking of syrup of ipecac—hopefully without the same unpleasant results.). The five processes interact with one another and allow the project manager, the project sponsor, the project team, and even the stakeholders to witness the progress, success, and, sometimes, failure of a project. These processes are cyclic, iterative, progressively elaborated, and chockablock full of work, documentation, and project manager participation. The following illustration shows the relationship between the five process groups.

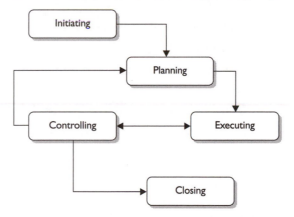

If you were to skim through the PMBOK Guide, you wouldn't see any chapters related directly to the five processes. Instead, you'd find chapters on knowledge areas. The five processes of the project management life cycle (IPECC) are spread across these knowledge areas. This book will cross-reference the five processes with the nine knowledge areas.

The material in the following sections will acquaint you with the knowledge areas.

e x a m
w a t c h

If you want to pass the PMP exam, learn and love the project management knowledge areas. These knowledge areas are the different facets of project management a project manager will work through in each of the processes. Chapters 4 through 12 will detail all of the

facts for each of the knowledge areas. A grid outlining the interaction of the process areas and the knowledge areas is on page 38 of the PMBOK Guide. You should be intimately familiar with this grid, and consider memorizing it to give yourself an edge up on the exam.

Project Integration Management

This knowledge area deals first with creating the official project plan. The project plan details can vary based on the size, impact, and priority of the project. Once the project plan is created, Integration Management ensures the plan is followed. Finally, Integrated Change Control is responsible for managing and controlling changes to the project. Project Integration Management includes

- The creation and approval of the project plan
- Executing the project plan
- Managing, controlling, and documenting changes to the project plan

Case Study: Implementing Project Integration Management

Zings Sweater Company, an international company that sells fancy cotton, silk, and wool sweaters, has hired you as their project manager. Zings Sweater Company uses old-fashioned machinery to create some of the finest and most comfortable sweaters in the world. Their busy manufacturing season is in late summer and again in early winter. They are thrilled to have you on board.

The Vice President of Sales for the Zings Sweater Company has a hot new idea to create a Frequent Customer Program for their clients. His idea is that customers can enroll in the program when purchasing sweaters in their stores, through www.zingsweaters.com, and even through a direct mail campaign. Once customers enroll, they'll receive coupons, discounts, and e-mail announcements about new sweaters.

Lucky you! You've been deemed the project manager of this massive, high-profile project. Through an initial feasibility study, the proposed project answers several business needs and has the potential to boost market share by seven percent.

To create your project, you'll have to complete plenty of research, break down the work into manageable chunks of activities, and rely on Subject Matter Experts (SMEs) from outside vendors and individuals on your recently recruited project team. As you work with your team, you'll have to rely on their findings, expert judgment, and evidence for decisions.

As the plan comes together, you'll document the current state of the company and make predictions about its future. Before any implementation begins, you and management will have to be in agreement regarding project requirements, expectations, and level of quality. Of course, this information will be documented in your project plan. Other inputs to your project plan will include related historical information, information gathered from stakeholders, and knowledge learned from your planning process.

Once your plan has been approved and you've been given the green light, the project team will get to work implementing the plan and working toward completion. You'll monitor and control project tasks through work authorization systems, guidelines set by the official project plan, and inputs from the experts on your project team. As you document the work, you'll report on the project's progress, the level of value, and the project's ability to end on schedule and on budget.

As this project moves forward, your project team may discover faster, better, or safer methods to complete the work than what was originally planned. Any deviation from the project plan will be documented, approved, and then updated (with your final approval) to the project plan—something Zings Sweater Company has not been used to doing.

Project Scope Management

The project scope encompasses all the required work, and only the required work, necessary to complete the project. Work that does not support the needs of the project is considered out of scope. Project Scope Management also includes verifying the work that the project team is completing is in alignment with project requirements. Project Scope Management includes

- ■ Initiating the project
- ■ Planning the project scope
- ■ Defining the exact project scope
- ■ Verifying the project scope
- ■ Controlling project scope

Case Study: Enacting Project Scope Management

Your project with the Zings Sweater Company has a project scope. In this instance, the scope of the work at the highest level is to create a Frequent Customer Program. Through your research, you and your project team will break down this work into a logical plan. Requested work that does not fit within the project scope is out of bounds and should not be completed as part of this project.

For example, Nancy Martin, the Director of Retail Locations, requests that since you'll be creating a few databases of customers you should also create a directory of all of the store employees with their photos, information regarding their favorite sweaters, and other neat facts. While this request may have some merit, it is not in the original scope of the Frequent Customer Program you've been assigned to create. Sorry, Nancy, your request is out of bounds, out of scope, and won't be added onto this project.

During the management of the Frequent Customer Program Project you discover that one of your team members is promising store managers that customers will be able to request custom-tailored sweaters as part of this project. Nope. That feature, while handy, is out of the project scope.

At the end of the project, and often at the end of each project phase, you will walk the project sponsor and key stakeholders through the deliverables you've created. This is scope verification—the activity of proving that what you have promised through the scope is a reality for the customer of the project.

The Vice President of Sales, the sponsor of the Frequent Customer Program Project, needs the database in place as soon as possible. Through the planning process you know several databases will need to be created to store the customer information. Marketing material will have to be developed. There'll be training for the store employees. And there's all the marketing material to write and produce. Also, don't forget the Internet site will have to be updated to support the discounts. You know, as an employee, that there are 220 Zings Sweater stores throughout the world and each will need their point-of-sale software updated either in person or through a remote access solution.

Hmm… Should it be done ASAP? This high-profile project will cost a considerable amount of money, time, and effort in order to obtain the targeted seven-percent increase in market share. Not exactly a project you want to rush through and wreck.

Next, you and your team estimate the amount of time each activity will actually take to complete. As you begin to assign your team tasks and arrange the order of activities, you build a time estimate.

During this process, you discover dependencies that have to be in place for the project to move forward. You map out the work in a logical order and discover there are several possible paths to completion. You must decide which solution has an acceptable amount of risk, as well as how it should be coordinated with business cycles, other projects, and separate business demands, and whether or not it is realistic enough for you and your project team to move forward with it.

Another part of time management is mathematical analysis of possible best- and worse-case scenarios for activity duration. Through this analysis, your project management software, and expert judgment, you will create a project calendar that everyone can live with and work through. As the project progresses, you'll have to monitor the performance and confirm its alignment with what you've predicted. When schedule variances occur, you'll have to follow your Communications Plan to report these variances to management.

Project Cost Management

There are several methods you can use to predict project expenses, depending on the project type. For example, if you've done a similar project, you could rely on your historical information to predict the costs of the current project. Another method you can use is a mathematical formula called parametric modeling. This formula works well with price per unit, like cost per square foot, cost per metric, and so on. In many instances, the proposed project may have widely different costs, and aspects that have never been completed before. In these instances, the project manager will rely on traditional bottom-up estimations. Bottom-up estimations start at zero, with each expense accounted for until a grand total is reached.

In your cost estimate, you will also need to calculate the cost of travel, hardware, and software needed to complete the project. Don't forget to factor in marketing material, training, petty cash, and monies for team rewards like tickets to ball games, movies, and other intermittent incentives.

Once the project moves into implementation, you'll be accountable for the approved budget and will have to keep track of procurements, fees, invoices, and the employees' time. You'll need some accounting software or a few sharp pencils. Just kidding—rely on the accounting software.

Throughout the project, management is going to want to see how things are progressing in dollars and sense. For starters, you'll rely on actual costs against your predicted project baseline. This will only tell you so much. For complex projects, you'll really need some advanced method to see the actual progress in monetary value. For this, you'll use nine different formulas to calculate the value of the project, any cost or schedule variances, and evidence that the project will likely finish on time and on budget. The nine formulas comprise Earned Value Management.

Managing project cost includes

- Planning for resource allocation
- Providing accurate cost estimates
- Creating the project budget
- Using project management cost control techniques
- Proving project financial accountability

Case Study: Enacting Project Cost Management

Your project for Zings Sweater Company is creating lots of excitement. Sales reps, managers, and customer service reps are eager to see the end results. The goal of a seven-percent boost in market share really has upper management excited about your project. But, of course, upper management is also concerned about the cost of the project. While they realize it takes money to make money, their concern is that the project expenses won't outweigh the benefits of the project.

Because Zings Sweater Company has never created a project of this magnitude before, much of your estimates are just that—estimates. Your initial estimate, called "the order of magnitude" estimate, has a range of variance from –25 percent to 75 percent. This initial estimate allows management to see the extremes of the project's likely costs.

As the project progresses, your initial estimate evolves into the budget estimate. This estimate accounts for the project work, vendors, and materials needed to deliver the project. You'll base this estimate on your conversations with the project team, the decomposition of the work into a work breakdown structure, and through proposals and quotes from vendors. This estimate gives management an estimate that is expected to vary no more than –10 percent and up to 25 percent. You've created a very accurate bottom-up estimate that everyone can live with.

To ensure the project stays within the accepted range of variance, you'll need a system to keep track of fees, invoices, travel, and other expenses. Management will need advance warning for capital expenses so they can plan cash flow accordingly.

The cost you assign to the project allows management to calculate the management horizon. *Management horizon* is the point in the future when the project will earn back the original investment and start creating new profits for the organization—a happy day.

Project Quality Management

In any project, there is a demand for quality. Project quality management planning is the process to ensure that the deliverables of the project satisfy its needs. Project quality management includes

- Planning for project quality
- Adhering to quality assurance
- Enforcing set quality control systems

Case Study: Ensuring Quality

You and your project team are very excited about the Frequent Customer Program Project. This project is high profile, will add a new service to your organization, and will help the company grow and become more profitable. The Vice President of Sales, the project sponsor, stops by during the initiating processes of the project to remind you how important this project is. He tells you that the entire company is counting on you and your team to deliver a superior, top-notch solution that is of utmost quality.

Nothing like some more pressure, eh?

You, being the expert project manager you are, have already been giving thoughts to the level of quality this project requires. The customers will use this service on a regular basis, the customer service reps in each of the retail locations will use this service, and all of the sales team will rely on the data from your creation to drive new sales and help the company grow.

As always, you begin with planning. Quality planning requires a look to your company's quality assurance policy or quality program such as ISO 9000 or Six Sigma. These quality methodologies, coupled with the requirements from the project stakeholders, will guide your team through the quality planning process.

With your quality plan in tow, you and your project team follow your company's quality assurance policy and begin implementing the quality plan. Throughout the implementation, you take measurements, respond to the measurements, and make adjustments as needed. For example, a manufacturer may take a sampling of one thousand units and expect no more than three defective units per one thousand. In your project, you have set a benchmark for acceptable levels of quality for the project deliverables.

You implement tools such as control charts and Pareto diagrams to measure quality and isolate reasons for defective results. With your team, you work on improving the results to meet the targeted quality benchmark. As you have planned, and as the project sponsor expects, if work falls below quality, it has to be redone before the project can move forward. No one, especially the project manager, likes to have to redo work since it means lost time and sunk costs. *Sunk costs* are funds already invested in a project regardless of the project's success.

Your project for Zings Sweater Company is progressing. Your team is working under extreme pressure to finish all of the different areas of the project—on time and on budget. You are monitoring the work schedule, costs, disruptions, delays, and are keeping a constant eye on the quality of the work created. Quality management is a knowledge area that spans not only the implementation of the project plan, but all of the project processes.

Project Human Resource Management

Project Human Resource Management is the process of successfully applying the right resource to the project work in the most effective way to accomplish the project goals while maintaining cost and schedule. Project Human Resource Management includes

- Developing a project organizational structure consistent with the organization's own structure
- Fulfilling staff acquisitions
- Developing the project team

Case Study: Applying Project Human Resources

Thankfully, you've been a project manager for years—just not with Zings Sweater Company. However, the level of confidence your company has in you is tremendous. They allow you to make decisions, control the budget, with some approval, and generally give you a fair amount of autonomy on the project. Of course, if the project fails, it's your entire fault. As this experienced project manager, you also have to take on the human resources issues such as bargaining with managers for specific employees, accounting for team members' time, and occasionally disciplining team members.

Your human resource knowledge area will be based on the structure of your company. In some organizations, the project manager has very little power, and all decisions flow through a functional manager. Other companies, like Zings, use a matrix structure which allows project managers some authority. Nevertheless, project managers and project team members still answer to a functional manager. Other entities use a projectized approach where the project manager is the manager and the project team answers directly to the project manager for the duration of the project.

During the planning process, you learn what roles and responsibilities will be required to complete the project. Based on your current team, you learn that several required roles are missing. Now you'll have to work with the project sponsor and functional managers to recruit new team members with the needed talent on the project team. In addition, there are some procurement issues since you've elected to bring in a few consultants and SMEs to join the project team.

With this large project, and equally large project team, there's an immediate need for the team members to get acquainted and learn about each other. You decide to take your team on a team-building outing: a wilderness survival camp. At the outing, the team will learn about each other, learn to work together, and to work towards a common goal.

Another facet of your human resource management plan is training. Many of the team members need their skills upgraded to complete the necessary work. In addition, there will be internal training on the usage of the Frequent Customer Program to ensure the team knows how the software and web site should work.

As the project moves through the implementation stage, you'll meet with the project team to discuss variances, problems, and other issues that may creep into the work. But not everything is bad. You also have created a method for recognizing the completion of work, completion of major milestones, and have set incentives for completing scheduled work on time and on budget.

Project Communications Management

Project managers spend the bulk of their time communicating. Half of communicating is listening. When it comes to project communications management know this: it's all about who needs what and when. We'll discuss communications in detail in Chapter 10. Project communication management includes

- Planning effective communications
- Designing information retrieval systems
- Reporting on the project team and on the project performance
- Following the Communications Management Plan to close out the project

Case Study: Applying Project Communications Management

Your project, the Frequent Customer Program, for Zings Sweater Company is huge and will require much of your time and attention to complete it as planned. A project of this magnitude will require special care for communicating the project progress. Your team, which is non-collocated, will require frequent updates, your sponsor will need weekly status reports, upper management has requested milestone reports, and even retail store managers would like information on the project status.

Your project team, however, is located around the world. Many of the team members speak different languages and, obviously, live in different time zones. You've created a method to allow for communications, timed meetings, and the creation of subteams with designated team leaders. The management of a collocated team requires additional thought and planning. Everything contained in this paragraph is part of communication planning.

You already know, based on past experience, that team meetings, vendor meetings, and status report meetings can eat up entire days of time—a necessary evil. You also know there'll be plenty of informal communications, such as hallway meetings, lunch meetings, and quick phone calls and e-mails. With all of these communication demands on top of the project, how will you be able to hold all of it together?

Ah, yes, the planning process. During the planning process, you'll research and discover the exact communication requirements—based on stakeholder analysis—and then set a schedule to satisfy those communication requirements. Your communications management plan will detail the reports, meetings, and summaries required by this project. And, of course, you'll be allowed to revisit the planning process as needed to update and amend the Communications Management Plan.

Communications, from meetings to memos, will need to be documented through minutes, organization, and consistency. Based on past projects, you've created an information retrieval system that allows qualified team members and stakeholders to search and retrieve information that has been recorded in a database of knowledge. This information retrieval system accomplishes a record of communications, helps you make decisions, and helps conclude the project based on the wealth of knowledge you've collected.

The Vice President of Sales, the project sponsor, drops by your office early in the project to chat. During this conversation, he reminds you that you'll be doing monthly reports on the project and team performance. Several of the project team members will be on this project full time and their managers want some accountability for their employees' time. Now you must update the communications management plan: more communications, more reports, more requirements.

As the project progresses, you'll follow your communications management plan for meetings, written communications, and record keeping. You'll also use several modalities for information distribution: e-mail, an intranet web site, memos, and printed reports are just a few options you've chosen. During the project, you'll also close out each project phase with a Lessons Learned document that you'll use again in the final project closure.

Project Risk Management

Risks are events that can affect a project for good or for bad. Project risk management is the process of identifying, classifying, and weighing the risks to determine their impact on the project should they come into play. Project risk management includes

- Planning for Risk Management
- Identifying risks
- Using qualitative risk analysis
- Using quantitative risk analysis
- Creating project risk response plans
- Actively monitoring and reacting to project risks

Case Study: Enforcing Project Risk Management

Zings Sweater Company requires an extensive analysis of risks within projects that could hinder the success of the project, interrupt business processes, or drive customers away. Your project, the Frequent Customer Program, will require extensive risk analysis as it will affect the way the company does business, the marketing campaigns aimed at frequent customers, and, if all goes well, an increase in market share.

Your reliance on planning requires you and the project team to break down the work into manageable chunks, map out the work from start to finish, and then begin identifying risks that could stop the project from completing. You'll have to discuss your work implementation strategy with key stakeholders to consider other business processes that may coincide with your plan, discuss areas of your plan that could result in loss of sales, and examine the plan for risks that are acceptable, unacceptable, or risks that can be easily neutralized.

Through qualitative risk analysis you will lead your team through risk planning sessions. In these sessions, you'll rank the risks according to probability and impact. Then, once the ranking is complete, you'll calculate an overall project risk score. Finally, you'll create plans for the major risks uncovered. You'll also use historical information for similar projects to look for trends in the risk analysis.

In conjunction with qualitative risk analysis, you'll use a more in-depth approach to study the risks you've discovered: quantitative analysis. In this process, you'll interview stakeholders, experience the work to see the risk impact, and apply tools such as decision trees, simulations, and formulas for the cost of mitigating the identified risks. Sounds like fun, right?

Once you've created the risk response plan you'll apply the plan as needed as the work progresses. With your project team and stakeholders you'll keep a lookout for signs that any identified risks are coming to fruition. In addition, you'll be allowed to revisit the planning process to update your risk management plan as new risks may come to light or old risks are taken out of play.

Through hard work and diligence you'll work with the project team and the project sponsor to ensure that risks are neutralized, documented, and that the risk management plan is updated and executed as needed.

Project Procurement Management

Project procurement management is the process of purchasing goods or services from vendors. Managing project procurement includes

- Planning for project procurement
- Planning for solicitation
- Management Project solicitation
- Selecting vendors
- Managing and creating procurement documents
- Administering and closing project contracts

Case Study: Utilizing Project Procurement Management

Your project, the Frequent Customer Program, has many demands: technology, travel, marketing, training, and more. Based on your initial project plan, there are not enough internal resources to complete the labor. Therefore, you'll be forced to contract vendors to help with the project work. This begins your procurement management.

During your planning process, you'll use make-or-buy analyses to determine what areas of the project must, or should be, outsourced, and then establish requirements for vendors. Zings Sweater Company has a qualified seller list that you'll use to request proposals and proposals for the project work. This vendor solicitation process will require expert judgment, historical information, and most likely input from management, the project team, and even other SMEs to help determine the best price and legal contracts.

Through bidder conferences, vendors will interview you on the project work, the level of quality, and the expected requirements for the work they may be completing. The vendors can then use this information to create estimates, proposals, and bids to complete the project contract.

Once the contracts have been awarded and the vendors go about completing the project work, you'll have to monitor the vendor's performance for quality, results, and schedule control. The vendors will provide their reports regarding the schedule and any variances to keep you abreast of their progress. You and the vendors will work together for the good of the project to ensure the integration of their work and your project team's work.

Finally, the vendors will want to be paid. You'll have contracts, statements of work, and invoices to confirm. You will review and approve invoices based on actual work completed, expedite the payment according to the contract terms, or meet with the vendor to discuss any issues with the invoices. At the end of the project, you will close out any project accounts, confirm that purchase orders have been fulfilled, and that invoices have been, or are being, processed.

INSIDE THE EXAM

The PMP exam is not for rookies. The application process alone can filter out the unqualified and the merely curious. You've purchased this book to find out more information on how to pass the exam, what the exam entails, and to prep for your exam— a wise decision. Now make another wise decision: begin completing your PMP exam application. The application process can be lengthy since you'll have to track down past information relating to projects you've completed.

By starting sooner, rather than later, in completing your exam application, you'll be focusing more on completing your exam studies than completing the exam application. In addition, response time from the Project Management Institute (PMI) to accept and approve your application can vary from a few days to weeks. Start now and you'll be on your way.

You won't see any questions about Zings Sweater Company on the exam. You will, however, be presented with similar scenarios that will test your project management abilities. Specifically, you'll need to know how the project manager works through the project processes. You should be familiar with the project management process groups, what a project deliverable is, and the requirements of a project scope.

Know that the project moves through phases to reach completion. The project manager oversees the project work as it moves through phases, but the project customer must approve the work. Specifically, the results of phases must pass through scope verification. Scope verification is the formal acceptance of the project work.

Adapting Management Expertise

Project management is a complex endeavor. Projects, like the previous example for Zings Sweater Company, have several knowledge areas that are unique to the discipline. Project managers typically need other managerial skills to be successful. Several of the skills you can learn from a book, but most skills come from experience, emulating others, and sheer talent. Let's take a quick look at some of the attributes of a successful project manager.

Communications

It's been said that project managers spend 90 percent of their time communicating.

That's understandable when you consider the meetings, the documentation of work, and the expression of ideas, requirements, and desired results that go into a project. Formal communications are mapped out in the Communication Management Plan, but the art of communicating comes from experience and practice.

Communication skills are included as part of the Professional Responsibility portion of the PMP exam. We'll cover the Professional Responsibility information in Chapter 13.

Budget *Management*

All businesses have a responsibility to the monies they are allotted, have earned, and have acquired through donations. In project management, the work completed within a project must be measured for value and accounted for. The budget the organization has set for the project must be guarded. Ultimately, the success of the project should generate an increase in funds, productivity, or efficiency for the sponsoring organization.

Project Organization

Project managers must be organized. How much time has been wasted looking for documentation, contracts, or permits? How much money has been lost due to disorganization? How many projects have failed because the project manager did not keep and maintain accurate records? Organization is a methodical approach to storing and retrieving information, as it is needed. Organization does not require a spotless desk, thousands of labeled file folders, or archives of every project-related document. Organization requires thorough, fast, and reliable access to project data.

Negotiation Skills

Negotiation is giving and taking so that both parties can live with the outcome of the "deal." For example, your project may need more electrical engineers, while another project manager needs more business analysts. Can you and the other project manager come to agreement to offset each other's business needs? Is one resource more valuable than the other? Another example of negotiation: a stakeholder demands the project be completed within three months at a set budget. You know that the project, with its proposed budget, will take five months. Can you and the stakeholder come to a compromise between the project budget and the project schedule?

Team Leadership

Managing a project team is different than leading a project team. It has been said that you manage things, but lead people. In project management, you must create a relationship between the project team members and yourself to excite, motivate, and inspire the workers to move toward the strategy and vision of the project deliverable. Management requires that you organize, document, and enforce the project plan so that the work progresses to completion. The marriage of leadership and management is necessary for truly successful project management.

Adapting Application Areas

Just as project management requires several general business skills, there are also instances when project management overlaps specific application areas. It is not necessary for you, the project manager, to know and participate in each of the application areas. It may be relevant, however, for a project manager in a given industry to understand the terminology, flow of work, and expectations of their given industry. Here are some common application areas you may encounter

- Legal issues such as contracts, statements of work, regulatory permits, and lawsuits
- Technical issues such as IT management, software development, electrical engineering
- Engineering requirements such as experience with pharmaceutical companies, civic engineering, or chemical engineering
- Manufacturing issues such as product development, automotive, plastics, and others

Examining Related Areas of Project Management

Project management is the management of activities to change the current state of an organization to a desired future state of the organization. Project management is a complex organization of decision-making, planning, implementation, control, and documentation of the experience from start to finish. In addition to traditional project management, there are related areas of project management that you may encounter, have encountered, or are actively participating in. These related endeavors often are superior to individual project management, are part of project management, or equate to less than the management of any given project.

In this section, we'll dissect the related areas of project management and see how they tie together to change a current state to a desired future state.

Program Management

Program management is the management of multiple projects all working in unison toward a common cause. Consider all of the work that could go into building a skyscraper. Within the overall work, there could potentially be several projects that lead to the end result, as demonstrated in Figure 1-2. You could have a project for the planning and design of the building. Another project could manage the legal, regulatory, and project inspections that would be required for the work to continue. Another project could be the physical construction of the building, while other projects could entail electrical wiring, elevators, plumbing, interior design, and more. Could one project manager effectively manage all of these areas of expertise? Possibly, but probably not.

A better solution could be to create a program that is comprised of multiple projects. Project managers would manage each of the projects within the program and report to the Program Manager. The Program Manager would ensure that all of the integrated projects worked together on schedule, on budget, and ultimately towards the completion of the program.

In other instances, the program is an ongoing effort that really does not have an end in sight. Consider the publication of a newspaper, newsletter, web site, or magazine. Essentially, the workers of these publications do the same activities for each issue, but each issue is unique and different than the last.

Another example is NASA's space program. It's a program to explore space, and is comprised of individual projects within that program. Each project under the program

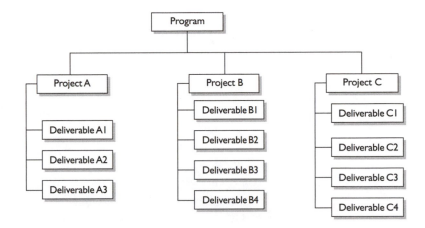

FIGURE 1-2

Programs contain multiple projects working towards one goal.

has its own goals, initiatives, and objectives that are in alignment with the overall mission of the space program. Programs are a collection of individual projects working in alignment towards a common end.

Case Study: Program in Action

Let's return to Zings Sweater Company. In this project, there are many tasks that could be turned into other projects. Based on your findings, you recommend that the Frequent Customer Program Project be converted into a program with a mission to increase market share by seven percent. Within this program, there are many different projects that can be established and operated by individual project managers. The project managers will work together under the guidance of the program manager to make certain that the completion of each project occurs in a logical order and in support of all the other projects.

Your company agrees that the creation of a program is a good idea and they create the following projects within the program:

■ **The IT Development Project**   This project will create the upgrade to the retail point of sale system to support the ID tags the customers will use to obtain their discounts. This project team will create the software and databases to support the technology facet of the project. The project manager for this project will work with the program manager on budget, schedule, and integration with the other projects.

- **The Web Sales Project**   Your company's web site, www.zingsweaters.com, does not currently have an e-commerce enabled utility. Customers can visit the site and see the catalog of sweaters, but they cannot make purchases online. This project will create a new web presence to allow customers to surf and purchase sweaters online and participate in the Frequent Customer Program.

- **The Frequent Customer Program Training Project**   This project will create training documentation, videos, and a web presence for internal training of how the new point of sale software, the ID tags, and the Frequent Customer Program will work to better the company. The training process will take 20 minutes to complete through the web-based training (WBT) application. The training for the retail managers will take one hour to complete through the WBT application. The documentation of how to use the point of sale software will be located at each register in the retail locations for quick reference.

- **The Manufacturing Upgrade Project**   The equipment used to create the wonderful Zings Sweaters will need to be upgraded in order to support the new demand of anticipated sales. This project will oversee the adjustment and fine-tuning of current equipment and the installation of two additional machines on the shop floor. The assigned project manager will work closely with the Director of Manufacturing and the Manufacturing Plant Manager in the procurement of the new equipment. In addition, there will be strong ties to the financial benefits of the new equipment, and the success of the other projects under this program.

- **The Customer Marketing Project**   In order for this project to be successful, customers will need to know about the new Frequent Customer Program. This project will work with writers and designers to create a flashy campaign that will drive sales at both the retail stores and the web site. In addition, the project will recruit customers into the program by offering a ten-percent discount on any sweaters purchased when they join.

Subproject Implementation

Subprojects are an alternative to programs. Some projects may not be wieldy enough to require the creation of a full-blown program, yet still be large enough that some of the work can be delegated to a subproject. A subproject exists under the parent project, but follows its own schedule to completion. Subprojects may be outsourced, assigned to other project managers, or managed by the parent project manager but with a different project team. The following illustration shows a project containing multiple subprojects.

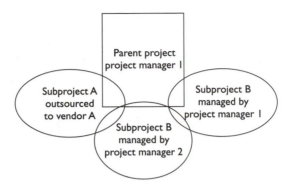

Subprojects are often areas of a project that are outsourced to vendors. For example, if you were managing a project to create a new sound system for home theaters, a subproject could be the development of the user manual included with the sound system. You'd hire writers and graphic designers to work with your project team. The writers and designers would learn all about the sound system and then retreat to their own space to create the user manual according to their project methodology. The deliverable of their subproject would be included in your overall project plan, but the actual work to complete the manual would not be in your plan. You'd simply allot the funds and time required by the writers and graphic designers to create the manual.

Subprojects do, however, follow the same quality guidelines and expectations of the overall project. The project manager has to work with the subproject team regarding scheduling, value, and cost to ensure the deliverables and activities of the subproject integrate smoothly with the "master" project.

Project Portfolio Management

Have you ever had a fantastic idea to implement a new technology, design a new product or service, or other project only to have it discarded by management? Most organizations, big and small, only have so much cash to invest in new projects.

Project Portfolio Management is a management process to select the projects that should be invested in. Specifically, it is the selection process based on the need, profitability, and affordability of the proposed projects. As you probably already know, not all proposed projects can realistically be implemented. Some projects cost too much, while others may not meet a required level of return on investment. The selection of projects can often be a political and gut-wrenching process. The planning process and the project initiation phase of a project allows a project to prove its worth.

Some projects, while valuable, still don't come into play for several reasons. One of the most obvious could be lack of money to implement the proposed project. Or there may already be too many investments in other projects. Or perhaps a lack of internal resources may require that the proposed project be shelved until a later date.

CERTIFICATION SUMMARY

This chapter covered the fundamentals of project management and the expectations for the PMP examination. The Project Management Body of Knowledge is the wealth of information relevant to the project management profession and what will be covered in the PMP exam.

We discussed the five process groups of project management and how they interrelate throughout a project's life cycle. Overlaying these five process groups are the nine knowledge areas that a project manager must have expertise in to be successful. These nine knowledge areas comprise the project management framework.

All projects, large or small, have a triple constraint: time, cost, and quality. The project manager must work with stakeholders to balance these three constraints or the project will run out of time, cost more than what was planned, or produce poor quality deliverables—or combinations of the three.

Finally, we discussed how projects may exist within large entities called programs. Recall that programs are a collection of projects working toward a common goal. Programs are led by a Program Manager that the project manager reports to.

KEY TERMS

To pass the PMP exams, you will need to memorize these terms and their definitions. For maximum value, create your own flashcards based on these definitions and review them daily. These definitions can be found within this chapter and in the glossary.

application areas	programs	project portfolio management
deliverable	progressive elaboration	subprojects
management by projects	project	Work Breakdown Structure
milestone	project framework	
PMBOK Guide	project manager	

TWO-MINUTE DRILL

Exploring Project Attributes

- ❏ Projects are temporary, unique, and create a product or service.
- ❏ All projects have their own life cycle, while the project management life cycle has five distinct phases: Initiation, Planning, Execution, Control, and Closure.
- ❏ Projects move from concept to completion through progressive elaboration.
- ❏ Not all projects get selected. The decisions to choose one project over another may vary from organization to organization. The process, however, is always called Project Portfolio Management.

Project Management Framework

- ❏ Within the project management framework, there are nine knowledge areas, which span the project management life cycle.
- ❏ Project Integration Management: focus is on managing all of the moving parts of a project.
- ❏ Project Scope Management: focus is on protecting, fulfilling, and delivering the project scope.
- ❏ Project Time Management: focus is on scheduling activities, monitoring the project schedule, and working with the project team and stakeholders to ensure the project completes on time.
- ❏ Project Cost Management: focus is on estimating and maintaining project costs.
- ❏ Project Quality Management: focus is on setting the quality expectations and then delivering the project product with the expected level of quality.
- ❏ Project Human Resources Management: focus in on developing the project team to work together to deliver the project as expected.
- ❏ Project Communications Management: focus is on delivering needed information to the correct parties, at the correct time.
- ❏ Project Risk Management: focus is on identifying, mitigating, and managing project risks.
- ❏ Project Procurement Management: focus is soliciting, selecting, and managing vendors to complete project work or supply project materials.

Identifying Project Manager Characteristics

❑ A project manager must have multiple skills to be successful, including the ability to communicate, manage a budget, be organized, negotiate, and provide leadership for the project.

❑ Project managers in different sectors of business and non-profit entities will encounter situations unique only to their area of expertise. For example, a project manager of a construction project will have different issues and concerns than a project manager of a manufacturing project.

❑ Project managers require organization.

SELF TEST

1. A series of activities to create a unique product or service by a specific date is best described as which one of the following?

    A. A program
    B. An operation
    C. A project
    D. A subproject

2. Which of the following is likely to be part of an operation?

    A. Providing electricity to a community
    B. Designing an electrical grid for a new community
    C. Building a new dam as a source for electricity
    D. Informing the public about changes at the electrical company

3. Of the following, which one is the best example of progressive elaboration?

    A. It is the process of decomposing the work into small, manageable tasks.
    B. It is the process of taking a project from concept to completion.
    C. It is the process of taking a project from concept to detailed project plan.
    D. It is the process of identifying the business needs of a potential project.

4. Of the following, which one is not a typical activity of a project manager?

    A. Controlling the project work
    B. Planning the project schedule
    C. Milestone completion
    D. Planning

5. In what process is the project manager selected to manage a project?

    A. Initiation
    B. Planning
    C. Controlling
    D. Design

6. What is the project scope?

    A. It is the design of experiments used to complete the project work.
    B. It is the combination of the cost and the schedule required to complete the project work.

C. It is the description of the required work, and only the required work, that is necessary to complete the project.

D. It is the description of the required work and resources needed to complete the project.

7. The closing process is also known as which of the following?

A. Project completion

B. Project postmortem

C. Project wake

D. Project parity

8. Which of the following is not a project management process?

A. Initiating

B. Planning

C. Controlling

D. Designing

9. You are the project manager of the Speaker Design Project. Your project sponsor wants to know why you believe the planning process will last throughout the project. Of the following, which is the best answer?

A. You are not very familiar with speakers and will have to revisit the planning process often.

B. The design of a new product requires planning throughout the closing process.

C. The design of any project should allow the project manager and the project team to revisit the planning phase as needed.

D. All processes within a project are iterative.

10. Of the following, which one is not part of Project Integration Management?

A. The creation of the project plan

B. The interaction between project teams

C. The execution of the project plan

D. The documentation of changes to the project plan

11. You are the project manager of the User Manual Project. The user manual your team is creating will be packaged with the office chairs your company makes. Nancy Martin, the Marketing Director and Sponsor of the project, requests that 30 additional pages be added to the user manual. These extra pages will describe the additional line of office products available through your company. What is your initial reaction to this proposed change?

A. Approve the change as the project sponsor has made it.

B. Deny the change as the project is already in the implementation phase.

    C. Approve the change if the budget can afford the expense.

    D. Deny the change as it falls outside of the project scope.

12. What activity must the project manager and the project customers do to complete the project? (Choose the best answer.)

    A. Approve the project budget

    B. Design the project schedule

    C. Close out the procurement documents

    D. Verify the project scope

13. You are the project manager for the Advertising Specialties Project. This project will mail each client a pen, coffee mug, and magnet—all to be designed with your company logo and mascot on it. You have worked on a similar project before, but have a new project team for this particular task. Of the following, which is the best source of information for creating the project schedule?

    A. Project team input

    B. Historical information input

    C. Project sponsor input

    D. Vendor input

14. Of the following, which is a mathematical model that can be used in assembling a project budget?

    A. Pareto formulas

    B. Parametric Modeling

    C. Parametric Estimating

    D. EVM

15. The company-wide policy that mandates all project quality is called what?

    A. Quality planning

    B. Quality control

    C. Quality policy

    D. ISO 9000

16. Which of the following can the project manager use to lead the project team to project completion?

    A. Project schedules

    B. EVM

    C. Lectures and motivational speeches

    D. Approved incentives

17. Sam is the project manager for a large, complex manufacturing project. There are many permits, regulatory filings, and accounting procedures for this project. In addition, there are technical guidelines and procedures that must be followed, verified, and approved. For a project of this nature, which of the following is most important?

- **A.** Internal politics
- **B.** Collocated teams
- **C.** Subprojects for minor details
- **D.** An information retrieval system

18. Of the following, which is not an example of risk?

- **A.** Interrupting a business process with project implementation
- **B.** Losing customers due to a project implementation
- **C.** Adding team members during the project implementation
- **D.** Updating the project plan during the implementation

19. Which document will guide the interaction between the project manager and a selected vendor on a project?

- **A.** The project plan
- **B.** The SOW
- **C.** The procurement management plan
- **D.** The contract

20. Of the following, what does the project manager typically do the most of?

- **A.** Communications
- **B.** Budget management
- **C.** Project organization
- **D.** Manage team negotiations

21. A program is which one of the following?

- **A.** A very large, complex project
- **B.** A collection of small projects with a common goal
- **C.** A collection of projects with a common cause
- **D.** A collection of subprojects with a common customer

22. Who manages programs?

- **A.** Management
- **B.** Project sponsors

    C. Project managers

    D. Program managers

23. You have an excellent idea for a new project that can increase productivity by 20 percent in your organization. Management, however, declines to approve the proposed project because too many resources are already devoted to other projects. You have just experienced what?

    A. Parametric modeling

    B. Management by exception

    C. Project Portfolio Management

    D. Management Reserve

24. Complete the following statement. All businesses are in business to…

    A. Make money

    B. Complete their company's vision

    C. Complete their company's mission statement

    D. Provide jobs and opportunities for others

25. Of the following, which is the most important person involved with a project?

    A. The project manager

    B. The project sponsor

    C. The CEO

    D. The customer

SELF TEST ANSWERS

1. ☑ **C.** A project is a temporary endeavor to create a unique product or service. Operations are ongoing activities.
   ☒ **A** is incorrect, because a program is a collection of projects with a common cause. **B** is not a valid choice as operations are ongoing activities. Subprojects (answer **D**) represent portions of a project broken off into smaller endeavors.

2. ☑ **A.** An electrical company's primary operation is to provide electricity.
   ☒ **B** and **C** are projects. While choice **D**, providing information could potentially be part of an ongoing operation, choice A is still the best answer presented.

3. ☑ **C.** Of the choices given, C is the best. Progressive elaboration is the process of taking a project concept through to the project plan. As the planning and research activities continue, the more detailed and focused the concept becomes. Progressive elaboration happens throughout the project. It is the process of elements within the project becoming more and more exact as additional information and details become available.
   ☒ **A** defines the process of creating a WBS. **B** is the process of completing the project, and **D** is one of the activities in the project initiation phase.

4. ☑ **C.** Milestones are not completed by the project manager, but by the project team. In addition, milestones are the results of activities, not activities themselves.
   ☒ **A, B,** and **D** are regular activities of the project manager. If the project manager isn't completing these activities, then the project will most likely fail.

5. ☑ **A.** The project manager is selected to manage a project in the Initiation process.
   ☒ **B, C,** and **D** are incorrect. Note that the design process is not one of the five project management processes. Design is often a project process that could fall into the planning process. Recall that the five processes in the project management life cycle are: Initiation, Planning, Execution, Control, and Closure.

6. ☑ **C.** The project scope is the description of the required work, and only the required work, to complete the project.
   ☒ **A** is incorrect because the design of experiments is a process to find solutions to problems by changing the variables that may be causing the problems. Answer **B** describes nothing more than the cost and time estimates and baselines. Answer **D** is incorrect because the scope is concerned only with the work, not the resource required to complete the work.

7. ☑ **B.** Project closure is also known as the project postmortem.
   ☒ Technically, the project postmortem comes after administrative closure in the closing process. **A, C,** and **D**, while tempting choices, are not terms that completely describe the project closure.

8. ☑ **D.** Designing is typically a phase of project management, but is not one of the five project management lifecycle processes.

    ☒ **A, B,** and **C** are valid project management lifecycle phases, so they are an incorrect choice for this question.

9. ☑ **C.** The planning process lasts through the project life cycle.

    ☒ **A** is not the best answer for this scenario. **B** may be correct in theory, but it does not answer the question as fully as C. Finally, **D** is incorrect since projects should be managed iteratively. Plus, D fails to answer the question fully.

10. ☑ **B.** Project Integration Management focuses on the project plan and the implementation of the project plan.

    ☒ While B could, in some instances, be considered incorrect if the project plan had some interaction with other project teams, the assumption cannot be made in this instance. **A, C,** and **D** are all part of Project Integration Management, so they are not a valid answer.

11. ☑ **D.** The project scope defines the required work, and only the required work, to complete the project.

    ☒ **A** is incorrect since a request comes from the project sponsor; remember that the scope must be protected from change. Once the change is properly submitted and approved, the scope will be updated to reflect the new work. Always, on the exam, protect the scope from changes. **B** is incorrect as changes may happen throughout the project as they are approved and warranted. **C** is incorrect since changes should be based on actual need rather than financial decisions.

12. ☑ **D.** Scope verification is the proof that the project manager has completed the project.

    ☒ **A, B,** and **D** are typically not done with the project customers.

13. ☑ **B.** Whenever you have access to historical information, this is your best source of input.

    ☒ While **A, C,** and **D** may offer some value, historical information is typically the greatest input for planning.

14. ☑ **B.** Parametric modeling is a mathematical formula to apply costs to a project. For example, cost per unit, cost per metric ton, and cost per yard.

    ☒ **A** is incorrect, as it refers to the Pareto rule of 80/20. B is not a viable choice for this question. **D,** Earned Value Management, is not applicable to this situation.

15. ☑ **C.** Quality policy is the organization-wide rules and requirements for quality.

    ☒ Choice **A,** quality planning is how you, the project manager, will plan to adhere to the quality standards set by the QA policy. Choice **B,** QC, is the method of inspecting the work results to ensure they map to the QA policy. Choice **D,** ISO 9000, is a quality assurance program, not a quality system. ISO 9000 is an adherence to a series of steps or processes to necessary to complete an action. This is not the best choice for this question.

16. ☑ **D.** The project manager should use approved rewards and incentives to move the project team towards completion.
    ☒ **A** is a requirement of all projects. Answer **B**, EVM, is a method of measuring project performance. While **C** may be effective, lectures and motivational speeches can include threats, punishments, or inspirational speeches—none of which work as well as approved incentives.

17. ☑ **D.** An information retrieval system is paramount for a project with so much documentation. Technically, all projects should have an information retrieval system.
    ☒ **A**, **B**, and **C**, while evident in many projects, do not offer solutions for the problems Sam is likely to experience on this project. Note that internal politics may also be known as "political capital."

18. ☑ **D.** All answers, with the exception of D, are an example of risk.
    ☒ The point of risk assessment is done to allow the project to successfully encounter business risks such as a loss of money or customers. Albeit, **C**, may not be a huge risk to most projects, D is the best choice. A project manager should update the project plan as discoveries and approved changes are made to the project.

19. ☑ **D.** The contract between the organization and the vendor supercedes all other work-related documents.
    ☒ The project plan will guide the project manager and the project team to completion, but will not supercede contracts. The SOW (statement of work), while needed and necessary, is not as important as a contract. The Procurement Management Plan will guide the user of the contract, but the contract is the most useful tool to govern contracts.

20. ☑ **A.** Communication, informal and formal, is the largest activity a project manager will undertake.
    ☒ **B**, **C**, and **D**. While budget management, project organization, and team negotiations may feel like they take the most time, communications are the bulk of a project manager's job.

21. ☑ **C.** Programs are a collection of projects with a common cause.
    ☒ **A** is incorrect because a program is a collection of projects, not just one large, complex project. **B** is incorrect because programs are not made up of just small projects. **D** is incorrect since projects with a common customer do not necessitate a program.

22. ☑ **C.** Program Managers manage programs.
    ☒ **A** is incorrect since Management doesn't manage programs. Project sponsors sponsor projects; they do not manage programs. **D** is incorrect, since within the program, project managers manage their projects and report to the Program Manager.

23. ☑ **C.** Project Portfolio Management is the process of choosing and prioritizing projects within an organization. An excellent project idea can still be denied if there are not enough resources to complete the project work.

☒ **A** is incorrect as it is a model to estimate costs, such as cost per ton, or cost per hour. **B** is incorrect because this is a management theory to manage people and problems. **D** is incorrect as it is an amount of time and money reserved for projects running late or over budget.

24. ☑ **A.** Businesses exist to make money.

☒ **B, C,** and **D** are incorrect. Businesses exist not to complete their mission statement, nor to complete their company's vision, or provide jobs. When answering questions dealing with business needs, think of the bottom line first.

25. ☑ **D.** Customers, internal or external, are the most important stakeholders in a project.

☒ **A** is incorrect, because the project manager manages the project for the customer. **B** is incorrect since the project sponsor authorizes the project. **C** is incorrect because the CEO may not even know about the project—and even then he would be interested in the success of the project for the customer.

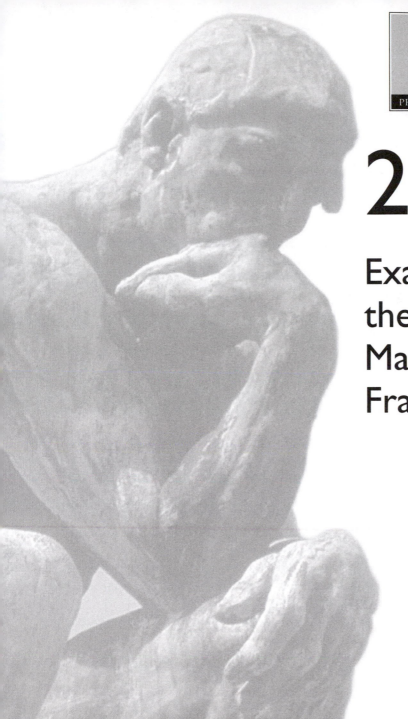

2

Examining the Project Management Framework

Project management, the ability to get things done, must support the higher vision of the organization the project management activities are occurring in. Projects must be in alignment with the organization's vision, strategy, tactics, and goals. Projects that are not in alignment with the higher vision of the organization won't be around long—or, at best, they are doomed to fail.

At the launch of a project, the project manager must have inherited the vision of the project. They must understand why the project is being created and what its purpose in the organization is. It's beneficial to also know the priority of the project and its impact on the organization. A project to install pencil sharpeners throughout the company's shop floor may be important, but not as significant as the project to install new manufacturing equipment on the shop floor.

In this chapter, we'll cover how the life of a project, the interest of stakeholders, and the organization's environment will influence the success and completion of projects.

Moving Through Project Phases

A project is an uncertain business; the larger the project, the more uncertainty. It's for this reason, among others, that projects are broken down into smaller, more manageable phases. A project phase allows a project manager to see the project as a whole and yet still focus on completing the project one phase at a time.

Projects are temporary endeavors to create a unique product or service. All projects must have an end date. Between the project launch and the coveted end date, a project will pass through multiple phases. Consider a project to create a new electronic gadget. This gadget will have several phases to complete from concept to completion: product description, prototype, revision, testing, and so on. The completion of each phase brings the project closer to completion.

Think of any project you may have worked on: a technology rollout, constructing a building, integrating a new service into a business. Each of these projects will have logical phases that move the project from concept to completion. The sum of the project phases comprises the project life cycle.

A project life cycle is the duration of a project. Consider our project to create a new electronic gadget. Once the gadget is completed, has passed testing and regulations, the project doesn't continue—it's done. The life of the project is over and the goal of the project, to create a unique product in this case, has been met. There's no reason for the project to keep going—so its life cycle is over.

Project Phase Deliverables

Every phase has deliverables. It's one of the main points to having phases. For example, your manager gives you a wieldy project that will require four years to complete and has a hefty budget of $16 million. Do you think management is going to say, "Have fun—see you in four years?"

Oh, if only they would, right?

Of course, in most organizations, that's not going to happen. Management wants to see proof of progress, evidence of work completed, and good news of how well the project is moving. Phases are an ideal method of keeping management informed of the project progression. The following illustration depicts a project moving from conception to completion. At the end of each phase there is some deliverable that the project manager can show to management and customers.

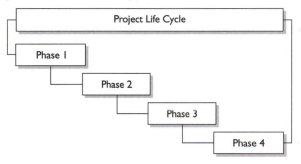

Project Advancement

Once a phase concludes, how does the project manager know it's safe to continue? Based on the size and type of the project, some form of scope verification must take place. Management and customers will want to see if the deliverable you have completed to date is in alignment with what they've expected.

Let's go back to that juicy project with the $16 million budget. We know management is not going to set us loose for four years. They'll want a schedule of when we'll be spending their money and what they'll be getting in return. And when will this fun happen? At the end of a project phase. The project manager will be accountable for several things at the end of a project phase:

- The performance of the project to date
- The performance of the project team to date
- Proof of deliverables in the project phase
- Verification of deliverables in alignment with the project scope

The verification of the performance and the project deliverables will be key to management determining if the project (cross your fingers) should continue or not. Imagine your project with $16 million has produced a lousy deliverable, outside of the project scope, and you've blown more than a few hundred thousand more than what you said it would take to get to this point in the project. Hmmm… Do you think the project will continue? An analysis by management will determine if the project should be killed or allowed to continue. The idea of killing a project at phases is why phase completion is also called a kill point. Uh, kill point for the project, not the project manager.

Stage Gates

Project phases are also known as stage gates. Stage gates are used often in manufacturing and product development. A stage gate allows a project to continue after performance and deliverable review against a set of predefined metrics. If the deliverables of the phase, or stage, met the predefined metrics, the project is allowed to continue. Should the deliverable not meet the metrics, the project may not be allowed to pass through the gate to move forward. In these unfortunate cases, the project may be terminated or sent through revisions to meet the predetermined metrics. The following illustration shows the advancement of the project through phases.

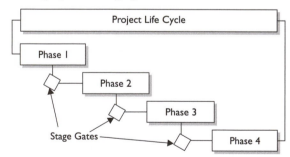

on the
job

As a project manager, you should identify the requirements as close to the project launch as possible. With the expectations and requirements, the project manager can know what the exit criteria for a phase may be and can plan accordingly. There are few things more frustrating than to get to the end of a project phase only to learn the exit criteria you had in mind is different than what the customer was expecting.

The completion of a phase may also be known as a phase exit. A phase exit requires the project deliverable meet some predetermined exit criteria. Exit criteria are typically inspection-specific and are scheduled events in the project schedule. Exit criteria can include many different activities, such as:

- Sign-offs from the customer
- Regulatory inspections and audits
- Quality metrics
- Performance metrics
- Security audits
- The end of a project phase

Completing a Project Phase

You know you are moving towards completion when management and customers agree with the results of a project phase. Each project will have its own logical phases to completion. Imagine you're the project manager for a project to build a new house. There'd be some very logical phases to the completion of the project to build the house:

1. **Requirements** What type of house are you building? What are the characteristics of the house? What are the expectations from the people that will be living in the home?

2. **Design** The architects and the designers would work with the requirements to create the specifications for the house in alignment with the requirements of the customer.

3. **Build** Within this phase, there'd be logical activities and mini-phases necessary to reach the project completion, such as the foundation, the framing, the roofing, and so on.

4. **Inspect** Before the home owners moved into their new home, they'd want to inspect the house for the quality of the building and confirm its functionality.

5. **Operational transfer** Ah, yes, the home is complete and the homeowners have moved in, approving the project and thereby heralding its end.

Each phase within the preceding project has logical activities that dictate the point of the phase, the goal of each, and what the deliverables of each phase likely will be. At the end of each of the listed phases, there'd likely be an inspection and confirmation that the project is moving towards its completion. The completion of a phase allows a project to move into the next phase.

Working with Project Life Cycles

Projects are like snowflakes: no two are alike. Sure, sure, some may be similar, but when you get down to it—each project has its own unique attributes, activities, and requirements from stakeholders. Within each project, one attribute that typically varies from project to project is the project life cycle. As its name implies, the project life cycle determines not only the start of the project, but also when the project should be completed. All that stuff packed in between starting and ending? Those are the different phases of the project.

In other words, the launch, series of phases, and project completion comprise the project life cycle. Each project will have similar project management activities, but the characteristics of the project life cycle will vary from project to project.

The PMP exam will test your knowledge on the outcome of project phases, rather than the idealistic outputs of a project phase. Know that each phase creates a deliverable of some sort and allows the project to move forward if the deliverables meet preset metrics.

on the Job *Project feasibility studies can be a separate project.*

Completing a Project Feasibility Study

The project's feasibility is part of the initiating processes. Once the need has been identified, a feasibility study is called for to determine if the need can realistically be met.

So how does a project get to be a project? In some organizations, it's pure luck. In most organizations, however, projects may begin with a feasibility study. Feasibility studies can be, and often are, part of the initiation process of a project. In some instances, a feasibility study may be treated as a stand-alone project. Let's assume that the feasibility of Project ABC is part of the project initiation phase. The outcome of the feasibility study may tell management several things:

- Whether the concept should be mapped into a project or not
- If the project concept is worth moving forward with
- The expected cost and time needed to complete the concept
- The benefits and costs to implement the project concept
- A report on the needs of the organization and how the project concept can satisfy these needs

Examining the Project Life Cycle

By now, you're more than familiar with the concept of a project's life cycle. You also know each project is different and that there are some attributes common across all project life cycles. For example, the concept of breaking the project apart into manageable phases to move towards completion is typical across most projects. As we've discussed, at the completion of a project phase, an inspection or audit is usually completed. This inspection confirms the project is in alignment with the requirements and expectations of the customer. If the results of the audit or briefing are not in alignment, then rework can happen, new expectations may be formulated, or the project may be killed.

Working Through a Project Life Cycle

Project life cycles, comprised of phases, move the project along. Project life cycles allow a project manager to determine several things about the project, such as:

- What work will be completed in each phase of the project?
- What resources, people, equipment, and facilities will be needed within each phase?
- What are the expected deliverables of each phase?
- What is the expected cost to complete a project phase?
- Which phases contain the highest amount of risk?

Armed with the appropriate information for each project phase, the project manager can plan for cost, schedules, resource availability, risk management, and other project management activities to ensure that the project progresses successfully.

While projects differ, there are also other common traits from project to project. The following lists a few examples:

- Cost and resource requirements are lower at the beginning of a project, but grow as the project progresses. Once the project moves into the final closing process, costs and resource requirements taper off dramatically.
- Projects fail at the beginning, not at the end. Projects are more likely to fail near their beginning—and more likely to succeed near the end of their life cycle. In other words, the odds of completing are low at launch and high at completion.
- The further the project is from completing, the higher the risk and uncertainty. Risk and doubt decrease as the project moves closer to fulfilling the project vision.

■ Changes are easier and more likely at the early phases of the project life cycle than at the completion. Stakeholders can have a greater influence on the outcome of the project deliverables in the early phases, but in the final phases of the project life cycle, their influence on change diminishes. Thankfully. Changes at the beginning of the project generally cost less and have lower risk than changes at the end of a project.

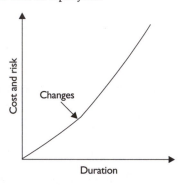

Project Life Cycles vs. Product Life Cycles

There must be some distinction between the project life cycle and the product life cycle. We've covered the project life cycle—the accumulation of phases from start to completion within a project, but what is a product life cycle?

A product life cycle is the parent of projects. Consider a company that wants to sell a new type of lemon soft drink. One of the projects the company may undertake to sell their new lemon soft drink is to create television commercials showing how tasty their beverage is. The creation of the television commercial may be considered one project in support of the product creation.

Many other projects may fall under the creation of the lemon soft drink: research, creation and testing, packaging, and more. Each project, however, needs to support the ultimate product: the tasty, lemon soft drink. Thus, the product life cycle oversees the smaller projects within the process.

on the
J o b

This example can also be mapped to a program. A program coordinates and controls all of the projects to create the product.

The Project Life Cycle in Action

You're the project manager for HollyWorks Productions. Your company would like to create a new video camera that allows consumers to make video productions that can be transferred to different media types such as VHS, DVDs, and PCs. The video camera must be small, light, and affordable. This project life cycle has several phases from concept to completion (see Figure 2-1). Remember, the project life cycle is unique to

FIGURE 2-1   The project life cycle for Project HollyWorks

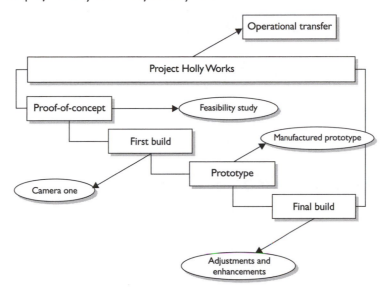

each project, so don't assume the phases within this sample will automatically map to any project you may be undertaking.

1. **Proof-of-concept**   In this phase, you'll work with business analysts, electrical engineers, customers, and manufacturing experts to confirm that such a camera is feasible to make. You'll examine the projected costs and resources required to make such a camera. If things go well, management may even front you some cash to build a prototype.

2. **First build**   Management loves the positive information you've discovered in the proof-of-concept phase—they've set a budget for your project to continue into development. Now you'll lead your project team through the process of designing and building a video camera according to the specifications from the stakeholders and management. Once the camera is built, your team will test, document, and adjust your camera for usability and feature-support.

3. **Prototype manufacturing**   Things are going remarkably well with your video camera project. The project stakeholders loved the first-build and have made some refinements to the design. Your project team builds a working model, thereby moving into prototyping the video camera's manufacture, testing its cost effectiveness and ease of mass production. The vision of the project is becoming a reality.

4. **Final build**   The prototype of the camera went fairly well. The project team has documented any flaws, and adjustments are being made. The project team is also working with the manufacturer to complete the requirements for materials and packaging. The project is nearing completion.

5. **Operational transfer**   The project is complete. Your team has successfully designed, built, and moved into production, a wonderful, affordable video camera. Each phase of the project allowed the camera to move towards completion. As the project came closer and closer to moving into operations, risk and project fluctuation waned.

Meeting the Project Stakeholders

Stakeholders are those fine folks and organizations who are actively involved in the project, or will be affected by its outcome—in other words, people, groups, businesses, customers, and communities that have a vested interest in the project.

Stakeholders may like, love, or hate your project. Consider an organization that is hosting a project to move all their workers to a common word-processing application. Everyone within this organization must now use the same word-processing application. Your job, as the project manager, is to see that it happens.

Now, within your project, you've got stakeholders that like the project, being in favor of the project deliverable. Other stakeholders love the project—they cannot wait for all of the organization to use the same application for word processing. And, sigh, there are those stakeholders who are diehard fans of the application your project will take away from them. These folks hate your project.

on the job

In high-profile projects, where stakeholders will be in conflict over the project purpose, deliverables, cost, and schedule, the project manager may want to use the Delphi Technique to gain anonymous consensus among stakeholders. The Delphi Technique allows stakeholders to offer opinions and input without fear of retribution from management.

Stakeholders, especially those not in favor of the project deliverable, may try to influence the project itself. This can be attempted in many ways, such as through:

- Political capital leveraged to change the project deliverable
- Change requests to alter the project deliverable
- Scope addendums to add to the project deliverable
- Sabotage, through physical acts or rumors, gossip, and negative influence

INSIDE THE EXAM

Projects don't last forever. Though projects may sometimes seem to last forever, they fortunately do not. Operations, however, do go on and on. Projects pass through logical phases to reach their completion, while operations may be influenced, or even created, by the outcome of a project.

The phases within a project create deliverables. The deliverables typically allow the project to move forward to the next phase—or allow the project to be terminated based on the quality, outcome, or condition of the phase deliverable. Some projects may use stage gates. Recall that stage gates allow a project to continue (after performance and deliverable review) against a set of predefined metrics. Other projects may use kill points. Kill points, like phase gates, are preset times placed in the project when it may, based on conditions and discovery within the phase, be "killed."

The project life cycle is different than the Project Management Life Cycle. The Project Management Life Cycle is comprised of the five project management processes (initiation, planning, execution, control, and closure). The project life cycle, meanwhile, is comprised of the logical phases within the project itself.

The project life cycle is affected by the project stakeholders. Project stakeholders have a vested interest in the outcome of the project. Stakeholders include the project manager, project team, management, customers, communities, and anyone affected by the project outcome. Project managers should scan the project outcome in order to identify all of the stakeholders and collect and record their expectations, concerns, and input regarding the project processes.

The project manager's power is relative to the organization structure he is operating within. A project manager in a functional organization will have relatively low authority. A project manager in a matrix environment can have low, balanced, or high authority over the project. A project manager in a projectized organization will have a high level of authority on the project. Essentially, the project manager's authority is typically inverse to the authority of the functional manager.

Your role as the project manager is to identify, align, and ascertain stakeholders and their expectations of the project. Stakeholder identification is not always as clear-cut as in the preceding example. Because stakeholders are identified as people that are affected by the outcome of your project, external customers may be stakeholders in your project, too.

Consider a company that is implementing a frequent customer discount project. External customers will use a card that tracks their purchases and gives them discounts on certain items they may buy. Is the customer in this instance a stakeholder? What if the customer doesn't want to use the card? Is she still a stakeholder?

Mystery Stakeholders

Stakeholders can go by many different names: internal and external customers, project owners, financiers, contractors, family members, government regulatory agencies, communities, cities, citizens and more. The classification of stakeholders into categories is not as important as realizing and understanding stakeholders' concerns and expectations. The identification and classification of stakeholders does allow, however, the project manager to deliver effective and timely communications to the appropriate stakeholders.

Key Project Stakeholders

Beyond those stakeholders affected by the project deliverable, there are key stakeholders on every project. Let's meet them.

- **Project manager** The project manager is the person—ahem, you—that is accountable for managing the project. They guide the team through the project phases to completion.

- **Project customer** The customer is the person or group that will use the project deliverable. In some instances, a project may have many different customers. Consider a book publisher for children. The bookstores distribute the children's book. The adults pay for the book. The children read the book. There is also some consideration given to the user versus the customer. The user uses the product; the customer pays for it. A stakeholder can be both a user and a customer.

- **Performing organization** On your project, you'll have a project team. Who do the team members work for? The performing organization is the entity that employs the people responsible for completing the prject work. In some instances, the performing organization can be a vendor whose project team is completing the project work for another entity, the customer.

- **Project team**   The project team is the collection of individuals that will, hopefully, work together to ensure the success of the project. The project manager works with the project team to guide, schedule, and oversee the project work. The project team completes the project work.

- **Project sponsor**   The sponsor authorizes the project. This person or group ensures that the project manager has the necessary resources, including monies, to get the work done. The project sponsor is someone within the performing organization that has the power to authorize and sanction the project work, and is ultimately responsible for the project's success.

Managing Stakeholder Expectations

Ever had an experience that didn't live up to your expectations? Not much fun, is it? With project management and the large number of stakeholders, it's easy to see how some stakeholders' expectations won't be realistic due to cost, schedule, or feasibility. A project manager must find solutions to create win-win scenarios between stakeholders.

Managing Expectations in Action

Consider a project to implement a new Customer Relationship Management software. In this project, there are three primary stakeholders with differing expectations:

- The Sales Director primarily wants a technical solution that will ensure fast output of order placements, proposals, and customer contact information—regardless of the cost.

- The Marketing Director primarily wants a technical solution that can track call volume, customer sales history, and trends with the least cost to implement.

- The IT Director wants a technical solution that will fan into the existing network topology, have considerable ease of use, and reliability—without costing more than 20 percent of his budget for ongoing support.

In this scenario, the project manager will have to work with each of the stakeholders to determine a winning solution that satisfies all of the project requirements while appeasing the stakeholders' demands. Specifically, the solution for the conflict of stakeholders is to satisfy the needs of the customer first. Customer needs, or the business need of why the project was initiated, should guide the project through the project life cycle. Once the project scope is aligned with the customer's needs, the project manager may work to satisfy the differing expectations of the stakeholders.

Identifying Organizational Models and Attributes

Projects are not islands. They are components of larger entities that work to create a unique product or service. The larger entities, organizations, companies, or communities will have direct influence over the project itself. Consider the values, maturity, business model, culture, and traditions at work in any organization. All of these variables can influence the progress and outcome of the project.

Project managers must recognize the role of the project as a component within an organization. The role of the project, as a component, is to support the business model of the organization as a whole—not to necessarily replace it. You can see in Figure 2-2 the major layers and purpose of the components within most organizations. Note that each layer of the pyramid answers a specific question in relation to the project.

- The Executive Layer sets the vision and strategy of the organization. The business layer asks, "Why is the project important to our organization? Our vision? Our strategy?"

- The Functional Management Layer of the pyramid must support the Executive Layer's objectives. Specifically, the Functional Management Layer is concerned with tactics to accomplish the vision and strategy as set by upper management. The Functional Management Layer asks, "What is the project purpose? What business processes are affected?"

- The Operational Layer of the pyramid supports the Executive and the Functional Management layers. This layer is concerned with the specifics of getting the work done. The Operational Layer asks, "How can the work be accomplished? How can we reach the desired future state with these requirements?"

FIGURE 2-2 Each layer of an organization supports the layer above.

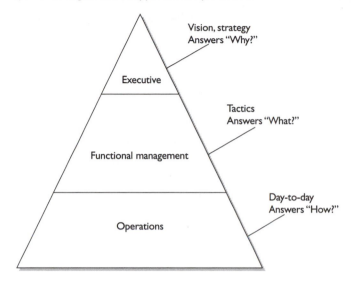

Vision, strategy
Answers "Why?"

Executive

Tactics
Answers "What?"

Functional management

Day-to-day
Answers "How?"

Operations

Considering Organizational Systems

What kind of an organization are you in? Does your organization complete projects for other entities? Does your organization treat every process of an operation as an operation? Or does your organization not know what to do with people like you: project managers?

When it comes to project management, organizations fall into one of three models:

- ■ **Completing projects for others** These entities swoop into other organizations and complete the project work based on specifications, details, and specification documents. Classical examples of these types of organizations include consultants, architectural firms, technology integration companies, and advertising agencies.

- ■ **Completing projects internally through a system** These entities have adopted management by projects (discussed in Chapter 1). Recall that organizations using management by projects have accounting, time, and management systems in place to account for the time, cost, and worth of each project.

- ■ **Completing projects as needed** These non-project-centric entities can complete projects successfully, but may not have the project systems in place to efficiently support projects. The lack of a project support system can cause the project to succumb to additional risks, lack of organization, and reporting difficulties. Some organizations may have special internal business units to support the projects in motion that are separate from the accounting, time, and management systems used by the rest of the organization.

Considering Organizational Culture

Imagine what it may be like to work as a project manager within a bank in downtown London versus working as a project manager in a web development company in New Orleans. Can you picture a clear difference in the expected culture within these two entities? The organizational culture of an entity will have a direct influence on the success of a project. Organizational culture includes

- Purpose
- Values
- Organization policies and procedures
- Type of business
- Maturity of business

As you can imagine, projects with more risk (and expected reward) may be welcome in an organization that readily accepts entrepreneurial ventures rather than in an organization that is less willing to accept chance and risk. Project formality is typically in alignment with the culture of an organization.

Another influence on the progress of a project is the management style of an organization. A project manager that is autocratic in nature will face challenges and opposition in organizations that allow and encourage self-led teams. A project manager must take cues from management as to how the management style of a project should operate. In other words, a project manager emulates the management style of the operating organization.

Completing Projects in Different Organizational Structures

Organizations are structured into one of six models, the organizational structure of which will affect the project in some aspect. In particular, the organizational structure will set the level of authority, the level of autonomy, and the reporting structure that the project manager can expect to have within the project. Figure 2-3 shows the level of authority in each of the organizational structures for the project manager and the functional manager. The organizational structures we'll discuss include

- Functional
- Weak matrix
- Balanced matrix
- Strong matrix
- Projectized
- Composite

on the

on the !Job *Being able to recognize your organizational structure in regard to project management will allow you to leverage and position your role as a project manager effectively.*

Functional Organizations

Functional organizations are entities that have a clear division regarding business units and their associated responsibility. For example, a functional organization may have an Accounting Department, Manufacturing Department, Research and Development Department, Marketing Department, and so on. Each department works as a separate entity within the organization and each employee works in a separate department. In these classical organizations, there is a clear distinction between an employee and a specific functional manager.

FIGURE 2-3   Project managers can expect varying levels of authority in each of the organizational structures.

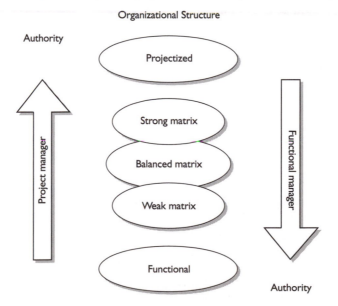

Functional organizations do complete projects, but these projects are specific to the function of the department the project falls into. For example, the IT Department could implement new software for the Finance Department. The role of the IT Department is separate from the Finance Department, but the coordination between the two functional departments would be evident. Communication between departments flows through functional managers down to the project team. Figure 2-4 depicts the relationship between business departments and the flow of communication between projects and departments.

Project managers in functional organizations have the following attributes:

- Little power
- Little autonomy
- Report directly to a functional manager
- The project manager may be known as a Project Coordinator or Team Leader
- The project manager's role is part-time
- The project team is part-time
- The project manager may have little or no administrative staff to expedite the project management activities

Matrix Structures

Matrix structures are organizations that have a blend of departmental duties and employees together on a common project. Matrix structures allow for project team members to be from multiple departments working toward the project completion. In these instances, the project team members have more than one boss. Depending on

FIGURE 2-4   Projects in functional organizations route communications through functional managers.

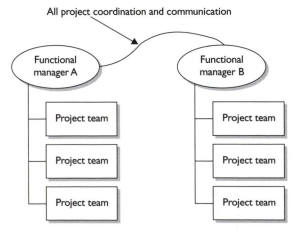

the number of projects a team member is participating in, they may have to report to multiple project managers as well as their functional manager.

Weak Matrix

Weak matrix structures map closely to a functional structure. The project team may come from different departments, but the project manager reports directly to a specific functional manager. In weak matrix organizations, the project manager has the following attributes:

- Limited authority
- Management of a part-time project team
- Project role is part-time
- May be known as a project coordinator or team leader
- May have part-time administrative staff to help expedite the project

Balanced Matrix

A balanced matrix structure has many of the same attributes as a weak matrix, but the project manager has more time and power regarding the project. A balanced matrix still has time accountability issues for all the project team members since their functional managers will want reports on their time within the project. Attributes of a project manager in a balanced matrix are

- Reasonable authority
- Management of a part-time project team
- Full-time role as a project manager
- May have part-time administrative staff to help expedite the project

Strong Matrix

Strong matrix equates to a strong project manager. In a strong matrix organization, many of the same attributes for the project team exist, but the project manager gains power and time when it comes to project work. The project team may also have more time available for the project even though they may come from multiple departments within the organization. Attributes of a project manager in a strong matrix include

- A reasonable to high level of power
- Management of a part-time to nearly full-time project team
- Full-time role as a project manager
- Has a full-time administrative staff to help expedite the project

Projectized Structure

At the pinnacle of project management structures is the projectized structure. These organizational types group employees, collocated or not, by activities on a particular project. The project manager in a projectized structure may have complete, or very close to complete, power over the project team. Project managers in a projectized structure enjoy a high level of autonomy over their projects, but also have a higher level of responsibility regarding the project's success.

Project managers in a projectized structure have the following attributes:

■ High to complete authority over the project team

■ Works full-time on the project with his team (though there may be some slight variation)

■ Has a full-time administrative staff to help expedite the project

Composite Organizations

On paper, all of these organizational structures look great. In reality, there are very few companies that map only to one of these structures all of the time. For example, a company using the functional model may create a special project consisting of talent from many different departments. Such project teams report directly to a project manager and will work on a high-priority project for its duration. These entities are called composite organizations, in that they may be a blend of multiple organizational types. Figure 2-5 shows a sample of a composite structure.

Table 2-1 shows the benefits and drawbacks of various organizational types.

FIGURE 2-5   Composite structures are blends of traditional organizational methods.

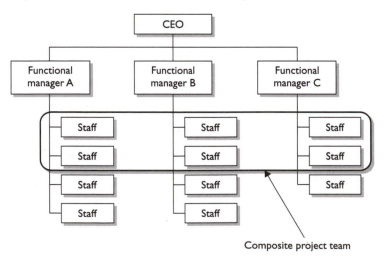

Composite project team

| TABLE 2-1 | Pros and Cons of Organization Types |

Organizational Type	Pros	Cons
Projectized	The project manager has autonomy of the project decisions. Improves communication as teams focus on current project work.	Encourages competition between project teams. Project teams may stockpile resources. The project team may also lose focus towards the end of the project since they are uncertain about their next assignment.
Strong matrix	Project team may be assigned to a project from 50 to 90 percent of its duration. The project manager has a high level of authority. This model also provides good communication.	Competition among project teams still exists. Overall costs may also increase due to redundant administrative staff among projects.
Balanced matrix	The project manager has balanced project authority with management. This model allows efficient use of functional resources.	The functional manager and the project manager may battle for project team members' time. Project team may feel they are reporting to multiple bosses.
Weak matrix	The project manager has little project authority and acts as a project coordinator.	The project is more a part of the functional department operations than a separate activity. Project team resources may be divided amongst too many projects at once.
Functional	Ideal for organizations with recurring projects, such as manufacturing. Everyone on the project knows who is in charge: the functional manager.	The project manager has little, if any, project authority and may be known as a project expeditor.

The Project Office

In the last several years, there has been a surge in the popularity of the project office. The project office is the central source for project management support within an organization. So what can a project manager expect from the project office? How about:

- Project management software
- Training and mentoring
- HR and project manager support
- Guidance
- Templates
- Administrative help

- Project oversight
- Access to knowledge repository

Defining Key General Management Skills

There is more to project management than just getting the work done. Inherent to the process of project management are general management skills that allow the project manager to complete the project with some level of efficiency and control. In some respects, managing a project is similar to running a business: there are risk and rewards, finance and accounting activities, human resource issues, time management, stress management, and a purpose for the project to exist.

The effective project manager will have experience, or guidance, in the general management skills we'll discuss in this section. These general management skills are needed in just about every project type—from architectural design to manufacturing. Other management skills are more specialized in nature, such as OSHA conformance in a manufacturing environment, and aren't needed in every project.

Leading the Project Team

Project managers manage things, but lead people. What's the difference? Management is the process of getting the results that are expected by project stakeholders. Leadership is the ability to motivate and inspire individuals to work towards those expected results.

---

e x a m

ⓦ a t c h

Leadership and management are interrelated. You won't have effective leadership without management, and vice-versa. Know that leadership can also come from project team members, not just from the project manager.

Ever work for a project manager that wasn't motivating or inspiring? A good project manager can motivate and inspire the project team to see the vision and value of the project. The project manager as a leader can inspire the project team to find a solution to overcome the perceived obstacles to get the work done. Motivation is a constant process that the project manager must have to help the team move towards completion—with passion and a profound reason to complete the work.

Finally, motivation and inspiration must be real; a personal relationship with the project team to help them achieve their goals is mandatory.

Communicating Project Information

Project Communication can be summed up as "who needs what information and when." Project managers spend the bulk of their time communicating information— not doing other activities. Therefore, they must be good communicators, promoting a clear, unambiguous exchange of information. Communication is a two-way street; it requires a sender and a receiver.

A key part of communication is *active listening*. This is the process by which the receiver restates what the sender has said in order to clarify and confirm the message. For example, a project team member tells the project manager that a work package will be done in seven days. The project manager clarifies and confirms by stating the work package will be done a week from today. This gives the project team member the opportunity to clarify that the work package will actually be done nine days from today, because of the upcoming weekend.

There are several communication avenues:

- Listening and speaking
- Written and oral
- Internal to the project, such as project team member to team member
- External to the project, such as the project manager to an external customer
- Formal communications, such as reports and presentations
- Informal communications, such as e-mails and "hallway" meetings
- Vertical communications, which follow the organizational flow chart
- Horizontal communications, such as director to director within the organizational flow chart

Within management communication skills, there are also variables and elements unique to the flow of communication. While we'll discuss communications in full in Chapter 10, here are some key facts for now:

- **Sender-receiver models** Communication requires a sender and receiver. Within this model, there may be multiple avenues to complete the flow of communication, but there may also be barriers to effective communication. Other variables within this model include recipient feedbacks, surveys, checklists, and confirmation of the sent message.

- **Media selection** There are multiple choices when it comes to sending a message. Which one is appropriate? Based on the audience and the message being sent, the media should be in alignment. In other words, an ad-hoc hallway meeting is probably not the best communication avenue to explain a large variance in the project schedule.

- **Style** The tone, structure, and formality of the message being sent should be in alignment with the audience and the content of the message.

- **Presentation** When it comes to formal presentations, the presenter's oral and body language, visual aids, and handouts all influence the message being delivered.

■ **Meeting management** Meetings are forms of communication. How the meeting is led, managed, and controlled all influence the message being delivered. Agendas, minutes, and order are mandatory for effective communications within a meeting.

Negotiating Project Terms and Conditions

Project managers must negotiate for the good of the project. In any project, the project manager, the project sponsor, and the project team will have to negotiate with stakeholders, vendors, and customers to reach a level of agreement acceptable to all parties involved in the negotiation process. In some instances, typically in less than pleasant circumstances, negotiations may have to proceed with assistance.

The purpose of negotiations is to reach a fair agreement among both parties.

Specifically, mediation and arbitration are examples of assisted negotiations. Negotiation proceedings typically center on:

■ Priorities

■ Technical approach

■ Project scope

■ Schedule

■ Cost

■ Changes to the project scope, schedule, or budget

■ Vendor terms and conditions

■ Project team member assignments and schedules

■ Resource constraints, such as facilities, travel issues, and team members with highly specialized skills

Active Problem Solving

Like riddles, puzzles, and cryptology? If so, you'll love this area of project management. Problem solving is the ability to understand the heart of a problem, look for a viable solution, and then make a decision to implement that solution. In any project, there are countless problems requiring viable solutions. And like any good puzzle, the solution to one portion of the problem may create more problems elsewhere.

The premise for problem solving is problem definition. Problem definition is the ability to discern between the cause and effect of the problem. This centers on root cause analysis. If a project manager treats only the symptoms of a problem rather than its cause, the symptoms will perpetuate and continue through the project life.

Root cause analysis looks beyond the immediate symptoms to the cause of the symptoms—which then affords opportunities for solutions.

Once the root of a problem has been identified, a decision must be made to effectively address the problem. Solutions can be presented from vendors, the project team, the project manager, or various stakeholders. A viable solution focuses on more than just the problem. It looks at the cause and effect of the solution itself. In addition, a timely decision is needed or the window of opportunity may pass and then a new decision will be needed to address the problem. As in most cases, the worst thing you can do is nothing.

e**x**a**m**
ⓦatch   *Completing the PMP exam*   *is not based on your environment. Learn*
is an example of problem-solving skills.   *the PMI method for passing the exam and*
Even though you may argue that things   *allow that to influence your "real-world"*
described in this book don't work this way *implementations.*
in your environment, know that the exam

Influencing the Organization

Project management is about getting things done. Every organization is different in its policies, modes of operations, and underlying culture. There are political alliances, differing motivations, conflicting interests, and power struggles within every organization. So where does project management fit into this rowdy scheme? Right smack in the middle.

e**x**a**m**
ⓦatch   *These exam questions are*
very shallow. Don't read too much into the
questions as far as political aspirations and
influences go. Take each question at face
value and assume all of the information
given in the question is correct.

A project manager must understand all of the unspoken influences at work within an organization—as well as the formal channels that exist. A balance between the implied and the explicit will allow the project manager to take the project from launch to completion. We all reference politics in organizations with disdain. However, politics aren't always a bad thing. Politics can be used as leverage to align and direct people to accomplish activities—with motivation and purpose.

Managing Social, Economical, and Environmental Project Influences

Social, economical, and environmental influences can cause a project to falter, stall, or fail completely. Awareness of potential influences outside of traditional management practices will help the project finish. The acknowledgement of such influences, from internal or external sources, allows the project manager and the project team to plan how to react to these influences in order for the project to succeed.

For example, consider a construction project that may reduce traffic flow to one lane over a bridge. Obviously, stakeholders in this instance are the commuters that travel over the bridge. Social influences are the people that are frustrated by the construction project, the people that live in the vicinity of the project, and even individuals or groups that believe their need for road repairs are more pressing than the repair of the bridge. These issues must all be addressed, on some level, for the project team to quickly and efficiently complete the project work.

The economical conditions in any organization are always present. The cost of a project must be weighed against the project's benefits and perceived worth. Projects may succumb to budget cuts, project priority, or their own failure based on the performance to date. Economic factors inside the organization may also hinder a project from moving forward. In other words, if the company sponsoring the project is not making money, projects may get axed in an effort to curb costs.

Finally, environmental influence on, and created by, the project must be considered. Let's revisit the construction project on the bridge. The construction project must consider the river below the bridge and how the construction may affect the water and wildlife. Consideration must not only be given to short-term effects that arise during the bridge's construction, but also to long-term effects that the construction may have on the environment?

In most projects, the social, economical, and environmental concerns must be evaluated, documented, and addressed within the project plan. Project managers can't have a come-what-may approach to these issues and expect to be successful.

Dealing with Standards and Regulations

Standards and regulations within any industry can affect a project's success. But what's the difference between a standard and a regulation? Standards are accepted practices that are not necessarily mandatory, while regulations are rules that must be followed—otherwise, fines, penalties, or even criminal charges may result.

For example, within information technology, there are standard sizes for CDs, DVDs, and floppy disks. Manufacturers generally map to these sizes for usability purposes. However, manufacturers can, and have, created other media that are slightly different in size and function than the standard. Consider the disposable, mini-CDs that hold short movies or advertisements for consumers. Some of these CDs come shaped like stars, footballs, and baseballs. Such products aren't exactly standard regarding format, but they don't break any regulations either. After a time though, standards can indeed become de facto regulations. They may begin as guidelines and then, due to marketplace circumstances, grow into an informal regulation.

An example of a regulation is a set rule or law. For example, the food packaging industry has some very particular regulations related to the packaging and delivery of food items. Violations of the regulations will result in fines and even more severe punishment. Regulations are more than suggestions—they are project requirements.

Every industry has some standards and regulations. Knowing which ones affect your project before you begin your work will not only help the project to unfold smoothly, but will also allow for effective risk analysis. In some instances, the requirements of regulations can afford the project manager additional time and monies to complete a project.

Considering International Influences

If a project spans the globe, how will the project manager effectively manage and lead the project team? How will teams in Paris communicate with teams in Sydney? What about the language barriers, time zone differences, currency differences, regulations, laws, and social influences? All of these concerns must be taken into consideration early in the project. Tools can include teleconferences, travel, face-to-face meetings, team leaders, and subprojects.

As companies and projects span the globe to offer goods and services, the completion of those projects will rely more and more on individuals from varying educational backgrounds, social influences, and values. The project manager must create a plan that takes these issues into account.

Cultural Influences

Project plans must deal with many cultural influences: geographical, political, organizational, even relationships between individual team members. Projects in Dallas, Texas, have different cultural influences than projects taking place in Dublin, Ireland. Culture consists of the values, beliefs, political ties, religion, art, aspiration, and purpose of being. A project manager must take into consideration these various cultural influences and how they may affect the project's completion, schedule, scope, and cost.

CERTIFICATION SUMMARY

This chapter detailed the framework of projects. Project managers operate within the framework of a project to coordinate all of the parts and to move the project toward completion. A project achieves momentum by completing project phases. Project phases comprise the project life cycle. The project lifecycle corresponds to the project management framework and provides several benefits:

- Each phase results in some type of deliverable.
- Phase completion shows accomplishment and progression.
- Phase completion allows time for review to determine if the project should move forward.
- Phases allow the project to be progressively elaborated.

Before projects can move into the implementation there must be a project plan. A project plan details what the project will accomplish and how it will be accomplished. Project plans, like project deliverables, pass through progressive elaboration. The project manager and the stakeholders work together to ascertain the priorities of the project requirements, the project constraints, and the project assumptions.

Projects must operate with the organization structure. Organizational structures control how the project manager can obtain resources, the level of authority the project manager can expect, and the participation of the project team. There are five organizational structures: functional, weak matrix, balanced matrix, strong matrix, and projectized.

The project management framework is like the skeleton of any project. It makes up the bones that support the project and provides strength and rigidity. The project management framework holds up the project and allows it to operate in the environment within which it was created.

KEY TERMS

To pass the PMP exams, you will need to memorize these terms and their definitions. For maximum value, create your own flashcards based on these definitions and review them daily. The definitions can be found within this chapter and in the glossary.

fast tracking	matrix structure	project office
functional structure	product life cycle	projectized structure
key management skills	project phases	stakeholders
kill point	project life cycle	

TWO-MINUTE DRILL

Project Management and Organizations

❑ The Project Management Framework is the inner construction of project management that allows it to operate and fluctuate from organization to organization.

❑ Projects within each organization will follow the culture and expected practices of the organization hosting the project. Projects, in any organization, operate to support the organization and its purpose.

Project Phase Create Projects

❑ Projects follow a logical sequence of phases to completion. Phases are typically different from project to project since the project work will differ from one to the next. The point of segmenting projects into phases is to allow for smaller, manageable sections, and to provide deliverables in support of the ongoing operations.

❑ The collection of the project phases, as a whole, is known as the project life cycle.

❑ Project life cycles define the beginning, middle, and end of a project. Projects have a greater risk and uncertainty in the early phases of the project life cycle than near its end. The project is also most susceptible to change, failure, and stakeholder influences at the beginning of the life cycle than near its end. In tandem, project costs and demand for resources are generally low at the beginning of the project, have a tendency to peak near the end of the project work, and then diminish.

Identifying Project Stakeholders

❑ Project stakeholders are individuals, businesses, or communities that have a vested interest in the project's outcome. Typically, project stakeholders are involved in the project process and their expectations drive the project requirements.

❑ It is essential to scan for hidden stakeholders early in the project life cycle to eliminate the need for change when addressing stakeholder needs later in the project.

❑ There are several key stakeholders that have direct influence over the project. They are

 ❑ **Project manager**   Manages the project

 ❑ **Customer**   Pays for the project; uses the project deliverable

 ❑ **Performing organization**   The organization hosting the project

 ❑ **Project team**   The collection of individuals completing the project work

 ❑ **Project Sponsor**   Authorizes the project work and budget

Organizational Structures

❑ Organizational structures have direct influence over the project. Organizational structures determine the procedures that the project manager must follow and the amount of authority the project manager possesses. A project office may oversee project management activities and provide additional support in any of the organizational structures. The organizational types and the level of authority a project manager can expect are shown in the following table:

Organizational Structure	Level of Power
Functional	Low to none
Weak matrix	Low
Balanced matrix	Low to moderate
Strong matrix	Moderate to high
Projectized	High to complete
Composite	Varies

❑ Beyond the concept of getting the work done, project managers must also consider the social, economic, and environmental influences that may sway a project. Specifically, the project manager must evaluate the project to see its social, economic, and environmental impact—as well as note the project's surroundings. The project manager may have some external guidance in these areas in the form of standards and regulations.

❑ Standards are guidelines that are generally followed but not enforced or mandated. Regulations come in the form of laws and industry demands, which are enforced by various governing bodies.

SELF TEST

1. The project life cycle is comprised of which of the following?
   A. Phases
   B. Milestones
   C. Estimates
   D. Activities

2. Marcy, the project manager for the ERP Project, is about to complete the Project Phase Review. The completion of a project phase is also known as which of the following?
   A. Lessons learned
   B. Kill points
   C. Earned Value Management
   D. Conditional advancement

3. Which of the following is not a key stakeholder in a project that creates a service internal to an organization?
   A. Project manager
   B. External customers
   C. Project vendors
   D. Project team members

4. Of the following management skills, which will a project manager use most?
   A. Leading
   B. Communication
   C. Influencing the organization
   D. Negotiations

5. Managing is best described as which one of the following?
   A. Establishing direction
   B. Functional controls over the project team and stakeholders
   C. Consistently producing key results expected by stakeholders
   D. Motivating and inspiring the project team to produce results that are expected by project stakeholders

6. Ron, the project manager, expects formal communications for change requests. Of the following, which is most likely not an example of formal communication?
   A. Reports
   B. Oral presentations

    C. E-mail

    D. Team meetings

7. Which of the following is an example of negotiation?

    A. Arbitration

    B. Formal communications

    C. Conferring

    D. Scope creep

8. You are the project manager for your organization. Influencing your organization requires which of the following?

    A. An understanding of the organizational budget

    B. Research and documentation of proven business cases

    C. An understanding of formal and informal organizational structures

    D. Positional power

9. Your global project is sabotaged by rumors and gossip about the project deliverable. This is an example of:

    A. Cultural achievability

    B. Cultural influences with the project team

    C. Project team mutiny

    D. Ineffective planning

10. What is the difference between a standard and a regulation?

    A. Standards are mandatory; regulations are not

    B. Standards are optional; regulations are not

    C. Regulations and standards are essentially the same

    D. Regulations are mandatory; standards may be seen as guidelines

11. You are the project manager of a project that spans the globe in its implementation. Your team is non-collocated and many of the project team members will need to travel between sites to complete the project work. Which of the following is least relevant to internationalization?

    A. Time zones

    B. Travel requirements

    C. Project schedule

    D. Teleconferences versus videoconferences

12. Which of the following is an example of a deliverable at the end of the requirements gathering phase in a software design project?

    A. Responsibility matrix creation
    B. Detail design document
    C. Business needs
    D. Project team assembled

13. You are the project manager for the ERP Project. Your organization uses a project office. The primary purpose of a project office is to:

    A. Support the project managers
    B. Support the Project Sponsor
    C. Support the project team
    D. Identify the stakeholders

14. Which of the following best describes a project deliverable?

    A. The resources used by the project to complete the necessary work
    B. The resources exported from the project as a result of the project work
    C. The end result of a project planning session
    D. The tangible good or service created by the project team

15. At what point in a project would a kill point be acceptable?

    A. When a project team member is not performing as planned
    B. When a project reaches the end of a project phase
    C. When a project reaches the end of its budget
    D. When a project manager determines the project cannot continue

16. Of the following, which is not an exit criterion?

    A. Customer sign-offs
    B. Quality metrics
    C. Stakeholder expectations
    D. Regulatory inspections

17. The compilation of all the phases within a project equates to _____.

    A. Project life cycle
    B. Product life cycle
    C. Project completion
    D. Project processes

18. Management has asked Nancy to determine if a project concept is valid and can be completed using a reasonable amount of time and finances. Management is asking for which of the following?

    A. Kill points

    B. Cost and time estimates

    C. A project case study

    D. A feasibility study

19. Henry, the project manager of the MHB Project, has allowed a subsequent project phase to begin before the predecessor phase is complete. This is an example of which of the following?

    A. Crashing

    B. Fast tracking

    C. Risk management

    D. Tandem scheduling

20. Which of the following describes the early stages of a project?

    A. High costs and high demand for resources

    B. A high demand for change

    C. A high demand for project team time

    D. Low costs and low demand for resources

21. At which point is the risk of failure the least, but the consequence of failure the highest?

    A. During the early stages

    B. During the middle stages

    C. During the final stages

    D. Risk of failure is even across all project phases

22. Tracey is the project manager of the KHG Project. Her organization is a classic functional environment. Her level of authority as a project manager can be best described as which of the following?

    A. Low

    B. Moderate

    C. Balanced

    D. High

23. Project team members are most likely to work full-time on a project in which of the following organizational structures?

A. Functional
B. Weak matrix
C. Strong matrix
D. Projectized

24. A project with much risk and reward is most likely to be accepted in which of the following?

A. An entrepreneurial company
B. A heavily regulated company
C. A non-profit organization
D. A community

25. Where can a project manager expect to receive templates?

A. Commercial databases
B. The project office
C. The project sponsor
D. PMIS

SELF TEST ANSWERS

1. ☑ **A.** The project life cycle is comprised of phases.
   ☒ **B** is incorrect since milestones may exist within the project plan, but they do not comprise the project life cycle. **C** is wrong because estimates are not directly related to the project life cycle. Choice **D,** activities, comprise the phases within the project life cycle, but not the project life cycle itself.

2. ☑ **B.** The completion of a project phase may also be known as a kill point.
   ☒ Lessons learned is a collection of information and knowledge gained through an experience, typically a phase, within the project, so **A** is wrong. EVM, earned value management, can happen at different times throughout the project, not just at the end of a project phase, therefore **C** is wrong. Choice **D,** conditional advancement, is a term that is used to describe the conditions that must be present for the work to continue on a project. Conditional advancement, however, does not have to happen only at the end of a project phase.

3. ☑ **B.** External customers are not key stakeholders in this instance as they are not actively involved in an internal project.
   ☒ **A** and **D** are actively involved in the project processes. Choice **C,** project vendors, is most likely a key stakeholder before an external customer since their ability to perform services and deliver goods may affect project schedule, budget, and completion.

4. ☑ **B.** Communication is the key general management skill a project manager will use the most.
   ☒ Choices **A, C,** and **D** are necessary, but communication accounts for the majority of a project manager's time.

5. ☑ **C.** Managing has to do with consistently producing key results that are expected by stakeholders.
   ☒ Choices **A** and **D** describe the leadership processes a project manager must possess, therefore they are wrong. Choice **B** is incorrect as it describes the functional management position over project team members.

6. ☑ **C.** Of all the choices presented, answer **C** is most likely not a formal communication.
   ☒ Choices A, B, and D are likely to be formal communications within a project.

7. ☑ **A.** Arbitration is a form of negotiation. Technically, it is a form of assisted negotiation.
   ☒ **B** is not a negotiation technique. Choice **C,** conferring, is not negotiating, but a process to seek consensus on a decision. **D** is incorrect as scope creep is the process of allowing additional activities into the project scope.

8. ☑ **C.** To influence an organization (in order to get things done), a project manager must understand the explicit and implied organizational structures within an organization.

☒   Choice **A** is incorrect since the project manager may not even have access to an organizational budget. **B** is incorrect because a proven business case may not map to every scenario when influencing an organization. Finally, **D** is incorrect because positional power may relate to only a small portion of an organization, not to multiple facets of influence.

9. ☑   **A.** Rumors and gossip can sabotage a project. This is an example of cultural achievability.
    ☒   **B** and **C** are incorrect since rumors and gossip may happen internally and externally to the project team. **D** may be tempting, but the rumors and gossip could happen outside of the effective planning completed by the project manager and the project team.

10. ☑   **D.** Of all the choices presented, **D** is the best answer since regulations are mandatory requirements.
    ☒   Choice **A** is incorrect because it does not accurately describe regulations and standards. Choice **B** is incorrect since regulations are not optional, they are mandatory. **C** is incorrect—standards and regulations are not the same.

11. ☑   **C.** The project schedule is the least relevant when compared to the other factors of internationalization.
    ☒   Choices **A, B,** and **D** are all greatly affected by the geographical locale, difference in time zones, and availability of resources in these different countries.

12. ☑   **B.** The detail design document is an output of the requirements gathering phase.
    ☒   Choice **A** is incorrect because the responsibility matrix creation is a process, not an output of itself. **C** is incorrect because business needs may prompt the project to begin, not an output of a phase. **D** is also wrong because the project team assembled is part of the project process; it is not an output.

13. ☑   **A.** The project office supports the project manager.
    ☒   **B** and **C** are incorrect because the project office does not support the Project Sponsor and project team. Choice **D** is incorrect because stakeholder objectives may vary from stakeholder to stakeholder.

14. ☑   **D.** Recall that projects are temporary endeavors to create a unique product or service.
    ☒   **A** is incorrect because resources devoted to the project do not constitute a project deliverable. **B** and **C** are incorrect since project work is not a deliverable and there will be multiple planning sessions on most projects. The work of a project often will result in a deliverable, not resources or a work product.

15. ☑   **B.** Kill points are typically at the end of a project phase. A kill point does not mean the project is killed, just that the potential for termination exists.
    ☒   Choices **A, C,** and **D** may appear to be correct, but they do not adequately describe a kill point.

16. ☑   **C.** Exit criterion are activities or evidence that allow a project to move forward. Stakeholder expectations are universal to the entire project, not just to one project phase.
    ☒   Choices **A, B,** and **D** are all examples of activities that can be considered exit criteria.

17. ☑ **A.** The project life cycle is comprised of all of the project phases within a project.
   ☒ **B** describes the life of many projects that create a unique product or service. **C** and **D** are incorrect since they do not accurately describe the project life cycle.

18. ☑ **D.** Management is looking for a feasibility study to determine if it is feasible for a project to exist.
   ☒ Choice **A** is incorrect since kill points are within a project and typically don't prove project feasibility. Cost and time estimates, answer **B,** are not the elements Nancy or management needs at this juncture. Choice **C,** Project Case Study, may seem correct, but **D** is a superior answer since it is the formal name for the report documenting the project's feasibility.

19. ☑ **B.** Fast tracking is the process of allowing successor phases (or activities) to begin before predecessor phases (or activities) are complete.
   ☒ **A** is incorrect because crashing is the process of adding more resources to the project in an attempt to complete the project sooner. **C,** risk management, happens throughout the project, therefore it is wrong. **D** is also wrong because tandem scheduling is not a relevant term in this instance.

20. ☑ **D.** Projects typically have low costs and low demand for resources early in their life cycle.
   ☒ Choices **A, B,** and **C** are incorrect statements in regard to projects.

21. ☑ **C.** As the project moves closer to completion, the likelihood of risk diminishes.
   ☒ Choices **A, B,** and **D** are incorrect in regard to risk assessment in a project.

22. ☑ **A.** Tracey will most likely have a low amount of authority in a functional organization structure.
   ☒ Choices **B** and **C** are incorrect because they describe the matrix structures. Choice **D** is incorrect since it is relevant to a projectized structure.

23. ☑ **D.** Projectized structures often have project team members assigned to the project on a full-time basis.
   ☒ Choices **A, B,** and **C** are incorrect since these structures have part-time project teams.

24. ☑ **A.** Projects with much risk and reward are most likely to be accepted within an entrepreneurial organization.
   ☒ Choices **B, C,** and **D** are typically more adverse to risk and likely wouldn't accept a project with a large amount of risk.

25. ☑ **B.** The project office is the best choice since its role is to support the project manager.
   ☒ Choice **A,** commercial databases, may be feasible, but it is not the best choice presented. Project Sponsors, Choice **C,** are not typically going to provide the project manager with templates. Choice **D,** project management information systems, may have project templates available, but the project office is the best choice presented.

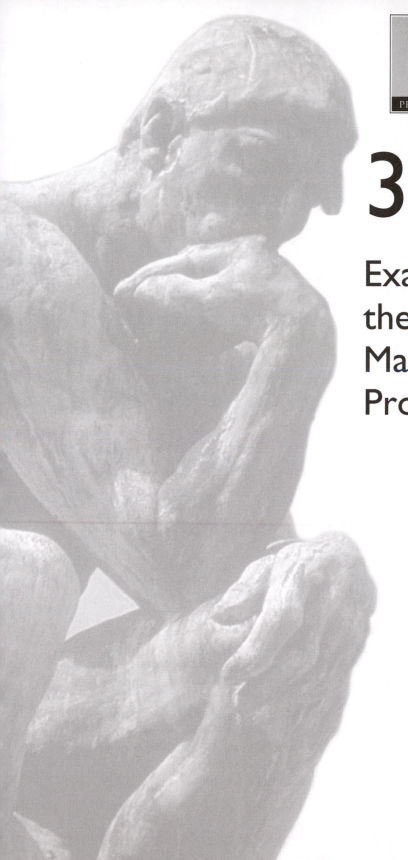

3

Examining the Project Management Processes

Did you ever have one of those Junior Scientist Chemistry Kits when you were a kid? These kits had recipes for different reactions, formulas, and experiments. You could make smoke, sparks, smells, and iridescent colors if you followed the step-by-step directions. Of course, if you were a "real scientist" you'd experiment and things could go haywire. One small change, an uncalculated variable, or a mistaken catalyst could cause your whole experiment to literally blow up in your face.

Sounds like project management, doesn't it?

All of the different elements in project management are integrated. The cost, time, scope, cultural achievability, technical achievability, and more are all related and interdependent. A small change, delay, decision (or lack thereof) can amplify into serious problems further down the project timeline.

Project management, unlike those Junior Scientist Chemistry Kits, doesn't come with exact step-by-step directions. It is a fluid process with general guidelines, stakeholder requirements, and you leading the project to reach the customer requirements. In this chapter, we'll talk about how all of the different parts of a project are interrelated. Specifically, we'll discuss the project processes and their interactions, the ability to customize the project processes, and how all of this business works towards your current project of passing the PMP examination.

Learning the Project Processes

All projects, from technology to architecture, are composed of processes. Recall that phases are unique to each project and that the goal of the phase is to conclude with a specific, desired result. The completion of phases is the end of the project, culminating in the creation of a unique product or service. Processes are a series of actions with a common, parent goal, to create a result. Processes within project management monitor and move the phases along.

on the **!** o b   *In your organization, you may treat equipment as a true resource. For example, manufacturing equipment, printing equipment, or even transactions may be treated as resources whose time is billable to project customers.*

People perform processes. It may be tempting to say that a piece of equipment, such as a manufacturing device, a computer, or a bulldozer, completes the process, but it is, technically for your exam, a person or group of people that complete the process. Think of the processes within a project you've worked on. Know that the processes are not the individual activities, but the control of individual activities to complete a project phase.

There are two types of processes:

■ **Product-orientated processes**   These processes are the activities that complete a project's phase and life cycle. Recall that the project's life cycle is comprised of the completion of the phases. In other words, the product-orientated processes within a project complete phases, which in turn complete the project. The processes within a project are unique to each project. The concept of project life cycles was discussed thoroughly in Chapter 2.

■ **Project management processes**   These processes are the activities that are universal to all projects. These activities comprise the bulk of the project management body of knowledge and will be discussed in detail in Chapters 4 through 12. These processes are common to all projects from construction to technology.

Project management processes are the processes you'll want to study. Product-orientated processes, on the other hand, are unique to the organization creating the product.

The two process types are interrelated and interdependent. Thus, a project manager must be familiar with the product-orientated processes in order to apply the project management processes. To use a real-world example, a project manager should be familiar with both how a house is constructed and the various phases involved in that construction in order to effectively apply the project management process.

Identifying the Project Management Process Groups

The following are the five project management process groups and what occurs under each:

■ **Initiating**   The project is authorized.

■ **Planning**   Project objectives are determined, as well as how to reach those objectives with the given constraints.

■ **Executing**   The project is executed utilizing acquired resources.

■ **Controlling**   Project performance is monitored and measured to ensure the project plan is being implemented to design specifications and requirements.

■ **Closing**   The project and its various phases are brought to a formal end.

The five process groups can be remembered as IPECC. Some think of syrup of ipecac to recall the processes.   *Hopefully, IPECC won't give you the same bitter aftertaste.*

FIGURE 3-1   Process groups overlap other groups.

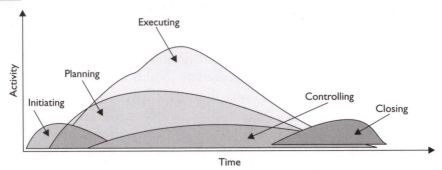

These process groups are not solo activities. The groups are a collection of activities that contribute to the control and implementation of the project management life cycle. The output of one process group will act as input for another process group. For example, one of the outputs of the initiating process is the project charter. The charter is thus input for the planning processes, being that it authorizes and sanctions the project, the project manager, and the resources required to complete the project work. While there is a logical succession and order to the flow of the processes, process groups will overlap other groups (as shown in Figure 3-1).

Not only will process groups overlap, but some process groups may be repeated based on the activities within the project. Specifically, planning, controlling, and executing processes are revisited throughout the project.

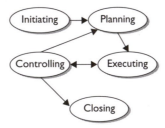

For example, within a project designed to create a new piece of software, there will be logical project phases: design, build, test, implement, and so on. Within each of the phases, project processes can also exist. Each phase of the project has project processes unique to the logical activities within that phase. The closing process of a project phase can serve as input for the next phase within the project.

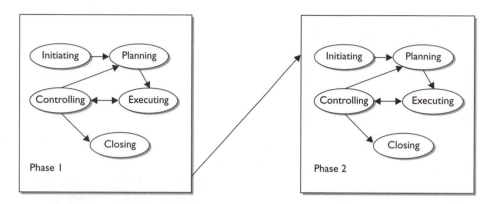

Identifying the Initiating Processes

This process launches the project process and allows the project manager to have the authority to begin the project. Project initiation, while simple on the surface, admits that there is some problem that a solution should solve. As a solution is considered, a level of authority is transferred from senior management to the project manager to lead the organization to the desired future state.

Identifying Needs

A project is generally called upon to provide a solution to a problem or to take advantage of an opportunity. The needs of the current state are then answered by the deliverables of the proposed project. These needs might have to do with:

- Reducing costs
- Increasing revenues
- Eliminating waste
- Increasing productivity and efficiency
- Solving a business or functional problem
- Taking advantage of market opportunities

This is just a short list. There are countless other needs that can be addressed through project plans.

on the **job**

Business reasons for why a project is created depend on your business objectives. If you're pitching a project to management, address the most prevalent business needs first. So first, from a business perspective, answer the following question: "Why is this important to my organization?"

Creating a Feasibility Study

A feasibility study is conducted to prove a problem actually exists, document the opportunities at hand, and then determine if a project can be created to resolve the problem or take advantage of the opportunity cited. A feasibility study may also look at the cost of the solution in relation to the possible rewards gained by its implementation.

Identifying the Business Needs

The business needs will examine the problem, opportunity, and solution to see how the potential project and its expected outcome fits within the realm of the business vision and goals. Recall the organizational pyramid in the following illustration? The business level of an organization asks, "Why is this important?" The focus of the business level is vision and strategy, so the results of the project must support that level.

Creating a Product Description

The initial product description will describe what the expected outcome of the project is to be. This may be a service, a product, or even a description of the desired future state. The initial product description does not have to be an exact specification document of what the project will create, though in some instances it may. Typically, the product description describes the solution or realized opportunity that the project will accomplish.

Creating a Project Charter

The project charter authorizes the project, officially naming the project manager and authorizing the project work. Such documents come from Senior Management and allow the project manager to begin the project work with the support, permission, and trust of management.

Project charters authorize. When you think of the project charter, think authority for the project manager.

Selecting the Project Manager

The project manager is officially named in the project charter, but the involvement of the project manager in the project will likely come early on in this process group. The project manager will need to know the expectations of his role in the type of organizational structure he is participating in (functional, matrix, projectized, or composite). The organizational structure recognition is important since it will determine the level of authority and power that the project manager can expect within a project.

Identifying the Planning Processes

The planning processes are iterative in nature; a project manager does not complete the planning processes and then move on to other activities within the project, never to return. Throughout the project the project manager, and the project team, will be returning to the planning processes as often as needed.

In particularly large projects, the project manager should include the stakeholders to obtain buy-in of the project deliverables. Including the project stakeholders not only accomplishes buy-in, but provides shared ownership of the project. This is important because shared ownership allows the customer to recognize the value and intensity of the project work and process. In addition, the project manager should include stakeholders to ensure the project deliverables are in alignment with what the stakeholders and the project team are expecting to receive.

Within large or highly technical projects, planning can also be known as rolling wave planning. Rolling wave planning focuses detailed planning on the immediate activities of the project, rather than on remote, future activities that may be affected by the outcome of the direct project results. The issues further downstream are addressed in rolling wave planning, but in high-level detail, rather than the specifics the pressing focus is on. This is an example of progressive elaboration.

exam
Watch

Rolling wave planning is an acceptable planning solution for long projects whose late activities in the project schedule are unknown or will be determined based on the results of early project phases.

Creating a Scope Statement

The scope statement is a document that describes the work, and only the required work, necessary to meet the project objectives. The scope statement establishes a common vision among the project stakeholders to establish the point and purpose of the project work. It is used as a baseline against which all future project decisions are made to determine if proposed changes or work results are aligned with expectations. The scope statement may, with adequate reason, be updated to reflect changes in the project work.

Recruiting the Project Team

The project team completes the project work. The project manager relies on the project team to do several tasks, including:

- Complete the project work
- Provide information on the work needed to complete the project scope
- Provide accuracy in project estimating
- Report on project progress

The project manager must use human resource and leadership skills to guide and lead the project team to project completion. In some organizations, the project team may be assigned to the project, while in other organizations the project manager may have the luxury of handpicking the project team members.

Creating the Work Breakdown Structure

The work breakdown structure (WBS) is an organized collection of the project-deliverable components to be created by project work. The project manager cannot complete this activity alone. The input and guidance of the project team is required as they are the individuals closest to the work and will be completing the actual activities within the project phases. The WBS will offer major input into planning, estimating, and scheduling processes throughout the project.

Completing the Initial Risk Assessment

Risk can be both good and bad. Generally, risk is a perceived threat (or opportunity) to the completion of the project. The initial risk assessment allows the project manager and the project team to determine what high-level risks may influence the feasibility, resources, and requirements to complete the project. The initial risk assessment may also steer the project toward a different solution.

Creating the Network Diagram

The network diagram, also called the Project Network Diagram (PND), illustrates the flow of activities to complete the project and/or the project phase. It identifies the sequencing of activities identified within the WBS and determines which activities may be scheduled sequentially versus in tandem.

Completing Estimates

Time and cost estimates are completed within the planning process. Time estimates reflect the amount of time to complete each activity within the WBS. Once the estimates are mapped to the PND, an accurate estimate of how long the project will take to complete may be created.

Cost estimates can be calculated a number of different ways, such as through top-down estimates, bottom-up estimates, or the dreaded informal "hallway estimates." All estimates should identify a range of variance reflective of the degree of confidence of the estimate, the assumption the estimate is based on, and how long the estimate is valid.

Discovering the Critical Path

The critical path is the chain of activities within the PND that cannot be delayed without delaying the project end date. There can be more than one critical path and it is possible for the critical path to change. The other paths within the PND have float or slack. Float or slack means these paths may be delayed, to a point, without delaying the end result of the project. Figure 3-2 shows a typical PND with the critical path in bold.

Creating the Project Schedule

The project schedule is dependent on the creation of the WBS, the PND, and the availability of the resources. Based on when the resources, the project team, and other required resources, such as equipment and facilities, are available the schedule can be determined. In many instances, the project must be scheduled from a time constraint. With a constraint of a deadline enforced on the project, all activities must be scheduled, from the project's start to its completion, to ensure the project can finish on time.

Completing the Project Budget

The project budget is the cost of the project, cash flow projections, and how the monies will be spent. The project budget should cover the cost of the team's time, facilities,

FIGURE 3-2   Network diagrams illustrate the sequence of events.

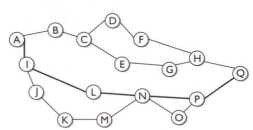

FIGURE 3-3   Cash flow projections allow an organization to plan for expenses.

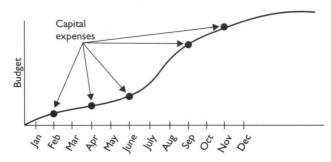

and all foreseeable expenses. Cash flow projections are needed to alert management as to when monies must be available for the project to continue. Figure 3-3 demonstrates a project with expected cash flow expenses.

Completing Risk Assessment

Risk assessment is an in-depth analysis of the project risks through qualitative and quantitative analysis. Qualitative risk analysis calls for a probability and impact matrix. Risks are typically categorized as high, medium, and low. Quantitative risk analysis is a more in-depth study of the identified risks. This technique calls for a risk matrix based on probability and impact. Quantitative analysis also uses simulations and decision tree models.

Completing Risk Response Planning

The risks are analyzed for both positive and negative impacts, entered through a risk matrix and then planned accordingly. Risks may be accepted, avoided, mitigated, countered, or planned for through contingency. Risks are also assigned to risk owners who will monitor thresholds and triggers.

Creating a Quality Management Plan

The quality management plan details how the project will map to the organizational quality policy; for example, ISO 9000 or Six Sigma specifics. The plan will provide specifics on how the project team will meet the quality expectations of the organizational quality assurance program. The quality management plan also sets the guidelines for how the project will adhere to quality control mechanisms and ongoing quality improvement. The following illustration demonstrates how QC fits within QA.

Completing Stakeholder Analysis

As part of planning, the stakeholders' expectations and requirements must be analyzed. The stakeholders' expectations must be documented, prioritized, and balanced between competing objectives. Managing stakeholders' expectations is crucial to project success, so having a complete understanding of their expectations is mandatory.

on the !ob

Stakeholder analysis allows the project manager and the project team to determine the expectations of the customer. If the customer doesn't know what their expectations are, the project manager cannot decide for them. The project manager and the customer must be in agreement with what the project should create before the creation begins.

Creating a Change Control Plan

Based on the scope statement, the project scope should not change—unless it is absolutely necessary. The project manager and the project team should create a change control plan that will specify how the project scope may be changed, what the procedure to change the scope is, and what the requirements are to make a change. On large or high-profile projects, the project manager may be working with a Change Control Board (CCB) to determine if changes should be approved and factored into a project scope.

Creating an Organizational Plan

The organizational plan determines who does what. Specifically, it documents the roles and responsibilities of the project stakeholders, including the project team, project sponsor, project manager, functional managers, and vendors. The organizational plan also defines the reporting structures within the organization. It is tightly integrated with the communications plan.

Creating a Communications Plan

The communications plan determines who needs what information, how they need it, and when it will be delivered. The plan specifies team meetings, reports, expectations for reports, and expectations of communication among team members. The communications plan must account for all needed communications within the project.

Consider a project manager of a high-profile project called Project XYZ. The project manager requires the project team members to report their progress on Project XYZ every Tuesday in the project status meeting. In addition to team members reporting their status, they will also need to update their work electronically through the Project Management Information System (PMIS). These communication requirements are defined in the communications management plan.

e x a m

W a t c h

It has been said that 90 percent of a project manager's time is spent communicating. Communicating equates to project management.

Completing the Project Plan

This formal document guides the project execution and control through the project phase(s). Senior Management must approve the plan prior to execution. The project plan's primary purpose is to communicate the assumptions, decisions, and risks to the involved stakeholders. In addition, the project plan documents the schedule, cost, and scope as baselines.

Officially Launching the Project

Planning is an iterative process. The result of planning is to allow the project work to begin. Once the project has reached a collective state of agreement between the project manager, management, the project team, and the customer, the project is officially allowed to begin.

Executing Processes

The executing processes allow the project work to perform. It is the execution of the project plan, the execution of the vendor management, and the management of the project implementation. The project manager works closely with the project team in this process to ensure that the work is being completed and that the work results are of quality. The project manager also works with vendors to ensure that their procured work is complete, of quality, and meets the obligations of the agreed contracts.

Authorizing the Project Work

A work authorization system is a method that allows work to begin according to schedule and circumstance. It provides for verification of predecessor activities and the permission to begin successor activities. The following illustration depicts the flow of work within a project's work authorization system.

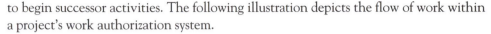

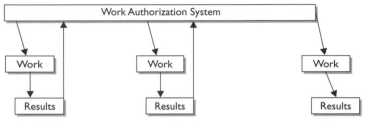

INSIDE THE EXAM

What, in this chapter, must you focus on for your PMP Exam? Hmm… could it be processes? Processes are activities that are completed by people, not things. On the exam you won't need to know facts like which process is the most important, but rather which activity should the project manager complete next? Just substitute "activity" for the appropriate process and you're on your way.

Product-orientated processes are unique to each project. Consider a construction project versus a technology project. Both projects have their own phases, but both also can share the project processes found within initiation, planning, execution, control, and closure. When you consider all of the different projects that happen in all of the different organizations, business types, and communities, you can imagine why the PMP exam will focus very little on product-orientated processes and more directly on project management processes.

Focus on the project management processes. Know the five process groups and how the processes among the groups are interrelated. Recall that the core processes follow a hard

logic in their sequencing and that the facilitating processes are more flexible and supportive to the core processes.

It will behoove you to know, if not memorize, Table 3-8 (shown later in the chapter). This table covers all of the processes and how they map to the knowledge areas. If you want to pass your exam, and I know you do, know which processes happen in which knowledge area. Create some witty acrostic to memorize the knowledge areas and the processes within each process group.

Here are a few other key exam tips to take from this chapter:

- Larger projects require more detail than smaller projects.
- Projects fail at the beginning, not the end.
- The processes may be customized to meet the demands or conditions of the project.
- Planning is iterative.
- Planning, executing, and controlling are tightly integrated.

Beginning Vendor Solicitation

In most projects, vendors are involved at some point. Part of the executing process is to solicit vendors should they need to be involved with the project. Adequate timing is required for the procurement process to allow the vendors to provide adequate, appropriate information for the project—and to allow the project manager to make an educated decision on which should be selected. Vendor solicitation includes obtaining quotations, bids, and proposals for the services or the goods to be purchased for the project completion.

Determining Vendor Source

This part of procurement involves making a decision as to which identified vendor will be the source of the service or good being procured. Source selection is based upon the selection criterion determined by the performing organization.

Administering Contracts

Procurement involves administering the contracts between the buyer and the seller. The contract must be fair and legal. The contract typically is a document that represents the offer and acceptance of both parties. Some organizations may utilize centralized contracting or a contracting office to manage all project contracts.

Mapping to Quality Assurance

As the project work continues, the project team and the project manager will need to verify that the project work results are mapping to the organization's quality assurance program as described in the quality management plan. Failure to adhere to the quality assurance program may result in rework, penalties, and project delays, as shown in the following illustration.

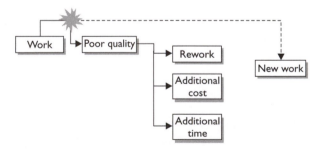

Dispersing Project Information

Information must be disseminated according to the communications plan. Stakeholders will need to be kept abreast of the project status. Management may want milestone reports, variance reports, and status reports. Customers will have specific communications requirements. All of these demands, from any stakeholder, should be documented within the communications plan—and then followed through in the execution process.

Ensuring Team Development

The project manager must work with the project team members to ensure that their level of proficiency is in agreement with their obligations on the project. This may involve classroom learning, shadowing between project team members, or on-the-job training. The success of the project work is dependent on the project team's ability. Should the team or team members be lagging in required knowledge to complete the project work, additional education and development is necessitated.

Controlling Processes

Controlling processes are the activities that ensure the project goes according to plan and the actions to implement when evidence proves the project is not going according to plan. Specifically, the controlling processes verify project work and the response to that work. In addition, the project manager must work to control the predicted cost and schedule of the project. Variances to the cost and schedule will affect the project's success.

Ensuring Quality Control

Quality control (QC) measures work results to determine if they are in alignment with quality standards. If the work results are not of quality, QC uses methods to determine why the results are inadequate and how to eliminate the causes of the quality deficiencies.

Providing Scope Verification

Scope verification is the process of verifying that the work results are within the expectations of the scope. It is typically done at project phase completion with the customer to formally accept the product of the project work. Should scope verification fail, the project scope must be compared against the work results. If the scope has not been met, the project may be halted, reworked, or delayed during a decision making process by the customer.

Implementing Scope Change Control

The project manager must follow the change management plan to ensure unneeded changes to the project scope do not occur. This includes scope creep that the project team may be completing on its own accord. For example, the project team members may be making additional adjustments to the equipment they are installing in a project, even through the project scope does not call for the additional adjustments. Scope change control ensures that the documented procedures to permit changes to scope are followed.

Leading Configuration Management

This process ensures the description of the project's product is precise, complete, and that it meets the demands of the stakeholder requirements. In addition, configuration management serves as a control agent for changes to the project deliverables. It monitors, guards, and documents changes to the scope. In some projects, configuration management may be the change control system. In other projects, it is part of the change control system.

Overseeing Change Control

The project manager must protect the project scope from unneeded change. Needed changes must be proven, documented, and analyzed for impacts on cost, schedule, and risks. The project manager must work within the confines of the change control plan and follow its guidelines regarding change requests, change approval or denials, and documentation. Overseeing change control may involve a Change Control Board that reviews, approves, or rejects the proposed changes for the project.

Managing Cost Control

Controlling the project's cost requires accurate estimates and then a check and balance against those estimates. Procurement management, cash flow, and fundamental accounting practices are required. Though cost control is dependent on project expenses, it also hinges on hidden and fluctuating expenses such as shipping, exchange rates for international projects, travel, and incidentals. Thus, accurate and thorough record keeping is imperative.

Enforcing Schedule Control

Schedule control requires constant monitoring of the project's progress, approval of phase deliverables, and task completion. Slippage must be analyzed early in the project to determine the root cause of the problem. Activities that slip may indicate inaccurate estimates, hidden work, or a poor WBS. Quality issues can also throw the project schedule when the time to redo project activities is taken into consideration, as shown in the following illustration. Finally, the project manager must also consider outside influences and their affect on the project—for example, weather, market conditions, cultural issues, and so on.

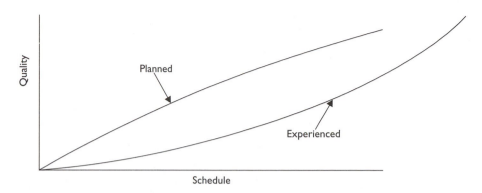

Monitoring Risk Response

Risk management requires risk ownership and monitoring by the project team members. As activities in the PND are completed, the project manager and the risk owners must pay special attention to the possible risks and the mitigation plans that may come into play. Risk responses, should they be acted on, may cause secondary risks, cost increases, and schedule delays. Risk response must be rapid and thorough—and their outcomes well-documented for historical reference for downstream activities and other projects.

on the
! o b

Risk response may also include risk impact statements that detail project risk, its possible impact on the project, and its probability. The project manager and management sign the risk impact statement for each identified risk beyond a predetermined score.

Ensuring Performance Reporting

The project manager and the project team must work together to report and record accurate completions of work. Performance reporting stems from accurate measurement by the project team, proof of work completion, and factual estimates. The project manager then churns the reported projects through earned value management, schedule baselines, cost baselines, and milestone targets. The status reports to management are reflective of where the project has been, where it stands now, and where it's heading.

Identifying Closing Processes

Closing a project is a wonderful feeling. Project closure has many requirements for it to be successful, however. Project closure requires a final, complete effort by the project manager, the project team, the project stakeholders, and management to officially close the project and move onto other opportunities. The activities in this process are typically associated with the end of a project, but most may also be completed within project phases, as shown in Figure 3-4.

FIGURE 3-4   Closing processes can be completed within projects and within project phases.

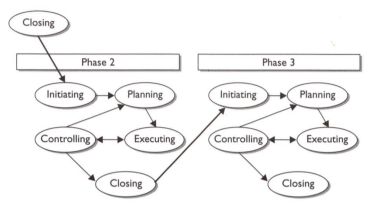

Auditing Procurement Documents

The project manager has spent the money, but on what? The procurement audit process requires accountability for the monies that have been invested in the project. In some instances, the financial audit is more formal, and an accountant or a finance professional reviews the project's accounting. In other instances, the process is considered a debriefing and is completed with the project manager and management. In practically all instances, the intensity of the procurement audit is relevant to the autonomy of the project manager: the more power and responsibility the project manager has in an organization, the more accountable he is for the project budget.

Completing Scope Verification

Scope verification is a control process. However, at the end of the project the scope must be verified for final acceptance. This process is completed with the project manager and the key stakeholders. Scope verification is the process of inspecting, touring, and "taking a walk-through" of the project deliverables to confirm that the requirements of the project have been met. Scope verification may happen at different intervals throughout the project, such as at key milestones or phase completions. Scope verification at the end of a project may require a formal sign-off from the customer that the project is complete and to their satisfaction.

Closing Vendor Contracts

At the completion of a project or project phase the vendor contracts must be closed out. Confirmation that vendor invoices and purchase orders have been fulfilled, met, and paid is needed to complete the vendor closeout process. Closing out vendor contracts may also require proof or delivery of the goods or services purchased. The vendor contracts may be audited to confirm the vendor responsibilities have been met.

Closing Administrative Duties

When the project is completed, the project manager must finalize all reports, document the project experience, and provide evidence of customer acceptance. The project manager will create a final report reflecting the project success, or failure. The project manager will also provide information reflective of the project product and how it met the project requirements, and then will complete the lessons learned documentation.

Submitting Final Reports

Once the project documentation has been completed, the project manager will submit the final reports to the appropriate parties as outlined in the communications management plan. The final reports will include variance reports, status reports, cost and schedule accountability, and team member performance reviews, as required by the performing organization.

Archiving Project Records

The project records should be archived so that other project managers can use the information on their projects. In addition, the archives should serve as a wealth of historical information for later reference, future project managers, and reference for versioning, updates, or potential changes to the current project deliverables.

Reassigning the Project Team Members

At some point in the project, based on the organizational structure, team members will be reassigned to new projects. Reassigning project team members is of utmost importance in a projectized organization where project team members are with a project full-time through completion. As the project in a projectized organization nears completion, the project team may be anxious about their next assignment. In a functional matrix environment, the project team may fluctuate at phases or milestones as they complete their assignments and then move onto other activities within the organization.

Celebrating!

At project completion, a celebration to thank and reward the project team for their hard work and dedication to the project is needed. Celebrations are also a good time to reflect on the work completed, the challenges of the project, and to come back together as a team before moving onto other projects and opportunities within the organization.

Examining the Process Interactions

The activities within each of the five processes all lead to one thing: project completion. The activities within one process allow the project to move into another. As these five processes, initiation, planning, execution, control, and closure, are not a series of events, but rather an integrated process, the activities within one process may coincide with an activity within another. For example, a project manager may be working through the execution process to administer the contracts of a vendor while simultaneously working with the vendor through scope verification.

To elaborate, consider a vendor that is not performing the contracted work to the agreed level of quality. Contract administration falls within the executing processes, but QC falls within the controlling processes. The agreement and execution of the contract will govern the expected level of quality the vendor will be required to provide. Figure 3-5 shows that all of the processes are interrelated and contribute to the other processes.

How Process Groups Interact

Imagine any project: building a new house, creating a new service, deploying a technology solution. Within any of these projects there will be a logical approach from start to finish. Within project management, and in particular for your PMP exam, the flow of activities must be documented from initiation to closure. The five processes don't necessarily allow the work to progress—they serve more as a control mechanism to identify and oversee the flow of actions within the project.

FIGURE 3-5   The processes within a project are interrelated.

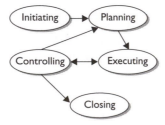

Each process has unique activities, as we've seen already in this chapter, but each of these activities contributes and coincides with the project work. The activities guide the project work from concept to completion. Specifically, the parts of the processes are the gears to the "project machine." The processes allow for a specific, manageable, and expected outcome of the project. Within each process, there are three common components:

- **Inputs**   Documented conditions, values, and expectations that start the given process
- **Tools and techniques**   The actions to evaluate and act upon the inputs to create the outputs
- **Outputs**   The documented results of a process that may serve as an input to another process

These three components are fundamental through all five processes. Typically, plans, documented evidence of problems, or documented outcomes of activities, are inputs to a project process. For example, resource planning requires the WBS. The WBS is an input to resource planning, but also an output of the planning process group. The tools and techniques used to plan for resources include expert judgment, alternative identification, and your nifty project management software. The relationship between inputs, tools and techniques, and outputs is shown in the following illustration.

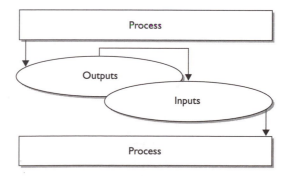

Recognizing the Process Types

Each of the five processes is tied to other processes in the realm of project management. Specifically, the outputs of one action within a process serve as inputs to the tools and techniques of another process.

Within the different process categories, there are two categories of process types:

- **Core processes**   These activities are required in practically every project. They follow a logical sequence to completion within the project. These core processes are also iterative in nature; they may be repeated until an acceptable solution is discovered.

- **Facilitating processes**   These activities are more flexible than the core processes, and their involvement in the project are not as stringent. Although these processes are flexible, they are not considered optional activities. You can think of the facilitating processes as supportive actions within a process, as shown in Figure 3-6.

The Initiating Process Group

The initiating process, as we've discussed, launches the five processes of a project. The key action to this process is authorizing. Initiating authorizes the project or the phase. Once initiation is complete, the project may move into the planning process.

The Planning Process Group

Projects fail at the beginning, not the end. Planning is the most important process within project management, because the work you are about to complete has likely

FIGURE 3-6   Facilitating processes support core processes.

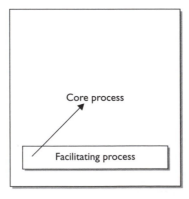

never been done before. While planning is of utmost importance—and has the most processes—it does not mean the bulk of a project is planning. Planning is relative to the scope of the project and the usefulness of research completed. As you know, planning is an iterative process throughout the project lifecycle. The core processes, their purpose, and their relationship with other processes within the planning process are defined in Table 3-1.

TABLE 3-1   Planning Core Processes Are Iterative

Core Process	Purpose	Precedes
Scope planning	To create a document that will guide project decisions.	Scope definition
Scope definition	To breakdown the project deliverables into manageable elements. The sum of the smaller elements equate to the project scope.	Activity definition Resource planning Cost estimating Risk management planning
Activity definition	To define the required activities, and only the required activities, to complete the project scope.	Activity sequencing Activity duration estimating
Resource planning	To ascertain the required resources to achieve the defined activities to complete the project work. Resources include people, equipment, and materials.	Activity duration estimating Cost estimating
Activity sequencing	To determine the best sequence of planned activities within the project work.	Schedule development
Activity duration estimating	To determine the estimated required work units to successfully complete the defined activities.	Cost estimating Schedule development
Cost estimating	To determine an estimated amount of monies to complete the project work using the defined facilities, services, and goods.	Cost budgeting
Risk management planning	To determine the risks within the project and how to react to the identified risks.	Schedule development Cost budgeting

TABLE 3-1   Planning Core Processes Are Iterative *(continued)*

Core Process	Purpose	Precedes
Schedule development	To determine the project schedule based on the sequence of activities, the required resources, and the required monies. The schedule development process reveals an estimated reflection of when all of the required work can be completed with the given resources.	Project plan development
Cost budgeting	To determine the estimated cost of the activities to complete the project work.	Project plan development
Project plan development	Creating a coherent compilation of the other planning processes to guide the project execution.	Executing processes

While the core processes follow a stringent pattern of completion, the facilitating processes are used as needed in no particular order. The facilitating processes are, however, linked to the core processes. They do not typically follow a particular flow from start to finish. The facilitating processes within the planning process are defined in Table 3-2.

TABLE 3-2   Facilitating Processes Support the Core Processes

Facilitating Process	Purpose	Precedes
Quality planning	To determine the quality assurance standards used by the organization. The quality assurance standards that are relevant to the project must be planned into the project.	
Communications planning	To determine who needs what, when they need it, and in what modality (paper, electronic, and so on) it may be needed.	

TABLE 3-2	Facilitating Processes Support the Core Processes (continued)	
Facilitating Process	**Purpose**	**Precedes**
Organizational planning	To determine the project roles and responsibility. This also determines the reporting structure between the project manager, the project team, and management.	Staff acquisition
Staff acquisition	To acquire the needed people to complete the determined project work.	
Risk identification	To identify the risks, rewards, and penalties associated with the project.	Qualitative risk analysis
Qualitative risk analysis	To prioritize the impact of the risks on the project (typically in a high, medium, and low ranking).	Quantitative risk analysis
Quantitative risk analysis	To measure and consider the probability and associated impact of the risks on the project.	
Risk response planning	To avoid, eliminate, reduce, or create a planned reaction to the identified risks within the project.	
Procurement planning	To determine what goods and services must be procured and when the goods and services will need to be procured in the project life cycle.	Solicitation planning
Solicitation planning	To determine the possible vendors to provide the goods and services for the project.	

The Executing Processes Group

The project work must be planned for, and then the project plan must be acted upon, followed, and adjusted. The executing processes are the activities that get the project work done. Within the executing processes there are also core processes and facilitating processes. Actually, there is only one core process, as Table 3-3 illustrates.

TABLE 3-3   The Core Process of Executing Is Following the Project Plan

Core Process	Purpose	Precedes
Project plan execution	To complete the project according to plan. The project plan may also be adjusted based on the outcome of the facilitating processes.	Facilitating processes

The facilitating processes support the core processes by allowing the project plan to be updated as needed. Table 3-4 shows the facilitating processes, their purpose, and what activities they precede.

TABLE 3-4   Facilitating Processes Support Project Plan Execution

Core Process	Purpose	Precedes
Solicitation	To accept quotes, bids, proposals, and offers to complete the solicited work as defined through solicitation planning.	Source selection
Source selection	To determine which source (vendor) will fulfill the procured good or service.	Contract administration
Contract administration	To manage a fair and balanced relationship between the buyer and the seller.	
Quality assurance	To meet the organization's quality standards. QA is an ongoing process that measures the quality of the work results against the demands of the quality standards of the performing organization.	
Team development	To develop the competencies of the project team as a whole and the individual members on the project team.	
Information distribution	To follow the details of the communications management plan; specifically to disperse the required information to the correct parties according to their identified needs and modalities.	

The Controlling Processes Group

Project management control requires measurement. Controlling a project requires active measurement against set goals, objectives, and expected outcomes. Should the measurements fall short of expectations, the planning processes are revisited. Within planning, variances to time and cost are reacted to with additional staffing, tradeoffs between schedule and budget, and the addition of possible resources necessary to complete the project on time. In addition, controlling processes allow for preventive action to squelch foreseen variances, failure, and quality control issues. There are two core processes within the controlling processes, as seen in Table 3-5.

The facilitating processes within the controlling processes contribute and support the core processes. The facilitating processes are listed in Table 3-6.

The Closing Processes Group

The closeout processes are typically associated with the project closure, but may also be applied to phase completion. Recall that the project phases are unique to each project, while the processes within project management exist within the project management life cycle. The core processes of the closing processes are shown in Table 3-7.

Customizing Process Interactions

The processes discussed in the previous section are the mainstream, generally accepted order of operations. You can count on the core processes existing and progressing in the preceding order. However, having said that, you can also count on these processes to be flexible, pliable, and customized to work in any order the project demands. Project processes are not made of stone, but flexible steel.

TABLE 3-5   Core Processes Interact with Each Other and the Facilitating Processes

Core Process	Purpose	Works with
Performance reporting	To determine variances, project performance, and forecasting of project outcome.	Integrated change control Facilitating processes
Integrated change control	To manage change across all facets of the project.	Performance reporting Facilitating processes

TABLE 3-6 Facilitating Processes Support the Core Processes

Facilitating Process	Purpose	Precedes
Scope verification	To verify that phase and project deliverables are in alignment with customer expectations. Scope verification formalizes the acceptance.	Scope change control
Scope change control	To protect the project scope from change.	
Schedule control	To prevent unnecessary changes to the schedule, to control the flow of activities, and to forecast completion.	
Cost control	To prevent unnecessary changes to the project budget.	
Quality control	To conform to the required organizational quality standards and to remove or improve faulty, below quality, performance.	
Risk monitoring and control	To monitor and maintain risks, responses to risk, introduction of new and secondary risks. In addition, allows for control of currently identified risks and the planned responses to the identified risks.	

TABLE 3-7 Closing Processes Close Out Procurement and Administrative Duties

Core Process	Purpose	Precedes
Contract closeout	To complete and finalize any procurement issues such as payment, inspection of procured services and goods, and any open project items.	Administrative closure
Administrative closure	To gather, evaluate, and disseminate the required information on the project or phase, its performance, quality, and completeness. Administrative closure also includes completing the lessons learned document and filing for future reference.	

Here are some general guidelines to know about customizing project processes:

■ Facilitating processes may be shifted in sequence to meet the demands of the project (such as the timing of the procurement processes).

■ All processes may not be needed on all projects, but the absence of a project doesn't mean it wasn't needed. The project manager and the project team should identify all of the processes required to make the project a successful one.

■ Projects that are resource dependent may define roles and responsibilities prior to scope creation. This is because the scope of the project may be limited by the availability of the resources to complete the scope.

■ The processes may be governed by a project constraint. Consider a predetermined deadline, budget, or project scope. The project constraint, such as a deadline, will determine the activity sequencing, the need for resources, risk management, and other processes.

■ Larger projects require more detail. Remember that projects fail at the beginning, not the end.

■ Subprojects and smaller projects have more flexibility with the processes based on the process usefulness. For example, a project with a relatively small team may not benefit from an in-depth communications plan the same as a large project with 35 project team members would.

Plotting the Processes

The first three chapters of this book have focused on the project management endeavor, the project management context, and the project management processes. Chapters 4 through 12 focus on the project management knowledge areas. In these chapters, we'll zoom in on the processes we've identified and breakdown the topics into exam specific information.

While the information we've covered in this chapter is important, it is more an umbrella of the nine knowledge areas you'll want to focus on for your PMP exam. Table 3-8 maps out the 39 project management processes to where they typically fall within the nine knowledge areas and which chapter in this book will cover the associated process.

TABLE 3-8 The Project Management Processes Map the Project Management Knowledge Areas.

	Initiating	Planning	Executing	Controlling	Closing	Chapter
Project integration management		Developing the project plan.	Project plan execution	Integrated change control		4
Project scope management	Project initiation	Creating and defining the project scope.		Scope verification and change control		5
Project time management		Defining activities, their sequence and their estimated duration. Developing the project schedule.		Schedule control		6
Project cost management		Determining the required resources, their estimated costs, and completing cost budgeting.		Enforcing cost control.		7
Project quality management		Planning for quality.	Adhering to the performing organization's quality assurance requirements.	Enforcing quality control on the project.		8
Project human resource management		Completing organizational planning and staff acquisition.	Ensuring team development.			9
Project communications management		Creating the communications management plan.	Distributing the required information to the appropriate parties.	Reporting on project performance.	Completing administrative closure.	10
Project risk management		Completing risk management planning, risk identification, qualitative and quantitative risk analysis, and risk responses.		Monitoring and controlling risk.		11

TABLE 3-8	The Project Management Processes Map the Project Management Knowledge Areas. *(continued)*

	Initiating	Planning	Executing	Controlling	Closing	Chapter
Project procurement management		Completing the procurement and solicitation planning.	Soliciting vendors to participate on the project. Completing source selection based on defined criterion, and then following-through with contract administration.		Completing the contract closeout.	12

CERTIFICATION SUMMARY

There are two types of processes: product-orientated processes and project-orientated processes. *Product-orientated processes* are the unique processes within a project to create the deliverable of the project. These processes are special because they are unique to each product. The *project management processes* are universal to all projects. For the PMP exam, and the rest of this book, your focus will be on these processes.

There are five processes groups within a project. You'll want to know what activity happens within each of these groups. Projects start in the Initiating process group, where projects get authorized. From here the project moves into the planning process group. Planning is an iterative process and allows the project objectives to be determined, as well as how the project will achieve those objects. The project plan is executed in the executing process group. The controlling process group is where project performance is monitored and measured. Finally, the project is completed and the scope is verified in the closing process.

You should know that a project can move between planning, controlling, and executing as conditions change. For example, a new risk may be identified. This risk is analyzed and then a risk response is created in the planning processes group. The project work moves on but the risk management is implemented during the executing processes. The response to the risk is monitored in controlling. Should the risk change, the project can revisit the planning processes. Don't subscribe to the theory that the project work stops as the project moves back into planning. Other project activities may continue to operate as the project planning processes group is revisited.

The project moves along according to the project schedule and the project network diagram. Activities on the critical path are actively monitored for slippage while non-critical path activities are periodically checked for slippage. This is important as activities on the critical path have no tolerance for delays, while non-critical path activities can be delayed as long as they do not delay the project's completion.

As the project progresses the project manager must monitor and communicate the project performance. Work results that are below an accepted level of performance must be adjusted with corrective actions to bring the project back into alignment with the cost, schedule, and scope baselines. Communication of the project performance is one of the key elements for successful project management—and for passing the PMP exam.

KEY TERMS

To pass the PMP exams, you will need to memorize these terms and their definitions. For maximum value, create your own flashcards based on these definitions and review them daily. The definitions can be found within this chapter and in the glossary.

closing	initiating	project charter
controlling	knowledge areas	project management processes
core processes	planning	scope statement
executing	process groups	
facilitating processes	product-orientated processes	

✓ TWO-MINUTE DRILL

Project Management Processes

❑ Projects are comprised of processes. People, not things, complete processes; processes move the project or phase to completion.

❑ There are two broad categories of processes across all project types: project management processes and product-orientated processes. Project management processes are universal to all projects as they control the project management life cycle. Product-orientated processes are unique to the product the project is creating.

❑ The five process groups, initiating, planning, executing, controlling, and closing comprise projects and project phases. These five process groups have sets of actions that move the project forward towards completion.

❑ Within the five process groups there are two categories of processes: core and facilitating. Core processes are logical in order and follow a somewhat stringent progression. Facilitating processes are more flexible and support the core processes.

Determining the Need for Projects

❑ Projects are created to provide a solution for a problem or to take advantage of an opportunity. Projects can be created to reduce costs, reduce waste, increase revenue, increase productivity and efficiency, or produce other results. The project manager should know why the project is created in order to aim towards the project purpose.

❑ Some projects require a feasibility study to prove that the problem exists or to conduct root cause analysis to find the root of a given problem. Feasibility studies also determine the possibility of the project to solve the identified problem for a reasonable cost and within a reasonable amount of time.

❑ The product description describes the expected outcome of the project. The product description should define what the project is creating. If the project is solving a problem, the product description should describe how the organization will perform without the problem in existence. If the project is seizing a market opportunity, it should describe the organization with opportunity seized. Basically, product descriptions describe life after a successful project.

Project Management Framework

❑ The three components of processes, inputs, tools and techniques, and outputs, spurn decisions, conditions, plans, and reactions to conditions and progress. The output of one process serves as the input to another. Within each process, the tools and techniques, such as expert judgment, guide and influence the output of a process. A faulty output will likely influence downstream processes negatively.

❑ Project processes can be customized to meet the needs and demands of the project. Some processes may be moved to better meet the conditions and requirements of a given project. In some instances, a process may be removed from a project. Use caution: a process that is not completed does not necessarily mean it was not needed.

❑ The nine knowledge areas are comprised of the project management processes we've discussed in detail in this chapter. The process groups discussed in this chapter map to the nine knowledge areas:

1. Project integration management

2. Project scope management

3. Project time management

4. Project cost management

5. Project quality management

6. Project human resource management

7. Project communications management

8. Project risk management

9. Project procurement management

SELF TEST

1. What is a project process?
   A. The creation of a product or service
   B. The progressive elaboration resulting in a product
   C. A series of actions that bring about a result
   D. A series of actions that allow the project to move from concept to deliverable

2. Within a project there are two distinct types of processes. Which of the following processes is unique to the project?
   A. EVM processes
   B. Project management planning
   C. IPECC
   D. A product-oriented process

3. There are five project management processes that allow projects to move from start to completion. Which one of the following is not one of the project management process groups?
   A. Initiating
   B. Planning
   C. Communicating
   D. Closing

4. Of the following, which is the logical order of the project management processes?
   A. Initiating, planning, controlling, executing, closing
   B. Planning, initiating, controlling, executing, closing
   C. Initiating, planning, executing, controlling, closing
   D. Planning, initiating, executing, closing

5. Which of the project management processes is progressively elaborated?
   A. Planning
   B. Communicating
   C. Contract administration
   D. Closing

6. The ongoing process of project planning is also known as _____.
   A. Constant integration planning
   B. Rolling wave planning
   C. Continuous planning
   D. Phase gates

7. You are the project manager for the AQA Project. You would like to include several of the customers in the project planning sessions. Your project leader would like to know why the stakeholders should be involved—your project team will be determining the best method to reach the project objectives. You should include the stakeholders because _____.

    A. It generates goodwill between the project team and the stakeholders

    B. It allows the stakeholders to see the project manager as the authority of the project

    C. It allows the project team to meet the stakeholders and express their concerns regarding project constraints

    D. It allows the stakeholders to realize the shared ownership of the project

8. You have requested that several of the stakeholders participate in the different phases of the project. Why is this important?

    A. It prevents scope creep.

    B. It allows for scope constraints.

    C. It improves the probability of satisfying the customer requirements.

    D. It allows for effective communications.

9. The information from the planning phase is input into which of the following processes?

    A. Initiating

    B. Controlling

    C. Executing

    D. Closing

10. The information from the initiating phase is input into which of the following processes?

    A. Planning

    B. Executing

    C. Controlling

    D. All of the project phases

11. Which process represents an ongoing effort throughout the project?

    A. Lessons learned

    B. Planning

    C. Closing

    D. EVM

12. Which of the following processes happen in the correct order?

    A. Scope planning, activity definition, activity duration estimating, cost budgeting

    B. Scope planning, resource planning, activity duration estimating, activity sequencing

    C. Scope definition, scope planning, activity definition, activity sequencing

    D. Scope planning, scope definition, activity definition, activity sequencing

13. Which of the following planning processes is a facilitating process?

    A. Activity definition

    B. Cost budgeting

    C. Resource planning

    D. Quality planning

14. Which of the following planning processes is concerned with reporting relationships?

    A. Organizational planning

    B. Resource planning

    C. Scope planning

    D. Activity definition

15. Of the following, which facilitating process is most concerned with mitigation?

    A. Quality planning

    B. Risk response planning

    C. Procurement planning

    D. Risk identification

16. You are the project manager for the FTG Project. This project will affect several lines of business and controversy on the project deliverables already abounds. You have 45 key stakeholders on this project representing internal customers from all areas of your organization. With this many stakeholders, what challenge will be the most difficult for the project's success?

    A. Communication

    B. Managing stakeholder expectations

    C. Managing scope creep

    D. Coordinating communications between the project manager, project team, and the project stakeholders

17. Which of the following is representative of a project constraint?

    A. A project that must be finished by year's end

    B. 45 stakeholders on a long-term project

    C. The requirement to complete EVM

    D. The requirement to produce a new product

18. You are a project manager of a large construction project. There are many different stakeholders involved in the project and each has their own opinion as to what the project

should create. To maintain communication, set objectives, and document all decisions, you can say that larger projects generally require _____.

A. A larger budget

B. More detail

C. Phase gate estimating

D. A large project team

19. In order to create a network diagram, the project manager needs which of the following?

A. Activity sequencing

B. Project sponsor approval of the WBS

C. The WBS dictionary

D. A cost baseline

20. Which of the following is considered an output of the cost budgeting process?

A. Cost estimating

B. Resource requirements

C. The risk management plan

D. The cost baseline

21. Which of the following is considered an output of risk management planning?

A. Activity lists

B. WBS

C. The risk management plan

D. The scope management plan

22. Which of the following is not an input to schedule development?

A. The cost baseline

B. Resource requirements

C. The risk management plan

D. The network diagram

23. Frances is the project manager of the JHG Project. This project is very similar to a recent project she completed for another customer. Which planning process will Frances need to finish first to ensure the project is completed successfully?

A. Solicitation planning

B. Scope definition

C. Activity sequencing

D. Quality planning

24. You are the project manager for the BKL Project. This type of project has never been attempted before by your organization. The stakeholders already have high requirements for the project deliverables and you need to create a change control system. This system should be controlled by which of the following?

    A. A formal change control form

    B. It should be completed by the team

    C. The Change Control Board

    D. It is specific to the organizational structure

25. Complete this statement: Projects fail _____.

    A. At the beginning, not the end

    B. During Initiating, not Closing

    C. Because of inadequate project managers

    D. Because of the project manager

SELF TEST ANSWERS

1. ☑ **C.** A process is a series of actions bringing about a result. Recall that processes exist in projects and in project phases.

   ☒ **A** is incorrect since this describes the project as a whole. **B** is incorrect since it also somewhat describes a phase or project as a whole. **D** is incorrect as it describes the series of processes moving through the project.

2. ☑ **D.** Product-orientated processes are unique to the product the project is creating.

   ☒ EVM processes, choice **A,** are part of project performance measurement. **B,** project management planning, is universal to project management. **C,** IPECC, is the acrostic for the five process groups: initiation, planning, executing, controlling, and closing.

3. ☑ **C.** Communications is an activity that will consume much of the project manager's time, but it is not one of the five process groups.

   ☒ **A, B,** and **D** are incorrect choices as initiating, planning, and closing are three of the five process groups.

4. ☑ **C.** Initiating, planning, controlling, executing, and closing is the correct order of the processes presented.

   ☒ **A** is incorrect since it is not the correct order of the processes. While **A** does list all five of the process groups, it does not list them in the correct order. **B** and **D** are incorrect since they do not list the processes in the proper order (nor, with D, in their entirety). Remember on the PMP exam you will need to choose the answer that is most correct according to the question presented.

5. ☑ **A.** Planning is an iterative process, which is also progressively elaborated. Throughout the project the project team and the project manager will revisit the planning processes to consider, update, and react to conditions and circumstances within the project.

   ☒ **B** is incorrect since communicating is not one of the process groups. **C** is incorrect as contract Administration is not a process group. **D** is incorrect since closing is not an iterative process, but a concluding process.

6. ☑ **B.** Rolling wave planning is a description of the planning process in most large projects. It requires the project manager and the project team to revisit the planning process to address the next phase, implementation, or piece of the project.

   ☒ **A** is incorrect since the planning process is not constant but iterative. **C** is incorrect since there is some pause to the planning processes. **D** is incorrect because phase gates are conditions that allow the projects to move from phase to phase.

7. ☑ **D.** Involving the stakeholders in the planning processes allows for shared ownership of the project.
☒ **A** is incorrect because, although it may generate goodwill between the project team and the stakeholders, this is not the prominent goal of stakeholder involvement. **B** is incorrect because the project charter and the project manager reputation will establish authority more than stakeholder involvement. **C** is incorrect because, though the stakeholders may express their concerns regarding the project constraints, such concerns should be addressed as part of the planning processes, not in addition to them.

8. ☑ **C.** By involving the stakeholders at different aspects of the project, their requirements are more likely to be met. Specifically, scope verification ensures that the stakeholders are seeing that phase deliverables, project progress, quality, and expectations are being met.
☒ **A** is incorrect because the untimely introduction of stakeholders can actually increase scope creep. **B** is incorrect because scope constraints will be evident early in the project, rather than during the implementation of the project work. **D** is incorrect since stakeholder presence does not ensure effective communications. Effective communications will stem from the project manager and the requirements identified and documented in the communications management plan.

9. ☑ **C.** The outputs of the planning phase are a direct input to the executing processes.
☒ **A** is incorrect since initiating processes precede planning processes. **B** is incorrect since conditions in the controlling processes are inputs to the planning processes, not the reverse. **D** is incorrect because planning processes do not serve as a direct input to the closing processes.

10. ☑ **A.** The initiating processes serve as a direct input to the planning processes.
☒ **B, C,** and **D** are incorrect because initiating processes do not directly serve as an input to the executing, controlling, and closing processes.

11. ☑ **B.** Planning is the iterative process evident throughout the project.
☒ **A** is incorrect since lessons learned is not a process group. Closing may be evident at the end of project phases and at the end of the project, but it is not an ongoing effort like the planning process. **D,** EVM, is not an ongoing process.

12. ☑ **D.** The correct order is scope planning, scope definition, activity definition, activity sequencing (Table 3-1 shows the order of these core planning processes).
☒ Choices **B, C,** and **D** do not show the processes in the correct order.

13. ☑ **D.** Quality Planning is the only facilitating process listed.
☒ **A** is incorrect since activity definition is a core process. **B** is incorrect since cost budgeting is also a core process. **C,** resource planning, is also a core process so it too is not a correct answer.

14. ☑ **A.** Organizational planning is the facilitating planning process which defines roles and responsibilities—and the reporting structure within the project.
    ☒ **B** is incorrect because resource planning is the determination of the required resources to complete the project objectives. **C** is incorrect since it is the determination of what the project will and will not do. **D** is incorrect since activity definition is the definition of the required activities to complete the project work.

15. ☑ **B.** Mitigation is a response to risk.
    ☒ **A,** quality planning, is incorrect since it focuses on QA and the enforcement of QC. **C** is concerned with procurement management. **D** is incorrect because the identification of risk does not guarantee, or in some instances warrant, mitigation.

16. ☑ **B.** On a project with 45 key stakeholders, the project manager must work to manage stakeholder expectations. Given the impact of the project and the identified controversy, the project manager will need to proceed with caution to ensure the project deliverables meet the required expectations of the stakeholders.
    ☒ **A** is incorrect because, though communications may be the most time-consuming activity for the project, it is not the most difficult to manage. **C** is incorrect because managing scope creep can be controlled through an effective change control system. Scope creep may be an issue, but it is likely not the largest issue with this number of key stakeholders. **D** is incorrect since the communication between the project manager, the project team, and the stakeholders will be governed by the communications management plan.

17. ☑ **A** is the best choice since it is a time constraint.
    ☒ Choice **B** is not a constraint, but a project attribute. **C** is incorrect since it describes a project requirement, not a project constraint. **D** is incorrect since the requirement to produce a new product may be the project itself, not the constraint.

18. ☑ **B.** Larger projects require more detail.
    ☒ **A** is incorrect since larger projects don't always require a larger budget; consider an Add/Move/Change project to replace a piece of equipment. The project work is shallow, but the piece of equipment may be very expensive. **C** is incorrect because not all large projects will implement phase gate estimating. **D** is incorrect because a large project does not always mandate a large project team; consider a large project with very few resources available to complete the project work.

19. ☑ **A.** The network diagram illustrates the sequence of events within the project.
    ☒ **B** is incorrect as the project sponsor may not approve, or need to approve, the WBS in all projects. **C** is incorrect because the WBS dictionary is not needed to create a network diagram. **D** is also incorrect since the cost baseline is not necessary to create a network diagram.

20. ☑ **D.** The cost budgeting process creates the cost baseline.
☒ **A** is incorrect since the cost estimates are an input to the cost budgeting process. **B** is incorrect because resource requirements serve as an input to cost estimating. **C** is incorrect because the risk management plan serves as an input to the cost budgeting process.

21. ☑ **C.** The risk management plan is the output of the risk management planning process.
☒ Answers **A** and **B,** Activity Lists and the WBS, are incorrect because they are neither inputs nor outputs of the risk management planning process. Choice **D,** the scope management plan, is incorrect since it is not an output of the risk management planning process.

22. ☑ **A.** The cost baseline is an output of the cost budgeting process; it is not an input to schedule development.
☒ **B.** Resource requirements are not an output of schedule development. Choice **C** is incorrect since the risk management plan is an output of the risk management planning process. **D** is incorrect because the network diagram is not an output of schedule development, but an input into schedule development.

23. ☑ **B.** Even though the projects are similar, Frances must still define the project scope.
☒ **A** is incorrect since not all projects will need procurement. **C** and **D** are incorrect because scope definition must precede activity sequencing and quality planning.

24. ☑ **C.** A Change Control Board (CCB) will review and approve changes to the project scope. Due to the high requirements of the stakeholders, a CCB can help fend off unneeded changes, and allow the project manager to focus on the project management activities, rather than the potential flood of change requests.
☒ **A** and **D,** while correct in theory, are incorrect since they do not answer the question as fully as choice **C** does. Choice **B** is incorrect because the project team should not review and approve changes in this scenario.

25. ☑ **A.** Projects fail at the beginning, not the end. A poor requirements document, inadequate needs assessments, unfulfilled planning, and more early processes can contribute to project failure.
☒ **B, C,** and **D** are not correct choices. Choice **A** is the best answer.

Part II

PMP Exam Essentials

4

Implementing Project Integration Management

W hat the heck is *project integration management?* Project integration management is the heart of project management and is made up of the day-to-day processes the project manager relies on to ensure that all of the parts of the project work together.

Put simply, project integration management is the way the gears of the project work together.

Within any project there are many moving parts: time management, cost management, schedule conflicts, human resource issues, iterative planning, and much, much more. Project integration management is the art and science of ensuring that your project moves forward, that your plan is fully developed and properly implemented. Project integration management requires your project, regardless of it size and impact, to mesh with the existing operations of your organization.

Project integration management requires finesse, as you, as the project manager, will have to negotiate with stakeholders for a resolution to competing project objectives. It requires organization, as you'll have to develop, coordinate, and record your project plan. It requires the ability to accomplish your project plan. It requires leadership, record-keeping, and political savvy, as you'll have to deal with potential changes throughout your project implementation. And, perhaps most importantly, it requires flexibility and adaptability throughout the project execution.

In this chapter we'll cover three big topics you'll have to master to pass your PMP exam, and you'll also need these skills to successfully implement projects out in the world. These topics are

- Developing the project plan
- Executing the project plan
- Managing change control

As you've learned already, all projects need a project plan—it's up to the project manager and the project team to create one. Then the project manager must work with the project team to ensure the work is being completed as it was planned. The project manager must follow all the subsidiary project plans, such as the Risk Management Plan, the Schedule Management Plan, and the Communications Plan. Finally, the project manager must work throughout the project to control changes across all facets of the project. Figure 4-1 shows the complete picture of project integration management.

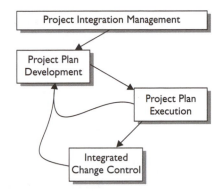

FIGURE 4-1

Project
integration
management uses
Development,
Execution, and
Integrated
Change Control.

Developing the Project Plan

The project plan is not a museum piece. You'll use, wrinkle, update, and depend on your project plan like a playbook for a Super Bowl coach. The project plan is developed with the project team, stakeholders, and management. It is the guide to how the project should flow and how the project will be managed, and it reflects the values, priorities, and conditions influencing the project.

Project plan development requires an iterative process of progressive elaboration. The project manager will revise and update the plan as research and planning reveal more information and as the project develops. For example, an initial project plan may describe a broad overview of what the project entails, what the desired future state should be, and the general methods used to achieve the goals of the plan. Then, after research, careful planning, and discovery, the project plan will develop into a concise document that details the work involved in and expectations of the project; how the project will be controlled, measured, and managed; and how the project should move. In addition, the project plan will contain all of the supporting detail, specify the project organization, and allow for growth in the plan.

e x a m

w a t c h   *The project plan guides the project manager through the Execution and Control process groups. The project plan is designed to control the project. As a whole,* *the point of the project plan is to communicate to the project team, stakeholders, and management how the project will be managed and controlled.*

Understanding the Project Plan's Purpose

The project plan is more than a playbook to determine what work needs to be accomplished. The project plan is a fluid document that will control several elements:

- **Provide structure** The project plan is developed to provide a structure to get the project to completion. It is a thorough, but concise, collection of documents that will serve as a point of reference through the project execution.

- **Provide documentation** "Noggin Plans"—the kind between your ears—are not good. A documented project plan is needed for truly successful projects—they provide a historical reference and the reasoning for why decisions were made. A project plan must provide documentation of the assumptions and constraints influencing the project plan development.

- **Provide communication** Project plans are documents that provide the information, explanations, and reasoning underlying the decisions made for the project. The project plan serves as a source of communication among stakeholders, the project team, and management on how the project plan will be controlled.

- **Provide baselines** A project plan contains several baselines. As the project moves toward completion, management, stakeholders, and the project manager can use the project plan to see what was predicted for costs, scheduling, quality, and scope—and then see how these predictions compare with what is being experienced.

Inputs to Project Plan Development

To effectively develop the project plan, the project manager and the stakeholders must be in agreement with the project objectives. For this agreement to exist, the project manager works with the stakeholders to negotiate a balance of expectations and required objectives. Competing objectives is a recurring theme in project management (and on the PMP exam). Project managers must be able to negotiate among stakeholders for the best solution to the problem or opportunity.

Planning Outputs Serve as Inputs

The outputs of the planning processes serve as an input to project plan development. As a refresher, the processes from the planning process group are shown in Table 4-1.

TABLE 4-1 An Overview of the Planning Processes

Planning Process	Purpose
Scope Planning	To create a document that will guide project decisions.
Scope Definition	To breakdown the project deliverables into manageable elements. The sum of the smaller elements equate to the project scope.
Activity Definition	To define the required activities, and only the required activities, to complete the project scope.
Resource Planning	To ascertain the resources required to achieve the defined activities for completing the project work. Resources include people, equipment, and materials.
Activity Sequencing	To determine the best sequence of planned activities within the project work.
Activity Duration Estimating	To determine the estimated required work units to successfully complete the defined activities.
Cost Estimating	To determine an estimated amount of monies to complete the project work using the defined facilities, services, and goods.
Risk Management Planning	To determine the risks within the project and how to react to the identified risks.
Schedule Development	To determine the project schedule based on the sequence of activities, the required resources, and the required monies. The Schedule Development process reveals an estimated reflection of when all of the required work can be completed with the given resources.
Cost Budgeting	To determine the estimated cost of the activities to complete the project work.
Project Plan Development	To create a coherent compilation of the other planning processes to guide the project execution.
Quality Planning	To determine the Quality Assurance standards used by the organization. The Quality Assurance standards that are relevant to the project must be planned into the project.
Communications Planning	To determine who needs what, when they need it, and in what modality (paper or electronic, for example) they need it.
Organizational Planning	To determine the project roles and responsibility. This also determines the reporting structure between the project manager, the project team, and management.
Staff Acquisition	To acquire the needed people to complete the determined project work.
Risk Identification	To identify the risks, rewards, and penalties associated with the project.

TABLE 4-1	An Overview of the Planning Processes *(continued)*

Planning Process	Purpose
Qualitative Risk Analysis	To prioritize the impact of the risks on the project (typically in a *high*, *medium*, and *low* ranking).
Quantitative Risk Analysis	To measure and consider the probability and associated impact of the risks on the project.
Risk Response Planning	To avoid, eliminate, reduce, or create a planned reaction to the identified risks within the project.
Procurement Planning	To determine what goods and services must be procured and when they will need to be procured in the project lifecycle.
Solicitation Planning	To determine the possible vendors to provide the goods and services for the project.

Historical Information

Historical information is used as an input to project plan development—and to the planning process group—and is always as excellent source of information to confirm, or deny, assumptions. Historical information can also serve as a point of reference for identifying alternatives during the planning processes. Historical information can come from:

- Previous projects
- Commercially available estimating databases
- Public records
- Organizational archives of past projects
- Performance records of other projects
- Other reliable sources

exam

watch   *Historical information is always a key source for project information—even more important than project team members' opinions. Why?*

Historical information is proven and documented and from reliable sources. If you must choose, choose historical information as a key input.

Organizational Policies

Consider the performing organization—the company hosting the project. The performing organization may have rules and regulations that the project must follow. During the project plan development consider the following:

- Quality Assurance programs and their influence over the project. The project manager must consider the standard operating procedures (SOPs) the project manager is expected to follow, the expected level of quality, and the target indexes the project manager may be expected to achieve. The QA requirements must be documented in the Quality Management Plan, and its activities must be accounted for in the project schedule.

- Human resource practices and the project manager requirements. An organization may have specific rules on how the project manager may recruit team members, release team members from the project, account for a team member's time, discipline team members, and so on. The project manager and project team must be familiar with the organization's HR practices, and the practices should be documented in the Human Resource Management Plan.

- Financial controls and requirements. An organization will have requirements for the project manager to account for the budget, expenses, and cash flow projections. The project manager will likely have to forecast expenses, account for project time, and have adequate bookkeeping for any project procurement. Throughout the Execution and Control processes (and also in the Closing process), the project manager can expect financial reviews and requests for projections. EVM can assist the project manager by providing time and cost variances, estimates to complete the project work, and information on the likelihood of the project completing on time and on schedule.

Project Constraints

Constraints are any restriction on the project. Constraints may be the availability of project resources, government requirements, budgetary limits, and so on. All projects have at least three constraints (as shown in the following illustration): scope, budget, and schedule. This is also known as the "triple constraint" of project management. A constraint is any force that may affect when, and if, a project activity can be completed. Consider a project with a deadline—that's a time constraint. Consider a project with a preset budget (I know, that one is tough to imagine)—that's a budget constraint, and it affects staffing, quality, scope, schedule, and more.

And what about a scope constraint? That's a project that has demands for the given requirements regardless of the time or cost to reach the demands. Consider a project to enforce a government regulation within a manufacturing industry. The government regulation must be met, regardless of the cost to enforce it. While projects with scope constraints are not as common as projects with financial and schedule constraints they do exist. Consider smaller projects such as the "Add/Move/Change Projects". Scope constraints are imposed by projects to implement safety standards, for example, and projects to document business processes within an organization.

The triple constraints of project management provide an excellent negotiation tool. No side of the equilateral triangle can change without affecting the other sides. The goal is for all of the sides of the triangle to always be even. Want to change to project end date to sooner than later? Okay, but we'll have to add more resources to get it done—which will mean more budget. Don't have enough cash in the old budget to complete the work? Okay, we'll just reduce the project scope. The triangle is sometimes called the "Iron Triangle".

Project Assumptions

Ever made an assumption? Assumptions are beliefs that are considered to be true, real, or certain for the sake of planning. For example, a project team can make the assumption that the weather will cooperate so that the construction project will finish by a given date. Assumptions should be documented, researched, and proven true—or untrue—as part of the planning process. This is part of progressive elaboration—the farther along the project moves to launch, the more detail the project needs.

Assumptions should be documented whenever they are used: estimates, planning, scheduling, and so on. Assumptions are considered as risks because false assumptions can alter the entire project.

Applying Tools and Techniques for Project Plan Development

All of the inputs to the project plan should be readily available for the project manager, because he or she may need to rely on this information for additional planning. With all of the "stuff" the project manager has to work with, it should be a snap to create the actual project plan, right? Well, not exactly. The project manager, the project team, stakeholders, and management will work together to finalize the project plan. The contributions from each include the following:

- **Project manager** leadership, facilitation, organization, direction, and expert judgment
- **Project team members** knowledge of the project work, time estimates, and they provide influence on the schedule, advice and opinions on risk, and expert judgment
- **Customer** requirements, objectives, quality requirements, expert judgment, influence over budget and schedule
- **Management** influence over budget, resources, project management methodology, quality requirements, and project plan approval

Adopting a Project Plan Methodology

A project plan methodology is a structured approach to developing the project plan. Methodologies can be simple or complex and based on the project type, the requirements of the performing organization, or multiple inputs. Organizations can use hard or soft tools to lead the project plan methodology. In its choice of hard tools, one organization may require the project team to create a project plan based on checklist of plan requirements, while another organization may require project teams to complete a computer-based project template.

Soft tools include project meetings, business analysts to investigate and research all facets of the problem or opportunity, and subject matter experts' interviews of stakeholders and project team members. A methodology to creating the project plan can include:

- Project templates
- Paper and electronic forms
- Monte Carlo simulations for risk management
- Project simulations for expected results
- Design of experiments
- Project startup meetings
- Interviews

Rely on the Stakeholder Skills and Knowledge

Stakeholders are individuals who are involved in the project creation, execution, or control; stakeholders are also the people affected by the project results. The project manager and the project team must consider the effects of the project on the stakeholders, and they must also interview and involve stakeholders so that they can make use of their knowledge of the project work and deliverables. The project manager must encourage participation and contribution from all stakeholders, as stakeholders provide valuable information for the project plan.

Stakeholders can include:

■ Sponsor

■ Client

■ End user

■ Team members

■ Functional manager

■ Vendors, the general public, subcontractors (and other "external" stakeholders)

Employ a Project Management Information Systems (PMIS)

A PMIS is typically a computer-driven system (though it can be paper-based) to aid a project manager in the development of the project. A PMIS is a tool for, not a replacement of, the project manager. A PMIS can calculate schedules, costs, expectations, and likely results. The PMIS cannot, however, replace the expert judgment of the project manager and the project team.

e x a m

w a t c h *Don't worry too much about PMIS brand names like Microsoft Project and Primavera. The exam doesn't fall in love with any PMIS systems—they are just tools for the project manager to work with.*

Count on Earned Value Management (EVM)

Earned value management (EVM) is a set of formulas that can measure a project's performance. EVM integrates scope, schedule, and cost to give an objective, scalable point in time assessment of the project. EVM calculates the performance of the project and compares current performance against where it should be. EVM can also be a harbinger of things to come. Poor results early in the project can predict the likelihood of the project's success. We'll cover EVM in Chapter 7.

Getting to Work: Project Plan Development

All the planning is done, right? Of course not. The planning processes are iterative and allow the project manager and the project team to revisit them as needed. But at what point do we push back from the planning buffet and move on with a working, feasible plan? Every project is different when it comes to planning, but a project team will continue in the planning stage until it is knowledgeable about the project work and has a clear vision of what needs to be done.

Figure 4-2 depicts the evolution of the Planning to Action process for a typical technology project. Once the business and the functional requirements have been established, the planning processes move into the specifics. Recall that the business requirements establish the project vision and that the functional requirements establish the goals for the project. The technical requirements and the design plan shift the focus onto the specifics the project will accomplish. Armed with this information, the project team and the project manager create the Work Breakdown Structure (WBS). The WBS is a decomposition of all the deliverables the project will create.

With the WBS, the project planning continues into schedule development, roles and responsibilities, and task assignments. The project manager must work within the confines of the organizational structure (functional, matrix, or projectized) to assign the project team members to the work. The project manager must consider project priority, availability of resources, and dependency of activities. The project manager must also factor in the demands of management, customers, and stakeholders for events like formal communications, quality assurance program requirements, and

FIGURE 4-2

The Planning Processes require documentation and a logical, systematic approach.

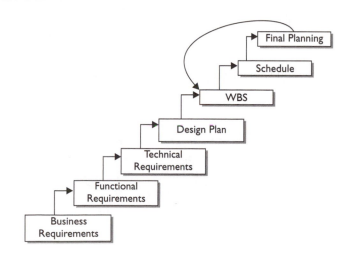

project status meetings. As the project plan moves toward reality, the project manager and the project team must evaluate risk, cost concerns, business cycles, procurement, and often a looming deadline.

Evaluating the Outputs of Project Plan Development

The project manager and the project team have finished, for now, a project plan. Before the project team can set about implementing it, the plan must be approved. Let's hear that again: the project plan is a formal, documented plan that must be approved by management. Once management has signed off on the project plan, the work is truly authorized to begin.

Examining the Typical Project Plan

So what's in this project plan, anyway? Let's take a peek:

Project Charter

When you think of the Project Charter, think of a formal document that *authorizes* the project manager to manage the project. The Project Charter comes from a manager external to the project. This manager must have the power within the organization to grant the project manager the expected level of authority within the organizational structure to apply resources (people, facilities, monies) to the project.

Project Management Approach

So how will the project be managed? The project management methodology is a summary of all the individual plans that comprise the project plan. The project

---

exam

watch   *Know this: the Project Charter does not come from the project sponsor; it comes from a manager outside of the project. It may work differently where you serve as a project manager—but on your exam, the charter is from Senior Management. In addition, the Project Charter doesn't launch the project—it authorizes the project manager.*

management approach describes how the work will be monitored, measured, and controlled. The project management approach summarizes the methods for QA, EVM, and risk response. Also included is an insight to the project accounting practices, cash flow projections, and expected outcome of the project. In other words, it describes how the project should advance, what the organization is achieving through the project, and how the project will react should things not go according to plan.

Project Scope Statement

This document establishes the purpose for doing the project and provides a high-level product description. The product description may list elements that are included in or excluded from the project. Its intent is to serve as a reference for future project decisions on what will—and will not—be accomplished within the project. The Scope Statement provides reasons for and justification of the project deliverables. In addition, the Scope Statement should provide detailed information on what the project objectives are, how they will be measured, and the expected level of quality.

Work Breakdown Structure

The WBS is a decomposition of the project work. The WBS should be thorough, organized, and small enough that progress can be measured but not so granular that it becomes a hindrance to implement the work. Tasks should be fully defined, measurable, and not open-ended. A heuristic for WBS work packages is that activities should fit into the "8/80 Rule." The 8/80 Rule demands that all activities be no smaller than 8 hours and no longer than 80 hours.

Plan Details

Within the project plan, you'll need a system to tie the activities to project team members, vendors, and stakeholders. You'll need to account for time, schedules, and cost. Specifically, you'll need cross-referencing to the WBS activities for the following:

- Cost estimates (and assumptions)
- Schedule estimates (and assumptions)
- Project start and finish dates (all projects have an end)
- Responsibility Assignment Matrix (who does what activities)

Project Schedule

The WBS and the network diagram coupled with the project resources will predict how long the project work should take. Your schedule should provide target dates, estimate the required resources to meet the targeted dates, and predict the project completion date. The schedule should, at a minimum, include target dates for phases and milestones.

Project Baselines

Baselines serve as evidence of what you've planned for. They allow you to compare what has been experienced in the project against what has been planned for in the project plan, with the differences being the variances. You'll need baselines for each of the following:

- WBS—Project scope: Did you deliver what you promised?
- Budget—Cost baseline: Did the project work cost what you estimated?
- Schedule—Schedule baseline: Is the project on the schedule you created?

Staffing Requirements

Who will do the work? The project plan should list the skills required to complete the project work and should indicate when those skills are required. The project plan should also identify the required personnel's time and associated cost. Required personnel may include vendors, subject matter experts, and employees within the company who are not considered project team members. Staff acquisition is an executing process.

Although the staffing requirements refer to personnel issues, don't forget to take into consideration the facilities, their schedules, and associated costs.

Risk Management Plan

The Risk Management Plan will detail the identified risks within the project, the risks associated with the constraints and project assumptions, and how the project team will monitor, react, or avoid the risks. The Risk Management Plan, and the processes to create it, will be detailed in Chapter 11.

Open Issues

Hmm...doesn't it always seem that there are open issues, pending decisions, and "we'll-see's" on projects? The project plan needs its own special section for pending decisions and open issues. This section of the plan documents issues that have not been resolved but are not preventing the project from starting. These issues should, however, be tied to a target date for a decision, so they do not grow into a halting point for project progress.

Subsidiary Management Plans

Depending on the size of the project, the conditions the project must operate within, and the demands of management and stakeholders, additional plans may be required. These are the *subsidiary plans*. It is worthwhile to note that each subsequent knowledge area has a subsidiary management plan, as seen in Table 4-2.

e x a m

ⓦatch   *Open issues are acceptable, as long as they are not related to major issues that will prevent the project from moving forward. For example, conflicting objectives and requirements between* *stakeholders can't be an open issue. A resolution and agreement on project requirements has to be in place before the project work can begin.*

TABLE 4-2	Plan	Content
Subsidiary plans support and organize the project work.	Scope Management Plan	How the project scope will be managed How scope changes will be integrated Assessment of scope stability Identification and classification of scope changes
	Schedule Management Plan	How changes to the schedule will be managed

TABLE 4-2	Plan	Content
Subsidiary plans support and organize the project work. *(continued)*	Cost Management Plan	How cost variances will be managed
	Quality Management Plan	How the quality policy will be implemented Quality control Quality assurance Quality improvement
	Staffing Management Plan	How resources are brought on and released from the team Resource histograms
	Communications Management Plan	Information collection and filing structure Information distribution structure Description of information to be distributed Production schedule Methods to access information between updates Methods to update the plan
	Risk Response Plan	Risk management methodology Risk roles and responsibilities Risk management budget Risk management timing Risk scoring and interpretation Risk thresholds Risk reporting formats Risk tracking
	Procurement Management Plan	Types of contracts that will be used Evaluation criteria Procurement roles and responsibilities Procurement documents How to manage multiple vendors Procurement coordination with project

Scope Management Plan The Scope Management Plan will detail how the project scope will be maintained and protected from change as well as how a change in scope may be allowed. The plan also provides information on how likely the project scope will change—and if changes do occur, how drastic the changes may be.

For example, a project to install additional electrical receptacles into an office building may have a very tightly controlled project scope that won't change often or much. Another project, to create a ten-acre park in a community, may change based on phase completion, discoveries in the land, natural resources, or conditions of the soil. The likelihood of change is directly related to the demands in the project scope. We'll discuss scope management and change control in Chapter 5.

Schedule Management Plan   The project plan details the scheduled work, milestones, and target completion dates for the project phases and the project itself. The Schedule Management Plan, on the other hand, identifies circumstances that may change the project schedule, such as the completion of project phases or the reliance on other projects and outside resources. The Schedule Management Plan identifies the likelihood that the schedule will change—and the impact of such changes should they occur. Finally, the Schedule Management Plan details the approval and accountability process for changes within the project. We'll discuss schedule management in Chapter 6.

Cost Management Plan   The project plan will include the project budget, cash flow forecast, and procedures for procurement and contract administration. The subsidiary Cost Management Plan explains how variances to the costs of the project will be managed. The plan may be based on a range of acceptable variances and the expected response to variances over a given threshold. For example, the project budget may have a range of variance of −10% to +15%. The following illustration demonstrates a variance range in the project budget.

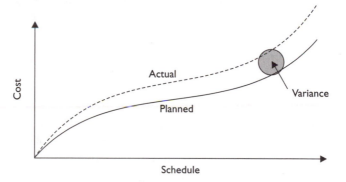

As an example, a cost variance of $5,000 may prompt a financial audit, whereas a cost variance of $500 may be within the accepted range of variance. The accepted range of cost variance can stem from cost estimates, assumptions, and risk. We'll cover cost management in Chapter 7.

Quality Management Plan   The Quality Management Plan describes how the project will operate and meet its quality expectations. The Quality Management Plan details the quality improvement, quality controls, and how the project will map to the Quality Assurance program of the performing organization. The Quality Management Plan will provide information on the required resources and time to meet the quality expectations. We'll discuss quality management in Chapter 8.

Staffing Management Plan The project plan will include information on the required resources needed to complete the project work. The Staffing Management Plan, however, provides details on how the project team members will be brought onto the project and released from the project. For example, a project may have a need for an electrical engineer for three months out of ten-month project. The Staffing Management Plan will determine how the engineer's time is accounted for on the project and how the employees can be released when they are no longer needed on the project. We'll discuss staffing management in Chapter 9.

Communications Management Plan It has been said that project managers spend 90 percent of their time communicating. When you consider all of the different requirements and communications of a project, it is easy to believe that statistic. The Communications Management Plan describes the required communications and how they will be fulfilled. The Communications Management Plan explains the methods used for gathering, storing, and dispersing information to appropriate parties.

In addition, the Communications Management Plan maps out the schedule of when the expected communication needs will be met. For example, milestone reports, timely status reports, project meetings, and other expected communication events are included in the Communications Management Plan. The communication schedule will also include accepted procedures to update, access, and revise communications between scheduled communication events. We'll discuss communications in Chapter 10.

Risk Response Plan This subsidiary plan, Risk Response, explains the actions the project team and the project manager may take on the basis of the identified risks coming to fruition. In some organizations, the Risk Response Plan is called the Risk Register. The plan includes specific information about the identified risks, their impact on the project, and what may cause the risks to come into play.

exam watch

In an ISO 9000 environment, the Quality Management Plan is called the project quality system. Also, an easy way to differentiate between QA and QC, is to remember that QA is organization-wide, and QC is project-wide. The clue is that there is an "A" in "organization", but not in project, and that there's a "C" in "project" but not in organization.

As part of the Risk Response Plan, the risk owners are identified along with what actions the owners may take should their risk events happen. Initial responses can include avoidance, transference, mitigation, or risk acceptance. We'll cover risk management in detail in Chapter 11.

Procurement Management Plan   If the project includes vendors, the project plan needs a Procurement Management Plan. This plan describes the procurement process from solicitation to source selection. The plan may also include the requirements for selection as set by the organization. The selected offers, proposals, and bids from vendor(s) should be incorporated into the Procurement Management Plan. We'll discuss procurement processes in Chapter 12.

Examining a Project's Supporting Detail

All of the decisions within the project are based on some reference, historical information, or expert judgment. The supporting detail provides the factual reasons for the decisions made in the project plan.

Outputs from Planning

Not every output of the planning process may be included in the project plan. For example, the planning process may have relied on industry whitepapers, vendor brochures, and magazine articles to guide the project planners to the decisions they've made. While all of this information is beneficial, it is not needed directly in the project plan. This research is an output of the planning processes, and may be needed for future reference, but it doesn't need to clutter up the working project plan.

Additional Project Information

The project manager will progressively elaborate the project plan until it is finalized and approved. Through this process. the requirements of the project will become more refined and the project vision will become clear. In addition, new constraints and project assumptions may be factored into the planning processes that were not accounted for in the early cost and time estimates. These additional constraints, assumptions, and requirements must be accounted for and their causes documented.

For example, an internal resource (such as a trainer) needed on the project may not be available during the months when the project schedule calls for the trainer. Now the project will need to hire a contracted resource to complete the work so the project schedule can be met. The new resource has a higher cost than the internal resource, so the cost constraint must be documented and the project costs are adjusted.

Technical Documentation

The technical decisions made in the project are typically based on the requirements of the stakeholders, industry standards and regulations, and project concepts. The information the technical decisions are founded on require documentation for future planning, reference, and inspection. The documentation of the industry standards can be included here or, based on the project type and size, in its own section.

For example, the customer may query why a particular material was used in the project deliverable. The technical documentation will provide the reason the material was chosen, its benefits to the project, and the associated cost to the customer.

Initial Planning Specifications

In the initial planning processes, the project manager and the project team may have ruled out alternatives to the project solution for quality, standards, or other reasons. Or, decisions may have been made to move the project toward a particular solution. These initial planning outputs should be documented to support the decisions that the project manager and the project team have made in the project solution.

For example, a customer may ask the project manager in the final phases of the project why a particular technology was chosen. The answer to the question may be the incompatibility with existing technology in the customer's environment. With appropriate documentation of the initial planning and supporting detail of the project decisions, the project manager can quickly and accurately answer the customer's questions.

e x a m

ⓦatch   *The whole point of the project plan is to communicate something to someone at some time. When stakeholders ask questions about the project, what does the project plan say? When project team members have* *questions about the project work, what does the project plan say? The only exception to this "rule" is when it comes to vendor disputes. With vendor disputes, refer to the contract, as it is the legal document for the client-vendor relationship.*

Executing the Project Plan

So you've got a project plan—great! Now the work of executing the project plan begins. The project manager and the project team will go about completing the promises made in the project plan to deliver, document, measure, and complete the project work. The project plan will communicate to the project team, the stakeholders, management, and even vendors what work happens next, how it begins, and how it will be measured for quality and performance.

The product of the project is created during these execution processes. The largest percentage of the project budget will be spent during the project execution processes. The project manager and the project team must work together to orchestrate the timings and integration of all the project's moving parts. A flaw in one area of the execution can have ramifications in cost and additional risk and can cause additional flaws in other areas of the project.

As the project work is implemented, the project manager refers to the project plan to ensure that the work is meeting the documented expectations, requirements, quality demands, target dates, and more. The completion of the work is measured and then compared against the cost, schedule, and scope baselines as documented in the project plan. Should there be—GASP!—discrepancies between the project work and the baselines, prompt and accurate reactions are needed to adjust the slipping components of the project.

Evaluating the Project Plan Execution Inputs

For a project to be successful, there must be adequate time allotted for planning. A project manager can't, or shouldn't, accept a project and immediately move into execution without planning. There are, however, additional inputs to the project execution besides planning. This shows the inputs of project plan execution:

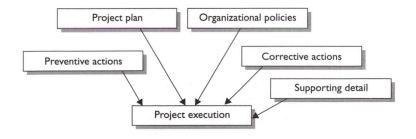

Consider the Project Plan

You've spent a great deal of time already in this chapter examining the outputs of planning—specifically, the project plan. The project plan is a composite of individual plans and summaries that guide and communicate the project work. As you may have expected, the project plan serves as a primary input to project execution. As a quick refresher, here are the details of the project plan that will guide the project execution:

- Project Charter
- Project management approach
- WBS
- Cost and schedule estimates
- Roles and responsibilities matrix
- Baselines for cost, schedule, and scope
- Target dates for milestones
- Staffing requirements and associated costs
- Risk Management Plan
- Subsidiary plans:
    - Scope Management Plan
    - Schedule Management Plan
    - Cost Management Plan
    - Quality Management Plan
    - Staffing Management Plan
    - Communications Management Plan
    - Risk Response Plan
    - Procurement Management Plan
    - Open issues at project plan completion

Rely on the Supporting Detail

Remember all of the stuff you based your decisions on in the project plan? That's the supporting detail you'll also use to guide your project execution. For example, if you based a technical solution on an article you read during your research, it'll be handy to have that article as you move in the project plan execution. Also consider historical information that you used to guide your project plan development. Historical information is an excellent guide the project manager can rely on during project planning and execution.

exam
watch

Don't fall in love with memorizing these different plans. You should be familiar with them and what they accomplish and know which plan you'd rely on in a given situation. On the exam you should choose the most appropriate and

specific plan for the condition described. For example, the Risk Management Plan is more specific than the whole Project Plan. Finally, remember that the project plan is a formal, management-approved, document.

Reference the Organizational Policies

Project execution must work with and in organizations. Projects cannot disrupt the ongoing operations of the performing organization. The policies of the performing organization will guide the methods used during the project plan execution. Recall that organizational policies can be formal or informal and can include any of the following:

- Quality management programs: quality expectations, requirements, audits, and documentation
- Human resource management policies: methods by which team members are recruited, released, hired, disciplined, and fired from the project team
- Financial Controls: Project manager responsibility for the project expenses and invoices and generally for the monies spent on the project

Consider the Preventive Actions

Do you wear your seat belt? Take an umbrella when there's chance of rain? These are preventive actions against some risk. In project management, preventive actions are steps the project manager and the project team can take to prevent the negative outcome of possible risk events. Preventive actions are documented methods to avoid risks from influencing the project success in a negative way. Preventive actions are actions to take risk events out of play.

Apply Corrective Action

Things go awry. Corrective actions are methods the project manager and the project team can take to bring the project back into alignment with the project plan. For example, a delay in the project work has now shifted the project schedule by a month.

The project manager, the project team, and even the stakeholders can examine the project schedule to see what possible alternatives can be taken in the project schedule to complete the project on time. Solutions may include additional resources, fast tracking, changing the order of work packages, and so on. Corrective actions bring the project performance back in alignment with the project plan. In addition to communicating, project managers spend a great deal of their time applying corrective actions.

Implementing Tools and Techniques for Project Execution

You have completed a workable, approved project plan. Now it's time to implement the thing. This is the heart of project management: taking your project plan and putting it into action. You'll act, do, adjust, and repeat. There are several tools and techniques the project manager will use to execute the project plan.

Using General Management Skills

The arsenal of general management tools help the project manager manage, lead, direct, and accomplish. You do remember the general management skills from Chapter 2, yes? Just in case, here's a brief recap:

- **Leading** Leadership is the ability to establish direction and align people, while motivating and inspiring them to accomplish.

- **Communicating** Ah, yes, communicating, the biggest requirement of a project manager is to communicate the correct information to the correct people when they need it. Communication to internal and external stakeholders can be oral or written and in many different modalities (e-mail, memos, reports, and so on). Communicating also includes everyone's favorite activity: managing meetings.

- **Negotiating** Negotiating is the art of working with others to reach a mutually beneficial and fair agreement. In most cases, the project manager will negotiate on project time, cost, and scope issues.

- **Problem Solving** This activity is a blend of problem definition, root cause analysis, and decision making. The project manager works with the project team to define the problem—the root of the problem, not the evidence of the problem. Next the project manager makes an educated decision on how best to squelch the problem.

■ **Influencing the Organization**   This activity is, as the PMBOK puts it, "the ability to get things done." It's the knowledge of how an organization operates: what it takes to get resources, time, and action.

Applying Skills and Knowledge

Here's some common sense: it's the project team that is going to be completing the work in the project, so the project team must know how to do the work. For the project work to be completed with accuracy, quality, and on schedule, the project team must be familiar with how to actually complete the activities in the project plan.

As part of the planning process group, the necessary resources to complete the project are identified. If the project team is lacking the necessary skills to complete the work, project team development is needed: educate the team. The project will obviously suffer if the project team doesn't have the skill set to complete the work you're about to assign to it. An alternative to additional training is to supplement or replace the project team with the appropriate resources to complete the project work.

There is inherent risk to moving into project plan execution with a project team that is unprepared to complete the required work. Delays, quality issues, reworkings, and fines may occur and even lives may be at stake. The project manager must work with the project team for honest assessments of members' abilities, knowledge, and skills needed to complete the project work.

Implementing a Work Authorization System

How will the project team know when they can go to work on their activities? Consider a project with a team that is non-collocated. In this project, a set of activities must be completed in London before the activities in Prague can begin. The coordination between the two cities must be managed, documented, and controlled. A Work Authorization System is a tool that can control the organization, sequence, and official authorization to begin the next piece of the project work.

Work Authorization Systems are typically influenced by the size of the project. For example, a large, non-collocated project may use a formal, documented approach to approve and confirm project work that has been completed. The documentation of completed work is then followed by a document to authorize the next project work package to begin.

In smaller projects, however, an elaborate system to sanction downstream work packages may be counterproductive. In these instances, a verbal authorization system is most appropriate. The project manager must consider the cost of the Work Authorization System against the priority and impact of the project, the effectiveness of such a system, and the overall need to implement the system in any given project.

on the **Job**

Collaborative PMIS packages can also serve as a Work Authorization System—if they are configured and used properly. Any PMIS, electronic or paper-based, is only as good as the person (or persons) keeping the information up-to-date.

Hosting Status Review Meetings

The project team is at work completing the project objectives—or so you think. In addition to providing a reason for getting out of the office and inspecting the project work, Status Review Meetings allow the project manager to interact and record the status of the team members' work efforts.

Status Review Meetings are regularly scheduled meetings to record the status of the project work. These common meetings provide a formal avenue for the project manager to query the team on the status of their work, and allows the project team to report delays and slippage These meetings also allow the project manager and the project team to forecast what work is about to begin. The goal of the meeting is to ascertain where the project stands, to hold the team accountable for their work, and to serve as motivation for the project team to complete their work on time.

Status Review Meetings are documented in the Communications Management Plan, as they are regularly scheduled communication events. A typical schedule of these meetings may call for the project team to meet with the project manager on a weekly basis, and the project manager and the project team to meet with customers on a monthly basis. The frequency of the meetings should reflect the project size, demand for status, and requirements of the performing organization.

Using a Project Management Information System

A PMIS is an excellent tool to help execute the project plan. A PMIS can be electronic or paper-based. The goal of a PMIS is to automate, organize, and provide control of the project management processes. A typical PMIS software system has

- WBS creation tools
- Calendaring features
- Scheduling abilities

- Work authorization tools
- EVM Controls
- Quality control charts, PERT charts, Gantt charts, and other charting features
- Calculations for critical path, EVM, target dates based on the project schedule, and more
- Resource tracking and leveling
- Reporting functionality

Organizational Procedures

Every performing organization has rules and regulations that are specific to the industry it operates within. In addition, the performing organization will likely have standard operating procedures that determine the order, approach, and autonomy of the project manager and the project team.

For example, an organization operating within the construction industry must operate according to the laws and regulations of the country, state or province, and city. In addition, the performing organization may require its construction crew to adhere to its safety standards, quality inspections, and other company rules that are not mandated by a government agency. The project manager must work within not only the law, but also the additional constraints the organization has added to the project.

Examining the Outputs of Project Plan Execution

The project is being completed; there is visible evidence that it is moving towards the desired future state. Inspections by the project manager and scope verification by the customer also prove the project team is completing their work as planned. Status Meetings provide opportunity for the project team to report their work and evaluate it against the WBS and the network diagram. Things are moving along smoothly.

And then it happens. The project team begins to slip on the quality of the project work. Team members begin to take longer than what was planned to complete their project work. The scope verification with the clients takes longer—and their satisfaction with the project work begins to wane. What's a project manager to do?

This scenario is typical of project plan execution. The team completes the work, the project manager reviews the work—and then makes adjustments to bring the project back into alignment with the baselines created in the project plan. There are two major components of project plan execution that happen throughout project execution, not just the end:

- Work results
- Change requests

Examining the Project Work Results

The team completes their work based on the project plan. The end result of the work should be measured against the quality metrics, scope requirements, and expected outcomes of the work as defined in the project plan. In addition, the project manager must examine the time and cost required to reach the work results and compare them against the baselines recorded in the project plan. Any difference between what was experienced and what was planned is a variance.

Work results are not always physical, tangible things: the creation of a service, the completion of a training class, the completion of a certification process—these too can be measured as work results.

Examining Change Requests

How many times have stakeholders begged, pleaded, or demanded a change in the project scope? Probably more times than you can count, right? Change requests are any requested deviation from or addition to the project scope, schedule, budget, quality, or staffing. Change requests will predominantly trickle (or flood) to the project manager during project plan execution. Change requests almost always affect one of four facets of a project:

- **Schedule** A desire to shorten or lengthen the project duration. For example, a key stakeholder would like the project to be completed before a particular business cycle begins. If the project can't be completed by that time, the project will be delayed until the business cycle has completed, so the project won't interfere with the business operations.

- **Cost** A reduction or increase in the project's budget. For example, the project's priority has been reduced in the organization so the budget may, unfortunately, be reduced as well. Budgets can also be increased: A functional manager may want to spend all of the remaining departmental budget at the end of the fiscal year so that next year's budget may meet or exceed the current year's budget. In this questionable instance, additional funds, new features, and more resources, needed or not, are added to a project's budget to "help" the functional manager spend the budget.

■ **Scope**   The most common instance of change. Stakeholder may request additional features, different features, or small changes to the project product. Each change must be evaluated against the project plan, the project scope, and supporting detail to determine the cost, time, and risks implied.

■ **Combination**   A change made to the schedule, cost, or scope affecting more than one facet, as is likely. This goes back to the idea of the triple constraints of project management. For example, a change to finish the schedule faster may be reasonable if more resources are applied to the project to complete the work faster. More resources, in turn, means more money.

Managing Integrated Change Control

Imagine you're the project manager for our old friends at Zings Sweater Works. The project you're working on now, the Customer Satisfaction Project, handles the marketing, customer relationship management, and sales follow-through activities for your organization. One component of this project is to allow customers to easily browse and purchase sweaters online.

The Vice President of Sales approaches you during project execution to congratulate you on how well the project is moving along. The work results are great, quality is proven, and the initial reaction from the stakeholders is outstanding. "However," he says, "I've got a great idea on how we can make the deliverables better."

Uh-oh…here comes the change request.

e x a m

w a t c h   *When competing objectives arise, such as fast completion and a small budget, remember: you can have it fast or you can have it cheap, but you cannot have it fast and cheap—unless the scope of the* *project is reduced to satisfy the available time and the available funds. Time costs money in project management because of the required resources to complete the work.*

The VP of Sales wants to include a feature that would allow customers to add sweater choices to a "wish list" because he saw it on a competitor's site. In addition, the VP wants to add:

- Options to remember users when they come back to the web site
- Options to allow visitors to join a newsletter for coupons and announcements
- Gift-services to remind customers of upcoming events in their personal calendar
- An online reward system that will allow customers to accumulate points as they purchase sweaters online

Now, you've got to deal with these change requests. The changes should flow through a Change Control System, be evaluated, and if approved for this project, be meshed into the existing work. As you're contemplating these change requests, Susan, a developer for the project, pops into your office.

Susan reports that she and the web designers have been adding some features to the web application and thought they should run it by you before proceeding. She says that the development team thought it'd be great to add a feature on each page that would track how long a customer spent on a particular web page. These stats would allow marketing to promote certain sweaters, evaluate sweaters that are being ignored, and track the amount of time a sweater is viewed before it is purchased. "Pretty clever, huh?" she says. "And it only takes about five additional minutes per sweater for us to write the code and hook it into a database."

Sounds good, right? And then you remember that, with all the different colors and sizes, there are at least 3,500 different sweaters in the web catalog. That's a ton of time at five minutes per sweater.

These incidents are reflective of the type of change requests a project manager faces regularly. Changes to the product often stem from the customer of the project. Changes from the project team may also stem from suggestions of the stakeholders—such as small, innocent changes that bloom into additional time and cost. Finally, changes may come from the project team, as with Susan in the above example. When it comes to Integrated Change Control the project manager must provide for:

- An evaluation of the change requests to determine whether changes are needed and wise for the project
- A determination that an unapproved or undocumented change has occurred within the project work

■ An acceptance of the change and methods for managing the changes that have occurred or are about to occur

Reaction to Change

When changes are proposed to the project, the project manager must route the proposed changes through a Change Control System (CCS). The CCS may also include the review of proposed changes through a Change Control Board (CCB). Changes may be discarded or approved on the basis of different criteria, such as Benefit Cost Ratios (BCRs), value-added changes, risk, and political capital.

When changes are approved, the project manager must then update the project baselines, as changes will likely affect a combination of scope, cost, and time. The updated baselines allow the project to continue with the new changes fleshed in and provide for accurate measurement of the performance of the project as changed.

This is an important concept: *update the project baselines*. Consider a project to which work has been added but for which the schedule baseline had not been updated: the project's end date will be sooner than what is possible, because the project baseline does not reflect the additional work that should extend that date. In addition, a failure to revise the project baseline could skew reporting, variances, future project decisions—and even future projects.

Consider a project manager who does not update the project baseline after a change. The completion of the project goes into the archives and can serve as historical information for future projects. The historical information is skewed, as it does not accurately account for the added work and the projected end date or budget.

Changes, small or large, must be accounted for throughout the project plan. Notice how the Integrated Change Control processes influence the communications of the change, including the change approval or denial. That's the whole point: to integrate proposed changes into the project processes. Figure 4-3 details Integrated Change Control.

e x a m
ⓦatch　　*Current projects become* 　　*through on the project execution, can*
future historical information. Inaccurate 　*cause long-term ill affects in other projects.*
data in the project plan, even if it is worked

FIGURE 4-3 All change requests must pass through Integrated Change Control.

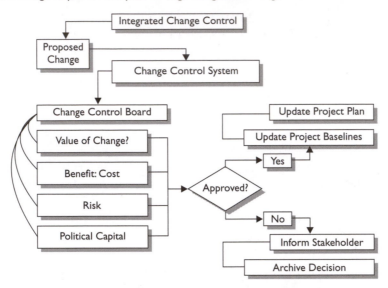

Consider the Inputs to Integrated Change Control

As with all processes in project management there are inputs to Integrated Change Control. There are three inputs to consider:

- **Project plan** Most projects have some change at some point in the project plan execution, so the management of the changes must be planned for. It is not so much the change incident, but the process of approving or denying the change that the project manager must anticipate. Recall that the project plan is the guide for all future project decisions.

- **Performance reports** The performance of the project is measured against the baselines defined in the project plan. Poor performance, a measurement below the project baselines, must prompt reactions to determine the cause and corrective actions to resolve the problems.

- **Change requests** Requests to change attributes of the project can come in many different modalities—written, oral, formal, informal, internal, external—and can even result from new laws, regulations, and industry mandates.

Implementing Tools and Techniques for Integrated Change Control

Given that changes, or requests for change, are likely to happen in the project, what tools are available to squelch, evaluate, and approve the proposed changes? And how can the project manager organize change requests in an orderly system so he or she's not constantly evaluating change requests instead of focusing on project completion? And how do change requests get approved, worked into the project plan, and accounted for in costs, schedule, and risk?

There are many tools to apply to requests for change: consistency, scope comparison, benefit-cost ratios, risk analysis, and the estimate of the time and cost to incorporate the change, among others. The tools will guide the project manager, the project team, and stakeholders through the process of approving and declining changes. The best approach for Integrated Change Control is a constant, purposeful process of reviewing, considering, evaluating, and then deciding if the change is needed or not.

Relying on a Change Control System

A Change Control System is a formal process of documenting and reviewing proposed changes. It establishes the flow of change from proposal to decision. The Change Control System is a process that describes how project performance will be monitored, how changes may occur, and then how the project plan may be revised and sent through versioning when the changes are approved.

A Change Control System is a collection of documented activities, factors for decisions, and performance measurements—not a computer program. While many electronic Project Management Information Systems offer a Change Control System, know that a Change Control System is a documented approach to change, not an automated approval structure.

Some organizations may have a Change Control System that is used across all projects and maps to common guidelines within the organization. If the performing organization does not have a Change Control System, it is the responsibility of the project manager and the project team to create one. A Change Control System is mandatory for effective project management.

Within a Change Control System there may be a collection of management, key stakeholders, and project team members that review the changes for approval or denial. This board is defined in the project plan, and its roles and responsibilities are defined prior to project plan execution. Common names for the board include:

- Change Control Board (CCB)
- Schedule Change Control Board

- Technical Review Board (TRB)
- Technical Assessment Board (TAB)
- Engineering Review Board (ERB)

Implement Configuration Management

Configuration management focuses on controlling the characteristics of a product or service. It is a documented process of controlling the features, attributes, and technical configuration of any product or service. When it comes to project management, configuration management has a focus on the project deliverables. In some organizations, configuration management is a part of the Change Control System, while in some industries, such as manufacturing; configuration management is control of existing operations. In a general sense, configuration management consists of the following:

- The documentation of the features, characteristics, and functions of a product or service
- The applied control to restrict changes to the features, characteristics, and function of the product or service
- The process of documenting any changes to the product or service
- The ongoing auditing of products and services to ensure their conformance to documented requirements

Applying Performance Measurement

The end result of project plan execution must be measured to see if the implementation of the plan meets the expected results of the project plan. The most common measurement of project plan execution is Earned Value. Earned Value is a collection of formulas to measure the project worth, performance, and likelihood of the project completing on time and on budget.

Revisiting Planning Processes

Planning is iterative. As project plans rarely, if ever, happen exactly the way the project team and project manager planned them, the project freely moves between the controlling, executing, and planning processes. This is most evident when changes enter the project scene. The project manager and the project team must evaluate the proposed changes for additional cost, time, and risk concerns.

If the project work slips from the expected performance, quality, or schedule, adjustments are needed. These adjustments will require consideration of project activities, the critical path, resources, cost, sequence of activities, and other refinements to the project plan.

Evaluating the Outputs of Integrated Change Control

As the project follows the project plan and changes are presented, the project manager will implement Integrated Change Control. Some changes will be denied, documented, and archived for reference if needed. Other changes will be approved and factored into the project scope and have their time, cost, and risks documented and accounted for. The process of Integrated Change Control is ongoing until project closure.

Updating the Project Plan

When changes are allowed into the project, their results must be included in the project plan. Any changes to scope, cost, time, risk, scheduling, and other attributes of the project plan must be revised and documented. In addition to having the project plan updated, any supporting detail used in the decision to include the change should be included in the project planning supporting detail. This may include information on new laws and regulations, proof of concept, rationalization for changes from management, and other information.

Applying Corrective Action

When the project work is measured and variances are evident, corrective actions are required. Corrective actions bring the project work results back into alignment with the project plan, increase project value, and attempt to ensure the project will end on time and on budget.

INSIDE THE EXAM

What must you know from this chapter to pass the exam? Know the purpose of the project plan: to guide the project manager through the Execution and Control groups. The project plan is also in place to provide communication to the project team, stakeholders, and management. The project plan guides all future project decisions.

You should know all of the components of the project plan. Know what each of the subsidiary project plans are used for, how they can be updated, and what their objectives are. Remember, the point of planning is to create the project plan. The project plan then is to provide leadership and direction for the project execution and control processes. The project plan is a formal, management-approved document. Once management approves the plan, then work can begin.

Remember the WBS? It's a major piece of the PMP exam. Know the attributes of the WBS, that it serves as an input to the planning process and execution, and that it requires input from the project manager and the project team. The WBS is an input to five planning processes:

1. Cost Estimating

2. Cost Budgeting

3. Resource Planning

4. Risk Management Planning

5. Activity Definition

After the WBS, historical information is another big factor on the exam. Why? Historical information is proof from other project managers. Historical information allows the project manager to rely on what has been proven, what has been accomplished, and what has been archived for reference. And remember: the current project plan will become a future historical reference.

Assumptions and constraints are present on every project. Assumptions are beliefs held to be true, but not proven to be true. Assumptions should be documented in the project plan. Constraints are restrictions the project must operate within. The triple constraint of project management—time, cost, and scope—will visit you on exam day, as will other internal and external constraints.

To begin the project, a project charter is needed. Project charters come from a manager external to the project. Once the charter is present, the project manager is named. The project manager then assembles the project team and begins the planning processes. The primary output of any planning is a project plan. The execution of the project plan cannot begin until management approves the plan. All work described in the project plan must pass through a Work Authorization System, either formal on a larger project, or informal on smaller projects.

Integrated Change Control requires evaluation of change requests to determine their worthiness for approval—or lack thereof for denial. Change requests can be written or verbal, internal or external. Change requests can stem from stakeholders or external sources such as government agencies, laws, or industry mandates.

Documenting the Lessons Learned

The project moves towards completion—what have you learned? Lessons Learned is a formal document that serves as a journal of the experience of the project manager, the project team, and the stakeholders. The project team and the project manager complete the Lessons Learned document. It becomes part of the project archives so that other project managers can learn from their experience. Lessons Learned documents are not completed only at the end of a project, but throughout a project. Lessons Learned can be incorporated into the Communications Management Plan as communication events.

CERTIFICATION SUMMARY

Project integration management is an ongoing process the project manager completes to ensure the project moves from start to completion. It is the gears, guts, and grind of project management – the day-in, day-out business of completing the project work. Project integration management takes your project plans, coordinates the activities, project resources, constraints, and assumptions and massages them into a working model.

Of course project integration management isn't an automatic process; it requires you, the project manager, to negotiate, finesse, and adapt to project circumstances. Project integration management relies on general business skills such as leadership, organizational skills and communication to get all the parts of the project working together.

The process of project management can be broken down into three chunks:

1. **Develop the project plan** Project plan development is an iterative process that requires input from the project manager, the project team, the project customers, and other stakeholders. It details how the project work will accomplish the project goals. The project plan provides communication.

2. **Execute the project plan** Now that the plan has been created it's time to execute it. The project execution processes authorizes work to begin, manages procurement, manages quality assurance, host project team meetings and manages conflict between stakeholders. On top of all these moving parts the project manager must actively work to develop the individuals on the project to work as a team for the good of the project.

3. **Manage changes to the project** Changes can kill a project. Change requests must be documented and sent through a formal change control system to

determine their worthiness for implementation. Integrated Change Control manages changes across the entire project. Change requests are evaluated, considered for impacts on risk, costs, schedule, and scope. Not all change requests are approved—but all change requests should be documented for future reference.

As the project moves from start to completion the project manager and the project team must update the Lessons Learned documentation. The Lessons Learned serves as future historical information to the current project and to other future projects within the organization. The project manager and project team should update the Lessons Learned at the end of project phases, when major deliverables are created, and at the project completion.

KEY TERMS

If you're serious about passing the PMP exams, memorize these terms and their definitions. For maximum value, create your own flashcards based for these definitions and review daily.

assumptions	earned value	project charter
Change Control Board	historical information	project integration management
Change Control System	Lessons Learned	project plan
configuration management	PMIS	status review meetings
constraints	project baselines	supporting detail

✓ TWO-MINUTE DRILL

Project Integration Management

Project integration management relies on project plan development, project plan execution, and Integrated Change Control. Integrated Change Control manages all the moving parts of a project.

❑ Project integration management is a fancy way of saying that the project components need to work together—and the project manager sees to it that they do. Project integration management requires negotiation between competing objectives.

❑ Project integration management calls for general management skills, effective communications, organization, familiarity with the product, and more. It is the day-to-day operations of the project execution.

Planning the Project

On your exam, you'll need to know that planning is an iterative process and that the results of planning are inputs to the project plan. The project plan is a fluid document, authorized by management, and guides all future decisions on the project.

❑ The project plan is a fluid work in progress. Updates to the plan reflect changes to the project, discoveries made during the project plan execution, and conditions of the project. The project plan serves as a point of reference for all future project decisions, and it becomes future historical information to guide other project managers. When changes occur, the cost, schedule, and scope baselines in the project plan must be updated.

❑ The WBS (Work Breakdown Structure) is one of the most important pieces in the project plan. It serves as an input to schedule development, roles and responsibility assignments, risk management, and other processes.

❑ The WBS is a decomposition of the project work into manageable portions. A heuristic of the WBS is that work packages should not be less than 8 hours nor more than eighty hours. The WBS is not created by the project manager alone, but with the project team.

Project Constraints

Projects have at least one or more constraints: time, cost, and scope. This is known as the triple constraint of project management. Constraints are factors that can hinder project performance.

❑ Time constraints include project deadlines, availability of key personnel, and target milestone dates. Remember that all projects are temporary: the have a beginning and an end.

❑ Cost constraints are typically predetermined budgets for project completion. It's usually easier to get more time than more money.

❑ Scope constraints are requirements for the project deliverables regardless of the cost or time to implement the requirements (safety regulations or industry mandates are examples).

Managing Change Control

Integrated Change Control is the process of documenting and controlling the features of a product, measuring and reacting to project conditions, and revisiting planning when needed.

❑ Projects need a Change Control System to determine how changes will be considered, reviewed, and approved or declined. A Change Control System is a documented approach to how a stakeholder may request a change and then what factors are considered when approving or declining the requested change.

❑ Configuration Management is part of change control. It is the process of controlling how the characteristics of the product or service the project is creating are allowed to changed.

SELF TEST

1. You are a project manager for your organization. Management has asked you to help them determine which projects should be selected for implementation. In a project selection model, the most important factor is which one of the following?

    A. Business needs

    B. Type of constraints

    C. Budget

    D. Schedule

2. On any project, the Lessons Learned document is created by which one of the following?

    A. Customers

    B. Project Sponsor

    C. Project team

    D. Stakeholders

3. Your project is moving ahead of schedule. Management elects to incorporate additional quality testing into the project to improve the quality and acceptability of the project deliverable. This is an example of which one of the following?

    A. Scope creep

    B. Change control

    C. Quality Assurance

    D. Integrated Change Control

4. All of the following are true about change requests except:

    A. They happen while the project work is being done.

    B. They always require additional funding.

    C. They can be written or verbal.

    D. They can be requested by a stakeholder.

5. You are the project manager for a pharmaceutical company. You are currently working on a project for a new drug your company is creating. A recent change in a law governing drug testing will impact your project and change your project scope. The first thing you should do as project manager is:

    A. Create a documented change request.

    B. Proceed as planned, as the project will be grandfathered beyond the new change in the law.

C. Consult with the project sponsor and the stakeholders.

D. Stop all project work until the issue is resolved.

6. During project integration activities, a project sponsor's role can best be described as doing which one of the following?

   A. Acting as a sounding board for the project stakeholders

   B. Helping the project manager and stakeholders to resolve any issues ASAP

   C. Deflecting change requests for the project manager

   D. Showing management the project progress and status reports

7. You are the project manager for the HALO Project. You and your project team are preparing the final project plan. Of the following, which one is a project plan development constraint you and your team must consider?

   A. The budget as assigned by management

   B. Project plans from similar projects

   C. Project plans from similar projects that have failed

   D. Interviews with Subject Matter Experts (SMEs) who have experience with the project work in your project plan

8. The primary purpose of your project plan is:

   A. To define the work to be completed to reach the project end date.

   B. To define the work needed in each phase of the project life cycle.

   C. To prevent any changes to the scope.

   D. To provide accurate communication for the project team, project sponsor, and stakeholders.

9. Of the following, which one is an input to project plan development?

   A. Assumptions

   B. Project planning methodology

   C. EVM

   D. Business needs

10. What is the difference between a project baseline and a project plan?

   A. Project plans change as needed, baselines change only at milestones.

   B. Project plans and baselines do not change—they are amended.

   C. Project plans change as needed; baselines are snapshots of the project plan.

   D. Baselines are control tools; project plans are execution tools.

11. Which one of the following is not beneficial to the project manager during the project plan development process?

    A. Gantt Charts

    B. PMIS

    C. EVM

    D. Stakeholder knowledge

12. Which one of the following represents the vast majority of a project's budget?

    A. Project planning

    B. Project plan execution

    C. Labor

    D. Cost of goods and services

13. The project plan provides a baseline for several things. Which one of the following does the project plan not provide a baseline for?

    A. Scope

    B. Cost

    C. Schedule

    D. Control

14. Which of the following can best help a project manager during project execution?

    A. Stakeholder analysis

    B. Change control boards

    C. PMIS

    D. Scope verification

15. You are the project manager for your organization. When it comes to Integrated Change Control, you must ensure which one of the following is present?

    A. Supporting detail for the change exists

    B. Approval of the change from the project team

    C. Approval of the change from an SME

    D. Risk assessment for each proposed change

16. The project plan provides what in regard to project changes?

    A. A methodology to approve or decline CCB changes

    B. A guide to all future project decisions

    C. A vision of the project deliverables

    D. A fluid document that may be updated as needed based on the CCB

17. You are the project manager for the DGF Project. This project is to design and implement a new application that will connect to a database server. Management of your company has requested that you create a method to document technical direction on the project and to document any changes or enhancements to the technical attributes of the project deliverable. Which one of the following would satisfy management's request?

   A. Configuration management

   B. Integrated Change Control

   C. Scope Control

   D. Change Management Plan

18. Baseline variances, a documented plan to management variances, and a proven methodology to offer corrective actions to the project plan are all part of which process?

   A. Change management

   B. Change Control System

   C. Scope Change Control

   D. Integrated Change Control

19. One of the requirements of project management in your organization is to describe your project management approach and methodology in the project plan. You can best accomplish this requirement through which one of the following actions?

   A. Establishing a project office

   B. Establishing a program office

   C. Compiling the management plans from each of the knowledge areas

   D. Creating a PMIS and documenting its inputs, tools and techniques, and outputs

20. You have just informed your project team that each team member will be contributing to the Lessons Learned documentation. Your team does not understand this approach and wants to know what the documentation will be used for. Which one of the following best describes the purpose of the Lessons Learned documentation?

   A. Offers proof of concept for management

   B. Offers historical information for future projects

   C. Offers evidence of project progression as reported by the project team

   D. Offers input to team member evaluations at the project conclusion

21. Which one of the following is a formal document to manage and control project execution?

   A. WBS
   B. Project plan
   C. Organizational management plan
   D. Work Authorization System

22. Configuration management is a process for applying technical and administrative direction and surveillance of the project implementation. Which activity is not included in configuration management?

   A. Controlling changes to the project deliverables
   B. Scope verification
   C. Automatic change request approvals
   D. Identification of the functional and physical attributes of the project deliverables

23. Which set of the following tools is part of the project plan execution?

   A. PMIS, WBS, EVM
   B. General management skills, status review meetings, EVM
   C. General management skills, status review meetings, Work Authorization Systems
   D. General management skills, status review meetings, EVM

24. EVM is used during the _____.

   A. Controlling processes
   B. Executing processes
   C. Closing processes
   D. Entire project

25. You are the project manager for your organization. Management would like you to use a tool that can help you plan, schedule, monitor, and report your findings on your project. This tool is which one of the following?

   A. PMIS
   B. EVM
   C. Status Review Meetings
   D. Project team knowledge and skill set

SELF TEST ANSWERS

1. ☑ **A.** Projects are selected based on business needs first.
   ☒ **B** is incorrect, as the project constraints are typically not an issue when a project is selected, the feasibility of a project to operate within the project constraints may be an issue, however. **C,** the project budget, is incorrect as the project budget is a project constraint. **D** is incorrect, as the project schedule is also a constraint.

2. ☑ **C.** The project team contributes to the Lessons Learned document. The project manager also contributes, if not leads, the creation, but this is not a choice in the question.
   ☒ **A** is incorrect, as the customers do not contribute to the Lessons Learned document. **B** is incorrect, as the project sponsor does not contribute to the Lessons Learned document. **D** is incorrect, as stakeholders, other than the project manager and the project team, do not contribute.

3. ☑ **D.** Additional quality testing will require additional time and resources for the project. This is an example of Integrated Change Control.
   ☒ **A** is incorrect, as scope creep are small, undocumented changes to the project execution. **B,** change control, is incorrect, as change control falls within Integrated Change Control. **C** is incorrect; as QA is an organization-wide program.

4. ☑ **B.** Change requests do not always require more money. Approved changes may require more funds, but not always. The change request may be denied, so no additional funds are needed for the project.
   ☒ **A, C,** and **D** are all incorrect choices, as these are characteristics of change requests during a project.

5. ☑ **A.** A formal, documented change request is the best course of action for a change request stemming from a law or regulation.
   ☒ **B** is incorrect, as the law or regulation will likely override any existing project implementation. **C** is incorrect, as the project manager should first document the change through a change request. **D** is incorrect, as all project work shouldn't stop just because of a change request.

6. ☑ **B.** The project sponsor can help the project manager and the stakeholders resolve issues during project integration management.
   ☒ **A** is incorrect, as the project sponsor is going to have an active rather than passive role in the process of integration management. **C** is incorrect, as the project sponsor will guide changes through the Change Control System. **D** is not a valid choice as the project sponsor is part of management and will do more than report status to other management roles.

7. ☑ **A.** If management has assigned the project constraint of a fixed budget, the project manager and the project team must determine how the project can operate within the constraint.

☒ **B** describes historical information, not a project constraint. **C** also is historical information and not a project constraint, so it too is incorrect. **D** is a valuable tool to use as input into the project plan development, but it is not a constraint.

8. ☑ **D.** Of all the choices presented, **D** is the best choice. Project plans communicate to the project team, the project sponsor, and stakeholders.

☒ **A** and **B** are incorrect, as they do not define the primary purpose of the project plan. **C** is also incorrect; the project plan is intended not to prevent changes, but to communicate.

9. ☑ **A.** Of the choices, assumptions are the only inputs to the project plan development.

☒ **B** is incorrect, as it describes a tool and technique used to develop the project plan. **C** is also a tool and technique to develop the project plan, rather than serve as input to the plan. **D** is incorrect, as it is an input to the planning processes.

10. ☑ **D.** A project baseline serves as a control tool. Project plan execution and work results are measured against the project baselines.

☒ **A** is incorrect, as baselines are changed with the project plan. **B** is incorrect, as project plans and baselines do change. **C** is also incorrect, as baselines are more than snapshots of the project plans; they are expectations of how the work should be performed.

11. ☑ **A.** Gantt charts are excellent tools to measure and predict the project progress, but are not needed during the project plan development process.

☒ Choices **B, C,** and **D** are needed, and expected, during the development of the project plan.

12. ☑ **B.** The project plan execution represents the majority of the project budget.

☒ **A,** project planning, does not reflect the majority of the project budget, although it may contain the most project processes. Choice **C,** labor, does not reflect the biggest project expense in all projects. Choice **D,** cost of goods and services, is incorrect, as the procurement of the goods and services will fall within the project plan execution; in addition, not every project will procure goods and services.

13. ☑ **D.** Control is not a baseline.

☒ Choices **A, B,** and **C** describe the project baselines contained within the project plan. Incidentally, **A, B,** and **C** are also the attributes of the Project Management Triple Constraint.

14. ☑ **C.** A PMIS can assist the project manager the most during project execution. It does not replace the role of the project manager, but only serves as an assistant.

☒ Choice **A** is incorrect, as stakeholder analysis should have been completed during the project planning processes. Choice **B** also incorrect; CCBs can assist the project manager, but not as much as the control and assistance offered through a PMIS. **D** is incorrect; scope verification is proof of the project work, but not an assistant to the project manager.

15. ☑ **A**. Integrated Change Control requires detail for implementing the change. Without evidence of the need for the change, there is no reason to implement it.

 ☒ Choice **B** is incorrect, as the project team's approval is not necessary for changes. **C** is incorrect, as a Subject Matter Expert is not always needed to determine the need for change. **D** is also incorrect; while risk assessment is needed for changes, some changes may be discarded based on reasons other than risk.

16. ☑ **B**. The project plan serves as a guide to all future project decisions.

 ☒ **A** is incorrect: the project plan details more than how changes may be approved or denied—recall that the Change Control Board (CCB) approves and declines changes. **C** is incorrect; the project plan describes how to obtain the project vision, not just what the project vision may be. **D** does describe that the project plan, but not as fully as choice **B**. In addition, the project plan can be updated without changing the project scope.

17. ☑ **A** configuration management is the documentation of the project product, its attributes and changes to the product.

 ☒ **B** is incorrect, as Integrated Change Control describes how to incorporate all of the project changes across the knowledge areas. **C** is incorrect, as scope control describes how to manage changes, or potential changes, to the project scope. **D** is also incorrect, as the Change Management Plan does not describe the project product, its features, or changes to the product.

18. ☑ **D**. Integrated Change Control is a system to document changes, their impact, response to changes, and performance deficits.

 ☒ **A** is incorrect, as change management does not respond to performance deficits as Integrated Change Control does. **B** is also incorrect, as the Change Control System is a documented procedure to manage change requests. **C** is incorrect, as Scope Change Control is the process of managing changes that only affect the work in the project scope.

19. ☑ **C**. The management approach is best described as a compilation of the individual plans in the project plan.

 ☒ **A** is incorrect, as a project office is not needed to describe the management approach. **B** is incorrect for the same reason as **A**. Choice **D** may be a good practice for project control, but it does not describe management approach and methodologies.

20. ☑ **B**. Lessons Learned is a document that offers historical information.

 ☒ **A** is incorrect; proof of concept likely comes early in the project's planning processes. **C** is also incorrect, as Lessons Learned may offer evidence of project progression, but it is not the purpose of the Lessons Learned document. **D** is also incorrect; Lessons Learned offers historical information for future projects.

21. ☑ **B.** The project plan is the formal document used to manage and control project execution.
☒ **A** is incorrect—the WBS is an input to the project plan. **C** is incorrect, as the organizational management plan is part of the project plan. **D** is also incorrect; the Work Authorization System allows work to be approved and for new work to begin.

22. ☑ **C.** Hopefully, in no project are there automatic change approvals. **C** is not a part of configuration management.
☒ **A, B,** and **D,** all describe the attributes of configuration management.

23. ☑ **C.** General management skills, status review meetings, and Work Authorization Systems are the best tools described here that serve as part of the project plan execution.
☒ **A** is incorrect, as EVM and the WBS are not part of the tools used in the project plan execution. **B** is incorrect, as it includes EVM. **D** is incorrect because it also includes EVM.

24. ☑ **D.** EVM, earned value management, is used throughout the project processes. It is a planning and control tool used to measure performance.
☒ Choices **A, B,** and **C** are correct in that EVM is used during these processes, but not as good a choice as **D**.

25. ☑ **A.** The PMIS is the best answer, as it helps the project manager plan, schedule, monitor, and report findings.
☒ Choice **B** is incorrect, as EVM does not help the project manager schedule. Choice **C** is incorrect; status review meetings do not help the project manager schedule. Choice **D** is incorrect, as the project team's knowledge and skills do not necessarily help the project manager plan, schedule, monitor, and report findings.

5

Managing the
Project Scope

H ave you ever set out to clean your garage and end up cleaning your attic? It usually starts by needing to move the car out of the garage so you can really dig in and clean. As you move your car you realize the car could really use a cleaning too.

So you clean out the car. You dust it down, clean the windows inside and out, and vacuum out pennies, old pens, and some green french fries. The vacuum, you discover, has something caught in the hose, so you have to fight to clear the blockage so you can finish cleaning out the car. Once the inside's spick-and-span, you think, "Might as well wash and wax the car, too."

This calls for the garden hose. The garden hose, you notice, is leaking water at the spigot by the house. Now you've got to replace the connector. This calls for a pair of channel-lock pliers. You run to the hardware store, get the pliers—and some new car wax. After fixing the garden hose, you finally wash and wax the car.

As you're putting the second coat of wax on, you see a few scratches on the car that could use some buffing. You have a great electric buffer—but can't recall where it is. Maybe it's in the attic? You check the attic only to realize how messy things are. So you begin moving out old boxes of clothes, baby toys, and more interesting stuff.

Before you know it, the garage is full of boxes you've brought down from the attic. The attic is somewhat cleaner, but the garage is messier than when you started way back this morning. As you admire the mess, you realize it's starting to rain on your freshly waxed car, the garden hose is tangled across the lawn, and there are so many boxes in the garage you can't pull the car in out of the rain.

So what does this have to do with project management? Plenty! Project management requires focus, organization, and a laser-like concentration. In this chapter, we'll be covering Project Scope Management: the ability to get the required work done—and only the required work—to complete the project. We'll look at how a project manager should create and follow a plan to complete the required work to satisfy the scope without wandering or embellishing the project deliverables.

Defining Project Scope Management

Project scope management, according to the PMBOK, constitutes "the processes to ensure that the project includes all of the work required, and only the work required, to complete the project successfully." Project scope management has several purposes:

- It defines what work is needed to complete the project objectives

- It determines what is included in the project
- It serves as a guide to determine what work is not needed to complete the project objectives
- It serves as a point of reference for what is not included in the project

So what is a project scope? A project scope is a description of the work required to deliver the product of a project. The project scope defines what work will, and will not, be included in the project work. A project scope guides the project manager on decisions to add, change, or remove the work of the project.

Project Scope vs. Product Scope

Project scope and product scope are different entities. A project scope deals with the required work to create the project deliverables. For instance, a project to create a new barn would focus only on the required work to complete the barn with the specific attributes, features, and characteristics called for by the project plan. The scope of the project is specific to the work required to complete the project objectives.

A product scope, on the other hand, is the attributes and characteristics of the deliverables the project is creating. As in the preceding barn project, the product scope would define the features and attributes of the barn. In this instance, the project to create a barn would not include creating a flower garden, a wading pool, and the installation of a fence. There would be very specific requirements regarding the features and characteristics of the barn: the materials to be used, the dimensions of the different rooms and stalls, the expected weight the hayloft should carry, electrical requirements, and more.

The project scope and the product scope are bound to each other. The product scope constitutes the characteristics and features of the product that the project creates. The end result of the project is measured against the requirements for that product. The project scope is the required work to deliver the product. Throughout the project execution, the work is measured against the project plan to verify that the project is on track to fulfill the product scope. The product scope is measured against requirements, while the project scope is measured against the project plan.

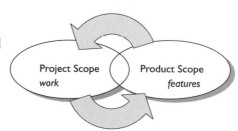

Initiating the Project

Initiation is the process to authorize a new project to begin. In addition, initiation can be the process to determine if a project should advance to the next phase of the project life cycle. In Chapter 2, we spent a good deal of time discussing the Initiation processes. Recall that initiation centers on two themes: determination of projects and authorization.

In many organizations, a formal determination process establishes the need for the project. This formal process can include the initial needs assessment, the feasibility study, a preliminary project plan, and so on. In other organizations, the determination process is more informal and is based on the project objectives: internal work orders, Add/Move/Change projects, and other conditions. In either case, there is some method of securing the needed resources and authority to move forward into the project management life cycle.

For a project to become authorized, formally or informally, management must recognize the need (or the perception of the need) and determine how to respond. The response can be yes, move forward with the project; no, the project is not authorized; or, the need may exist but additional information is needed to make a decision.

The need and authorization for projects, regardless of the selection methods, can come from one or more sources:

- **Marketplace opportunity**   A demand in the marketplace calls for the performing organization to meet the need in order to realize new profits.

- **Business need**   The project is created to grow the business, support the organization's vision, or to create a new product or service in a commercial venture.

- **Customers**   The performing organization's customers have requested the project to create a new product or service.

- ■ **Advances in technology** New technology has surpassed current implementations. The benefits of the new technology are valued.

- ■ **Legal** New laws or mandates require organizations to change their practices, adjust to safety requirements, provide additional services, and so on.

- ■ **Social** A project may be created to resolve a problem within a community or culture based on identified needs.

Examining the Product Description

For a project to be authorized, there must be some consensus among the stakeholders regarding what the project is to accomplish. The product description details the product the project will create. The product description will generally be vague in the early portions of the project and become more detailed as the project moves towards a solution. As the project moves forward, it passes through progressive elaboration. Progressive elaboration is the process of allowing the project to evolve and the project characteristics to come into focus based on the needs of the stakeholders and the feasible solution.

Here's a simple example: CDRX, a CD duplication company, has a CD duplicator machine that is not keeping up with the demands of customers. Orders for CDs are causing the duplicator equipment to process orders on two shifts—and jobs are still backlogged. A new project is created to find a solution for the problem. The initial product description addresses the issue with the duplicator machine. The objective of the project is to solve the backlogged problem so customers won't take their orders to the competition. A competing objective is to determine if the new demand is short-term or long-term. If the demand is short-term, then a solution is needed to address the immediate problem. If the demand is long term, then a solution is needed to address the new opportunities.

In the preceding example, the project is to address the problem of the backlogged orders. The project will, through research, stakeholder interviews, and analysis of the organization's work, pass through progressive elaboration. Through root cause analysis, the project objective is now to add an additional, faster duplicator to the manufacturing process. With this direction, the project will pass through additional refinements until the exact vision for the project exists. The product description is a document to provide recognition to the original need for the project to exist.

Considering Client-Vendor Relationships

When it comes to organizations, such as consultants, integrators, architectural firms, and more, that perform projects for other entities, the product description is provided by the buyer. The product description, from the buyer, may not be a formal document, but a conversation or informal document of what the final product should be. The vendor should document and create the product description for several reasons:

- It confirms that the buyer and the seller are in agreement regarding the project's purpose.
- It allows the seller to guide progressive elaboration.
- It allows the buyer to refine the product description.
- It provides accurate communications between the buyer and the seller.
- It provides clear input to scope planning processes.

Working with Strategic Plans

All projects should "fit" within the performing organization. Specifically, all projects should map to the strategic plans of the performing organization. For example, an organization that creates packaging supplies for a food manufacturer has a very specific market. The packing supplier focuses on food manufacturers and their need for labels, shrink-wrap, food containers, boxes, and other food-packaging products. It would most likely not be within the packaging supplier's strategic plan to begin manufacturing and packaging their own food products.

The strategic plan of the performing organization focuses on the reason the business, community, or not-for-profit group is in existence. Projects that don't support the strategic plan of an organization are not likely to be selected—or be successful if they do manage to get initiated.

Examining the Project Selection Criteria

Meet Tracy. Tracy has a great project she'd like to see authorized. She has to "sell" the project to management in order to have it authorized. She needs to determine what's so great about her project—and why management should buy into it. She is looking for project selection criteria—reasons why her project should be authorized. Possible considerations Tracy can include:

- Return on investment
- Realized opportunities

- Market share
- Customer perspective
- Demand for the product
- Social needs
- Increased revenues
- Reduced costs

Historical Information

Has anyone ever done something like this before? Historical information provides proven documentation of the success or failure of performance, and can be referenced for project selection criteria. For instance: Has management squelched similar projects for specific reasons? Historical information can be referenced for similar projects and how they performed through execution, as well as how the deliverables of the project performed according to prediction.

In addition, historical information is one of the key elements to determining if an existing project should move forward into the next project phase. If the completed project phase has proven successful, and provided some merit or value, it's likely to move forward. Projects that don't prove valuable—based on the performance of the phase or less-than-desirable phase results—will likely be axed.

Considering the Initiation Tools and Techniques

Projects get initiated, authorized, and then the real work begins. As you know, project initiation can be formal or informal depending on the organization, and the type and size of the project. Project initiation boils down to selecting projects—and then authorizing those projects to begin.

Selecting Projects

When it comes to management selecting projects, the "attractiveness" of the project to the project owner is a weighty factor. The attractiveness can be measured through proven worth, suspected worth, and the level of uncertainty within the project. When a potential project is evaluated, the project owner, customer, or management wants to reduce business risk—specifically the risk of project failure—which could result in lost monies, lost customers, lost time, fines, inconvenience, and more. Projects with many variables carry more business risk than projects with few variables.

Project selection methods are about resolving the unknown, predicting the likelihood of project success, and the expected value of that project's success—or the cost of its failure. The process of selecting projects to keep and selecting projects to discard is based on two different methods.

- Benefit measurement methods
- Constrained optimization methods

on the **Job**

Project selection is also known as Go/No Go decision-making. Projects with many variables are excellent candidates for phase gates. The project is allowed a Go decision to the end of the first phase. Another Go/No Go decision happens at the end of each phase based on the performance and deliverables.

Examining Benefit Measurement Methods

There are several different benefit measurement methods. These methods are all about comparing values of one project against the values of another. As you might expect, the projects with higher, positive values typically get selected over projects with low values. Here are some common benefit measurement methods you may encounter:

Murder Boards

Murder boards are committees full of folks that ask every conceivable negative question about the proposed project. Their goal is to expose strengths and weakness of the project—and kill the project if it's deemed worthless for the organization to commit to. Not a pleasant decision-making process.

Scoring Models

Scoring models (sometimes called weighted scoring models) are models that use a common set of values for all of the projects up for selection. For example, values can be profitability, complexity, customer demand, and so on. Each of these values has a weight assigned to them—values of high importance have a high weight, while values of lesser importance have a lesser weight. The projects are measured against these values and assigned scores by how well they match to the predefined values. The projects with high scores take priority over projects will lesser scores. Figure 5-1 demonstrates the scoring model.

FIGURE 5-1 The weighted model bases project selection on predefined values.

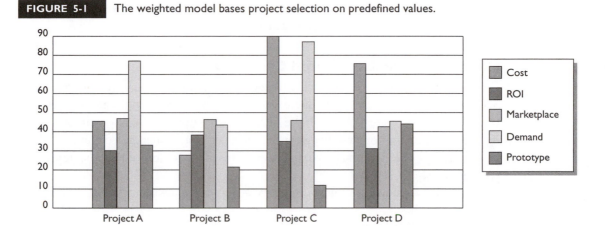

Benefit/Cost Ratios

Just like they sound, benefit/cost ratio (BCR) models examine the cost-to-benefit ratio. For example, a typical measure is the cost to complete the project, the cost of ongoing operations of the project product, compared against the expected benefits of the project. For example, consider a project that will cost $575,000 to create a new product, market the product, and provide ongoing support for the product for one year. The expected gross return on the product, however, is $980,000 in year one. The benefit of completing the project is greater than the cost to create the product.

exam

watch *BCR statements can be written as ratios. For example, a BCR of 3:2 has three benefits to two costs—a good choice. A BCR of 1:3, however, is not a good choice. Pay special attention to which side of the ratio represents the cost; it should not be more than the benefit to be selected.*

Payback Period

How long does it take the project to "pay back" the costs of the project? For example, the AXZ Project will cost the organization $500,000 to create over five years. The expected cash inflow (income) on the project deliverable, however, is $40,000 per quarter. From here it's simple math: 500,000 divided by $40,000 is 12.5 quarters, or a little over three years to recoup the expenses.

This selection method, while one of the simplest, is also the weakest. Why? The cash inflows are not discounted against the time to begin creating the cash. This is the time value of money. The $40,000 per quarter five years from now is worth less than $40,000 in your pocket today. Remember when sodas were a nickel? It's the same idea—the soda hasn't gotten better, the nickel is just worth less today than it was way back then.

Considering the Discounted Cash Flow

Discounted cash flow accounts for the time value of money. If you were to borrow $100,000 for five years from your uncle you'd be paying interest on the money, yes? (If not, you've got a great uncle.) If the $100,000 were invested for five years and managed to earn a whopping six percent interest per year, compounded annually it'd be worth $133,822.60 at the end of five years. This is the future value of the money in today's terms.

The magic formula for future value is $FV = PV (1 + I)^n$, where:

- FV is future value
- PV is present value
- I is the interest rate
- N is the number of time periods (years, quarters, and so on)
- Here's the formula with the $100,000 in action:

    $FV = 100,000(1 + .06)^5$

    $FV = 100,000(1.338226)$

    $FV = 133,822.60$

The future value of the $100,000 five years from now is worth $133,822.60 today. So how does that help? Now we've got to calculate the discounted cash flow across all of the projects up for selection. The discounted cash flow is really just the inverse of the preceding formula. We're looking for the present value of future cash flows: $PV = FV \div (1 + I)^n$

In other words, if a project says it'll be earning the organization $160,000 per year in five years, that's great, but what's $160,000 five years from now really worth today? This puts the amount of the cash flow in perspective with what the projections are in today's money. Let's plug it into the formula and find out (assuming the interest rate is still six percent):

$PV = FV \div (1 + I)^n$

$PV = 160,000 \div (1.338226)$

$PV = \$119,561$

So… $160,000 in five years is really only worth $119,561 today. If we had four different projects of varying time to completion, cost, and project cash inflows at completion we'd calculate the present value, and choose the project with the best PV as it'll likely be the best investment for the organization.

Calculating the Net Present Value

The net present value (NPV) is a somewhat complicated formula, but allows a more precise prediction of project value than the lump sum approach found with the PV formula. NPV evaluates the monies returned on a project for each time period the project lasts. In other words, a project may last five years, but there may be a return of investment in each of the five years the project is in existence, not just at the end of the project.

You should be able to look at the PV of two proposed projects and make a decision as to which one should be green-lighted. The project with the highest PV is the best choice if that's the only factor you're presented with.

For example, a retail company may be upgrading the facilities at each of their stores to make shopping and purchasing easier for their customers. The company has 1000 stores. As each store makes the conversion to the new facility design, the project deliverables will begin, hopefully, generating cash flow as a result of the project deliverables. (Uh, we specifically want cash inflow from the new stores, not cash outflow. That's some nerdy accounting humor.) The project can begin earning money when the first store is completed with the conversion to the new facilities. The faster the project can be completed, the sooner the organization will see a complete return on their investment.

Here's how the NPV formula works:

1. Calculate the project's cash flow for time unit (typically quarters or years).
2. Calculate each time unit total into present value.
3. Sum the present value of each time unit.
4. Subtract the investment for the project.
5. Take two aspirins.
6. Examine the NPV value. An NPV greater than one is good and the project should be approved. An NPV less than one is bad and the project should be rejected.

When comparing two projects, the project with the greater NPV is typically better, though projects with high returns (PV) early in the project are better than those with low returns early in the project. Here's an example of an NPV calculation:

Time Period	Cash Flow	Present Value
1	15,000.00	14,150.94
2	25,000.00	22,249.91
3	17,000.00	14,273.53
4	25,000.00	19,802.34
5	18,000.00	13,450.65
Totals	$100,000.00	83,927.37
Investment		78,000.00
NPV		$5,927.37

on the job

The CD accompanying this book contains an Excel spreadsheet called "Project Selection Formulas." This spreadsheet has formulas to walk you through the formulas for present value, future value, and the net present value.

Considering the Internal Rate of Return

The last benefit measurement method is the internal rate of return (IRR). The IRR is a complex formula to calculate when the present value of the cash inflow equals the original investment. Don't get too lost in this formula—it's a tricky business and you won't need to know how to calculate the IRR for the exam. You will need to know, however, that when comparing multiple projects' IRRs, projects with high IRRs are better choices than projects with low IRRs. This makes sense. Would you like an investment with a high rate of return or a lower rate of return?

Examining Constrained Optimization Methods

Constrained optimization methods are complex mathematical formulas and algorithms that are used to predict the success of projects, the variables within projects, and tendencies to move forward with selected project investments. For the exam, thankfully all you need to know about these selection methods are that they are not typically used for most projects, but large, complex projects. Here are the major constrained optimization methods:

- Linear programming
- Nonlinear programming

- Integer algorithms
- Dynamic programming
- Multiobjective programming

Relying on Expert Judgment

Have you ever heard the expression "To be successful surround yourself with smarter people"? That's the idea of expert judgment. When it comes to project selection, another tool management (and the project manager throughout the project) can rely on is expert judgment. Expert judgment is referenced over and over as a tool and technique in the PMBOK. So, what is it? Expert judgment is a technique to rely on the experts within your organization, consultants, stakeholders (including the project customers), professional associations, or industry groups for advice. These experts can contribute to the project selection method by offering their opinion, research, and experience.

Examining the Outputs of the Initiation

The potential project has moved through the initiation process, passed through the project selection methods, and has been deemed worthy to become an official project. The outputs of the initiation process will serve as inputs to many downstream processes. Let's examine the specifics of what the outputs are.

Examining the Project Charter

The project charter is an output of the initiation processes and serves as an input to scope planning. The project charter, as you know by now, authorizes the project. Projects, as far as the PMP exam goes, do not exist without a project charter. In some instances, however, a contract can serve as the project charter. As a quick review, here are some exam essentials you should know about the project charter:

- The project charter names the project and provides a description of the product.
- The project charter names the project manager and assigns the project manager a level of authority for managing resources, finances, and decisions on the project.
- The project charter details the business case of the project. The business case identifies the business need behind the project, and establishes why the project has been created.

- The project charter provides detailed product description. This is a description of the desired future state the project will create.

- The project charter is signed and approved by a member of management that has the proper authority to ascertain the needed resources and charge the project manager with the management duties. The person signing the charter is high enough in the organization to be considered "over" the project team members and functional managers.

- The project charter should be written so as not to require change as the project progresses.

Recognizing the Project Manager

An output of the initiation processes is to identify the project manager. This is evident through the project charter, but, according to the PMBOK, the project manager should be named as early as possible in the project process. If you cannot have a project with a charter, then the project manager cannot be named until the charter is written—a classic "Catch-22" scenario. For the exam, know that the project manager is identified by the project charter, must be identified before project plan execution begins, and hopefully be identified before much project planning begins.

Identifying the Project Constraints

You've seen project constraints already: time, cost, and scope. Constraints can come from contracts, social conditions, and stakeholder requests, all of which contribute to conditions placed upon time, cost, and scope. Generally speaking, it's easier to get more time than money. Stakeholders and the project team identify constraints.

Planning the Project Scope

Planning the project scope involves progress elaboration. The project scope begins broad and through refinement becomes focused on the required work to create the product of the project. Like any process in project management, scope planning has inputs, tools and techniques, and outputs. The following table lists the inputs, tools and techniques, and outputs of scope planning.

Inputs	Tools and Techniques	Outputs
Product description	Product analysis	Scope statement
Project charter	Benefit/cost analysis	Supporting detail

Inputs	Tools and Techniques	Outputs
Constraints	Alternatives identification	Scope management plan
Assumptions	Expert judgment	

Using Scope Planning Tools and Techniques

The goal of scope planning is to create a scope statement and the scope management plan, two of the outputs of the scope planning process. The project manager and the project team must have a full understanding of the project requirements, business need of the project, and stakeholder expectations to be successful creating the scope statement and the scope management plan. Recall that there are two types of scopes:

- **Product scope**   Features and functions of the product of the project
- **Project scope**   The work needed to create the product of the project

Using Product Analysis

Product analysis is, as the name implies, analyzing the product the project will create. Specifically, it involves understanding all facets of the product, its purpose, how it works, and its characteristics. Product analysis can be accomplished through one or more of the following:

- **Product breakdown**   This method breaks down the product into components, examining each component individually and how it may work with other parts of the product. This approach can be used in chemical engineering to see how a product, such as a pharmaceutical, is created and how effective it is.

- **Systems engineering**   This process focuses on satisfying the customers' needs, cost requirements, and quality demands through the design and creation of the product. There is an entire science devoted to systems engineering in various industries.

- **Value engineering**   Deals with reducing costs and increasing profits, all while improving quality. Its focus is on solving problems, realizing opportunities, and maintaining quality improvement.

- **Value analysis**   Similar to value engineering, this focuses on the cost/quality ratio of the product. For example, your expected level of quality of a $100,000 automobile versus a $6,700 used car is likely relevant to the cost of each. Value analysis focuses on the expected quality against the acceptable cost—also known as the cost of quality.

- **Function analysis** Related to value engineering, this allows team input to the problem, a search for a logical solution, and tests the functions of the product so the results can be graphed.
- **Quality function** This deployment is a philosophy and a practice to fully understand the customer needs—both spoken and implied—without gold-plating the project deliverables.

Using the Benefit/Cost Analysis

The analysis of benefits to costs is straightforward business. The project manager records the tangible and intangible benefits and costs and creates a ratio between the two. For example, a project to create an addition onto an existing home may have a cost outlay of $75,000, but also have costs that are not financial, such as loss of yard space, additional heating and cooling requirements, risk of expansion for resale purposes, and so on. The benefits of the expansion can include more living space for the family, added comfort to the home, not having to move to a new house, and so on. The benefit/cost ratio lists the key benefits against the key costs and can be written as 3:2—three benefits, against two costs.

Finding Alternatives

Project managers, project team members, and stakeholders must resist the temptation to fall in love with a solution too quickly. Alternative identification is any method of creating alternative solutions to the project need. This is typically accomplished through brainstorming and lateral thinking.

Examining the Scope Statement

The scope statement, an output of scope planning, is the guide for all future project decisions. It is the key document to provide understanding of the project purpose. The scope statement provides justification for the project existence, lists the high-level deliverables, and quantifies the project objectives. The scope statement is a powerful document that the project manager and the project team will use as a point of reference for potential changes, added work, and any project decisions. The scope statement includes or references the following:

- **Project justification** Identifies the business needs of the project. It answers why the project has been authorized. This is important since it provides guidance should the project undergo cuts and tradeoffs of deliverables.

- **Project's product**   The scope statement reiterates the details of the project product.

- **Project deliverables**   The high-level deliverables of the project should be identified. These deliverables, when predefined metrics are met, signal that the project scope has been completed. When appropriate, the scope statement should also list what deliverables are excluded from the project deliverables. For example, a project to create a new food product may state that it is not including the packaging of the food product as part of the project. Items and features not listed as part of the project deliverables should be assumed to be excluded.

- **Project objectives**   Project objectives are specific conditions that determine the success of a project. Conditions are typically cost, schedule, and quality metrics. Vague metrics, such as customer satisfaction, increase risk for the project, as the metric "customer satisfaction" is subjective and not quantified.

Examining the Supporting Detail

Have you ever wondered how and why a project manager made a particular decision? Supporting detail provides information on why decisions were made. Supporting detail serves as point of reference in the project. It provides information for identified constraints and assumptions made during the scope planning processes.

Implementing the Scope Management Plan

The scope management plan explains how the project scope will be managed and how scope changes will be factored into the project plan. Based on the conditions of the project, the project work, and the confidence of the project scope, the scope management plan should also define the likelihood of changes to the scope, how often the scope may change, and how much the scope can change. The scope management plan also details the process of how changes to the project scope will be documented and classified throughout the project life cycle.

e x a m

ⓦatch

Generally, you do not want the project scope to change. The implication of the scope management plan concerns how change to the project scope will be permitted—and what the justification is to allow the change.

INSIDE THE EXAM

There are three big themes from this chapter you'll encounter on the project exam: initiation, scope, and the WBS. For initiation, you should know several facts based on the processes found within initiation:

1. Projects are initiated based on business and customer needs, as well as opportunities.

2. Feasibility studies can help determine if a project should be selected for authorization.

3. The product description is created to help direct the project planning and selection method.

4. The project charter is created and signed by senior management to authorize the project.

5. The project manager is named and appointed in the project charter.

There are two types of scope, project scope, and product scope. Unless the exam is talking about features and characteristics of the project deliverables, it will be referring to the project scope. If you think this through,

it makes sense: think of all the billions of different product scopes that can exist... the exam will offer big, old hints if its talking about product scope.

Project scope, on the other hand, focuses on the work that has to be done in order to create the product. Recall that the project scope is concerned with the work required—and only the required work—to complete the project.

Your favorite project management tool, the WBS, is the most important tool in your project management toolbox. It is used as input to five planning processes:

- Cost estimating
- Cost budgeting
- Resource planning
- Activity definition
- Risk management planning

Here's a nifty hint: WBS templates come from previous projects and/or the project management office if the organization has one. WBS activities are defined in the WBS dictionary.

Creating the Scope Definition

The process of scope definition is all about breaking down the work into manageable chunks. If you had a desire to create a new house, you probably wouldn't stop by the lumberyard, pick up a truck of lumber, some cement, and nails and set about building your dream house. You'd follow a logical approach to designing, planning, and then creating the house.

The same is true with project management. Your organization and stakeholders may have a general idea of where the project should end up, but a detailed, fully developed plan is needed to get you there. Scope definition is the process of taking the broad vision for the project and breaking it down into logical steps to reach the completion.

In this section, we'll examine the inputs, tools and techniques, and outputs of scope definition, as defined in Table 5-1:

Examining the Inputs to Scope Definition

You should be very familiar with the inputs to scope definition; you've seen these several times already throughout the book. Here's a quick refresher of each and their role in this process:

- **Scope statement**   Guide for all future project decisions. It is the key document to understanding the project purpose.
- **Constraints**   This includes factors such as cost, time, and scope requirements.
- **Assumptions**   Beliefs, held to be true, that the project is operating under.
- **Other planning outputs**   Outputs from the planning processes in other knowledge areas, such as risk, can influence the scope.
- **Historical Information**   Past projects can serve as inputs to scope definition. Consider errors and omissions from past projects against similar issues in the current project.

Using a Work Breakdown Structure Template

One of the tools you can use in scope definition in a WBS template. We'll detail how a WBS gets created from scratch in a moment. A WBS breaks down work into a deliverables-orientated collection of manageable pieces (see Figure 5-2). It is not a list of activities necessary to complete the project.

TABLE 5-1	Inputs	Tools and Techniques	Outputs
The Inputs, Outputs, and Tools and Techniques of Scope Definition.	Scope statement	Work breakdown structure templates	Work breakdown structure
	Constraints	Decomposition	Scope statement updates
	Assumptions		
	Other planning outputs		
	Historical information		

FIGURE 5-2 A sample WBS structure for a technology project.

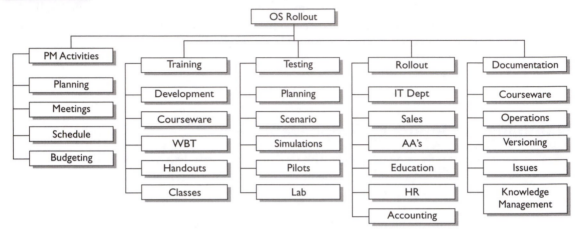

A WBS template uses a similar project's WBS as a guide for the current work. This approach is recommended since most projects in an organization are similar in their project life cycles—and the approach can be adapted to fit a given project.

Depending on the organization and its structure, an entity may have a common WBS template that all projects follow. The WBS template may have common activities included in the form, a common lexicon for the project in the organization, and a standard approach to the level of detail required for the project type.

Decomposing the Project Deliverables

Decomposition is the process of breaking down the major project deliverables into smaller, manageable components. So what's a manageable component? It's a unit of the project deliverable that can be assigned resources, measured, executed, and controlled. So, how does one decompose the project deliverables? It's done this way:

1. The major deliverables of the project are identified. This includes the project management activities. A logical approach includes identifying the phases of the project life cycle or the major deliverables of the project.

2. Determine if adequate cost and time estimates can be applied to the lowest level of the decomposed work. Adequate is subjective to the demands of the project work. Deliverables that won't be realized until later portions of the project may be difficult to decompose since there are many variables between now and when the deliverable is created. The smallest component of the WBS is

the work package. A simple heuristic of decomposition is the 8/80 rule: no work package smaller than eight hours and no work package larger than 80.

3. Identify the deliverable's constituent components . This is a fancy way of asking whether the project deliverable can be measured at this particular point of decomposition? For example, a decomposition of a user manual may have the constituent components of assembling the book, confirming that the book is complete, shrink-wrapping the book, and shipping it to the customer. Each component of the work can be measured, and may take varying amounts of time to complete, but it all must be done to complete the requirement.

4. Verify the decomposition. The lower-level items must be evaluated to ensure they are complete and accurate. Each item within the decomposition must be clearly defined and deliverable-orientated. Finally, each item should be decomposed to the point that it can be scheduled, budgeted, and assigned to a resource.

5. Other approaches include breaking it out by geography or functional area, or even breaking the work down by in-house and contracted work.

Working Through a WBS

As you hopefully know by now, the WBS is a deliverables-orientated collection of project components. Work that doesn't fit into the WBS does not fit within the project. The point of the WBS is to organize and define the project scope. As you can see in Figure 5-3, each level of the WBS becomes more detailed.

The WBS is more than a shopping list of activities—it is a visual representation of the high-level deliverables broken down into manageable components. A WBS is not a chart of the activities to complete the work—it is a breakdown of the deliverables. The smallest element in the WBS is called the work package. The components in the WBS are typically mapped against a code of accounts. The code of accounts is a tool to number and identify the elements within the WBS. For example, a project manager and a stakeholder could reference work package 7.3.2.1 and both would be able to find the exact element in the WBS.

The components in the WBS should be included in a WBS dictionary. A WBS dictionary is a reference tool to explain the WBS components, the nature of the work package, the assigned resources, and the time and billing estimates for each element. The WBS also identifies the relationship between work packages. Finally, the WBS should be updated to reflect changes to the project scope.

Here are some essential elements you must know about the WBS:

FIGURE 5-3

This section of the WBS has been expanded to offer more detail.

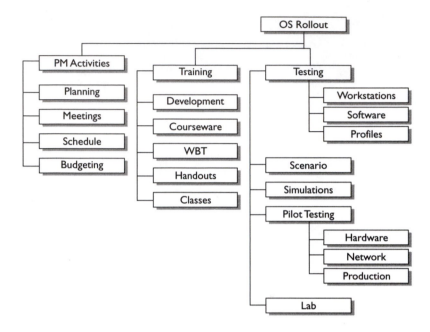

- Serves as the project scope baseline
- One of the most important project management tools
- Serves as the foundation for planning, estimating, and project control
- Visualizes the entire project
- Work not included in the WBS is not part of the project
- Builds team consensus and buy-in to the project
- Serves as a control mechanism to keep the project on track
- Allows for accurate cost and time estimates
- Serves as deterrent to scope change

As you can tell, the WBS is pretty darn important. If you're wondering where exactly the WBS fits into the project as a whole, the WBS is an input to five core processes.

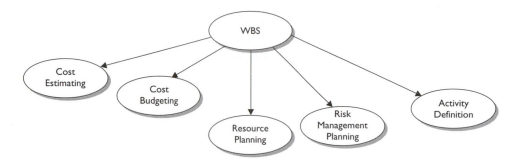

- ■ Cost estimating
- ■ Cost budgeting
- ■ Resource planning
- ■ Risk management planning
- ■ Activity definition

Updating the Scope Statement

The second output of scope definition is scope updates. During the decomposition of the project deliverables, the project manager and the project team may discover elements that were not included in the scope statement but should be. Or the project manager and the team may discover superfluous activities in the scope statement that should be removed. For whatever reason, when updating the scope statement, the appropriate stakeholders must be notified of the change and the justification of why the change is being made.

Verifying the Project Scope

Imagine a project to create a full-color, slick catalog for an electronics manufacturer. The project manager has completed the initiation processes, moved through planning, and is now executing the project work. The only trouble is the project manager and the experts on the project team aren't sharing the work progress with the customer. The work they are completing is not in alignment with the product description or the customer requirements.

The project team has created a trendy 1950s style catalog with funky green and orange colors, lots of beehive hairdo models, horn-rimmed glasses, and tongue-in-cheek jokes about "the future" of electronics. The manufacturer wants to demonstrate a professional, accessible, current look for its publications. What do you think will happen if the project manager presents the catalog with his spin rather than following the request of the customer?

Scope verification is the process of the project customer accepting the project deliverables. Scope verification happens at the end of each project phase—or as major deliverables are created. Scope verification is ensuring that the deliverables the project creates are in alignment with the project scope. Scope verification is concerned with the acceptance of the work. A related activity, quality control, is concerned with the correctness of the work. Scope verification and quality control happen in tandem as the quality of the work contributes to scope verification. Poor quality will typically result in scope verification failure.

Should a project get cancelled before it has completed the scope, scope verification is measured against the deliverables to the point of the project cancellation. In other words, scope verification measures the completeness of the work up to the cancellation, not the work that was to be completed after project termination.

The inputs, tools and techniques, and outputs of scope verification are shown in the Table 5-2.

Examining the Inputs to Scope Verification

To verify the project scope, which is accomplished through inspection, there must be something to inspect—namely work results. The work results are compared against the project plan to check for their completeness and against the quality control measure to check their correctness of the work.

TABLE 5-2	Inputs	Tools and Techniques	Outputs
The Inputs, Outputs, and Tools and Techniques of Scope Verification.	Work results	Inspection	Formal acceptance
	Product documentation		
	WBS		
	Scope statement		
	Project plan		

One of the biggest inputs of scope verification is the product documentation. This information describes the requirements and expectations of the product, its features, and attributes. The product documentation may go by many different names depending on the industry. A few project documentation names include:

- Plans
- Specifications
- Technical documentation
- Drawings
- Blueprints

As you know, the WBS is a collection of deliverables-orientated components. This collection of components can be used to ensure that the defined project work has been completed to obtain all of the components of the product. The WBS allows the project manager, the project team, and the customer to verify the necessary work was completed to create the deliverable.

The scope statement and the project plan serve as input to the project plan since they provide details on the project work, the product, and the expectations of the customer. A reference to these documents may be needed to clarify any issues during scope verification.

Inspecting the Project Work

To complete scope verification, the work must be inspected. Inspection may require measuring, examining, and testing the product to prove that it meets the customer requirements. Inspection usually requires the project manager and the customer to inspect the project work for verification, which in turn results in acceptance. Depending on the industry, inspections may also be known as:

- Reviews
- Product reviews
- Audits
- Walk-throughs

Formally Accepting the Project Deliverables

e x a m

⊕ a t c h *If a project scope has been completed, the project is complete. Resist the urge to do additional work once the project scope has been fulfilled. Also be cautious of instances where the scope is fulfilled, the product description is exact, but the customer is not happy with the product. Technically, for the exam, the project is complete even if the customer is not happy.*

Assuming the scope has been verified, the customer accepts the deliverable. This is a formal process that requires signed documentation of the acceptance by the sponsor or customer. Scope verification can also happen at the end of each project phase or at major deliverables within the project. In these instances, scope verification may be conditional based on the work results. When the scope is not verified, the project may undergo one of several actions. It may be cancelled and deemed a failure, sent through corrective actions, or put on hold while a decision is made based on the project or phase results.

Protecting the Scope from Change

When it comes to project management, the one constant thing is change. Changes happen, or try to happen, all the time in projects. The project manager must have a reliable system to track, monitor, manage, and review changes to the project scope. Change control focuses on three things:

- ■ Facilitates scope changes to determine that changes are agreed upon.
- ■ Determines if a scope change has happened.
- ■ Manages the scope changes when, and if, they happen.

Table 5-3 shows the inputs, tools and techniques, and outputs of scope change control.

TABLE 5-3	Inputs	Tools and Techniques	Outputs
The Inputs, Tools and Techniques, and Outputs of Scope Change Control.	Work breakdown structure	Scope change control system	Scope changes
	Performance reports	Performance measurement	Corrective actions
	Change requests	Additional planning	Lessons learned
	Scope management plan		Adjusted baseline

Examining the Inputs to Scope Change Control

Throughout a project's life, the need and desire for change will come from project team members, the sponsor, management, customers, and other stakeholders. All of these change requests must be coupled with supporting evidence to determine the need of the change, the change's impact on the project scope (and usually on other processes as well), and the required planning, schedule, and budget to account for the changes.

Using the WBS

Your favorite project management tool, the WBS, serves as an input to the scope change control. It represents the sum of the components, and ultimately the project work, that make up the project scope. It characterizes the project scope baseline. The change requests may be for additional components in the project deliverables, changes to product attributes, or changes to different procedures to create the product. The WBS is referenced to determine which work packages would be affected by the change, and which may be added or removed as a result of the change.

Evaluating Performance Reports

The Communications Management Plan, which we'll cover in Chapter 10, includes specific requirements on the need for performance reports. Performance reports indicate how the project is going—good or bad. Performance reports can lead to change requests. How? When a project is going bad, operating beyond its budget, or off schedule, changes may be made to reduce the project scope, add corrective actions, or add quality activities to ensure the product is correct.

Considering Change Requests

Some project managers despise change requests. Change requests can mean additional work, adjustments to the project, or a reduction in scope. They mean additional planning for the project manager, time for consideration, and can be seen as a distraction from the project execution and control. Change requests, however, are a very real and expected part of project management. They can come in several modalities:

- Oral or written
- Direct or indirect
- Internal or external
- Legally mandated or optional

Why do change requests happen? And which ones are most likely to be approved? Most change requests are a result of:

- **Value-added** The change will reduce costs (this is often due to technological advances since the time the project scope was created)
- **External events** These could be such things as new laws or industry requirements.
- **Errors or omissions** Ever hear this one: "Oops! We forgot to include this feature in the product description and WBS!" Errors and omissions can happen to both the project scope, which is the work to complete the project, and the product scope, and typically constitute an overlooked feature or requirement.
- **Risk response** A risk has been identified and changes to scope are needed to mitigate the risk.

Relying on the Scope Management Plan

Remember this plan earlier in the chapter? It's an output of scope planning and controls how the project scope can be changed. The scope management plan also defines the likelihood of the scope to change, how often the scope may change, and how much it may change. You don't have to be a mind reader to determine how often the project scope may change—and by how much; you just have to rely on your level of confidence in the scope, the variables within the project, and the conditions the project must operate under. The scope management plan also details the process of how changes to the project scope will be documented and classified throughout the project life cycle.

Implementing a Scope Change Control System

The most prominent tool applied with scope change control is the Scope Change Control System. Because changes are likely to happen within any project, there must be order to process, document, and manage the changes. The Scope Change Control System is the answer. This system includes:

- Cataloging the documented requests and paperwork
- Tracking the requests through the system

- Determining the required approval levels for varying changes
- Supporting the integrated change control policies of the project
- In instances when the project is performed through a contractual relationship, the scope change control system must map to the requirements of the contract.

on the job

The Scope Change Control System is likely to be computer-driven, automated to some extent, and provide workflow to route change requests to appropriate stakeholders and decision makers within the project.

Revisiting Performance Measurement

Performance Reports are inputs to scope change control—the contents of these reports, the actual measurements of the project—are evaluated to determine what the needed changes may be. The reports are not meant to expose variances as much as they are done to drive root cause analysis of the variances. Project variances happen for a reason: the correct actions required to eliminate the variances may require changes to project scope.

There is a distinct difference between performance reports and performance measurement, as shown in Table 5-4:

Completing Additional Planning

Planning is iterative. As change requests are presented, evidence of change exists, or corrective actions are needed within the project—the project manager and the project team will need to revisit the planning processes. Change within the project may require alternative identification, study of the change impact, risks introduced by the change, and solutions to problems within the project execution. Changes made as part of this planning could cause the project plan, project WBS, and the project baselines to be revised.

TABLE 5-4	Performance Reports	Performance Measurement
Performance Reports vs. Performance Measurement	Signal an inconsistency	Evaluates the degree of inconsistency
	Serve as an output of performance reporting	Defines expected and experienced performance levels
	Serve as an input to change control	Measures current performance against what was planned

Updating the Project Scope

When changes to the project scope have been approved, the documented project scope must be updated to reflect these new changes. The stakeholders affected by the scope changes must be notified. The WBS must also be updated to reflect the components added, or removed, from the project. Scope changes can include cost updates, schedule updates, quality updates, or changes to the project deliverables.

When the project scope is to be changed, the new requirements must pass through the planning processes. The changes must be evaluated for cost and time estimates, risk, work considerations, product specification, and technical specification.

Correcting the Project

Often the reason for change is due to faulty deliverables, quality problems, or poor performance of the project deliverables. Corrective actions are activities that will make an effort to bring the project back in alignment with the project plan. Errors and omissions in the product specifications are scope changes, not corrective action changes.

Updating the Lessons Learned

The lessons learned documentation should be updated as an output of scope change control. The project manager should document reasons why changes were approved, corrective actions were taken, components were added or removed from the scope— and the reasoning behind these decisions. Lessons learned will serve as future historical information and help guide other project managers.

Adjusting the Project Baselines

When changes are made, the project baselines will need to be adjusted to reflect these changes. Such changes can affect time, cost, schedule, and scope. The changes that affect the appropriate baseline should be updated to reflect the new project scope. The new baselines serve as a point of reference for the remainder of the project (assuming there are no additional changes). Should other changes occur, the baseline should be updated—enabling the project to continue.

CERTIFICATION SUMMARY

Project scope management is the ability to complete all of the project's required work—and only the required work. This means no extras, no favors, and no cutting corners. The project scope is the focus of the project—it is the necessary work to complete the project. Project scope management is a tool the project manager uses to determine what work is in the project and what work is extraneous.

Projects, big or small, fit within the confines of the performing operation's strategic plans. Projects don't meander, at least not often, outside of the business focus of the organization. You won't find too many car manufacturers creating projects to make chocolate pies. Projects fit within the vision and function of the organization they operate within.

Most projects undergo a process to determine their cost and value. The selection process based on the perceived worth is typically a benefit/cost ratio (BCR). These models examine the cost-to-benefit ratio to determine if the project is worth doing. Selected projects should always have a higher benefits-than-costs ratio.

Another selection model is the constrained optimization method. You won't need to know how to complete one of these beasts for your exam, but you should be familiar with some common models: linear programming, nonlinear programming, integer algorithms and multi-objective programming to name a few.

In order to determine what the project scope actually is, there's plenty of scope planning. The project manager and the project team must have a clear vision of the project, the business need for the project, the requirements, and the stakeholder expectations for the project. The end result of the scope planning processes is the scope statement. The scope statement says, in no uncertain terms, what is within the project and what is without.

For your PMP exam, focus on protecting the project scope. This includes finding the real purpose of the project so the scope is in alignment with identified need. Once the scope has been created, the project team, stakeholders, the project sponsor, and even the project manager should not change the scope—unless there is overwhelming evidence of why the scope needs to be changed.

KEY TERMS

To pass the PMP exams, you will need to memorize these terms and their definitions. For maximum value, create your own flashcards based on these definitions and review them daily. The definitions can be found within this chapter and in the glossary.

benefit measurement methods	product scope	time value of money
benefit/cost ratios	project scope	value added change
constrained optimization methods	project scope management	WBS
future value	ROI	WBS dictionary
internal rate of return	scope statement	WBS template
net present value	scope verification	
present value	scoring models	

✓ TWO-MINUTE DRILL

Selecting Projects

❑ Projects are selected based on many different conditions: opportunity, need, customer demands, and so on. The project purpose and business need must be identified so the project scope can be created to support this purpose.

❑ When there are multiple projects up for approval, management may use one of two methods to choose between them: benefit measurement methods (which are comparative models), or, for large complex projects, constrained optimization methods (which focus on complex mathematical equations).

Authorizing Projects

❑ Once a project is selected, it moves through the initiation processes. One of the major outputs of initiation is the project charter; it's major because it provides authority for the project. Specifically, the project charter provides authority, names the project title and the project manager. The charter defines the business needs the project product will satisfy.

❑ The charter should be written in open terms and dialogue so it does not have to be re-written because it is too narrow. The charter should be written and signed by senior management in order to gain access to the necessary project resources.

❑ A project does not exist until a charter has been created.

Project Scopes

❑ Projects move through product-orientated processes to create the project's product. These processes are typically marked by phases unique to the project work. For example, foundation, framing, roofing, finishing, and so on. Project management processes are the activities universal to all projects.

❑ There are two scopes: the project scope and the product scope. The project scope is the work to be completed to create the product. The product scope describes the features of the product and its characteristics.

❑ Scope management is the process that follows the scope management plan. It ensures that the scope includes all of the required work—and only the required work—to complete the project. It documents how changes may enter into the scope, and how frequently the scope is expected to change.

❑ At the end of the project or project phase—or even at major deliverables within the project—scope verification happens. Scope verification is the process of formally accepting the project work as defined in the product documentation, the project scope, or in the contractual agreement, if relevant. Formal acceptance requires signoff for acceptance of the product.

SELF TEST

1. Of the following, which is not part of project scope management?

    A. Scope planning

    B. Scope verification

    C. Quality assurance

    D. Initiation

2. You are probably going to be the project manager for the HGD Project and will need as many inputs to the initiation phase as possible. Of the following, which is the best source of information for your project?

    A. Business plans

    B. Historical information

    C. WBS

    D. The project charter

3. You are a project manager for your organization. Sarah, a project manager in training, wants to know when the project manager is assigned to a project? Your answer should be:

    A. During the initiation stage

    B. During the planning stage

    C. When the stakeholders approve the budget

    D. After the project is proven feasible

4. You are the project manager for a technical project. The project product is the complete installation of a new operating system on 4500 workstations. You have, in your project cost and time estimates, told the customer that the estimates provided will be accurate if the workstations meet the hardware requirements of the new operating system. This is an example of which of the following?

    A. Risk

    B. Assumption

    C. Constraint

    D. Order of magnitude

5. You are the project manager for the NBG Project. This project must be completed within six months. This is an example of which of the following?

   A. Schedule
   B. Assumption
   C. Constraint
   D. Planning process

6. Which of the following best describes project scope?

   A. The description of the project deliverables
   B. The authorizing document that allows the project manager to move forward with the project and to assign resources to the tasks
   C. The process of managing all of the required work—and only the required work—to complete the project
   D. The process of planning and executing all of the required work to deliver the project to the customer

7. During the planning phase of your project, your project team has discovered another method to complete a portion of the project scope. This method is safer for the project team, but may cost more for the customer. This is an example of:

   A. Risk assessment
   B. Alternative identification
   C. Alternative selection
   D. Product analysis

8. Of the following, which does the scope statement not provide?

   A. Project justification
   B. Project product
   C. Project manager authority
   D. Project objective

9. You are the project manager for the JHN Project. Mike, a project manager you are mentoring, does not know which plan he should reference for guarding the project scope. Which of the following plans does Mike need?

   A. The scope management plan
   B. The scope change control system
   C. The scope verification
   D. The scope charter

10. You are the project manager for the JKL Project. This project has over 45 key stakeholders and will span the globe in implementation. Management has deemed the project's completion should not cost more than $34 million. Because of the global concerns, the final budget must be in U.S. dollars. This is an example of which of the following?

A. Internationalization

B. Budget constraint

C. Management constraint

D. Hard logic

11. You are the project manager for your organization. You need to ensure the customer formally accepts the deliverables of each project phase. This process is known as _____?

A. Earned value management

B. Scope verification

C. Quality control

D. Quality assurance

12. Which of the following is an output of scope verification?

A. WBS template

B. Rework

C. Formal acceptance

D. SOW acceptance

13. Complete the statement: Most change requests are a result of _____.

A. Improvement to the project scope

B. Schedule constraints

C. Regulatory constraints

D. Value-added change

14. You are a project manager for a large manufacturer. Your current project is to create a new manufacturing assembly line that will allow your organization to create its products with less downtime and faster turnaround time for its clients. Which of the following is an example of value-added change in this project?

A. Adding more team members to the project to get the project work done faster

B. Outsourcing portions of the project execution to transfer risk

C. Adding a recently created computer program to control and monitor the manufacturing assembly

D. Documenting the project and how the manufacturing assembly should work

15. A project team member has, on his own initiative, added extra vents to an attic to increase air circulation in the attic. The project plan did not call for these extra vents, but the team member decided they were needed based on the geographical location of the house. The project team's experts concur with this decision. This is an example of:

    A. Cost control

    B. Ineffective change control

    C. Self-led teams

    D. Value added change

16. Which of the following is an output of scope change control?

    A. Workarounds

    B. Corrective action

    C. Transference

    D. Risk assessment

17. You are the project manager for the JHG Project. Your project is to create a new product for your industry. You have recently learned your competitor is also working on a similar project but their offering will include a computer-aided program and web-based tools, which the project does not offer. You have implemented a change request to update your project. This is an example of which of the following?

    A. A change due to an error and omission in the initiation phase

    B. A change due to an external event

    C. A change due to an error or omission in the planning phase

    D. A change due to a legal issue

18. You are the project manager for a pharmaceuticals company. A new government regulation will change your project scope. For the project to move forward and be in accordance with the new regulation, your next action should be?

    A. Prepare a new baseline to reflect the government changes

    B. Notify management

    C. Present the change to the CCB

    D. Create a feasibility study

19. You have finished the project scope according to plan. For the customer to accept the project what must happen next?

    A. Nothing. The plan is complete so the project is complete.

    B. Scope verification should be conducted

    C. Lessons learned should be finalized

    D. Proof-of-concept should be implemented

20. You are the project manager for an airplane manufacturer. Your project concerns the development of lighter, stronger material for commercial jets. As the project moves towards completion, the material is defined in more detail after each phase of materials testing. This is an example of which of the following?

    A. Program management

    B. Progressive elaboration

    C. Quality assurance

    D. Regulatory guidelines

21. You are the project manager of a large project. Your project sponsor and management have approved you to outsource portions of the project plan. The _____ must ensure that all of the project work is authorized, contracted properly, and funded.

    A. Project sponsor

    B. Organization's management

    C. Vendor(s)

    D. Project manager

22. A project team member has asked you what a scope statement is. Which of the following is a characteristic of a scope statement?

    A. Defines the baseline for project acceptance

    B. Defines the requirements for each project within the organization

    C. Defines the cost, schedule, and quality metrics

    D. Defines the functional managers assigned to the project

23. One of the stakeholders of the project you are managing asks why you consider the scope statement so important in your project management methodology. You answer her question with which of the following?

    A. It is mandatory to consult the plan before authorizing any change.

    B. Project managers must document any changes before approving or declining them.

    C. The project scope serves as a reference for all future project decisions.

    D. The project plan and EVM work together to assess the risk involved with proposed changes.

24. A WBS serves as an input to many of the project management processes. Of the following, which is not true?

    A. WBS serves as an input to activity sequencing.

    B. WBS serves as an input to activity definition.

    C. WBS serves as an input to resource planning.

    D. WBS serves as an input to cost budgeting.

25. You are the project manager of the WIFI Project. You would like to meet with a stakeholder for scope verification. Which of the following is typical of scope verification?

    A. Reviewing changes to the project scope with the stakeholders

    B. Reviewing the performance of the project deliverables

    C. Reviewing the performance of the project team to date

    D. Reviewing the EVM results of the project to date

SELF TEST ANSWERS

1. ☑ **C.** Quality Assurance is not part of project scope management. It is the quality assurance program of the entire organization.
   ☒ **A, B,** and **D** are all part of project scope management.

2. ☑ **B.** Historical information is the best input of the choices presented.
   ☒ **A** is incorrect since business plans are not a likely input to the initiation process, although business needs may be. **C,** the WBS, is incorrect since the WBS has not been created at this point of the project. **D,** the project charter, is an output of the initiation process, not an input.

3. ☑ **A.** Project managers are assigned during the initiation process of the project.
   ☒ Choices **B, C,** and **D** are incorrect because **A** is the best choice of those presented.

4. ☑ **B.** This is an example of an assumption since the workstations must meet the hardware requirements.
   ☒ **A** and **C** are incorrect because the scenario did not describe a risk or constraint. **D** is incorrect because order of magnitude refers to the level of confidence in an estimate.

5. ☑ **C.** A project that must be completed by a deadline is dealing with time constraints.
   ☒ **A** is incorrect since the condition does not offer a schedule, but a "must finish no later than" constraint. **B** is incorrect because the condition is not an assumption. **D** is also incorrect because this is not a planning process.

6. ☑ **C.** A project scope focuses on completing all of the required work, and only the required work, to complete the project.
   ☒ Choice **A** is a product description, not a scope. **B** is incorrect because this choice describes the charter. **D** is incorrect because it does not define the project scope as completely as choice **C.**

7. ☑ **B.** Alternative identification is a planning process to find alternatives to completing the project scope.
   ☒ **A** is incorrect because this is not a risk assessment activity. **C** is incorrect because the team has identified the alternative, but has not selected it. **D** is incorrect because this is not product analysis.

8. ☑ **C.** The project charter provides the project manager with authority.
   ☒ **A, B,** and **D** are incorrect because these items are all provided within the project scope statement.

9. ☑ **A.** The scope management plan provides details about how the project scope may be changed.
    ☒ **B** is not a valid choice because it refers to the scope change control system, not the plan to guard the scope from changes. **C** is incorrect because scope verification is the process of formally accepting the product. **D** is incorrect, because the charter does not define how changes to the project may happen.

10. ☑ **B.** This is an example of a budget constraint. The budget must not exceed $34 million. In addition, the metric for the values to be in U.S. dollars can affect the budget if most of the product is to be purchased in a foreign country.
    ☒ **A** is incorrect because this does not define a constraint. Internationalization focuses on time zones, languages, cultural differences, and so on. **C** is incorrect because this is not an adequate answer. **D** is also incorrect because hard logic describes the most logical or required method for events or conditions to happen.

11. ☑ **B.** Scope verification is the process of formally accepting the deliverable of a project or phase.
    ☒ **A** is incorrect because EVM measures project performance. **C** is incorrect because quality control is concerned with the correctness of the work, not the acceptance of the work. **D**, QA, is incorrect because this described the quality program for the organization as a whole.

12. ☑ **C.** Scope verification results in one thing: formal acceptance.
    ☒ **A** is incorrect; WBS templates come from past projects or the PMO. **B** is incorrect because rework does not come from verification. **D** is incorrect because SOW (statement of work) acceptance is not the best choice.

13. ☑ **D.** Value added change is the only choice that is a correct answer.
    ☒ Choices **A**, **B**, and **C** are incorrect because change requests do stem from these options. **A** may seem correct, but **D** is the best choice because an improvement to the project scope would likely be a value-added change.

14. ☑ **C.** Value added change centers on adding some element that was not available to the project scope to reduce costs at scope creation.
    ☒ **A** is incorrect because this describes crashing. **B** is incorrect because transference is not a value-added change. **D** is incorrect because this process should be part of the product description already included in the project plan.

15. ☑ **B.** The project team member did not follow the change management plan's method of incorporating changes into the scope.
    ☒ **A** is incorrect because this scenarios describe change control, although the decision may lead to additional expenses. **C** is incorrect because self-led teams are not described in this scenario. **D** is incorrect, because the added vents do not apparently reduce cost in this example.

16. ☑ **B.** Corrective actions are outputs of change control. Poor performance leads to corrective actions to bring the project back in alignment with the project plan.
☒ **A** is incorrect because a workaround is a reaction to an identified risk or issue. **C** and **D** are also incorrect because transference is the process of transferring the risk. Risk assessment is the process of identifying and analyzing risk within the project or phase.

17. ☑ **B.** The change is requested to remain competitive with the competition—an external event.
☒ **A, C,** and **D** are all incorrect choices based on the conditions of the change request.

18. ☑ **C.** Presenting the change to the Change Control Board is the best choice.
☒ **A** is incorrect because the change has not been approved—the project could be stopped based on the required change. **B** is incorrect, though tempting. It is wrong for two primary reasons: the project manager should never contact management with a problem and no solution to offer for the problem. It is also incorrect because **C** more fully answers the question, since management is likely part of the appropriate stakeholders. **D** is incorrect because it is not appropriate for the conditions surrounding the change.

19. ☑ **B.** Scope verification concerns itself with the formal acceptance of the product.
☒ Choice **A** is incorrect, acceptance must happen for closure. **C** is incorrect, lessons learned do not close out the project. **D** is incorrect because it is not relevant to the issue.

20. ☑ **B.** Progressive elaboration is typical of all projects.
☒ **A** is incorrect; Program Management is not relevant. **C** is incorrect because QA describes the quality system of an organization. **D** is incorrect because regulatory guidelines do not refine the project scope.

21. ☑ **D.** The responsibility to ensure that the project work is authorized, contracted, and funded rests with the project manager.
☒ **A, B,** and **C** are all incorrect because these stakeholders do not have the responsibility of the project manager in this scenario.

22. ☑ **C.** Scope statements must at least include the quantifiable criteria of cost, schedule, and quality metrics.
☒ **A** is incorrect because the scope statement provides information on the project product acceptance. **B** is incorrect, because a scope statement does not address all projects within an organization. **D** is also incorrect because functional managers are not addressed in the scope statement.

23. ☑ **C.** The scope statement serves as a point of reference for all future project decisions.
☒ **A** is incorrect because it is too vague. **B** is incorrect because some changes may come orally and be declined immediately based on historical information or other factors. **D** is incorrect because EVM is not an issue in this scenario.

24. ☑ **A.** The WBS does not directly serve as an input to activity sequencing.
    ☒ **B, C,** and **D** are incorrect choices because the WBS does serve as an input to these processes. Incidentally, the WBS also serves as input to the cost estimating and the risk management planning processes.

25. ☑ **B.** When it comes to scope verification, the customer is concerned with the performance of the product.
    ☒ Choice **A** may seem correct, but the stakeholder should already know about the changes prior to scope verification. **C** and **D** are incorrect because these reviews are not relevant to scope verification.

6

Introducing Project Time Management

There's an old joke when it comes to project management time: "The first 90 percent of a project schedule takes 90 percent of the time. The last 10 percent takes the other 90 percent of the time."

And isn't that the way it goes? Hopefully not, but far too often, yes. Projects, especially projects that are running behind schedule, fail at the beginning, not the end. The importance of planning a project is never as evident until the rush to completion. The final actions to complete a project are dependent on the plans and motivations set in the project planning processes.

Effective project management requires adequate time for planning—and based on the results of planning, adequate time for implementation of those plans. In this chapter, we'll discuss how project activities are decomposed and then how the work packages are sequenced, calculated, and accounted for. We'll also discuss the art and science of estimating the time for work packages in new and familiar projects. Once the work's been decomposed, we'll create and visualize the network diagram.

Time management is an essential element on the PMP exam. You'll need a solid understanding of the activities and methods to predict and account for project time. Time management is crucial to not only passing the PMP exam, but also to successful project management.

Defining the Project Activities

Projects are temporary undertakings to create a unique product or service. The idea of time is inherent to the very definition of a project in that all projects are temporary. Projects may seem to last forever, but sooner or later they must end. Adequate planning of the temporary project can predict when a project will end. Within this short, limited time, the project manager must create something: a product or a service. The creation is about change—and change, as you may have guessed, takes time. Figure 6-1 shows the components of project time management.

Creation of the product or service comes about due to the work the project team completes. The sum of the time of the work equates to when the project is completed. In addition to the duration of activities, there are other factors of time to consider:

- Project management activities
- Planning processes
- The sequence of activities

FIGURE 6-1

Time
management
relies on several
inputs to help
build and control
the schedule.

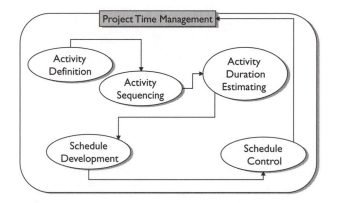

- Procurement
- Reliance on internal and external events
- Known and unknown events affecting the project

Project time management is based predominantly on planning, and then it's all control and execution. Planning for project schedules may stem from deadlines, customer demands, hard and soft logic, and a bit of prediction.

Considering the Inputs to Activity Definition

The activity list is an output of activity definition, and includes all of the activities to be performed within the project. The list must be in alignment with the project scope. Remember the project scope? It's a description of all the required work, and only the required work, to complete the project. In a sense, the activity list is a further definition of the project scope since it includes only those actions needed to complete the project scope.

Creating the activity list relies on several completed documents, knowledge, and actions. The creation of the activity list uses the following as inputs to the process:

- **WBS** The WBS serves as a major input in the creation of the activity list. Recall from Chapter 5 that the WBS is a deliverables-orientated collection of project components. It is not a collection of activities to create the deliverables.

- **Scope statement** It is a description of the required work, and only the required work, to complete the project.

■ **Historical information**   If the project's been done before, what activities were included in the similar project? Historical information is proven information that the project manager can rely on for creating activity lists.

■ **Constraints**   What restrictions are imposed on the project manager and the project team? For example, is there a deadline for the project? A predetermined budget? Demanded quality metrics? These are examples of constraints.

■ **Assumptions**   What assumptions have been identified for the project work? For example, consider the availability of resources, acceptable weather, and time allotments to complete the project.

■ **Expert judgment**   Expert judgment allows experts to influence decisions in regard to the needed work packages.

Decomposing the Project Work Packages

The WBS, the collection of deliverable-orientated components, must now be broken into activities. Specifically the work packages within the WBS must be decomposed into manageable work elements. What's the difference between decomposing the project deliverables and the project work? The elements in the WBS are deliverables; this process is concerned with the actions needed to create the deliverables.

It's quite possible to create the WBS and the activity list in tandem. Don't get too caught up in the timing of the activity list definition and the WBS. Simply put, the WBS describes the components of the deliverables; the activity list defines the actions to create the deliverables.

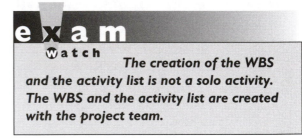

The creation of the WBS and the activity list is not a solo activity. The WBS and the activity list are created with the project team.

Relying on Templates

Why reinvent the wheel? If similar projects have been completed in the past, rely on the WBS and activity lists from this historical information to serve as a template for the current project. Even if a portion of a project is similar, a project manager can use the activity list and focus on the similarities of the current project.

A template can include several elements to make a project manager's life easier and the new project more successful:

- Required actions to complete the project scope
- Required resources and skills
- Required hours of duration for activities
- Known risks
- Outputs of the work
- Descriptions of the work packages
- Supporting details

Compiling the Activity List

Ta-dah! The primary output of decomposing the work is the activity list. The activity list is a collection of all of the work elements required to complete the project. The activity list is actually an extension of the WBS, and will serve as a fundamental tool in creating the project schedule. The activity list is needed to ensure that all of the deliverables of the WBS are accounted for and that the necessary work is mapped to each of the deliverables as shown in Figure 6-2.

The activity list also ensures that there is no extra work included in the project. Extra work costs time and money—and defeats the project scope. The correlation between the WBS and the work package is a one-to-one ratio: the deliverables in the WBS map to the required work. In other words, the WBS is comprised of all of the components the project will create. The activities list is comprised of all of the work required to create the components within the WBS.

FIGURE 6-2

Activity lists are organized as extensions of the WBS.

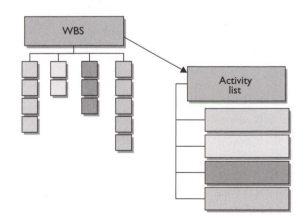

In addition, the work on the activity list includes descriptions of each identified activity. This accomplishes three things:

- Ensures the team members are in agreement on what the work package accomplishes
- Ensures the work supports and creates the WBS deliverables
- Ensures the work is within the project scope

Organizing the Supporting Detail

The supporting detail of the activity list must be documented, organized for fast reference, and accessible throughout the project implementation. The supporting detail allows the project manager, the project team, and other interested parties to reference the activity list definition process and recall why decisions were made and how the activity list was created. The supporting detail includes:

- Assumptions
- Constraints
- Reasoning behind identified work package
- Information specific to the industry that the project is operating within

Updating the Work Breakdown Structure

When creating the activity list, the project team and the project manager may discover discrepancies or inadequacies in the existing WBS. Updates to the WBS allow the project manager to ensure that all of the needed project deliverables are included in the WBS and then map the discovered deliverables to the identified work in the activity list.

In addition, the elements within the WBS may not be defined fully or correctly. During the decomposition of the work, elements of the WBS may need to be updated to reflect the proper description of the WBS elements. The description of the WBS should be complete and full—and leave no room for ambiguity or misinterpretation. Finally, updates to the WBS may also include cost estimates to the discovered deliverables.

Mapping the Activities

Now that the activity list has been created, the activities must be arranged in a logical sequence. This process calls on the project manager and the project team to identify the logical relationships between activities—and the preferred relationship between activities. This can be accomplished a few different ways:

- **Computer driven** There are many different scheduling and project management software packages available. These programs can help the project manager and the project team determine which actions need to happen in what order—and with what level of discretion.

- **Manual process** In smaller projects, and on larger projects in the early phases, manual sequencing may be preferred. An advantage of manual sequencing is that it's easier to move around dependencies and activities than in some programs.

- **Blended approach** A combination of manual and computer-driven scheduling methods is fine. It's important to determine the finality of the activity sequence, however. Sometimes a blended approach can be more complex than relying on just one or another.

on the job *"Sticky notes" can help sequence events. Put your activities on sticky notes and then plot them out on a white board. Draw arrows to show the relationship between activities. Want to make a change? It's easy to rearrange the notes and the relationships.*

Considering the Inputs to Activity Sequencing

Figure 6-3 shows the complete process of activity sequencing. There are many approaches to completing the activity sequencing. Perhaps the greatest approach, however, is that activity sequencing is done with the project team, not as a solo activity.

FIGURE 6-3

Activity
sequencing relies
on inputs to
create the final
sequence of
events.

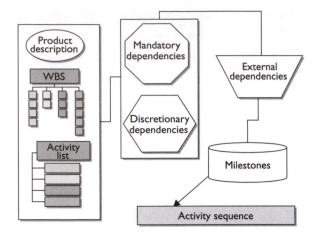

The project manager must rely on the project team and the inputs to activity sequencing:

- **Activity list**   The activity list we've just discussed—it's the list of actions needed to complete the project deliverables.

- **Product description**   The product description is needed since it may influence the sequence of events. For example, in construction, technology, or community planning (among other project types), the product description may include requirements that will logically affect the planning of activity sequencing.

- **Mandatory dependencies**   These dependencies are the natural order of activities. For example, you cannot begin building your house until your foundation is in place. These relationships are called hard logic.

- **Discretionary dependencies**   These dependencies are the preferred order of activities. Project managers should use these relationships at their "discretion" and document the logic behind the decision. Discretionary dependencies allow activities to happen in a preferred order because of best practices, conditions unique to the project work, or external events. For example, a painting project typically allows the primer and the paint to be applied within hours of each other. Due to the expected high humidity during the project, however, all of the building will be completely primed before the paint can be applied. These relationships are also known as soft logic, preferred logic, or preferential logic.

- **External dependencies** As its name implies, these are dependencies outside of the project's control. Examples include delivery of equipment from a vendor, the deliverable of another project, or the decision of a committee, lawsuit, or expected new law.

- **Milestones** Milestones must be considered and evaluated when sequencing events to ensure all of the work needed to complete the milestones is included.

Creating Network Diagrams

Network diagrams visualize the project work. A network diagram shows the relationship of the work activities and how the work will progress from start to completion. Network diagrams can be extremely complex or easy to create and configure. Most network diagrams in today's project management environment use an approach called "activity-on-node" to illustrate the activities and the relationship between activities. Older network diagramming methods used "activity-on-arrows" to represent the activities and their relationships.

Using the Precedence Diagramming Method

The Precedence Diagramming Method (PDM) is the most common method of arranging the project work visually. The PDM puts the activities in boxes, called nodes, and connects the boxes with arrows. The arrows represent the relationship and the dependencies of the work packages. The following illustration shows a simple network diagram using PDM.

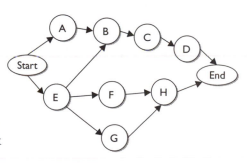

PDM is also known as AON— activity-on-node. It's the most common approach to network diagramming since it's used by most project management information systems but can also be done manually.

Relationships between activities in a PDM constitute one of four different types (as shown in Figure 6-4):

FIGURE 6-4

PDM
relationships can
vary, but most
use the finish-to-
start approach.

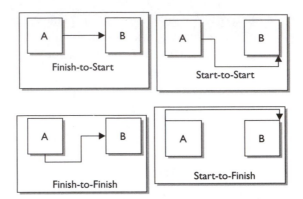

■ **Finish-to-start (FS)** This relationship means Task A must complete before
Task B can begin. This is the most common relationship. Example: The
foundation must be set before the framing can begin.

■ **Start-to-start (SS)** This relationship means Task A must start before Task
B can start. This relationship allows both activities to happen in tandem.
For example, a crew of painters is painting a house. Task A is to scrape the
flecking paint off the house and Task B is to prime the house. The workers
scraping the house must start before the other workers can begin priming the
house. All of the scraping doesn't have to be completed before the priming
can start, just some of it.

■ **Finish-to-finish (FF)** This relationship means Task A must complete
before Task B does. Ideally, two tasks must finish at exactly the same time,
but this is not always the case. For example, two teams of electricians may be
working together to install new telephone cables throughout a building by
Monday morning. Team A is pulling the cable to each office. Team B is
connecting the cables to wall jacks and connecting the telephones. Team A
must pull the cable to the office so Team B can complete their activity. The
activities need to complete at nearly the same time, by Monday morning, so
the new phones are functional.

■ **Start-to-finish (SF)** This relationship is unusual and is rarely used. It
requires that Task A start so that Task B may finish. Such relationships may
be encountered in construction and manufacturing. It is also known as just-
in-time (JIT) scheduling. An example is a construction of a shoe store. The
end of the construction is soon, but an exact date is not known. The owner of
the shoe store doesn't want to order the shoe inventory until the completion
of the construction is nearly complete. The start of the construction tasks
dictates when the inventory of the shoes is ordered.

Using the Arrow Diagramming Method

The Arrow Diagramming Method (ADM) approach to activity sequencing uses arrows to represent the activities. The arrows are "connected" on nodes. ADM only uses finish-to-start relationships. In some instances, dummy activities are required to express the logical relationship between two activities. A dummy activity is illustrated with a dashed arrow between the nodes. The following illustration is a simple example of an ADM network diagram.

ADM is an example of activity-on-arrow (AOA) networks. This approach is not as popular as PDM, but may still be prevalent in some industries. ADM can be created manually or through a PMIS.

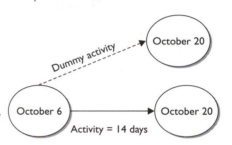

Using Conditional Diagramming Methods

Conditional diagramming methods are more complex and structured than ADM or PDM. Conditional diagramming methods include system dynamics and the graphical evaluation and review technique (GERT). These models allow for loops and conditional branching. For example, GERT may require that tests of the product be performed several times before the project may continue. Based on the outcome of the testing, the project may use one of several paths to enable its completion. In addition, GERT allows for probabilistic clarification of work package estimates.

Utilizing Network Templates

Just as a project manager can rely on WBS templates, there may be network templates available to streamline the planning process or to conform to a predetermined standard. Network templates can represent an entire project if appropriate, though portions of a network template, such as the required project management activities, are common.

The portions of a network template are also known as subnets or fragnets. Subnets are often associated with repetitive actions within a network diagram. For example, each floor in a high-rise apartment building may undergo the same or similar actions during construction. Rather than complete the network diagram for each floor, a subnet can be implemented.

Examining the Sequencing Outputs

There are many approaches to using activity sequencing: a project manager and the project team can use software programs, the approach can be done manually, or the team can manually do the scheduling and then transfer the schedule into a PMIS. Whichever method is selected, the project manager must remember four things:

- Only the required work should be scheduled.
- Finish-to-start relationships are the most common and preferred.
- Activity sequencing is not the same as a schedule.
- Scheduling comes after activity sequencing.

Using a Project Network Diagram

Once the activity list has been put into sequential order, the flow of the project work can be visualized. A project network diagram (PND) illustrates the flow of the project work and the relationship between the work packages. PNDs are typically activity-on-node (AON) and most PMIS packages use the PDM method. The following illustration is typical example of a network diagram.

Network diagrams may also include summary activities, also known as hammock activities. Accompanying the network diagram, there should be an explanation of the workflow, why decisions were made, and details on any preferred logic the project manager may have used. Network diagrams may also be known as a PERT chart, though this term may be slightly inaccurate. PERT, Program Evaluation and Review Technique, is a specific network diagram using weighted averages. (More on PERT in a moment.)

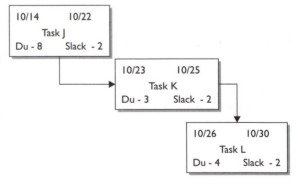

Updating the Activity Lists

During the creation of the network diagram, assumptions about the activity sequence may reveal missing activities in the activity list. Just as the creation of the activity list may prompt the project team and the project manager to update the WBS, the creation of the network diagram may prompt the project team to update the activity lists.

While this may seem redundant, to update the activities list illustrated in the project network diagram, it is essential documentation. A reflection of the WBS, the activity list, and the network diagram should all support the project scope. A key stakeholder should be able to follow the logic of the WBS to the activity list, and from the activity list find all of the activities mapped in order.

Estimating Activity Durations

Ready for a loaded question? "Now how long will all of this take?" Project managers hear this one all the time, right? And maybe right after that: "How much will all of this cost?" We'll talk about cost estimates in Chapter 7. For now, let's talk about time.

The answer to the question "How long will it take?" depends on the accuracy of the estimates, the consistency of the work, and other variables within the project. The best a project manager can do is create honest estimates based on the information he's been provided. Until the schedule is finalized, no one will know the duration of the project.

The tasks are first identified, their duration is estimated, and then the sequencing of the activities takes place. These activities are required to complete the project schedule and the estimated project duration. These three activities are iterated as more information comes available. If the proposed schedule is acceptable, the project can move forward. If the proposed schedule takes too long, the scheduler can use a few strategies to compress the project. We'll discuss the art of sequencing in a few moments.

Activity duration estimates, like the activity list and the WBS, don't come from the project manager—they come from the people completing the work. Activity duration estimates may undergo progressive elaboration. In this section, we'll examine the approach to completing activity duration estimates, the basis of estimates, and allow for activity list updates.

Considering the Activity Duration Estimates Inputs

The importance of accurate estimates is paramount. The activity estimates will be used to create the project schedule, and predict when the project should end. Inaccurate estimates could cost the performing organization thousands of dollars in fines, lost opportunities, loss of customers, or worse. To create accurate estimates, the project manager and the project team will rely on several inputs:

- **Activity lists**   You know this right? Activity lists are the work elements necessary to create the deliverables.

- **Constraints**   An identification of the project constraints is needed since they may influence the estimates. A deadline is an example of a constraint.

- **Assumptions**   An identification of the assumptions is needed since work estimates may be influenced by the assumptions. For example, the team may be operating under an assumption that the project must be completed within one calendar year.

- **Resource requirements**   Activity durations may change based on the number of resources assigned to the activity. For example, Task A may take eight hours with one person assigned to the work, but Task A may be completed in four hours with two team members assigned. Some activities, such as installing a computer operating system, will take the same amount of time regardless of how many resources are assigned. Project managers must also take care not to overload resources in an effort to complete a task; too many resources can be counterproductive.

- **Effort vs. duration**   Effort is the amount of labor that is applied to a task. Duration is how long the task is expected to take with the given amount of labor. For example, a task to unload a freight truck may take eight hours with two people assigned to the task. If the effort is increased by adding more labor to the task (in this instance, more people), then the duration of the task is decreased. Some activities, however, have a fixed duration and are not affected by the amount of labor assigned to the task. For example, to install a piece of software on a computer will take the same amount of time if one computer administrator is completing the work or if two computer administrators are attempting to complete the work.

- **Resource capabilities**   The abilities of the project team members must be taken into consideration. Consider a task in an architectural firm. Reason says that if a senior architect is assigned to the task, he will be able to complete it faster than if a junior architect were assigned to the same task. Material resources are also considered to influence activity time. Consider predrilled cabinets versus cabinets that require the carpenter to drill each cabinet as it is installed. The predrilled cabinets allow the job to be completed faster.

- **Historical information**   Historical information is always an excellent source for information on activity duration estimates. Historical information can come from several sources:

- Historical information can come from project files of other projects within the organization.

- Commercial duration estimating databases can offer information on how long industry-specific activities should take. These databases should take into consideration the materials, the experience of the resources, and define the assumptions the predicted work duration is based upon.

- Project team members may recollect information regarding the expected duration of activities. While these inputs are valuable, they are generally less valuable than documented sources such as other project files or the commercial databases.

- **Identified risks**   We'll discuss risk in detail in Chapter 11. Risks, good or bad, can influence the estimated duration of activities. The risks on each activity should be identified, analyzed, and then predicted as to their probability and impact. If risk mitigation tasks are added to the schedule, the mitigation activities will need their duration estimated and then sequenced into the schedule in the proper order.

Applying Expert Judgment

The project manager and the project team should utilize expert judgment if possible to predict the duration of project activities. Expert judgment can come from subject matter experts, project team members, and other resources, internal or external to the performing organization, that are familiar with the activities the project demands.

Estimating durations is not easy as there are many variables that can influence an activity's duration. Consider the amount of resources that can be applied to the resources, the experience of the resources completing this type of work, and their competence with the work packages.

on the
job
A big dose of reality is also needed with activity duration estimates. Imagine an activity that has been estimated to take 40 hours. While on paper that looks like a typical workweek, it's pretty unlikely the task will be completed within one week. Why? Consider all the phone calls, impromptu meetings, e-mail, and other interruptions throughout the day. These slivers of time chip away at the actual productive hours within a workday. The project manager should find a base of actual productive hours per day based on typical interruptions, meetings, and so on; for example, six productive hours out of eight working hours is typical. Based on this assumption (that six hours out of a day are productive), this means a task slated to last 40 hours will actually take nearly seven working days to complete.

Creating an Analogy

Analogous estimating relies on historical information to predict what current activity durations should be. Analogous estimating is also known as top-down estimating and is a form of expert judgment. To use analogous estimating, the activities from the historical project are similar in nature and are used to predict what the similar activities in the current project will take.

A project manager must consider if the work has ever been done before, and if so, what help will the historical information provide. The project manager must consider the resources, project team members, and equipment that completed the activities in the previous project compared to the resources available for the current project. Ideally, the activities should be more than similar; they should be identical. And the resources that completed the work in the past should be the same resources used in completing the current work.

When the only source of activity duration estimates is the project team members, instead of expert judgment and historical information, your estimates will be uncertain and inherently risky.

Analogous estimating uses historical information and is more reliable than predictions from the project team members.

Applying Quantitative Estimates

Quantitatively-based durations use mathematical formulas to predict how long an activity will take based on the "quantities" of work to be completed. For example, a commercial printer needs to print 100,000 brochures. The workers include two pressman and two bindery experts to fold and package the brochures. Notice how the duration is how long the activity will take to complete, while the effort is the total number of hours (labor) invested because of the resources involved. The decomposed work, with quantitative factors, is shown in Table 6-1.

TABLE 6-1	Workers	Units per hour	Duration for 100,000	Effort
Decomposed Work, with Quantitative Factors	Pressman (two)	5,000	20 hours	40 hours
	Bindery (two)	4,000	25 hours	50 hours
	Totals		45 hours	90 hours

e x a m
w a t c h

e x a m

w a t c h
Duration is how long an activity takes, while effort is the billable time for the labor to complete the activity. Consider an activity that is scheduled to last 40 hours. The project manager must consider the cost of the person's time assigned to complete project work—for example, a senior full-time engineer versus a part-time person, at a lower cost. The
senior engineer may be able to complete the activity in 40 consecutive work hours, but the cost of this employee's time may be more than the value of the activity. The part-time employee may be able to complete the task in two segments of 20 hours, but their time is billed at a substantially lower rate.

Factoring in Reserve Time

Parkinson's Law states: "Work expands so as to fill the time available for its completion." This little nugget of wisdom is oh-so-true. Consider a project team member that knows an activity should last 24 hours. The team member decides, in his own wisdom, to say the activity will last 32 hours. This extra eight hours, he figures, will allow plenty of time for the work to be completed should any unforeseen incidents pop-up. The trouble is, however, that the task will magically expand to require the complete 32 hours. Why does this happen? Consider the following:

- **Hidden time** Hidden time, the time factored in by the project team member, is secret. No one, especially the project manager, knows why the extra time has been factored into the activity. The team member can then "enjoy" the extra time to complete the task at leisure.

- **Procrastination** Most people put off starting a task until the last possible minute. The trouble with bloated, hidden time is people may wait through the additional time they've secretly factored into the activity. Unfortunately, if something does go awry in completing the activity, the work result is later than predicted.

- **Demands** Project team members may be on multiple projects with multiple demands. The requirement to move from project to project can shift focus, result in loss of concentration, and require additional ramp-up time as workers shift from activity to activity. The demand for multitasking allows project team members to take advantage of hidden time.

- **On schedule** Activities are typically completed on schedule or late, but rarely early. Users that have bloated the activity duration estimates may finish their task ahead of what they promised, but have a tendency to hold the results until the activity was due. This is because workers aren't usually rewarded for completing work early. In addition, workers don't want to reveal the inaccuracies in their time estimates. Workers may believe future estimates may be based on actual work durations, rather than estimates, so they'll "sandbag" the results to protect themselves—and finish "on-schedule."

So what's a project manager to do? First off, the project manager should strive to incorporate historical information and expert judgment to predicate accurate estimates. Second, the project manager should stress a genuine need for accurate duration estimates. Finally, the project manager can incorporate a reserve time.

A reserve time is a percentage of the project duration or a preset number of work periods and is usually added to the end of the project schedule. Reserve time may also be added to individual activity durations based on risk or uncertainty in the activity duration. When activities are completed late, the additional time for the activity is subtracted from the reserve time. As the project moves forward, the reserve time can be reduced or eliminated as the project manager sees fit. Reserve time decisions should be documented.

Evaluating the Estimates

The end result of estimating activities provides three things:

- **Activity duration estimates**   Activity duration estimates reflect how long each work package will take to complete. Duration estimates should include an acknowledgement of the range of variance. For example, an activity whose duration is expected to be one week may have a range of variance of one week ± three days. This means the work can take up to eight days, or as little as two days. This is assuming a week is five days.

- **Basis of estimates**   Any assumptions made during the activity estimating process should be identified. In addition, any historical information, subject matter experts, or commercial estimating databases that were used should also be documented for future reference.

- **Activity list updates**   During the estimating process, there may be discoveries of missing activities within the activity list. The project manager should confirm that the new work packages are reflected in the activity list for the project.

INSIDE THE EXAM

There's a ton of information in this chapter—all of it important—but there are some key things you must know to pass the PMP exam. For starters, you should understand how activity estimates are created.

Analogous estimates use historical information to predict how long current project activities will take place. These estimates are considered top-down estimates and are part of expert judgment. Quantifiable estimates, on the other hand, use a quantity to predict how long activities will take. Consider any unit such as square feet painted per hour or number of units created per day.

GERT is the only network diagram that allows for loops and conditional branching based on what the project has experienced to date. System dynamics is another example of conditional advancement.

When developing the schedule, the most common method is the CPM, though PERT and GERT may also be used. Lag is a positive time added to a task to indicate waiting. Lead is negative time added to a task to "hurry up." Fast tracking arranges activities to happen in tandem rather than in succession—this increases risk. Crashing adds more resources to activities to decrease their duration, which typically adds cost.

Monte Carlo Analysis is typically a computer program to estimate the many possible variables within a project schedule. Monte Carlo simulations predict probable end dates, not an exact end date. Another tool the project manager can use is *resource leveling*. Resource leveling smoothes out the project schedule so resources are not over-allocated. A result of this is that projects are often scheduled to last longer than initial estimates.

The critical path in a project has zero float, and is the path with the longest duration to completion. There can be more than one critical path in a network diagram. Should delays happen on noncritical paths, and all float is consumed, the critical path may change.

The project schedule is a calendar-based system used to predict when the project, and work, will start and end. Gantt charts map activities against a calendar and may show the relationship between activities. Milestone charts show when key deliverables are expected; they do not show the relationship between activities.

Developing the Project Schedule

Now that the estimates for the activities are completed, it's time to work some magic and see how long the entire project will take. The project manager specifically pursues the start date, and more importantly, the completion date. Projects that don't provide realistic schedules aren't likely to get approved. Or worse, the projects will get approved, but they will most likely fail, as the project team will not be able to meet the unrealistic schedule.

The creation of the project schedule is iterative. It's rare for a schedule to get created, approved, and implemented without some iterative examination, arrangement, and management input—though on smaller projects it may be possible. When activity list updates, constraints, assumptions and other inputs are considered, it's easy to see why scheduling can become complex.

Revisiting the Project Network Diagram

The PND illustrates the project. Recall that the PND shows the sequence of activities and the relationship between activities. The PND is important during schedule creation because it allows the project manager and the project team to evaluate the decisions, constraints, and assumptions that were made earlier in the process to determine why certain activities must occur in a particular order.

Hard logic and soft logic must be evaluated to confirm that the decisions and logic are feasible, accurate, and fit within the expected completion of the project. The following illustration is a simple PND for a small project.

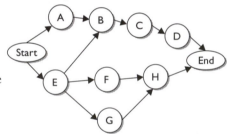

Relying on Activity Duration Estimates

Another key input to schedule creation is the activity duration estimates. Makes sense, right? The project manager needs to know how long the whole project will take, so the activity duration estimates will help calculate that number. Recall, however, the range of variances for each activity—these possible variances need to be accounted for in the actual project schedule creation. We'll discuss the schedule creation in a few moments.

Considering the Resource Requirements

The identified resource requirements will affect the project schedule. Remember the difference between duration and effort? Duration is how long the activity will take, effort is the labor applied to the task. For example, painting a building may take 80 hours to complete with two workers assigned to the job. Add two more workers and now the work will take only 40 hours.

The duration in the preceding example is 40 hours to complete the painting, but there will be 160 hours of effort on the activity. At some point in the work, the "duration to effort ratio" becomes saturated, and adding additional laborers will actually become counterproductive. This is subject to the law of diminishing returns. The following illustration demonstrates the previous example.

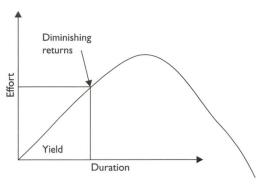

Considering the Resource Pool Availability

In a perfect world, all of the needed resources for a project would be available whenever the project manager says so. In the real world, and on your PMP exam, the availability of project resources fluctuate due to demands of other projects, demands of ongoing operations, personal lives, vacations, sick days, and more.

The availability of the project pool must be evaluated. If certain activities require a worker with a highly specialized skill, these activities are resource-dependent. Should the worker not be available for the timeframe of the required activity, one of several things must happen:

- The project manager must negotiate to make the resource available for the activity in the project schedule.
- The activity must be moved in the schedule for when the resource is available.
- The activity, and possibly the project, must wait for the resource to become available.
- The project may incur additional costs by finding other resources to complete the scheduled work.

Considering the Calendars

There are two calendar types that will affect the project:

■ **Project calendar** This calendar shows when work is allowed on the project. For example, a project may require the project team to work nights and weekends so as not to disturb the ongoing operations of the organization during working hours. In addition, the project calendar accounts for holidays, working hours, and work shifts that the project will cover.

■ **Resource calendar** The resource calendar controls when resources, such as project team members, consultants, and SMEs are available to work on the project. It takes into account vacations, other commitments within the organization, or restrictions on contracted work, overtime issues, and so on.

The consideration of the project calendar and the resource calendar is mandatory to predict when a project may realistically begin and end. Figure 6-5 shows the project calendar setting from Microsoft Project. Keep in mind the PMP exam is not concerned with which PMIS system is used, but the understanding of the role of the PMIS.

FIGURE 6-5

Project calendars determine when the project work will take place.

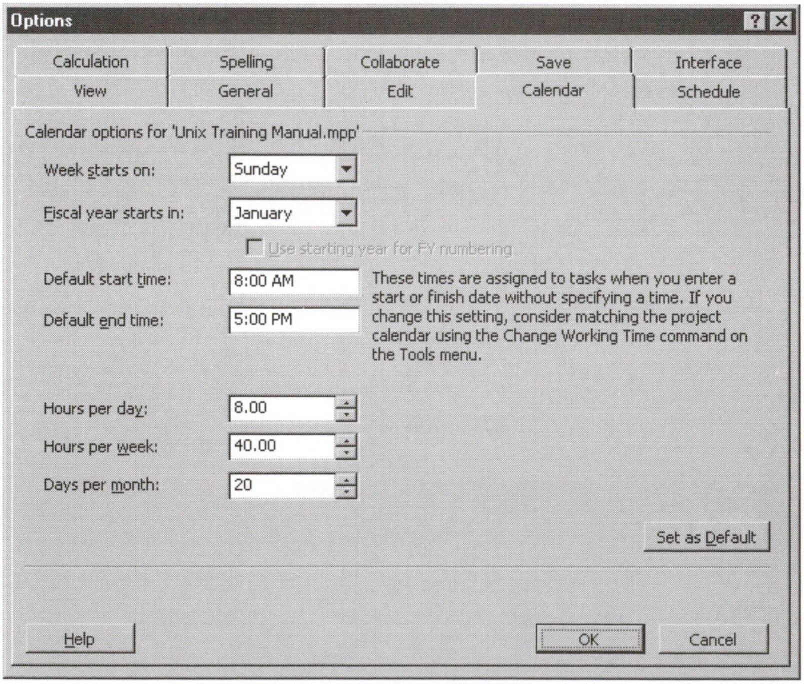

Evaluating the Project Constraints

Constraints will restrict when and how the project may be implemented. Constraints are added to a project for a purpose, not just to rush the work to completion. It is important to understand why the constraint has been imposed. Here are a few common examples of why constraints exist:

- To take advantage of an opportunity to profit from a market window for a product or service
- To work within the parameters of expected weather conditions (for seasonal or outdoor projects)
- To adhere to government requirements
- To adhere to industry regulations, best practices, or guidelines
- To work within timeframes that incorporate the expected delivery of materials from vendors or other projects

Perhaps one of the biggest constraints is the predetermined project deadline. Imagine a company creating a product to take to a tradeshow. If the creation of the product is running late, the tradeshow isn't going to move so that the product has enough time to be completed for the show. There are four time constraints to consider:

- **Start No Earlier Than (SNET)**   This constraint requires that the project or activity not start earlier than the predetermined date. Consider an activity to add software to an existing network server in a technology project. The project manager adds a "Start No Earlier Than" constraint on the activity to ensure the activity begins on a Saturday when the server is not in use by the organization. The activity can begin any time after the preset date, but not before it.

- **Start No Later Than (SNLT)**   This constraint requires the activity to begin by a predetermined date. For example, the creation of a community flower garden must "Start No Later Than" May 15. The creation of the garden may, weather permitting, begin earlier than the preset date, but it must start by that date.

- **Finish No Later Than (FNLT)**   This constraint requires the project or activity to finish by a predetermined date. For example, the installation of flooring tile in a restaurant must be finished by October 25 so the kitchen equipment can be installed. The constraint "Finish No Later Than" is tied to the date of October 25. The activity can end sooner than October 25, but not after it.

- **Finish No Earlier Than (FNET)**   This somewhat unusual constraint requires the activity to be in motion up until the predetermined date. Consider a project to create a special blend of wine. The wine must be aged a specific amount of time before the winemaking process can continue; the process requires a set amount of time so it may "Finish No Earlier Than" the determined time. The activity can end any time after the preset date, but not before it.

Project constraints can also include milestones. The project sponsor may request, for example, a milestone for a deliverable within the project on April 28. Based on this milestone all of the work needed to create a deliverable must be scheduled against the expected due date. In addition, once these milestones are set, it's pretty darn tough to change them.

Milestone constraints can also be tied to activities outside of the project. Consider a scheduled walk-through with a customer on a construction project. Or consider the demands of a project to create a product or service by a scheduled milestone that another project within the performing organization is expecting.

Reevaluating the Assumptions

Assumptions are beliefs held to be true, but that may not necessarily be so. Assumptions, such as being able to have access to a building 24 hours a day, seven days a week, can wreak havoc on the project schedule if they are proved false. Consider a schedule that plans on working three shifts during a remodeling of an office building only to discover late in the project planning that the customer will not allow the work to happen during daytime hours. Assumptions factored into the project should be documented and accounted for.

Considering Leads and Lags

Leads and lags are values added to work packages to slightly alter the relationship between two or more work packages. For example, a finish-to-start relationship may exist between applying primer to a warehouse and applying the paint. The project manager, in this scenario, has decided to add one day of lead-time to the work package painting the warehouse. Now the painting can begin one day before the priming is scheduled to end. Lead time is considered a negative value because time is subtracted from the downstream activity to bring it closer to the start of the project.

Lag time is waiting time. Imagine a project to install wood floors in an office building. Currently, there is a finish-to-start relationship between staining the floors and adding a layer of shellac to seal the wood floors. The project manager has elected, because of the humidity in the building, to add two days of lag time to the downstream activity of sealing the floors. Now the shellac cannot be applied immediately after the stain, but must wait two additional days. Lag is considered a positive value since time is added to the project schedule.

The following illustration shows the difference between lead and lag. Leads and lags must be considered in the project schedule since an abundance of lag time can increase the project duration. An abundance of lead time, however, may increase risks.

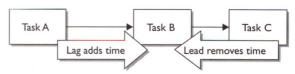

Evaluating the Risk Management Plan

We'll discuss risk and risk management completely in Chapter 11. For now, know that risks can alter the project schedule—for better or for worse. This isn't difficult to see. A risk in the project may be identified as delays from the vendor for the equipment needed to complete the project. The response to this risk, should it happen, may be to secure an alternate vendor that charges slightly more for the same equipment but has it in stock. The delay of the equipment with the original vendor may throw the project off schedule, and the additional time to find, purchase, and ship the needed equipment could also add extra time to the project.

Examining the Activity Attributes

The activity attributes can have a direct impact on the project schedule. Some activities are effort driven, which means more effort can reduce the duration. Other activities are of fixed duration—that is, additional effort does nothing to reduce their expected duration. Activity attributes are the characteristics of the work to be completed, including

- Person(s) responsible for completing each work package
- Where the work will take place (building, city, outdoors)
- Type of activity (electrical, technical, supervised, and so on)
- When the activity must take place (business hours, off-hours, more unusual times)

Creating the Project Schedule

The project manager, the project team, and possibly even the key stakeholders, will examine the inputs previously discussed, and apply the techniques discussed in this section to create a feasible schedule for the project. The point of the project schedule is to complete the project scope in the shortest amount of time possible without incurring exceptional costs, risks, or a loss of quality.

Creating the project schedule is part of the planning process group. It is calendar-based and relies on the project network diagram and the accuracy of time estimates.

Applying Mathematical Analysis

Mathematical analysis is the process of factoring theoretical early and late start dates and theoretical early and late finish dates for each activity within the PND. The early and late dates are not the expected schedule, but rather a potential schedule based on the project constraints, likelihood of success, and availability of resources, and other constraints. There are three common methods for mathematical analysis:

- **Program Evaluation and Review Technique (PERT)** PERT uses a weighted average formula to predict the length of activities and the project. Specifically, PERT uses a "pessimistic," "optimistic," and "most likely" estimate to predict when the project will be completed. Figure 6-6 shows the formula and typical outcome of using PERT. Note that PERT is rarely used in today's project management practices.

FIGURE 6-6

PERT uses a
weighted average
to predict when
the activities
will end.

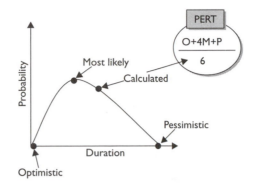

- **Graphical Evaluation and Review Technique (GERT)** GERT uses conditional advancement, branching, and looping of activities and is based on probable estimates. Activities within GERT are dependent on the results of other upstream activities. For example, the results of a work package may determine if additional testing is needed, rework is required, or the project may continue as planned.

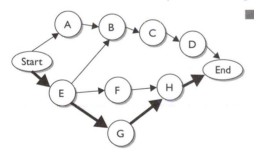

- **Critical Path Method (CPM)** This is the most common approach to calculating when a project may finish. It uses a "forward" and "backward" pass to reveal which activities are considered critical. Activities on the critical path may not be delayed; otherwise, the project end date will be delayed. The critical path is the path with the longest duration to completion. Activities not on the critical path have some float (also called slack) that allows some amount of delay without delaying the project end date. The following illustration is an example of the critical path.

Calculating Float in a PND

Float, or slack, is the amount of time a delayed task can delay the project's completion. Technically, there are three different types of float:

- **Free float**   This is the total time a single activity can be delayed without delaying the early start of any successor activities.
- **Total slack**   This is the total time an activity can be delayed without delaying project completion.
- **Project slack**   This is the total time the project can be delayed without passing the customer-expected completion date.

Most project management software will automatically calculate float, on the PMP exam; however, candidates will be expected to calculate float manually. Don't worry; it's not too tough. Here's the process:

Examine the PND and find the critical path. The critical path is typically the path with the longest duration and will always have zero float. The critical path is technically found once you complete the forward and backward pass. Start with the forward pass, after the backward pass you can identify the critical and near critical path, as well as float.

1. The Early Start (ES) and Early Finish (EF) dates are calculated first by completing the "forward pass." The ES of the first task is one. The EF for the first task is its ES, plus the task duration, minus one. Don't let the "minus one value" throw you. If Task A is scheduled to last one day, it would only take one day to complete, right? The ES would be 1, the duration is 1, and the EF would also be one because the activity would finish within one day, not two days. The following illustration shows the start of the forward pass.

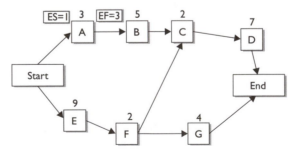

2. The ES of the next task(s) will be the EF for the previous activity, plus one. In other words, if Task A finishes on day eight, Task B will begin on day nine.

3. The EF for the next task(s) equals its ES plus the task duration, minus one. Sound familiar?

4. Now each task moves forward with the forward pass. Use caution when there are predecessor activities; the EF with the largest value is carried forward. The following illustration shows the completed forward pass.

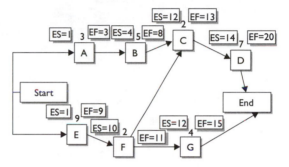

5. After the forward pass is completed, the backward pass starts at the end of the PND. The backward pass is concerned with the Late Finish (LF) and the Late Start (LS) of each activity. The LF for the last activity in the PND equals its EF value. The LS is calculated by subtracting the duration of the activity from its LF, plus one. The one is added to accommodate the full day's work; it's just the opposite of subtracting the one day in the forward pass. Here's a tip: the last activity is on the critical path, so its LS will equal its ES.

6. The next predecessor activity's LF equals the LS of the successor activity minus one. In other words, if Task Z has an LS of 107, Task Y will have an LF of 106. The following illustration shows the process of the backward pass.

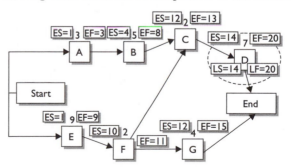

7. The LS is again calculated by subtracting the task's duration from the task's LF, plus one. The following shows the completed backward pass.

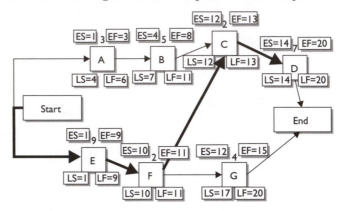

8. To officially calculate float, the LS is subtracted from the ES and the LF is subtracted from the EF. Recall the total float is the amount of time a task can be delayed without delaying the project completion date. The next illustration shows the completed PND with the float exposed.

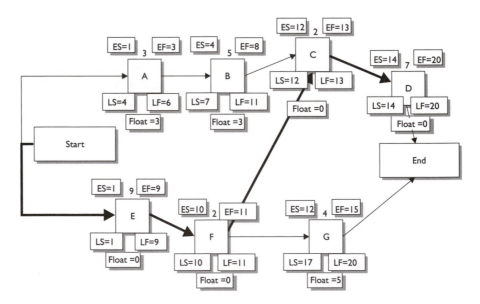

You'll have to calculate float on the exam. "Du" means duration when shown in a PND. Always neatly draw the PND on your paper. The same network diagram may be used over and over   *throughout the exam—this saves time! Finally, find and mark the critical path first on your scratch paper. The question may want to know the float for a task on the critical path, which is zero, of course.*

Encountering Scheduling on the PMP Exam

You'll encounter float, scheduling, and critical path activities on the PMP exam. You should count these questions as "gimmies" if you remember a few important rules:

- Always draw out the network diagram presented on your scratch paper; it may be used in several questions.

- Know how to calculate float. (The complete process was shown earlier in the "Calculating Float in a PND" section)

- You may encounter questions that ask on what day of the week a project will end if no weekends or holidays are worked. No problem. Add up the critical path, divide by 5 (Monday through Friday), and then figure out which day of the week the activity will end on.

- You may see something like Figure 6-7 when it comes to scheduling. When three numbers are presented, think PERT; optimistic is the smallest number, pessimistic is the largest, most likely is somewhere between the two. When a number is positioned directly over the tasks, it is the task duration. When a number is positioned to the upper-right of a task, this represents the Early Finish date.

Applying Duration Compression

Duration compression is also a mathematical approach to scheduling. The trick with duration compression, as its name implies, is calculating ways the project can get done sooner than expected. Consider a construction project. The project may be slated to last eight months, but due to the expected cold and nasty weather typical of month seven, the project manager needs to rearrange activities, where possible, to end the project as soon as possible.

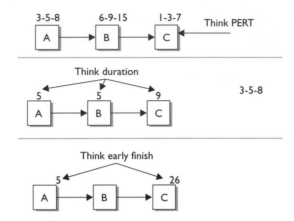

FIGURE 6-7

Scheduling follows many rules to arrive at the project destination.

In some instances, the relationship between activities cannot be changed due to hard or soft logic. The relationships must remain as scheduled. Now consider the same construction company that is promised a bonus if they can complete the work by the end of month seven. Now there's incentive to complete the work, but there's also the fixed relationship between activities.

To apply duration compression, the performing organization can rely on two different methods. These methods can be used independently or together and are applied to activities or the entire project based on need, risk, and cost. The methods are:

- **Crashing** This approach adds more resources to activities on the critical path to complete the project earlier. When crashing a project, costs are added as the labor expenses increase. Crashing doesn't always work. Consider activities that have fixed duration and won't finish faster with additional resources. The project manager must also consider the expenses in relation to the gains of completing on time. For example, a construction company may have been promised a bonus to complete the work by a preset date, but the cost incurred to hit the targeted date is more than what the bonus offers.

- **Fast Tracking** This method changes the relationship of activities. With fast tracking, activities that would normally be done in sequence are allowed to be done in parallel or with some overlap. Fast tracking can be accomplished by changing the relation of activities from FS to SS or by adding lead time to downstream activities. For example, a construction company could change the relationship between painting the rooms and installing the carpet by

e x a m

ⓦ a t c h   *It's easy to remember the*
difference between these two actions.
Crashing and cost both begin with C; we're
adding resources and too many people will
"crash" into each other. Fast tracking is
about speeding things up: haste makes
waste—risky.

adding lead time to the carpet installation
task. Before the change, all of the rooms had
to be painted before the carpet installers
could begin. With the added lead time, the
carpet can be installed hours after a room is
painted. Fast tracking increases risk and may
cause rework in the project. Can't you just
imagine those workers getting fresh paint on
the new carpet?

Using a Project Simulation

Project simulations allow a project manager to examine the feasibility of the project
schedule under different conditions, variables, and events. For example, the project
manager can see what would happen to a project if activities were delayed, vendors
missed shipment dates, and external events affected the project.

Simulations are often completed with the Monte Carlo Analysis. The Monte Carlo
Analysis, named after the world-famous gambling city, predicts how scenarios may
work out given any number of variables. The process doesn't actually churn out a
specific answer, but a range of possible answers. When Monte Carlo is applied to a
schedule it can examine, for example, the optimistic completion date, the pessimistic
completion date, and the most likely completion date for each activity in the project.

As you can imagine in a typical network diagram, there are likely thousands, if not
millions, of combinations of tasks that complete early, late, or as expected. Monte Carlo
analysis shuffles these combinations, usually through computer software, and offers a range
of possible end dates coupled with an expected probability for achieving each end date.

In other words, Monte Carlo Analysis is an odds-maker; the project manager
chooses, or is at least influenced, by the end date with the highest odds of completion
in ratio to the demands for completion by an expected time. The project manager
can then predict with some certainty that the project has an 85 percent chance of
completion by a specific date.

Simulations also provide time to factor in
"what-if" questions, worst-case scenarios, and
potential disasters. The end result of simulations
is to create responses to the feasible situations.
Then, should the situations come into play, the
project team is ready with a planned response.

e x a m

ⓦ a t c h   *Monte Carlo Analysis can*
be applied to more than just scheduling. It
can be applied to cost, project variables,
and most often, risk analysis.

Using Resource Leveling Heuristics

First off, a heuristic is a fancy way of saying "rule of thumb." A resource leveling heuristic is a method to flatten the schedule when resources are over-allocated. Resource leveling can be applied using different methods to accomplish different goals. One of the most common methods is to ensure that workers are not overextended on activities. Figure 6-8 is a screenshot from Microsoft Project 2002 where resource leveling has been applied.

For example, Sarah is assigned to Task C and Task H which both are planned to happen concurrently. Sarah cannot be in two places at once, so resource leveling changes the timing of the activities so Sarah can complete Task C and then move onto Task H. As expected, however, resource leveling often extends the project end date.

Another method for resource leveling is to take resources off of noncritical path activities and apply them to critical-path activities to ensure the project end date is met. This method takes advantage of available slack and balances the expected duration of the noncritical path with the expected duration of the critical path.

Resource leveling also provides for changing the project schedule to allow for long work hours to complete the project work—such as weekends, evenings, or even adding a second or third shift to bring the project back in alignment. Another approach, also part of resource leveling, is to change the resources, tools, or equipment used to

FIGURE 6-8

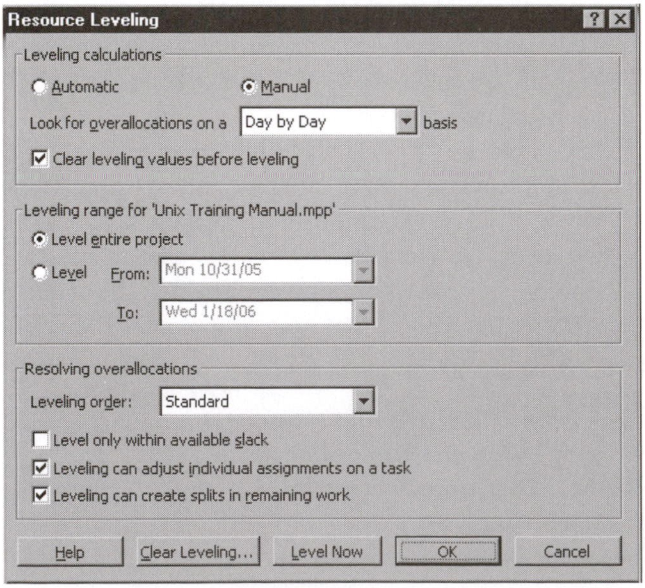

Resource leveling smoothes the schedule, but may extend the project end date.

complete the project work faster. For example, a project manager could request the printer to use a different, faster printing press to complete the printing activity than what was originally planned for. Of course, these approaches often increase cost.

Finally, some resources may be scarce to the project. Consider a highly skilled technician or consultant that is only available on a particular date to contribute to the project. These resources are scheduled from the project end date, rather than the start date. This is known as reverse resource allocation scheduling.

Using a Project Management Software

When it comes to project management software, take your pick: the market is full of them. Project management applications are tools, not replacements, for the project management process. Many of the software titles today automate the processes of

scheduling, activity sequencing, work authorization, and other activities. The performing organization must weigh the cost of the PMIS against the benefits the project managers will actually use.

Relying on a Project Coding Structure

The coding structure identifies the work packages within the WBS and is then applied to the PND. This allows the project manager, the project team, experts, and even key stakeholders, to extract areas of the project to examine, evaluate, and inspect. For example, a project to create a catalog for a parts distributor may follow multiple paths to completion. Each path to completion has its own "family" of numbers that relate to each activity on the path. Consider Table 6-2:

TABLE 6-2	Path	Coding for Path	Typical Activities
Possible Paths in Creating a Catalog	Artwork	4.2	Concept (4.2.1) Logos (4.2.2) Font design (4.2.3)
	Photography	4.3	Product models (4.3.1) Airbrushing (4.3.2) Selection (4.3.3)

TABLE 6-2	Path	Coding for Path	Typical Activities
Possible Paths in Creating a Catalog (continued)	Content	4.4	Message (4.4.1) Copywriting (4.4.2) Editing (4.4.3) Rewrites (4.4.4)
	Print	4.5	Signatures (4.5.1) Plates (4.5.2) Four-color printing (4.5.3)
	Bind	4.6	Assembly (4.6.1) Bindery (4.6.2) Trimming (4.6.3) Shrink-wrap (4.6.4)
	Distribution	4.7	Packaging (4.7.1) Labeling (4.7.2) Shipping (4.7.3)

Considering the Outputs of Schedule Development

After all the challenges of examining, sequencing, and calculating the project activities, a working schedule is created. Schedule development, like most of project management's planning processes, moves through progressive elaboration. As the project moves forward, discoveries, risk events, or other conditions may require the project schedule to be adjusted. In this section, we'll discuss the project schedule and how it is managed.

Examining the Project Schedule

The project schedule includes, at a minimum, a date for when the project begins and a date when the project is expected to end. The project schedule is considered proposed until the resources needed to complete the project work are ascertained. In addition to the schedule, the project manager should include all of the supporting details. Project schedules can be presented in many different formats, such as:

- **Project Network Diagram** Illustrates the flow of work, the relationship between activities, the critical path, and the expected project end date. PNDs when used as the project schedule should have dates associated with each project activity to show when the activity is expected to start and end.

- **Bar charts**   These show the start and end dates for the project, and the activity duration against a calendar. They are easy to read. Scheduling bar charts are also called Gantt charts.
- **Milestone charts**   Plot out the high-level deliverables and external interfaces, such as a customer walk-through, against a calendar. Milestone charts are similar to a Gantt chart, but with less detail regarding individual activities. The following is an example of a milestone chart.

Milestone	July	Aug	Sep	Oct	Nov	Dec
Customer	△▼					
Architect signature		△	▼			
Foundation				△		
Framing					△ ▼	
Roofing						△

Legend

△ Planned
▼ Actual

Utilizing the Schedule Management Plan

The schedule management plan is a subsidiary plan of the overall project plan. It is used to control changes to the schedule. A formal schedule management plan has procedures that control how changes to the project plan can be proposed, accounted for, and then implemented. An informal schedule management plan may consider changes on an instance-by-instance basis.

Updating the Resource Requirements

Due to resource leveling, additional resources may need to be added to the project. For example, a proposed leveling may extend the project beyond an acceptable completion date. To reach the project end date the project manager elects to add additional resources to the critical path activities. The resources the project manager adds should be documented, the associated costs accounted for, and approved.

Controlling the Project Schedule

Schedule control is part of Integrated Change Management, as discussed in Chapter 4. Throughout a typical project, events will happen that may require updates to the project schedule. Schedule control is concerned with three processes:

- The project manager works with the factors that can cause schedule change in an effort to confirm that the changes are agreed upon. Factors can include project team members, stakeholders, management, customers, and project conditions.
- The project manager examines the work results, conditions, and demands to know the schedule has changed.
- The project manager manages the actual change in the schedule.

Managing the Inputs to Schedule Control

Schedule control, the process of managing changes to the project schedule, is based on several inputs:

- Project schedule
- Performance reports
- Change requests
- The schedule management plan

Applying a Schedule Control System

A Schedule Control System is a formal approach to managing changes to the project schedule. It considers the conditions, reasons, requests, costs, and risks or making changes. It includes methods of tracking changes, approval levels based on thresholds, and documentation of approved or declined changes. The Schedule Control System process is part of integrated change management.

Measuring Project Performance

Poor performance may result in schedule changes. Consider a project team that is completing a work on time, but all of the work results are unacceptable. The project team may be rushing through their assignments to meet their deadline. To compensate for this, the project may be changed to allow for additional quality inspections, and more time for activity completion. Project performance is often based on earned value management, which we'll discuss in Chapter 10.

Returning to Planning

Planning is an iterative process. If the schedule, work results, or performance is unacceptable, the project manager should revisit the planning processes to determine the root cause. Additional planning is also needed when the scope may be changed, risks are discovered, and when other project events happen. Additional planning is expected throughout most projects.

Relying on Project Management Software

Most project management software can simulate the result of changes to a project schedule. Project management software can predict what may happen when a task is delayed, additional tasks are added, or the relationship between activities is edited. Project management can streamline schedule control.

Examining the Schedule Variance

The project manager must actively monitor the variances between when activities are scheduled to end and when they actually end. An accumulation of differences between scheduled and actual dates may result in a schedule variance.

The project manager must also pay attention to the completion of activities on paths with float, not just the critical path. Consider a project that has eight different paths to completion. The project manager should first identify the critical path, but should also identify the float on each path. The paths should be arranged and monitored in a hierarchy of the path with smallest float to the path with the largest float. As activities are completed, the float of each path should be monitored to identify any paths that may be slipping from the scheduled end dates.

Updating the Project Schedule

So what happens when a schedule change occurs? The project manager must ensure that the project schedule is updated to reflect the change, document the change, and follow the guidelines within the schedule management plan. Any formal processes, such as notifying stakeholders or management, should be followed.

Revisions are a special type of project schedule change, which cause the project start date, and more likely, the project end date to be changed. They typically stem from project scope changes. Because of the additional work the new scope requires, additional time is needed to complete the project.

Schedule delays, for whatever reason, may be so drastic that the entire project has to be rebaselined. Rebaselining is a worst-case scenario and should only be used when adjusting for drastic, long delays. When rebaselining happens, all of the historical information up to the point of the rebaseline is eliminated. Schedule revision is the preferred, and most common, approach to changing the project end date.

Applying Corrective Action

Corrective action is any method applied to bring the project schedule back into alignment with the original dates and goals for the project end date. Corrective actions are efforts to ensure future performance meets the expected performance levels. It includes:

- Extraordinary measures to ensure work packages complete as scheduled
- Extraordinary measures to ensure work packages complete with as little delay as possible
- Root-cause analysis of schedule variances
- Implementing measures to recover from schedule delays

Writing the Lessons Learned

Lessons learned on creating the schedule, changes to the project schedule, and response to variances are needed as part of the project's historical information. Recall that lessons learned documentation happens throughout the project plan, not just at the conclusion of the project.

CERTIFICATION SUMMARY

Projects cannot last forever—thankfully. To effectively finish and manage a project, a project manager must be able to effectively manage time. Within a project there can be many factors that affect the project length: activity duration, project calendars, resource calendars, vendors, activity sequencing, and more. Time management begins with the constraints of the product schedule, the project calendar, the resource calendars, as well as the activities and their expected duration.

Many projects can rely on project templates that have worked before. Other projects, new and never-attempted technology, require that a project schedule be created from scratch. The WBS contributes to the activity list, which in turn, allows the project manager and the project team to begin activity sequencing.

Activities to be sequences must be estimated. The project manager and the project team must evaluate the required time to complete the work packages. The project manager can rely on a number of estimating methods to come to a predicted duration for activities. For example, a project manager may use analogous estimation of historical data to provide the needed estimate. Or, the project manager may use a parametric model to predict the amount of time for the activities. The importance of estimating is that each work package is considered and its duration calculated.

Within the process of activity sequencing there will be hard logic and soft logic. Hard logic is the mandatory relationships between activities: the foundation must be in place before the house framing can begin. Soft logic allows the relationship and order of activities to be determined based on conditions, preferences, or other factors. For example, the landscaping will happen before the house is painted so that dirt and dust won't get onto the fresh paint.

The relationships of activities are illustrated within a network diagram. Network diagrams show the path from start to completion and identify which activities are on the critical path. Of course, the critical path is the path with the longest duration and typically has zero slack or float. Activities on the noncritical paths may be delayed to the extent that they do not delay activities on the critical path.

Finally, project team members may have a tendency to bloat their duration estimates. Bloating the work to allow for "wiggle room" on assignments can cause durations to swell way beyond the practical completion of the project. In lieu of bloated estimates, project team members and the project manager should use a percentage of the project time as management reserve. When activities are late, the tardiness of the work is borrowed from management reserve rather than tacked onto the conclusion of the project.

KEY TERMS

To pass the PMP exams, you will need to memorize these terms and their definitions. For maximum value, create your own flashcards based on these definitions and review them daily. The definitions can be found within this chapter and in the glossary.

activity list	FNET	quantitative estimating
activity on arrow	fragnets	resource calendar
activity on node	GERT	resource leveling heuristics
activity sequencing	hard logic	schedule control
analogous estimating	lag	schedule management plan
CPM	lead	schedule variance
crashing	mandatory dependencies	SNET
discretionary dependencies	Monte Carlo Analysis	soft logic
fast tracking	network templates	start-to-finish
finish-to-finish	PERT	start-to-start
finish-to-start	Precedence Diagramming Method	subnets
float	project calendar	

TWO-MINUTE DRILL

Sequencing Activities

❑ Projects are made up of sequential activities to create a product. The WBS and the activity list serve as key input to the sequencing of project activities. The science of arranging, calculating, and predicting how long the activities will take to complete allows the project manager to create a schedule and then predict when the project will end.

❑ Hard logic is the approach that requires activities to happen in a specific order due to the nature of the work. For example, configure a computer workstation's operating systems before adding the software.

❑ Soft logic is a "preferred" method of arranging activities based on conditions, guidelines, or best practices. For example, the project manager prefers all of the photocopying of a user manual to be complete before any bindery work on the manual begins.

❑ The sequence of activities is displayed in a network diagram. The network diagram illustrates the flow of activities and the relationship between activities. The Precedent Diagramming Method is the most common approach to arranging activities visually.

Estimating Activity Durations

❑ Activity duration estimates are needed to calculate how long the project will take to complete. Estimates can come from project team members, commercial databases, expert judgment, and historical information.

❑ Analogous estimating relies on historical information to predict how long current project activities should last.

❑ Quantitative estimates use a mathematical model to calculate how long activities should take based on units, duration, and effort.

Evaluating Time and Duration

❑ The resources to complete the project activities must be considered. The project manager must evaluate the skill set, the experience, and ability to get the work done.

❑ The project manager must evaluate applying additional resources to effort-driven activities to reduce their duration. Adding resources does not reduce fixed-duration activities' durations.

❑ The calendar of the project is the time when the project work may take place. The project manager must consider access to the workplace, project schedule, organization holidays, and events that affect the project calendar.

❑ The resource calendar reflects when the project resources (project team members, consultants, and so on) are available to complete the project work.

Determining the Project Duration

❑ The critical path is the longest path to completion in the network diagram. Activities on the critical path have no float or slack. Free float is the amount of time an activity can be delayed without affecting the next activity's scheduled start date. Total float is the amount of time an activity can be delayed without affecting the project end date.

❑ Duration compression is applied to reduce the length of the project or to account for project delays. Crashing adds resources to project activities and usually increases cost. Fast tracking allows activities to happen in tandem and usually increases risk.

❑ The schedule management plan must be consulted when project schedule changes occur, are proposed, or are needed. The Schedule Control System implements the schedule management plan and is part of integration change management.

SELF TEST

1. You are the project manager of the JHG Project. This project has 32 stakeholders and will require implementation activities in North and South America. You have been requested to provide a duration estimate for the project. Of the following, which will offer the best level of detail in your estimate?

   A. WBS
   B. Order of magnitude
   C. Requirements document
   D. Stakeholder analysis

2. Michael is the project manager of the 78GH Project. This project requires several members of the project team to complete a certification class for another project the week of November 2. This class causes some of the project activities on Michael's activities to be delayed from his target schedule. This is an example of which of the following?

   A. Hard logic
   B. External dependencies
   C. Soft logic
   D. Conflict of interest

3. Which of the following best describes GERT?

   A. PDM
   B. Network template
   C. Conditional diagramming methods
   D. ADM

4. As the project manager for the DFK Project, you are reviewing your project's network diagram (as shown in the following illustration):

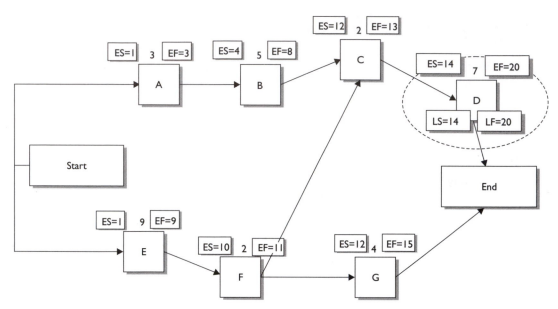

Given the diagram, what is the relationship between tasks F and G?

A. FS

B. SS

C. FF

D. SF

5. You are the project manager for the LLL Project. Steven, a project team member, is confused about network diagrams. Specifically, he wants to know what the critical path is in a network diagram. Your answer is which one of the following?

A. The critical path is the network that hosts the activities most critical to the project success.

B. The critical path is the path with the longest duration.

C. The critical path is always one path that cannot be delayed or the entire project will be delayed.

D. The critical path is the path from start to completion with no deviation from the project plan.

6. What is the difference between PDM and ADM?

A. ADM places activities on arrows; PDM places activities on nodes.

B. ADM is also known as AOA, while PDM is also known as GERT.

C. ADM hosts activities on nodes, while PDM hosts activities on arrows.

D. PDM can have two types of relationships between tasks, while ADM can have only type of relationship between tasks.

7. The purpose of using GERT is which of the following?

   A. Allows for float to be distributed across all paths to completion

   B. Allows for loops and conditional branches

   C. Requires all paths to completion to intersect at quality audits

   D. Requires all paths to completion to intersect at scope verification checkpoints

8. Where is a project manager most likely to experience a subnet?

   A. WBS

   B. Kill points

   C. GERT charts

   D. Network template

9. You are the project manager for the POL Project. This project will use PERT to calculate the estimates for activity duration. For activity D, you have the following information: P=9, O=4, M=5. What is the result of PERT?

   A. 18 weeks

   B. 5.5 weeks

   C. 33.33 days

   D. 3 weeks

10. You are the project manager for the YKL Project. This project will impact several lines of business at completion. Each milestone in the project is scheduled to end so the work does not impact current business cycles. This is an example of which one of the following?

   A. Constraint

   B. Expert judgment

   C. WBS scheduling

   D. Soft logic

11. You are the project manager for the MNB Project. You and your project team are about to enter into the activity duration estimating process. Which of the following will not be helpful in your meeting?

   A. Constraints

   B. Assumptions

   C. The project charter

   D. Identified risks

12. You are the project manager for a new training program at your customer's site. This program will require each of the customer's employees to attend the half-day class and complete an assessment exam. You will be completing the training at the customer's facility, and will need a trainer for the duration of the training, which is six months. This is an example of which of the following?

    A. Resource requirements
    B. Assumption
    C. Cost constraint
    D. A human resource issue

13. You are the project manager for a construction company. Your firm has been contracted to complete the drilling of a well for a new cabin in Arkansas. The specification of the well is documented, but your company has little experience in well drilling in Arkansas. The stakeholder is concerned your time estimates are not accurate as the soil and rock in Arkansas are much different than the soil in your home state. Which one of the following can you use to ensure your project estimates are accurate?

    A. Order of magnitude
    B. Commercial duration estimating databases
    C. Local contractors
    D. Soil samplings from the Arkansas government

14. You are the project manager for your organization. You and your project team are in conflict on the amount of time allotted to complete certain activities. Several of the team members are wanting to bloat the time associated with activities to ensure they will have enough time to complete their tasks should something go awry. The law of economics that these tasks may suffer from is which one of the following?

    A. Parkinson's Law
    B. The law of diminishing returns
    C. Hertzberg's theory of motivation
    D. Oligopoly

15. You are the project manager for your organization. You and your project team are in conflict on the amount time allotted to complete certain activities. Several of the team members are wanting to bloat the time associated with activities to ensure they will have enough time to complete their tasks should something go awry. Instead of overestimating their project activities, the project team should use which of the following?

    A. Capital reserve

    B. Contingency plans

    C. Contingency reserve

    D. Assumptions of plus or minus a percentage

16. Which of the following is not an output from the activity duration estimating process?

    A. WBS

    B. Activity list updates

    C. Basis of estimates

    D. Duration estimates

17. You are the project manager for the 987 Project. Should this project run over schedule, it will cost your organization $35,000 per day in lost sales. With four months to completion, you realize the project is running late. You decide, with management's approval, to add more project team members to the project plan to complete the work on time. This is an example of which of the following?

    A. Crashing

    B. Fast tracking

    C. Expert judgment

    D. Cost benefit analysis

18. You are the project manager for the 987 Project. Should this project run over schedule, it will cost your organization $35,000 per day in lost sales. With four months to completion, you realize the project is running late. You decide, with management's approval, to change the relationship between several of the work packages so they begin in tandem rather than sequentially. This is an example of which one of the following?

    A. Crashing

    B. Fast tracking

    C. Expert judgment

    D. Cost benefit analysis

19. Chris, a project manager for his company, is explaining the difference between a Gantt chart and a milestone chart. Which of the following best describes a Gantt chart?

    A. A Gantt chart depicts what was planned against what actually occurred.

    B. A Gantt chart depicts the work in the project against the work that has been completed.

    C. A Gantt chart depicts the work in the project against a calendar.

    D. A Gantt chart depicts the work in the project against each resource's calendar.

20. Which of the following is a correct attribute of the critical path?
    A. It determines the earliest completion date
    B. It has the smallest amount of float
    C. It has the most activities in the PND
    D. It is the path with the most expensive project activities

21. You are the project manager for a construction project. Your foreman informs you that, due to the humidity, the concrete will need to cure for an additional 24 hours before the framing can begin. To accommodate the requirement, you add _____ time to the framing activity.
    A. Lead
    B. Lag
    C. Delay
    D. Slack

22. A heuristic is a _____?
    A. Rule of thumb
    B. Regulation
    C. A regulation internal to an organization
    D. A best method of implementing an activity

23. You are the project manager for a project with the following network diagram.

    Studying the diagram, which path is the critical path?
    A. ABCD
    B. EBCD
    C. EFH
    D. EGH

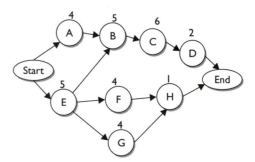

24. Bertha is the project manager for the HAR Project. The project is behind schedule and Bertha has elected, with management's approval, to crash the critical path. This process adds more what? (Choose the best answer.)
    A. Cost
    B. Time
    C. Risk
    D. Documentation

25. Bertha is the project manager for the HAR Project. The project is behind schedule and Bertha has elected, with management's approval, to fast track the critical path. This process adds more what? (Choose the best answer.)

A. Cost

B. Time

C. Risk

D. Documentation

SELF TEST ANSWERS

1. ☑ **A.** The WBS is the best choice for this scenario.
   ☒ **B** is incorrect because the order of magnitude provides little information for accurate estimating. **C**, while tempting, is incorrect because the requirements document lists the high-level deliverable, while the WBS provides more detail. **D** is incorrect because stakeholder analysis does not provide enough information to accurately predict when the project will end.

2. ☑ **B.** Before the work can begin, the certification class must be completed.
   ☒ **A** is incorrect; hard logic is the mandatory sequencing of particular events. **C** is incorrect because there is no preferential logic. **D** is incorrect because it does not apply to this scenario.

3. ☑ **C.** GERT, Graphical Evaluation and Review Technique, allows for conditional advancement.
   ☒ **A, B,** and **C** are all incorrect because these describe other network diagrams.

4. ☑ **A.** G is slated to start immediately after F, so this is a finish-to-start relationship. In other words, F must finish so G may start.
   ☒ **B, C,** and **D** are all incorrect relationships.

5. ☑ **B.** The critical path is always the path with the longest duration.
   ☒ **A** is incorrect because the critical path hosts the activities, not a network. **C** is a distracter and is incorrect because there can be more than one critical path in a network diagram. **D** is incorrect because it does not adequately describe the critical path.

6. ☑ **A.** ADM, the Arrow Diagramming Method, is also known as "Activity-on-Arrow," while PDM, the Precedence Diagramming Method, places activities on nodes. PDM is also known as "Activity-on-Nodes."
   ☒ **B** and **C** are incorrect because they do not accurately describe ADM and PDM. **D** is incorrect because PDM is allowed four different relationship types: FS, SF, FF, and SF.

7. ☑ **B.** GERT allows for branching and loopbacks.
   ☒ **A, C,** and **D** are all incorrect because they do not accurately describe GERT.

8. ☑ **D.** Subnets are often included in network templates to summarize common activities in a project.
   ☒ **A, B,** and **C** do not use subnets.

9. ☑ **B.** The formula for pert is (P+4M+O)/6. In this instance, the outcome is 5.5 weeks.
   ☒ **A, C,** and **D** are incorrect calculations, so they are incorrect.

10. ☑ **D.** Soft logic allows the project manager to make decisions based on conditions outside of the project, best practices, or guidelines.
    ☒ **A** is incorrect because this is not an example of constraints since the project manager is not required to use soft logic. **B** and **C** are incorrect; they do not describe the scenario fully.

11. ☑ **C.** The project charter is not an input to the activity duration estimating process.
☒ Choices **A, B,** and **D** are all correct choices because they are inputs to activity duration estimating.

12. ☑ **A.** The trainer is required for the project for six months.
☒ **B, C,** and **D** are incorrect because they do not describe the resource requirement of the trainer on the project.

13. ☑ **B.** Commercial duration estimating databases are valid resources to confirm or base time estimates upon.
☒ **A** is incorrect because order of magnitude offers very little detail on time estimates. **C** is incorrect because local contractors are not the best source for confirming time estimates; the question does not define if the contractors are local to Arkansas or to your home state. **D** is incorrect because commercial duration estimating databases are much more reliable in this scenario.

14. ☑ **A.** Parkinson's Law states that work will expand to fulfill the time allotted to it.
☒ Bloated tasks will take all of the time allotted. Management reserve should be used instead. **B** is incorrect because this describes the relationship between effort, duration, and the maximum yield. **C** is incorrect because it describes personalities and worker motivation. **D** is incorrect because an oligopoly is a procurement issue where there are few vendors available to choose from; the vendors may seemingly have checks and balances with each other.

15. ☑ **C.** Rather than bloat activities, projects should use contingency reserve. Contingency reserve is a portion of the project schedule allotted for time overruns on activities.
☒ **A** is incorrect because it does not describe the scenario. **B** is incorrect because contingency plans are a response to risk situations. **D** is incorrect because it describes a range of variance.

16. ☑ **A.** The WBS is not an output of activity duration estimating.
☒ Choices **B, C,** and **D** are incorrect because they are outputs of activity duration estimating.

17. ☑ **A.** When more resources are added to a project to complete the work on time, this is called crashing.
☒ **B** is incorrect; fast tracking is the process of changing the relationship between activities to allow tasks to overlap. **C** is incorrect because expert judgment is not used in this scenario. **D** is incorrect; cost benefit analysis may be part of the process to decide the value of adding more workers to the schedule, but it is not the process described.

18. ☑ **B.** Fast tracking allows activities to operate in tandem with each other rather than sequentially.
☒ **A** is incorrect; when more resources are added to a project to complete the work on time, this is called crashing. **C** is incorrect, because expert judgment is not used in this scenario. **D** is

incorrect; cost benefit analysis may be part of the process to decide the value of fast tracking the schedule, but it is not the process described.

19. ☑ **C.** A Gantt chart is a bar chart that represents the duration of activities against a calendar. The length of the bars represent the length of activities while the order of the bars represent the order of activities in the project.
☒ **A** and **B** are incorrect because this describes a tracking Gantt. **D** is incorrect because this does not describe a Gantt chart.

20. ☑ **A.** Of all the choices presented, **A** is the best description of the critical path. The critical path is the path with the longest duration. There can be instances, however, when the project's expected end date is well beyond the duration of the scheduled work. In such cases, the critical path is considered the path with the least amount of float.
☒ Choices **B, C,** and **D** are incorrect because they are false descriptions of the critical path. The critical path has no float, has the longest duration, and does not necessarily have the most expensive activities.

21. ☑ **B.** You will add lag time to the framing activity. Lag is waiting time.
☒ **A** is incorrect; lead time allows activities to overlap. **C** is not the correct choice. **D** is also incorrect because slack is the amount of time a task can be delayed without delaying the scheduled start date of dependent activities.

22. ☑ **A.** Heuristic is simply a rule of thumb.
☒ **B, C,** and **D** are all incorrect; these choices do not describe heuristics.

23. ☑ **B** is the critical path because EBCD is the longest path to completion at 18 days.
☒ **A, C,** and **D** are incorrect because these paths have float.

24. ☑ **A.** Crashing involves adding resources, which typically increases cost.
☒ **B** is incorrect because crashing is an effort to reduce time, not add it. **C** may be correct, but it is not the best answer. **D** is incorrect.

25. ☑ **C.** Fast tracking adds risk as tasks are allowed to overlap.
☒ **A** may be correct in some instances, but it is not the best choice here. **B** is incorrect because Bertha wants to remove time, not add it. **D** is also incorrect.

7

Introducing Project Cost Management

Projects cost. Have you ever worked with a client who had a huge vision for a project, but had little capital to invest into the vision? Or have you worked with a client who gasped when you revealed how much it would cost to complete their desired scope of work? Or have you been fortunate and had a customer who accepted the costs for the project at face value, made certain the funds were available, and sent you on your way to complete the work? As a general rule, management and customers are always concerned with how much a project is going to cost in relation to how much a project is going to earn.

Most likely there is more negotiating, questioning, and evaluating for larger projects than for smaller ones. The relation between the project cost and the project scope should be direct: you get what you pay for. Think it's possible to buy a mansion at ranch home prices? Not likely. Think it's possible to run a worldwide marketing campaign at the cost of a postcard mailer? Not likely. A realistic expectation of what a project will cost will give great weight to the project's scope.

As the business need undergoes analysis, progressive elaboration and estimates are completed based on varying levels of detail, and eventually the cost of the project will emerge. Often, however, the predicted costs and the actual costs vary. Poor planning, skewed assumptions, and overly optimistic estimates all contribute to this. A successful project manager must be able to plan, predict, budget, and control the costs of a project.

Costs associated with projects are not just the costs of goods procured to complete the project. The cost of the labor may be one of the biggest expenses of a project. The project manager must rely on time estimates to predict the cost of the labor to complete the project work. In addition, the cost of the equipment and materials needed to complete the project work must be factored into the project expenses. This chapter examines the management of project costs, how to predict them, account for them, and then, with plan in hand, to control them. We'll examine exactly how costs are planned for and taken into consideration by the performing organization and how the size of the project affects the cost estimating process.

Planning the Project Resources

As part of the planning process, the project manager must determine what resources are needed to complete the project. Resources include the people, equipment, and materials that will be utilized to complete the work. In addition, the project manager must identify the quantity of the needed resources and when the resources are needed for the project. The identification of the resources, the needed quantity, and the schedule of the resources are directly linked to the expected cost of the project work, as shown here:

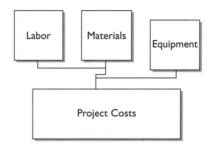

Consider a project to fully automate a new home: the lights, heating and cooling, appliances, and home security are all connected through a central computer operating system. The resources to complete the project work would include technicians, HVAC experts, electricians, and other people with the knowledge to install and configure the components. The resources in this case, however, would also include the network cabling to connect the components, diagnostic tools to monitor and test the installation, and the equipment and tools to physically install the components.

In addition, services and sites are considered resources as well. Your project may require a vendor's service, such as a commercial printer, a carpenter, or other service. If these services are not available for the project as planned, the project will suffer. Some projects require you to lease space; the leased space is considered a resource.

In some instances, it is most cost effective to hire a consultant or subject matter expert (SME) to identify details unique to the project work, such as mandates, laws, standards, and so on. The expense of relying on the SME may be far less than the cost of the time to research the unique details and requirements of the project. The knowledge gained from the SME can offset the expenses that would otherwise result from not having specialized knowledge of the project work.

e x a m

ⓦ **a t c h**   *If time is an issue in a complex project, rely on an SME to provide input to the decision-making process. If the project team is lacking a needed project skill set, a seminar or training class is appropriate to get the team member up to speed.*

Consider the Inputs to Resource Planning

Resource planning is the process of examining the project work and determining what resources, people, and equipment are needed to complete the project. Resource planning also includes identifying the expected quantity of the needed resources so the predicted cost can be calculated. These are some familiar inputs to resource planning:

- **Work breakdown structure** The WBS is a deliverables-orientated breakdown of the components of the project. It helps the project manager and the project team identify the components requiring specific people, equipment, and materials. The WBS is the primary input to resource planning.

- **Historical information** If similar projects have been completed, what resources were required on these projects? Historical information should be used if it's available, as it is proven information rather than speculation.

- **Scope statement** The scope statement serves as a key input to resource planning; the scope statement defines the project work. The scope statement should guide the resource planning process, as it identifies why the project was undertaken and the required work to complete the project. The required work, therefore, can help identify the required resources to complete the project.

- **Resource pool description** The project manager should identify what resources are available for the project. These include people, materials, and equipment. As the project passes through progressive elaboration, the identified pool of resources may vary. For example, in the early phases of a marketing campaign, the pool may include copywriters, designers, computer professionals, the individuals that operate the printing equipment, and photographers. As the project moves through its phases to completion, the resource pool may be limited to only those people who have worked on the project in the early phases.

- **Organizational policies** The performing organization's policies regarding staff acquisition must be taken into consideration. In addition, any procurement policies to ascertain, lease, or rent equipment must be evaluated. The project manager should be aware of these requirements before planning the resources— time invested identifying resources may be lost if the process conflicts with the organizational policies.

- **Activity duration estimates** The duration of the activities are needed so the project manager and the project team can consider the costs and benefits of assigning more effort to reduce tasks' duration where feasible, as seen next. The activity duration estimates should be readily available from the time management processes.

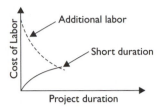

Applying Expert Judgment

Armed with the inputs to resource planning, the project manager and the project team should be ready to identify and plan the need for the project resources. The project manager and the project team will examine the project work and the available resources and then apply reason, logic, and experience in evaluating the available resources in relation to the project requirements.

A person or group can offer expert judgment on the project resource needs. The person or group offering the expert judgment should have the expertise, experience, or training needed to evaluate and analyze the resources that the project needs. Expert judgment can come from several sources:

- Internal subject matter experts, such as resources from other departments
- External subject matter experts, such as consultants
- Trade and professional associations
- Industry groups

Identifying Alternative Solutions

Alternatives-identification is any process that identifies other solutions to an identified problem. These approaches typically use brainstorming and lateral thinking. In this process, alternatives-identification may include buy-versus-build scenarios, outsourcing, cross training, and other activities. The idea of using alternatives-identification is to ensure that the identified resources are complete and that the cost of the resources are the best fit for the project work.

Value analysis is an approach to find more affordable, less costly, methods of accomplishing the same work. For example, a project manager may change the sequencing of activities to shorten the project duration, while saving labor costs by assigning high-cost resources only to the activities that demand it.

Relying on Project Management Software

Project management software can help the project manager identify and organize the resource pools. Project management software can be configured to organize common resources, talents, skill sets, calendars, rates, contact information, and more. While there are many different project management applications available, the ability to easily use and update the information an application stores is critical. Figure 7-1 is a screen shot of Microsoft Project accessing resources from a central repository.

Identifying Resource Requirements

Once the project manager and the project team have completed resource planning, the required resources to complete the project will have been identified. The resource identification is specific to the lowest level of the WBS. The identified resources will need to be obtained through staff acquisition or through procurement. We'll cover staff acquisition in Chapter 9 and procurement in Chapter 12. Figure 7-2 is a recap of all the inputs, tools, and techniques, and outputs of resource planning.

FIGURE 7-1

Project management software can assist in resource planning.

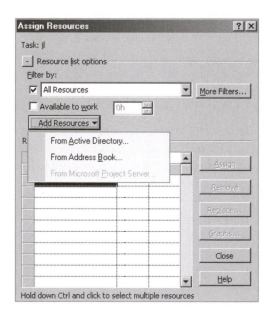

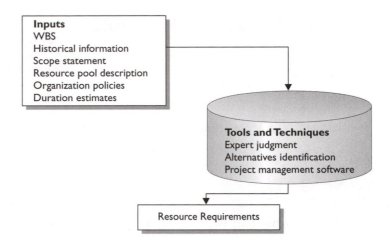

FIGURE 7-2

Resource
planning identifies
all of the required
resources.

Cost Estimating

Cost estimating is the process of calculating the costs of the identified resources needed
to complete the project work. The person or group doing the estimating must consider
the possible fluctuations, conditions, and other causes of variances that could affect the
total cost of the estimate.

There is a distinct difference between cost estimating and pricing. A cost estimate
is the cost of the resources required to complete the project work. Pricing, however,
includes a profit margin. In other words, a company performing projects for other
organizations may do a cost estimate to see how much the project is going to cost to
complete. Then, with this cost information, they'll factor a profit into the project work,
as shown here:

*More and more companies are requiring the project manager to calculate the
project costs and then factor the ROI, and other benefit models, into the project
product. The goal is to see the value of the project once its deliverables are in
operations.*

Considering the Cost Estimating Inputs

Cost estimating relies on several project components from the Initiation and Planning process groups. This process also relies on historical information and policies from the performing organization.

Using the Work Breakdown Structure

Of course the WBS is included—it's an input to five major planning processes: cost estimating, cost budgeting, resource planning, risk management planning, and activity definition.

Relying on the Resource Requirements

The only output of resource planning serves as a key input to cost estimating. The project will have some requirement for resources—the skills of the labor, the ability of materials, or the function of equipment must all be accounted for.

Calculating Resource Rates

The estimator has to know how much each resource costs. The cost should be in some unit of time or measure—such as cost per hour, cost per metric ton, or cost per use. If the rates of the resources are not known, the rates themselves may also have to be estimated. Of course, skewed rates on the estimates will result in a skewed estimate for the project. There are four categories of cost:

- **Direct costs** These costs are attributed directly to the project work and cannot be shared among projects (airfare, hotels, and long distance phone charges, and so on).

- **Variable costs** These costs vary depending on the conditions applied in the project (number of meeting participants, supply and demand of materials, and so on).

- **Fixed costs** These costs remain constant throughout the project (the cost of a piece of rented equipment for the project, the cost of a consultant brought onto the project, and so on).

- **Indirect costs** These costs are representative of more than one project (utilities for the performing organization, access to a training room, project management software license, and so on).

Estimating Activity Durations

Estimates of the duration of the activities, which predict the length of the project, are needed for decisions on financing the project. The length of the activities will help the performing organization calculate what the total cost of the project will be, including the finance charges. Recall the formula for present value? It's $PV = FV/(1+R)^n$; PV is the present value, FV is the future value, R is the interest rate, and n is the number of time periods. The future value of the monies the project will earn may need to be measured against the present value to determine if the project is worth financing, as shown here:

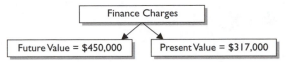

Calculations of the duration of activities are needed in order to extrapolate the total cost of the work packages. For example, if an activity is estimated to last 14 hours and Suzanne's cost per hour is $80, then the cost of the work package is $1,120. The duration shows management how long the project is expected to last and which activities will cost the most and provides the opportunity to re-sequence activities to shorten the project duration—which consequently shortens the finance period for the project.

Another aspect the project manager and management may have to determine is the long-term worth of a product in regard to tax deductions. There are three approaches to deduct the product's cost:

- *Straight-line depreciation* allows the organization to write off the same amount each year. The formula for straight-line depreciation is Purchase Value minus Salvage Value divided by Number of Years in Use. For example, if the purchase price of a photocopier is $7,000 and the salvage value of the photocopier in five years is $2,000, the formula would read 7,000–2,000/5=$1,000.

- *Double-declining balance* is considered accelerated depreciation. This method allows the organization to double the percentage written off in the first year. In our preceding example, a single deduction was $1,000 per year, which is 20 percent of the total deduction across the five years. With double-declining, the customer would subtract 40 percent the first year, and then 40 percent of the remaining value each subsequent year. In our example, the deducted amount for year one would be $2,000. For year two it would be $1,200, and year three it would be $720. This is a great method for equipment that you don't anticipate to have around for a very long time—such as computer equipment.

- *Sum of the years depreciation* is like a magic trick. It works by writing out the number of years the equipment is in production and adding each year to the year before. In our example it was five years, so we'd do this: 5+4+3+2+1=15 (note the largest to smallest). The sum of the years, 15, becomes our denominator; the five, for the first year, is our numerator. So for the first year, we'd deduct 5/15ths (or one third) of the photocopier cost after the salvage amount, which would be $1,650. The second year the four would be the numerator and we'd deduct $1,250, and so on. Each year we'd deduct a slightly smaller percentage than the year before.

e x a m

ⓦatch *You may encounter a general question on straight-line versus double-declining depreciation on the PMP Exam. You should be familiar with the concept, but don't invest too much time memorizing these formulas for the exam.*

Using Estimating Publications

There are, for different industries, commercial estimating publications. These references can help the project estimator confirm and predict the accuracy of estimates. If a project manager elects to use one of these commercial databases, the estimate should include a pointer to this document for future reference and verification.

Using Historical Information

Historical information is proven information and can come from several places:

- **Project files**   Past projects within the performing organization can be used as a reference to predict costs and time. Caution must be taken that the records referenced are accurate, somewhat current, and reflective of what was actually experienced in the historical project.

- **Commercial cost-estimating databases**   These databases provide estimates of what the project should cost based on the variables of the project, resources, and other conditions.

- **Team members**   Team members may have specific experience with the project costs or estimates. Recollections may be useful, but are highly unreliable when compared to documented results.

e x a m

ⓦatch *The project team members' recollections of what things cost should not be trusted as fact. It's advice and input, but documented information is always better.*

Referencing the Chart of Accounts

This is a coding system used by the performing organization's accounting system to account for the project work. Estimates within the project must be mapped to the correct code of accounts so that the organization's ledger reflects the actual work performed, the cost of the work performed, and any billing (internal or external) that was charged to the customer for the completed work.

Acknowledging the Cost of Risk

The impact of risks, for positive or negative effect, must be evaluated and considered in the cost estimates. Risks, which we'll cover in Chapter 11, can impact the cost of the project. For example, should a risk come into play, the mitigation of the risk may require adding several activities to squelch the risk. The expense of the activities would add cost to the project.

Estimating Project Costs

Management, customers, and other interested stakeholders are all going to be interested in what the project is going to cost to complete. There are several approaches to cost estimating, which we'll discuss in one moment. First, however, understand that cost estimates have a way of following the project manager around—especially the lowest initial cost estimate.

The estimates you'll want to know for the PMP exam, and for your career, are reflective of the accuracy of the information the estimate is based upon. The more accurate the information, the better the cost estimate will be.

Using Analogous Estimating

Analogous estimating relies on historical information to predict the cost of the current project. It is also known as top-down estimating. The process of analogous estimating takes the actual cost of a historical project as a basis for the current project. The cost of the historical project is applied to the cost of the current project, taking into account the scope and size of the current project as well as other known variables.

Analogous estimating is a form of expert judgment. This estimating approach takes less time to complete than other estimating models, but is also less accurate. This top-down approach is good for fast estimates to get a general idea of what the project may cost.

Here's an example of analogous estimating: The Carlton Park Project was to grade and pave a sidewalk around a pond in the community park. The sidewalk of Carlton Park was 1,048 feet by 6 feet, used a textured surface, had some curves around trees, and cost $25,287 to complete. The current project, King Park, will have a similar surface and will cover 4,500 feet by 6 feet. The analogous estimate for this project, based on the work in Carlton Park, is $108,500. This is based on the price per foot of material at $4.02—note that $4.021 is not the same as $4.21.

Using Parametric Modeling

Parametric modeling uses a mathematical model based on known parameters to predict the cost of a project. The parameters in the model can vary based on the type of work being completed. A parameter can be cost per cubic yard, cost per unit, and so on. A complex parameter can be cost per unit with adjustment factors based on the conditions of the project. In addition, the adjustment factors may have additional modifying factors depending on additional conditions.

To use parametric modeling, the factors the model is based on must be accurate. The factors within the model are quantifiable and don't vary much based on the effort applied to the activity. And finally, the model must be scalable between project sizes. The parametric model using a scalable cost-per-unit approach is depicted here:.

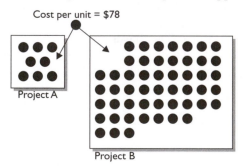

There are two types of parametric estimating:

■ **Regression analysis** This is a statistical approach to predict what future values may be, based on historical values. Regression analysis creates quantitative predictions based on variables within one value to predict variables in another. This form of estimating relies solely on pure statistical math to reveal relationships between variables and predict future values.

■ **Learning curve**   This approach is simple: the cost per unit decreases the more units workers complete; this is because workers learn as they complete the required work. The more an individual completes an activity, the easier it is to complete. The estimate is considered parametric, as the formula is based on repetitive activities, such as wiring telephone jacks, painting hotel rooms, or other activities that are completed over and over within a project. The cost per unit decreases as the experience increases because the time to complete the work is shortened.

e x a m
ⓦatch   *Don't worry too much about regression analysis for the exam. Learning curve is a topic you'll more likely have questions on.*

Using Bottom-Up Estimating

Bottom-up estimating starts from zero, accounts for each component of the WBS, and arrives at a sum for the project. It is completed with the project team and can be one of the most time-consuming methods to predict project costs. While this method is more expensive, because of the time invested to create the estimate, it is also one of the most accurate. A fringe benefit of completing a bottom-up estimate is the project team may buy into the project work as they see the cost and value of each cost within the project.

Using Computer Software

While the PMP examination is vendor-neutral, a general knowledge of how computer software can assist the project manager is needed. There are several different computer programs that can streamline and make accurate estimates for the project work. These tools can include project management software, spreadsheet programs, and simulations.

Analyzing Cost Estimating Results

The output of cost estimating is the actual cost estimates of the resources required to the complete the project work. The estimate is typically quantitative and can be presented in detail against the WBS components or summarized in terms of a grand total, by phases of the project, or by major deliverables. Each resource in the project must be accounted for and assigned to a cost category. Categories include the following:

■ Labor costs
■ Material costs

- Travel costs
- Supplies
- Hardware costs
- Software costs
- Special categories (inflation, cost reserve, and so on)

The cost of the project is expressed in monetary terms, such as dollars, euros, or yen, so management can compare projects based on costs. It may be acceptable, depending on the demands of the performing organization, to provide estimates in staffing hours or days of work to complete the project along with the estimated costs.

As projects have risks, the cost of the risks should be identified along with the cost of the risk responses. The project manager should list the risks, their expected risk event value, and the response to the risk should it come into play. We'll cover risk management in detail in Chapter 11.

Refining the Cost Estimates

Cost estimates can also pass through progress elaboration. As more details are acquired as the project progresses, the estimates are refined. Industry guidelines and organizational policies may define how the estimates are refined, but there are three generally accepted categories of estimating accuracy:

- **Rough order of magnitude**   This estimate is "rough" and is used during the Initiating processes and in top-down estimates. The range of variance for the estimate can be –25 percent to +75 percent.

- **Budget estimate**   This estimate is also somewhat broad and is used early in the planning processes and also in top-down estimates. The range of variance for the estimate can be –10 percent to +25 percent.

- **Definitive estimates**   This estimate type is one of the most accurate. It is used late in the planning processes and is associated with bottom-up estimating. The range of variance for the estimate can be –5 percent to +10 percent.

Considering the Supporting Detail

Once the estimates have been completed, supporting detail must be organized and documented to show how the estimates were created. This material, even the notes that contributed to the estimates, may provide valuable information later in the project. Specifically, the supporting detail includes the following:

- **Information on the project scope work** This may be provided by referencing the WBS.
- **Information on the approach used in developing the cost estimates** This can include how the estimate was accomplished and the parties involved with the estimate.
- **Information on the range of variance in the estimate** For example, based on the estimating method used, the project cost may be $220,000 ± $15,000. This project cost may be as low as $205,000 or as high as $235,000.

Developing the Cost Management Plan

The cost management plan details how variances from the project costs will be managed. The performing organization may have policies and procedures on the expected reactions to cost variances within the project. For example, variances over a set dollar amount may prompt the project manager to create a Variance Report, meet with management, or even initiate an audit.

Completing Cost Budgeting

Cost budgeting is the process of assigning a cost to an individual work package. The goal of this process is to assign costs to the work in the project so that the work may be measured for performance. This is the creation of the cost baseline, as shown here:

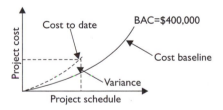

Cost budgeting and cost estimates may go hand-in-hand, but estimating should be completed before a budget is requested—or assigned. Cost budgeting applies the cost estimates over time. This results in a time-phased estimate for cost, allowing an organization to predict cash flow needs. The difference between cost estimates and cost budgeting is that cost estimates show costs by category, whereas a cost budget shows costs across time.

Consider the Inputs to Cost Budgeting

Because cost budgeting and cost estimating are so closely related, you can expect many of the same inputs for both. Here are the inputs to cost budgeting:

- **Cost estimates** These serve as key inputs; they're the predicted cost for the project work.

- **Work breakdown structure** It's a key input to this process, as it is the deliverables of the project—it's what the project is buying.

- **Project schedule** The project schedule is needed to determine when the monies in the budget will be spent. The schedule should reflect the sequenced activities against a projected timeline. This allows management not only to plan financially, but also to compare expected cash inflows against the cash outflows the project will demand.

- **Risk management plan** The risk management plan is considered because of information it provides of the probability of identified risks and their associated costs. In addition, the risks may have an expected risk value that contributes to the contingency reserve for the project.

Developing the Project Budget

The tools and techniques used to create the project cost estimates are also used to create the project budget. Here's a quick reminder of the four components:

- **Analogous budgeting** This is a form of expert judgment that uses a top-down approach to predict costs. It is generally less accurate than other budgeting techniques.

- **Parametric modeling** This approach uses a parametric model to extrapolate what costs will be for a project (for example, cost per hour and cost per unit). It can include variables and points based on conditions.

- **Bottom-up budgeting** This approach is the most reliable, though it also takes the longest to create. It starts at zero and requires each work package to be accounted for.

- **Computerized tools** The same software programs used in estimating can help predict the project budget with some accuracy.

Creating the Cost Baseline

A project's cost baseline shows what is expected to be spent on the project. It's usually shown in an S-curve, as in Figure 7-3. The idea of the cost baseline allows the project manager and management to predict when the project will be spending monies and over what time period. The purpose of the cost baseline is to measure and predict project performance.

Large projects that have multiple deliverables may have multiple cost baselines to illustrate the costs within each phase. Additionally, larger projects may have cost baselines to predict spending plans, cash flows of the project, and overall project performance.

The purpose of a cost baseline is to measure performance, and a baseline will predict the expenses over the life of the project. Any discrepancies early on in the predicted baseline and the actual costs serve as a signal that the project is slipping.

Implementing Cost Control

Cost control focuses on the ability of costs to change and on the ways of allowing or preventing cost change from happening. When a change does occur, the project manager must document the change and the reason why the change has occurred and, if necessary, create a variance report. Cost control is concerned with understanding why the cost variances, both good and bad, have occurred. The "why" behind the variances allows the project manager to make appropriate decisions on future project actions.

Ignoring the project cost variances may cause the project to suffer from budget shortages, additional risks, or scheduling problems. When cost variances happen they must be examined, recorded, and investigated. Cost control allows the project manager to confront the problem, find a solution, and then act accordingly. Specifically, cost control focuses on these activities:

- Controlling causes of change to ensure the changes are actually needed
- Controlling and documenting changes to the cost baseline as they happen

FIGURE 7-3

Cost baselines show predicted project and phase performance.

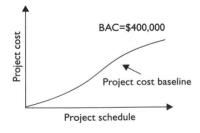

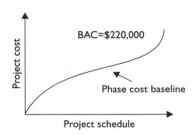

- Controlling changes in the project and their influence on cost
- Performing cost monitoring to recognize and understand cost variances
- Recording appropriate cost changes in the cost baseline
- Preventing unauthorized changes to the cost baseline
- Communicating the cost changes to the proper stakeholders
- Working to bring and maintain costs within an acceptable range

Considering Cost Control Inputs

To implement cost control, the project manager must rely on several documents and processes:

- **Cost baseline** The cost baseline is the expected cost the project will incur. This time-phased budget reflects the amount that will be spent throughout the project. Recall that the cost baseline is a tool used to measure project performance.

- **Performance reports** These reports focus on project cost performance, project scope, and planned performance versus actual performance. The reports may vary according to stakeholder needs. We'll discuss performance reporting in detail in Chapter 10.

- **Change requests** When changes to the project scope are requested, an analysis of the associated costs to complete the proposed change is required. In some instances, such as removing a portion of the project deliverable, a change request may reduce the project cost.

- **Cost management plan** The cost management plan dictates how cost variances will be managed.

Creating a Cost Change Control System

Sometimes a project manager must add, or remove, costs from a project. The Cost Change Control System is part of the Integrated Change Control System and documents the procedures to request, approve, and incorporate changes to project costs.

When a cost change enters the system, there is appropriate paperwork, a tracking system, and procedures the project manager must follow to obtain approval on the proposed change. Figure 7-4 demonstrates a typical workflow for cost change approval. If a change gets approved, the cost baseline is updated to reflect the approved changes. If a request gets denied, the denial must be documented for future potential reference.

FIGURE 7-4

A Cost Change
Control System
tracks and
documents cost
change issues.

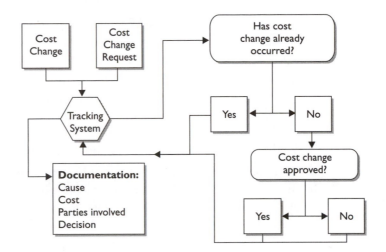

Measuring Project Performance

Earned Value Management (EVM) is the process of measuring performance of project
work against a plan to identify variances. It can also be useful in predicting future
variances and the final costs at completion. It is a system of mathematical formulas
that compares work performed against work planned and measures the actual cost of
the work performed. EVM is an important part of cost control as it allows a project
manager to predict future variances from the expenses to date within the project.

EVM, in regard to cost management, is concerned with the relationships between
three formulas that reflect project performance. Figure 7-5 demonstrates the relation
between these EVM values:

- **Planned Value (PV)**   Planned Value is the work scheduled and the
  authorized budget to accomplish that work. For example, if a project has a
  budget of $100,000 and month six represents 50 percent of the project work,

FIGURE 7-5

Earned value
management
measures project
performance.

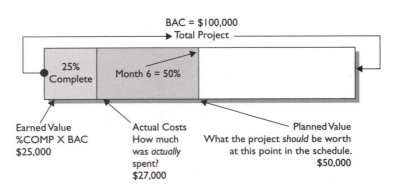

the PV for month six is $50,000. Planned Value used to be known as the Budget Cost of Work Schedule (BCWS), and you may see this term on the PMP Exam.

- **Earned Value (EV)** Earned Value is the physical work completed to date and the authorized budget for that work. For example, if a project has a budget of $100,000 and the work completed to date represents 25 percent of the entire project work, its EV is $25,000. Earned Value used to be known as the Budgeted Cost of Work Performed (BCWP).

- **Actual Cost (AC)** Actual Cost is the actual amount of monies the project has required to date. For example, if a project has a budget of $100,000 and $35,000 has been spent on the project to date, the AC of the project would be $35,000. Actual Cost used to be known as Actual Cost of Work Performed (ACWP).

These three values are key information about the worth of the project to date (EV), the cost of the project work to date (AC), and the planned value of the work to date (PV). These values will be revisited later in this chapter and in Chapter 10.

Additional Planning

Planning is an iterative process. Throughout the project there will be demands for additional planning—and an output of cost control is one of those demands. Consider a project that must complete by a given date and that also has a set budget. The balance between the schedule and the cost must be kept. The project manager can't assign a large crew to complete the project work if the budget won't allow it. The project manager must, through planning, get as creative as possible to figure out an approach to accomplish the project without exceeding the budget.

The balance between cost and schedule is an ongoing battle. While it's usually easier to get more time than money, this isn't always the case. Consider deadlines that can't move, or the company may face fines and penalties, or a deadline that centers on a tradeshow, an expo, or the start of the school year.

Using Computers

It's hard to imagine a project, especially larger projects, moving forward without the use of computers. Project managers can rely on project management software and spreadsheet programs to assist them in calculating actual costs, earned value, and planned value.

It's not hard to create a spreadsheet with the appropriate earned value formulas. Once the spreadsheet has been created, you can save it as a template and use it on multiple projects. If you want, and your software allows it, you can tie in multiple earned value spreadsheets to a master file to track all of your projects at a glance.

Considering the Cost Control Results

Cost control is an ongoing process throughout the project. The project manager must actively monitor the project for variances to costs. Specifically, the project manager always does the following:

- Monitor cost variances and then understand why variances have occurred.
- Update the cost baseline as needed based on approved changes.
- Work with the conditions and stakeholders to prevent unnecessary changes to the cost baseline.
- Communicate to the appropriate stakeholders cost changes as they occur.
- Maintain costs within an acceptable and agreed range.

Revising the Cost Estimates

As the project progresses and more detail comes available, there may be a need to update the cost estimates. A revision to the cost estimates requires communication with the key stakeholders to share why the costs were revised. A revision to the cost estimates may have a ripple effect: other parts of the project may need to be adjusted to account for the changes in cost, the sequence of events may be reordered, and resources may have to be changed. In some instances, the revision of the estimates may be expected, as with phased-gate estimating in a long project.

Updating the Budget

Updating the budget is slightly different than revising a cost estimate. Budget updates allow the cost baseline to be changed. The cost baseline is the "before project snapshot" of what the total project scope and the individual WBS components should cost. Should the project scope grow, as shown here, the cost will also likely change to be able to fulfill the new scope.

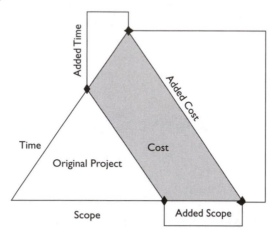

If a project undergoes drastic changes—due to large changes to the project scope, false assumptions, or new demands from the customer—it may be necessary to rebaseline the project cost. Rebaselining is done only in drastic changes, as it essentially resets the project. All historical information up to the rebaseline is cleared, and the project starts fresh.

Applying Corrective Actions

Throughout a project, the project manager will apply corrective actions. Corrective actions are any actions applied to project performance to bring the project back into alignment with the project plan. Corrective actions can be scheduling changes, a shift in resources, a different approach to completing the project work—any action, even nudges or shoves, to bring the project back to its expected level of performance.

Preparing for the Estimate at Completion

The Estimate at Completion (EAC) is a hypothesis of what the total cost of the project will be. Before the project begins, the project manager completes an estimate for the project deliverables based on the WBS. As the project progresses, there will be in most projects some variances between what the cost estimate was and what the actual cost is. The difference between these estimates is the variance for the deliverable.

EAC is part of the Earned Value Management approach. We've talked about Earned Value, Planned Value, and Actual Costs earlier in this chapter. To complete this discussion on EAC, we'll need another formula from the EVM family. We'll discuss the entire EVM process in Chapter 10; for now, the one we're after is the Cost Performance Index (CPI).

Calculating the CPI

CPI is a value that demonstrates how the project costs are performing. CPI is a value that reveals how much money the project is losing. Or, if you're an optimist, how much money the project is making. For example, a project with a CPI of .93 is losing seven cents on the dollar, assuming U.S. dollars. Or, for the optimist, it's making .93 cents on the dollar. The fact of the matter is, a project with this CPI value is likely to be over budget because for every dollar spent seven cents evaporates. This shows the CPI in action:

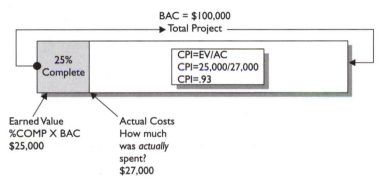

CPI is a value that shows how the project costs are performing to plan. It relates the work you have accomplished to the amount you have spent to accomplish it. A project with a CPI of .93 means you are spending 1.00 for every .93 worth of work accomplished. Therefore, a CPI under 1.00 means the project is performing poorly against the plan. However, a CPI over 1.00 does not necessarily mean that the project is performing well. It could mean that estimates were inflated or that an expenditure for equipment is late or sitting in accounts payable and has not yet been entered into the project accounting cycle.

If you don't want to think of the CPI value as making or losing money, that's fine too. Just know the CPI value should be as close to 1.00 as possible. Oh, and don't celebrate too loudly if the CPI is greater than 1.00. A CPI greater than 1.00 may just reflect poor, bloated estimates, rather than an over-performing project.

Calculating Estimate at Completion

Now that the CPI is known, the project manager can calculate the Estimate at Completion. There are actually a few different ways to calculate the EAC. The project manager should choose the approach that best matches what has been experienced in the project. Figure 7-6 shows all of the EAC formulas in action. The next sections describe the different formulas and the conditions in which to use them.

Experiencing Expected Conditions

If the project is going as planned with little variances, the project manager can use the most basic EAC formula to predict the EAC. Here's the formula for this condition: EAC=Budget at Completion (BAC)/Cost Performance Index (CPI); you can also write this formula as EAC=BAC/CPI.

For example, if the project's BAC is $575,000 and the CPI is .91, the EAC for this project is $631,868. Those nine cents on every dollar sure do add up!

Accounting for Flawed Estimates

Imagine a project to install a new operating system on 1,000 workstations. One of the assumptions the project team made was that each workstation had the correct hardware to install the operating system automatically. As it turns out, this assumption was wrong, and now the project team must change their approach to installing the operating system.

Because the assumption to install the operating system was flawed, a new estimate to complete the project is needed. This new estimate to complete the work is known as the "Estimate to Complete (ETC)." The ETC represents how much more money is needed to complete the project work, and its formula is ETC=EAC-AC.

FIGURE 7-6			
There are many approaches to calculating the EAC.	$EAC = \dfrac{BAC}{CPI}$	$EAC = \dfrac{\$575,000}{.91}$	EAC= $631,868
	EAC=AC+ETC	EAC=$20,000+175,000	EAC=$195,000
	EAC=AC+BAC-EV	EAC=$7,000+24,000-$2,450	EAC=$29,050
	$EAC = \dfrac{AC+(BAC-EV)}{CPI}$	$EAC = \dfrac{\$45,000+(\$250,000-37,500)}{.83}$	EAC+$301,024

In this scenario of a flawed assumption, the project manager will use a slightly different formula to predict the EAC: EAC = AC +ETC. For example, if the project's original BAC was $100,000 and the project team had spent $20,000 before realizing the project assumption was flawed, they'd have to create a new estimate to complete the remaining work. Let's pretend the ETC the project team arrived at was $175,000. The formula EAC=AC+ETC would result in $20,000+$175,000=$195,000. This is because the project had spent $20,000, and $175,000 more is needed to complete the work.

Accounting for Anomalies

Sometimes in a project weird stuff happens. These anomalies, or weird stuff, can cause project costs to skew. For example, consider a project to construct a wooden fence around a property line. One of the project team members makes a mistake while installing the wooden fence and reverses the face of the fencing material. In other words, the material for the outside of the fence faces the wrong direction.

The project now has to invest additional time to remove the fence material, correct the problem, and replace any wood that may have been damaged in the incorrect installation. This anomaly likely won't happen again, but it will add costs to the project.

For these instances, when events happen but the project manager doesn't expect similar events to happen again, this EAC formula should be used: EAC=AC+BAC-EV. Let's try this out with our fencing project. The project's AC so far was $7,000; the BAC was $24,500; the EV is only $2,450, as the project has barely started. The formula would read EAC=$7,000+$24,500-$2,450 and result in an EAC of $29,050— a costly mistake.

Accounting for Permanent Variances

This last EAC formula is used when existing variances in the project are expected to be typical of the remaining variances in the project. For example, a project manager has overestimated the competence of the workers to complete the project work. Because the project team is not performing at the level the project manager had expected, work is completed late and in a faulty manner. Rework has been a common theme for this project.

The EAC formula for these instances is EAC=AC+((BAC-EV)/CPI). In our example, let's say the AC is $45,000; the BAC is $250,000; the EV is $37,5000; and our CPI is calculated to be .83. The EAC formula for this project is EAC= $45,000+(($250,000–$37,500)/.83). The result of the formula (following the order of operations) is $301,024.

Closing Out the Project

Cost control requires accountability for the funds spent. As part of project closeout, phase closeout, or even project cancellation, there must be identified processes and procedures on how to shut down the project. A formal audit may be called for to review the time, costs, materials, and budget of the project. In some instances, a review may happen with management or the Project Sponsor to account for the project budget and how well cost control was managed within the project.

Updating Lessons Learned

As part of Cost Control, the project manager should update the Lessons Learned document to reflect the decisions behind the actions taken. For example, the project manager should identify:

- Changes to cost baseline and why they were approved
- Corrective actions and why they were implemented
- Cost control challenges and issues and how they were resolved
- Other cost control information that may be beneficial for other projects

CERTIFICATION SUMMARY

There are several contributing factors to cost on any project: the expense of the labor to complete the project, the expense of materials needed to complete the project, and the expense of the equipment needed to complete a project. These expenses must be estimated, planned for, and monitored for a project to finish on budget.

Management and customers will want to know how much a project is going to cost so they can determine if the project is worth doing, if the project deliverable will be worth the cost, and if the project will be profitable. The estimates for project costs can come in several forms:

- **Analogous estimating** Uses similar historical information to predict the cost of the current project.
- **Parametric modeling** Uses a parameter, such as cost per metric ton, to predict project costs.
- **Bottom-up estimating** Starts from zero and adds the expenses from bottom-up.
- **Top-down estimating** Uses a similar project as a cost baseline and factors in current project conditions to predict costs.

The resources needed to complete a project may be one of the biggest expenses in the project's budget. The activities the resources complete must be worthy of the resource's time. In other words, the project manager does not want to assign a $125 per hour engineer to filing activity that a $15 per hour administrative assistant is qualified to do. Accurate assignment of project resources to project activities helps prevent waste.

Projects also have four different kinds of cost:

- **Direct costs** These are costs that attributed directly to the project and cannot be shared with operations or other projects.
- **Variable costs** Costs that vary depending on the conditions within the project.
- **Fixed costs** Costs that remain the same throughout the project.
- **Indirect costs** These costs can be shared across multiple projects that use the same resources—such as training room or piece of equipment.

There is one last cost, called opportunity cost. This is a special cost because it really doesn't cost the organization anything out of pocket, but rather the cost of a lost opportunity. Opportunity costs are an expense companies that complete projects for other organizations realize. When an organization that completes projects for others must forgo one project in order to complete the other, the value of the forgone project is the opportunity cost. For example, a company has two projects it can complete but it must choose only one of them. Project A is worth $75,000 and Project B is worth $50,000. If the company chooses Project A the opportunity cost is $50,000 because the company misses out on the opportunity.

KEY TERMS

If you're serious about passing the PMP exams, memorize these terms and their definitions. For maximum value, create your own flashcards based on these definitions and review daily.

Actual costs	Cost control	Estimating publications
Analogous estimating	Cost estimating	Parametric modeling
Bottom up estimating	Cost management plan	Planned value
Budget at completion	Cost Performance Index	Risk
Chart of accounts	Earned value	Top-down estimating
Cost baseline	Earned value management	Variance
Cost budgeting	Estimate at completion	
Cost change control	Estimate to complete	

TWO-MINUTE DRILL

Resources and the Project Work

❑ The project manager must know what resources are needed to complete the project work. How will the project ever be completed without the resources? The project manager must know the people, the equipment, materials, and other resources needed to make the vision of the project a reality.

❑ The resources also must be known so the project manager may predict, monitor, and control what the project costs are expected to be. The relation between the project vision and the needed resources can help the project manager work within the predicted costs.

❑ Resources to complete a project also include services, leases, real estate, and other components that contribute to the project work being completed.

Creating Project Estimates

❑ The identified resource requirements and the WBS are two key tools to identify what resources are needed for what component of the project. The cost of the resources help the project manager calculate the estimated costs based on the duration of the project activities or the amount of materials applied to the project.

❑ Analogous estimating uses a similar project to predict what the costs of the current project should be. It is less accurate, but easier and faster to complete than other methods.

❑ Bottom-up estimating starts with zero, and each component of the WBS is accounted for to reach a grand total of the project. It is the most accurate method, but it takes longer to complete.

❑ Parametric estimating uses a parameter for units of goods and time to calculate what the project will cost. For example, cost per hour, cost per metric ton, or cost per cubic yard.

Management Project Costs

❑ The cost management plan documents how the project manager will react to cost variances within the project. The performing organization will likely have policies and procedures on unacceptable variances.

❑ Variances that cross a given threshold may require the project manager to create a variance report to explain the variance, why it has happened, and what corrective action has been applied to prevent the variance from recurring.

❑ Cost control is the process of monitoring and documenting cost changes, whether they are allowed to occur or prevented from occurring. The project manager studies the cost changes to understand why the change has happened and then makes corrective actions to the project if needed.

Applying Earned Value Management

Earned value management is a method to measure project performance. The formulas we covered in this chapter are

❑ BAC=Our predicted budget at completion

❑ EV=%Complete X BAC

❑ PV= What the project should be worth at this point in the schedule

❑ AC=The actual costs of the project work to date

❑ CPI=EV/AC

❑ EAC=BAC/CPI

❑ ETC=EAC–AC

INSIDE THE EXAM

The PMP examination requires the exam candidate to know how to estimate, budget, and manage costs. The WBS is an input to estimating costs, as it reflects the whole of the project. When creating the estimates, rely on documented historical information over team members' recollections. There are three estimating approaches:

- **Analogous** A top-down approach that is less costly and less accurate than others and provides just an idea of what the project will cost.

- **Bottom-up** Starts with zero and adds up all the expenses. This is more costly and takes longer, but gains team buy-in to the project.

- **Parametric modeling** Uses a parameter for labor and goods to calculate the cost of the project.

The accuracy of the estimates is based on available information. As the project manager and the project team progressively elaborate the project plan, more details become available. The more details a project has, the more accurate the estimate. Know these facts on estimating:

- **Rough order of magnitude** The accuracy of the estimate is –25 percent to +75 percent and is used in the initiation process and in top-down estimating.

- **Budget estimate** The accuracy of the estimate is –10 percent to +25 percent. This is used early in the planning process and also in top-down estimating.

- **Definitive estimate** The accuracy of the estimate is –5 percent to +10 percent. This is used late in the planning process and in bottom-up estimating.

The resources on a project can include people, materials, and equipment. If the people on a project do not have the necessary skill set to complete the work, either hire an SME to guide the project implementation, outsource the project work, or train the current people for the needed skills.

Earned value management is a tool to measure project performance. Earned value is the budget at completion multiplied by the percentage of the project work that has been completed. The Cost Performance Index shows how well the project is performing financially. It is calculated by dividing EV by the actual costs spent on the project. Use the most common formula for finding the estimate at completion, EAC=BAC/CPI.

SELF TEST

1. Which one of the following best describes analogous estimating?
   A. Regression analysis
   B. Bottom-up estimating
   C. Less accurate
   D. More accurate

2. You are the project manager for GHG Project. You are about to create the cost estimates for the project. Which input to this process will help you the most?
   A. Parametric modeling
   B. WBS
   C. Project scope
   D. Requirements document

3. You are the project manager for the JKH Project. You have elected to use parametric modeling in your cost estimating for the project. Which one of the following is an example of parametric modeling?
   A. $750 per ton
   B. Historical information from a similar project
   C. Estimates built bottom-up based on the WBS
   D. Estimates based on top-down budgeting

4. You are the project manager for a new technology implementation project. Management has requested that your estimates be as exact as possible. Which one of the following methods of estimating will provide the most accurate estimate?
   A. Top-down estimating
   B. Top-down budgeting
   C. Bottom-up estimating
   D. Parametric modeling

5. Your company has been hired to install the tile in 1,000 hotel rooms. All rooms will be identical in nature and will require the same amount of materials. You calculate the time to install the tile in each hotel room as six hours. The cost for labor for each room is calculated at $700. Your Project Sponsor disagrees with your labor estimate. Why?

   A. You haven't completed one hotel room yet so you don't know how long the work will actually take.

   B. You have not factored in all of the effort applied to the work.

   C. You have not considered the law of diminishing returns.

   D. You have not considered the learning curve.

6. You are the project manager for a construction project to build 17 cabins. All of the cabins will be identical in nature. The contract for the project is set at a fixed cost, the incentive being the faster the project work is completed, the more the profitable the job. Management has requested that you study the work method to determine a faster, less costly, and better method to complete the project. This is an example of which one of the following?

   A. Time constraint

   B. Schedule constraint

   C. Value analysis

   D. Learning curve

7. You are the project manager for a technical implementation project. The customer has requested that you factor in the after-the-project costs, such as maintenance and service. This is an example of which one of the following?

   A. Life cycle costs

   B. Scope creep

   C. Project spin off

   D. Operations

8. Which one of the following provides the least accurate in estimating?

   A. Rough order of magnitude

   B. Budget estimate

   C. Definitive estimate

   D. WBS estimate

9. Which one of the following is true?

   A. The cost management plan controls how change management affects the BAC.

   B. The cost management plan controls how cost variances will be managed.

   C. The cost management plan controls how the project manager may update the cost estimates.

   D. The cost management plan controls how the BAC may be adjusted.

10. You have just started a project for a manufacturer. Project team members report they are 30 percent done with the project. You agree with their completion status but do not change any of the progress in your report to the customer. This is an example of which one of the following?

   A. 50/50 rule

   B. 0/100 rule

   C. Percent Complete Rule

   D. Poor project management

11. You and your project team are about to enter a meeting to determine project costs. You have elected to use bottom-up estimating and will base your estimates on the WBS. Which one of the following is not an attribute of bottom-up estimating?

   A. People doing the work create the estimates.

   B. Creates a more accurate estimate.

   C. More expensive to do than other methods.

   D. Less expensive to do than other methods.

12. What is the present value if the organization expects to make $100,000 four years from now and the annual interest rate is six percent?

   A. $100,000

   B. $58,000

   C. $25,000

   D. Zero

13. You are the project manager for the construction of a new hotel. Before you begin the cost budgeting process, what is needed?

   A. Costs estimates and project schedule

   B. Cost estimates and supporting detail

   C. EAC and BAC

   D. Parametric model used to arrive at the costs submitted

14. You are the project manager of the MNJ Project. Your project is falling behind schedule and you have already spent $130,000 of your $150,000 budget. What do you call the $130,000?

   A. Planned value

   B. Present value

   C. Sunk costs

   D. Capital expenditure

15. You are the project manager of the JHD Project. Your project will cost your organization $250,000 to complete over the next eight months. Once the project is completed, the deliverables will begin earning the company $3,500 per month. The time to recover the costs of the project is which one of the following?

    A. Not enough information to know
    B. Eight months
    C. 72 months
    D. 5 years

16. You are the project manager for the consulting company. Your company has two possible projects to manage, but they can only choose one. Project KJH is worth $17,000, while Project ADS is worth $22,000. Management elects to choose Project ADS. The opportunity cost of this choice is which one of the following?

    A. $5,000
    B. $17,000
    C. $22,000
    D. Zero, as project ADS is worth more than Project KJH

17. You are the project manager for the CSR Training Project, and 21,000 customer service reps are invited to attend the training session. Attendance is optional. You have calculated the costs of the training facility, but the workbook expense depends on how many students register to the class. For every 5,000 workbooks created the cost is reduced a percentage of the original printing cost. The workbook expense is an example of which one of the following?

    A. Fixed costs
    B. Parametric costs
    C. Variable costs
    D. Indirect costs

18. You are the project manager of a construction project scheduled to last 24 months. You have elected to rent a piece of equipment for the duration of a project, even though you will need the equipment only periodically throughout the project. The costs of the equipment rental per month are $890. This is an example of _____.

    A. Fixed costs
    B. Parametric costs
    C. Variable costs
    D. Indirect costs

19. You are the project manager for the Hardware Inventory Project. You have a piece of equipment that was purchased recently for $10,000 and is expected to last five years in production. At the end of the five years the expected worth of the equipment is $1,000. Using straight-line deprecation, what is the amount that can be written off each year?

A. Zero

B. $1,000

C. $1,800

D. $2,000

20. You are the project manager of the LKG Project. The project has a budget of $290,000 and is expected to last three years. The project is now ten percent complete and is on schedule. What is the BAC?

A. $29,000

B. $290,000

C. $96,666

D. $9,666

21. Your project has a budget of $130,000 and is expected to last ten months, with the work and budget spread evenly across all months. The project is now in month three, the work is on schedule, but you have spent $65,000 of the project budget. What is your variance?

A. $65,000

B. $39,000

C. $26,000

D. $64,999

22. You are the project manager of the Carpet Installation Project for a new building. Your BAC is $600,000. You are now 40 percent done with the project, though your plan called for you to be 45 percent done with the work at this time. What is your earned value?

A. $240,000

B. $270,000

C. $30,000

D. –$30,000

23. You are the project manager of the Carpet Installation Project for a new building. Your BAC is $600,000. You have spent $270,000 of your budget. You are now 40 percent done with the project, though your plan called for you to be 45 percent done with the work at this time. What is your CPI?

    A. 100

    B. 89

    C. .89

    D. .79

24. You are the project manager for the Facility Installation Project. The project calls for 1500 units to be installed into a new baseball stadium. Your team wants to know why you have not assigned the same amount of time for the last 800 units as you had for the first five hundred units. You tell them it is because of the learning curve. Which one of the following best describes this theory?

    A. Production increases as workers become more efficient with the installation procedure.

    B. Efficiency increases as workers become more familiar with the installation procedure.

    C. Costs decrease as workers complete more of the installation procedure.

    D. Time decreases as workers complete more of the installation procedure in the final phases of a project.

25. Of the following, which one is the most reliable source of information for estimating project costs?

    A. Historical information from a recently completed project

    B. An SME's opinion

    C. Recollections of team members that have worked on similar projects

    D. Vendor's white papers

SELF TEST ANSWERS

I. ☑ **C.** Analogous estimating is less accurate than other estimating methods.
☒ **A** is incorrect, as regression analysis is a type of parametric modeling. **B** is incorrect, as bottom-up estimating starts with zero and adds up the project costs. **D** is incorrect, as analogous estimating is not more accurate.

2. ☑ **B.** The WBS is the input that can help you the most with the cost estimates.
☒ **A** is incorrect, as parametric modeling is a form of estimating, not an input. **C** is incorrect, as the project scope is not an input to the estimating process. **D** is incorrect, as the requirements document is also not an input to the estimating process.

3. ☑ **A** is correct; $750 per ton is an example of parametric modeling.
☒ **B** is incorrect, as historical information is analogous, not parametric. **C** and **D** are incorrect, as these do not describe parametric modeling.

4. ☑ **C.** Bottom-up estimating provides the most accurate estimates. The project manager starts at zero, the bottom, and accounts for each cost within the project.
☒ **A, B,** and **D** are all incorrect as they do not reflect the most accurate method to create an estimate.

5. ☑ **D** is the best choice. As the project team completes more and more units, the time to complete a hotel room should take less and less time.
☒ Choices **A, B,** and **C** are incorrect as they do not answer the question as fully as answer **D.**

6. ☑ **C.** Value analysis is a systematic approach to find less costly ways to complete the same work.
☒ **A** and **B** are not correct, as this situation does not describe a specific time or cost constraint. **D** is incorrect, as the learning curve happens as the project team completes the work. Value analysis is a study of a process to complete the work faster and more affordably.

7. ☑ **A.** The after-project costs are known as the life cycle costs.
☒ Choices **B** and **C** are incorrect, though tempting, because they do not describe the process of calculating the ongoing expenses of the product the project is creating. **D** is incorrect; operations do not fully describe the expenses unique to the product.

8. ☑ **A.** The rough order of magnitude is the least accurate approach, as it may vary from –25 percent to +75 percent.
☒ Choices **B** and **C** are more accurate estimates than the rough order of magnitude. Choice **D** is not a valid answer for this question.

9. ☑ **B.** The cost management plan controls how cost variances will be managed.
☒ Choices **A, C,** and **D** are incorrect descriptions of the cost management plan.

10. ☑ **B.** This is an example of the 0/100 rule. This completion method allows for zero percent credit on an activity until it is 100 percent complete.

☒ Choice **A** allows for 50 percent completion when the work begins and 50 percent when the work is completed. Choices **C** and **D** are incorrect responses, as they do not describe the scenario.

11. ☑ **D.** Using bottom-up estimating is not less expensive to do.

☒ **A, B,** and **C** are not correct choices, as these are attributes of a bottom-up estimating process.

12. ☑ **B.** The present value of $100,000 four years from now can be calculated through this formula: Present Value = $FV/(1+R)^n$. FV is the future value, R is the interest rate, and n is the number of time periods.

☒ Choices **A, C,** and **D** are all incorrect answers, as they do not reflect the present value.

13. ☑ **A.** Cost estimates and the project schedule are inputs to the cost budgeting process.

☒ Choices **B, C,** and **D** are all incorrect as they are not inputs to cost budgeting.

14. ☑ **C.** Sunk costs are monies that have been spent.

☒ **A** is incorrect, as planned value is the amount the project should be worth at this point in the schedule. **B** is incorrect; present value is the current value of future monies. **D** is incorrect; a capital expenditure is money spent to purchase a long-term asset, such as a building.

15. ☑ **C.** The time to recoup the monies from the project is 72 months. This is calculated by dividing the ROI of $3,500 per month into the project cost.

☒ **A** is an incorrect answer. **B** is incorrect; eight months is the amount of time left in the project schedule. **D,** five years, is also incorrect.

16. ☑ **B.** The opportunity cost is the amount of the project that was not chosen.

☒ **A** is incorrect; $5,000 is the difference between the two projects, it is not the opportunity cost. **C** is incorrect, as $22,000 is the amount of the project that was selected. **D** is an incorrect answer.

17. ☑ **C.** This is an example of variable costs. The more students that register to take the class the more the cost of the books will be.

☒ **A** is incorrect, as the cost of the book varies depending on the number of students that register for the class. **B** is incorrect, as the cost of each book diminishes as more books are created. A parametric cost would remain the same regardless of how many books were created. **D** is not correct, as this is not an example of an indirect cost.

18. ☑ **A.** This is a fixed cost expense of $890 per month—regardless of how often the piece of equipment is used.
☒ **B** is incorrect, as a parametric cost is a value used to calculate cost per use, cost per metric ton, or cost per unit. While it may appear **B** is a correct choice, there is no historical information mentioned to base the parametric model on. **C** is incorrect, as the cost does not vary within the project. **D** is also incorrect; this is a cost attributed directly to the project work.

19. ☑ **C.** The straight-line depreciation takes the purchase value of the item, minus the salvage price of the item, divided by the number of time periods. In this instance, it would be $10,000 minus $1,000, or $9,000. The $9,000 is divided by five years and equates to $1,800 per year.
☒ **A, C,** and **D** are all incorrect, as they do not reflect the correct calculation.

20. ☑ **B.** The BAC is the budget at completion, which is $290,000.
☒ **A** is incorrect, as it describes the earned value for the project. **C** and **D** are both incorrect values.

21. ☑ **C.** $26,000 is the variance. This is calculated by subtracting the actual costs of $65,000 from the earned value of $39,000. EV is calculated by taking the 30 percent completion of the project against the BAC. The project is considered to be 30 percent complete because it's slated for ten months, is currently in month three, and is on schedule.
☒ **A, B,** and **D** are all incorrect calculations for the problem.

22. ☑ **A.** The earned value is calculated by multiplying the percentage of completion, 40 percent, by the BAC, which is $600,000, for a value of $240,000.
☒ **B, C,** and **D** are incorrect calculations of the earned value formula.

23. ☑ **C** is the correct answer. The EV of $240,000 is divided by the AC of $270,000 for a value of .89.
☒ **A** and **D** are incorrect calculations. **B** is incorrect, as the value needs a decimal.

24. ☑ **B.** The learning curve allows the cost to decrease as a result of decreased installation time as workers complete more of the installation procedure.
☒ Choices **A, C,** and **D** are all incorrect choices, as they do not correctly describe the learning curve in relation to time and cost.

25. ☑ **A.** Of the choices presented, historical information from a recently completed project is the most reliable source of information.
☒ **B,** while valuable, is not as proven as historical information. **C** is incorrect, as recollections are the least reliable source of information. **D** is also incorrect, though it may prove valuable in the planning process.

8

Introducing Project Quality Management

W hat is quality? Quality is the "totality of characteristics of an entity that bear on its ability to satisfy stated or implied needs." Every project has an anticipated level of quality for the project deliverables. Project quality management is the process to ensure that the project fulfills its obligations to satisfy the project needs. As projects vary, so too will the anticipated level of quality.

Picture this: it's late on a hot summer night and you're hungry. You pull up a gravel road and see a diner with a neon "open" sign. The sign, you notice, really says "Ope" since the "n" is burned out. Inside the diner, stale smoke drifts around like fog. Grease, onions, and garlic seep into your clothes. You opt for a booth only to find the table smeared with catsup, a little gravy, and, guessing by the stickiness, a glob of maple syrup.

Now picture this: You step off the elevator on the 43rd floor. A maitre d' welcomes you and guides you to a table next to a window offering a sweeping view of the city. A piano player massages a song into the evening. The waiter snaps open a napkin and drapes it across your lap. Another waiter pours you a glass of cold, crisp water and presents the menu. By the soft candlelight, everything looks, and feels, grand.

With these two contrasting scenarios, which one do you think will have better quality? Or can they both have an acceptable level of quality? For the first scenario— the diner—you expect a certain level of quality when it comes to service, food, and atmosphere. With the second scenario—the fancy restaurant—you also have an expected level of quality regarding service, food, and atmosphere. Both experiences are measured by that expected level of quality.

In the diner, you might get one of the best bacon cheeseburger/milkshake combos you can find late at night in the middle of nowhere. Just what you'd expect from this kind of place. And the fancy downtown restaurant? A fancy meal cooked to perfection— also what you'd expect. The difference between the two restaurants is grade. The expected level of service, food, and atmosphere is the quality of the experience.

The Big Quality Picture

Before we hop into the three different facets of project quality management, let's establish a few "PMI-isms" on quality. Because quality means so many different things to so many different people, it's important to confirm we're working with a common understanding of what quality is and what quality management hopes to accomplish— from PMI's point of view.

Accepting the Quality Management Approach

The details and specifications set out by the customer determine what the expected level of quality is. Project quality management, as far as your exam goes, is compatible with ISO 9000 and ISO 10000 quality standards and guidelines.

Project quality management also is concerned with the management of the project and the product of the project. It's easy to focus on the product (the thing or service the project creates), but project managers must also provide quality for the project management activities. Aspects of the downside of focusing too much on the product include:

■ Overworking the project team in order to complete the project. This may result in unacceptable work, decline in team morale, and the slow, steady destruction of the project team's willingness to work.

■ A hurry to complete the project work by speeding through quality inspections. This can result in unacceptable deliverables

Quality vs. Grade

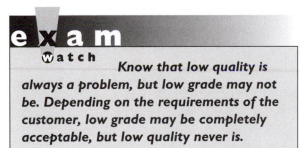

Know that low quality is always a problem, but low grade may not be. Depending on the requirements of the customer, low grade may be completely acceptable, but low quality never is.

Quality and grade are not the same.

Quality is the sum of the characteristics of a product that allow it to meet the demands or expectations of the project. Grade, according to the PMBOK, "is a category or rank given to entities having the same functional use but different technical characteristics." For example, there are different grades of paint, different grades of metal, and even different grades of travel.

Implementing Quality Project Management

Quality management and project management have similar characteristics:

■ **Customer satisfaction** The project must satisfy the customer requirements by delivering what it promised in order to satisfy the needs of the customer. The PMBOK puts it as "conformance to requirements" and "fitness for use."

■ **Prevention** Quality is planned into a project, not inspected in. It is always more cost-effective to prevent mistakes than to correct them.

- **Management responsibility** The project team must work towards the quality goal, but management must provide the needed resources to deliver on the quality promises.

- **Plan-do-check-act** Deming, arguably the world's leader in quality management theory thanks to his management methods implemented in Japan after World War II, set the bar with his "plan-do-check-act" approach to quality management. This approach is similar to the project management processes every project passes through.

- **Kaizen technology** Kaizen is a quality management philosophy of applying continuous small improvements to reduce costs and ensure consistency or project performance.

- **Marginal analysis** Marginal analysis studies the cost of the incremental improvements to a process or product and compares it against the increase in revenue made from the improvements. For example, the price of the added feature may cost the company $7.50 per unit, but the amount of gained sales per year because of the improvement will meet or exceed the cost of the improvement.

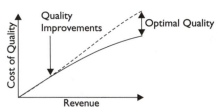

Preparing for Quality

Before a project manager can plan for quality, he must know what the quality expectations are. Specifically, what are the quality standards of the performing organization and which quality standards are applicable to the project? As part of the planning processes, the project manager and the project team must identify the requirements of planning, determine how the requirements may be met, and identify the costs and time demands to meet the identified requirements.

One of the key principles of project quality management is that quality is planned in, not inspected in. Planning for quality is more cost-effective than inspecting work results and doing the work over, or correcting problems to adhere to quality demands.

The project manager must consider the cost of achieving the expected level of quality in contrast to the cost of nonconformance. The cost of quality includes training, safety measures, and action to prevent poor quality. The cost of nonconformance can far outweigh the cost of quality: loss of customers, rework, lost time, lost materials, and danger to workers.

Determining the Quality Policy

Top management should define the quality policy. The quality policy of the organization may follow a formal approach such as ISO 9000, Six Sigma, or Total Quality Management (TQM), or it may have its own direction and approach to satisfying the demand for quality.

The project team should adapt the quality policy of the organization to guide the project implementation. This ensures the management of the project and the deliverables of the project are in alignment with the performing organization's quality policy. In addition, the project manager should document how the project will fulfill the quality policy in both management and in the project deliverable.

But what if the performing organization doesn't have a quality policy? Or what if two different entities are working together on a project and they use differing quality policies? In these circumstances, the project management team should create the quality policy. The quality policy, in these instances, will accomplish the same goals as a company's quality policy: to define quality requirements and determine how to adhere to them.

Regardless of where the quality policy comes from—management or the project team—the project stakeholders must be aware of the quality policy. This is important because the quality policy, and associated quality methodology, may require actions that could lengthen the project schedule. For example, quality audits, peer reviews, and other quality-centric activities. In addition to the required time to fulfill the quality requirements, there may be additional costs incurred.

Reviewing the Project Scope Statement

Just as project quality management is focused on fulfilling the needs of the project, the scope statement is a key input to the quality planning process. Recall that the scope statement defines what will and will not be delivered as part of the project, as well as objectives regarding cost, schedule, and scope. The deliverables, and the expectations of the customers, will help guide the quality planning session to ensure the customer requirements in regard to quality are met.

Reviewing the Product Description

While the project scope will define the initial product description, the product description may have supporting detail that the project manager and project team will need to review.

Consider a project to create an apartment building. The requirements, specifications, and details of the building will need to be evaluated and reviewed since this information will, no doubt, affect the quality planning.

Reviewing the Standards and Regulations

The standards and regulations of each industry will need to be reviewed to determine that both the project plan and the plan for quality are acceptable. For example, a project to wire a building for electricity will have certain regulations it must adhere to. The relevance of the regulations must be planned into the project to conform to the requirements.

Reviewing Other Process Outputs

The project manager will need more than just the scope statement and the product description to plan for quality. The outputs of other processes will need to be evaluated for quality considerations. For example, procurement, which we'll discuss in Chapter 12, may have special needs for contractors. The organization purchases products and services from vendors. If the vendors' level of quality is unacceptable, the project can suffer, get off schedule, or result in failure.

Planning for Quality

Once the project manager has assembled the needed inputs, and evaluated the product description and project scope, he can get to work creating a plan on how to satisfy the quality demands. He'll need to rely on the documentation created to date, his project team, and the project's key stakeholder for much of the input. In addition, the project manager will use several different techniques to plan on meeting quality.

As planning is an iterative process, so too is quality planning. As events happen within the project, the project manager should evaluate the events and then apply corrective actions. This is a common PMI theme: plan, implement, measure, react—and document! Throughout the project implementation, things will go awry, team members may complete less-than-acceptable work, stakeholders will demand changes, and so on; all of these variables must be evaluated for their impact on project quality. What good is a project if it's "completed" on time, but the quality of the deliverable is unacceptable? Technically, if the product is unacceptable, the project is not finished since it failed to meet the project scope. Let's look at some tools and techniques the project manager will use to plan for quality.

Using a Benefit/Cost Analysis

Benefits should outweigh costs.

A benefit/cost analysis is a process of determining the pros and cons of any process, product, or activity. The straightforward approach, when it comes to project management, is concerned with the benefits of quality management activities versus the costs of the quality management activities. There are two major considerations with the benefit/cost analysis in quality management:

- **Benefit**   Completing quality work increases productivity because shoddy work does not have to be redone. When work is completed correctly the first time, as expected, the project does not have to spend additional funds to redo the work.

- **Costs**   Completing quality work may cost more monies than the work is worth. To deliver a level of quality beyond what is demanded costs the project additional funds. The types of quality management activities that guarantee quality may not be needed for every project.

- **Gold plating**   The customer does not need or want more than what was requested. Gold plating is the process of adding extra features that may drive up costs and alter schedules. The project team should strive to deliver what was expected.

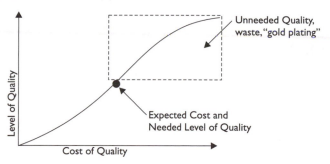

While quality is needed on every project, not every project has the same quality expenses based on the demands. For example, consider a project to create a temporary drainage ditch for a field. There are specifications for the ditch, but the project may not require the expense of a landscape architect to evaluate the slant and descent of the temporary ditch.

Another project, to create and secure an information technology department, may require the expense of a security consulting firm to evaluate, test, and certify the security of the software code, the network servers, and the physical security of the department. The cost of the quality requirements is in alignment with the demands of the project.

Applying Benchmarking Practices

Benchmarking, when it comes to quality project management, is all about comparing this project to another. Benchmarking is a technique to take what the project manager has planned or experienced regarding quality and compare it to another project to see how things measure up. The current project can be measured against any other project—not just projects within the performing organization or within the same industry.

The goal of benchmarking is to evaluate the differences between the two projects and then to make corrective actions to the current project. For example, Project A may have better quality performance than Project B. When the project manager compares the two projects, he'll want to find out what the differences are between them. He'll look for what's missing in Project B, or what activities the folks in Project A are doing that he's not.

Benchmarking allows the project manager and the project team to see what's possible and then strive toward that goal. Benchmarking can also be used as a measurement against industry standards, competitors' pricing, or competitors' level of performance.

on the
job

Benchmarking, if used improperly, can create some false goals and internal competition. If the projects that are being compared to each other are active, truth in reporting is mandatory; otherwise, the results of the benchmarking will be skewed. Ideally, benchmarking is compared against similar, completed projects early in the quality planning, rather than late in the process.

Creating a Flow Chart

Technically, a flow chart is any diagram illustrating how components within a system are related. An organizational flow chart shows the bottom crew of operations up to the "little squirt" on top. A HVAC blueprint shows how the air flows through a building from the furnace to each room. Flow charts show the relation between components, as well as help the project team determine where quality issues may be present and, once done, plan accordingly.

There are two types of flow charts you'll need to be concerned with for this exam:

■ **Cause-and-effect diagrams**   These diagrams show the relation between the variables within a process and how those relations may contribute to inadequate quality. This diagram can help organize both the process and team opinions, as well as generate discussion on finding a solution to ensure quality. Figure 8-1 is an example of a cause-and-effect diagram. These diagrams are also known as Ishikawa diagrams and fishbone diagrams.

FIGURE 8-1

Cause-and-effect
diagrams show
the relation of
variables to the
quality problem.

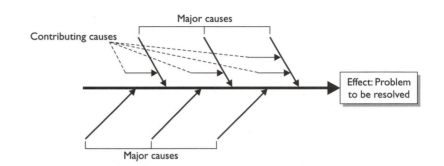

*A cause-and-effect diagram
is also called an Ishikawa diagram. Same
thing; fancier name.*

■ **System or process flow charts** These flow
charts illustrate the flow of a process through
a system, such as a project change request
through the change control system, or work
authorization through a quality control
process. A process flow chart does not have
to be limited to the project management
activities; a process flow chart could
demonstrate how a manufacturer creates, packages, and ships the product
to the customer as seen in Figure 8-2.

Design of Experiments

The design of experiments approach relies on statistical what-if scenarios to determine
what variables within a project will result in the best outcome. Design of experiments

FIGURE 8-2

Process flow
charts illustrate
how a system
process unfolds.

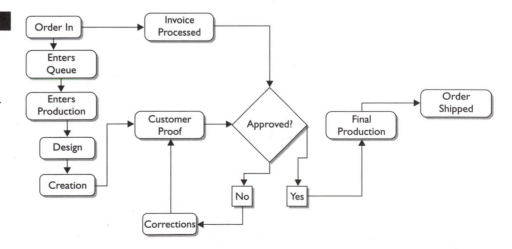

approach is most often used on the product of the project, rather than the project itself. For example, a project team creating a new bicycle may experiment with the width of the tires, the weight of the frame, and the position of the handlebars in relation to the bike seat to determine the most comfortable ride at an acceptable cost to the consumer.

Although design of experiments is most associated with product design, it can be applied to project management activities. For example, a project manager may evaluate the activities within a project and determine the time and cost of activities depending on which employees are assigned to complete the work. A more experienced worker may cost the project more money on an hourly basis, but this individual is expected to complete the work in a third of the time a less experienced worker would. This is design of experiments: experimenting with different variables to find the best solution at the best cost.

Design of experiments is also used as a method to identify which variables within a project, or product, are causing failures or unacceptable results. The goal of design of experiments is to isolate the root cause of an effect and then make adjustments to that cause to eliminate the unacceptable results.

Considering the Cost of Quality

The cost of quality considers the expense of all the activities within a project to ensure quality. The cost of quality is broken into two major categories:

- **Cost of conformance to requirements** This approach is the cost of completing the project work to satisfy the project scope and the expected level of quality. Examples of this cost include training, safety measures, and quality management activities to ensure that quality is met.

- **Cost of nonconformance** This approach is the cost of completing the project work without quality. The biggest issue here is the money lost by having to redo the project work; it's always more cost effective to do the work right the first time. Other nonconformance costs include loss of sales, loss of customers, downtime, and corrective actions to fix problems caused by incorrect work.

Implementing the Quality Policy

The end result of the quality planning is to find a method to implement the quality policy. Because planning is iterative, the quality planning sessions may need, often do require, several revisits to the quality planning processes. On longer projects, there may be scheduled quality planning sessions to compare the performance of the project in relation to the quality that was planned.

Creating the Quality Management Plan

One of the major outputs of quality planning is the quality management plan. This document describes how the project manager and the project team will fulfill the quality policy. In an ISO 9000 environment, the quality management plan is referred to as the "project quality system."

The quality management plan addresses three things about the project and the project work:

ISO 9000 is an international standard that helps organizations follow their own quality procedures. ISO 9000 is not a quality system, but a method of following procedures created internally to an organization.

- **Quality control** Work results are monitored to see if they meet relevant quality standards. If the results do not meet the quality standards, the project manager applies root cause analysis to determine the cause of the poor performance and then eliminates the cause. Quality control is inspection orientated.

- **Quality assurance** The overall performance is evaluated to ensure the project meets the relevant quality standards. Quality assurance maps to an organization's quality policy and is typically a managerial process. Quality assurance is generally considered the work of applying the quality plan.

- **Quality improvement** The project performance is measured and evaluated, and corrective actions are applied to improve the product and the project. The improvements can be large or small depending on the condition and the quality philosophy of the performing organization.

Identifying the Operational Definitions

Operational definitions, also known as metrics, are the quantifiable terms and values to measure a process, activity, or work result. An example of an operational definition could be an expected value for the required torque to tighten a bolt on a piece of equipment. By testing and measuring the torque, the operational definition would prove or disprove the quality of the product. Other examples can include hours of labor to complete a work package, required safety measures, cost per unit, and so on.

Operational definitions are clear, concise measurements. Designating that 95 percent of all customer service calls should be answered by a live person within 30 seconds is a metric. A statement that all calls should be answered in a timely manner is not.

Applying Checklists

Checklists are simple approaches to ensure work is completed according to the quality policy. It's usually a list of activities that workers will check off to ensure each task has been completed. Checklists can be quick instructions of what needs to be done to clean a piece of equipment, or questions that remind the employee to complete a task: "Did you turn off the printer before opening the cover?"

Creating Quality Assurance

Quality assurance (QA) is the sum of the planning and the implementations of the plans the project manager, the project team, and management does to ensure the project meets the demands of quality. QA is not something that is done only at the end of the project, but before and during the project.

In some organizations, the Quality Assurance department or another entity will complete the QA activities. QA is interested in finding the defects and then fixing the problems. There are many different approaches to QA, depending on the quality system the organization or project team has adapted. There are two types of QA:

- **Internal QA**   Assurance provided to management and the project team
- **External QA**   Assurance provide to the external customers of the project

Preparing for Quality Assurance

There are three inputs the project manager and the project team will need to prepare for QA:

- **The quality management plan**   This plan defines how the project team will implement and fulfill the quality policy of the performing organization.
- **Results of quality control measurements**   Quality control tests will provide these measurements. The values must be quantifiable so results may be measured, compared, and analyzed. In other words, "pretty close to on track" is not adequate; "95 percent pass rate" is more acceptable.

■ **Operational definitions** The metrics that define the project processes, their attributes, and units of measure are needed for QA.

Applying Quality Assurance

The QA department, management, or in some instances, even the project manager can complete the requirements for QA. QA can be accomplished using the same tools used for project planning:

■ Benefit cost analysis

■ Benchmarking

■ Flowcharting

■ Design of experiments

■ Cost of quality

Completing a Quality Audit

Quality audits are about learning. The idea of a quality audit is to identify the lessons learned on the current project to determine how to make things better for this project—and other projects within the organization. The idea is that Susan the project manager can learn from the implementations of Bob the project manager and vice versa.

Quality audits are formal reviews of what's been completed within a project, what's worked, and what didn't work. The end result of the audit is to improve performance for the current project, other projects, or the entire organization.

Quality audits can be scheduled at key intervals within a project or—Surprise!—they can come without warning. The audit process can vary depending on who is completing the audit: internal auditors or hired, third-party experts.

Improving the Project

The lone output of QA? Quality improvement.

Quality improvement requires action to improve the project's effectiveness. The actions to improve the effectiveness may have to be routed through the change control system, which means change requests, analysis of the costs and risks, and involvement from the Change Control Board.

Implementing Quality Control

Quality control (QC) requires the project manager, or other qualified party, to monitor and measure project results to determine that the results are up to the demands of the quality standards. If the results are not satisfactory, root cause analysis follows the quality control processes. Root cause analysis is needed so the project manager can determine the cause and apply corrective actions. On the whole, QC occurs throughout the life of a project, not just at its end.

QC is also not only concerned with the product the project is creating, but with the project management processes. QC measures performance, scheduling, and cost variances. The experience of the project should be of quality—not just the product the project creates. Consider a project manager that demands the project team work extreme hours to meet an unrealistic deadline; team morale suffers and likely so does the project work the team is completing.

The project team should have the following skill sets to be competent at quality control:

- Statistical quality control, such as sampling and probability
- Inspection to keep errors away from the customer
- Attribute sampling to measure conformance to quality on a per unit basis
- Variable sampling to measure conformance to quality as a whole
- Special causes to determine anomalies to quality
- Random causes to determine expected variances of quality
- Tolerance range to determine if the results are within, or without, an acceptable level of quality
- Control limits to determine if the results are in, or out, of quality control

Preparing for Quality Control

Quality control relies on several inputs:

- **Work results**   The results of both the project processes and the product results are needed to measure and compare to the quality standards. The expected results of the product and the project can be measured from the project plan.
- **Quality management plan**   This plan defines how the project team will meet the quality policy.
- **Operational definitions**   The operational definitions that define the metrics for the project are needed so QC can measure and react to the results of project performance.

■ **Checklists** If the project is using checklists to ensure project work is completed, a copy of the checklists will be needed as part of quality control. The checklists can serve as an indicator of completed work—and expected results.

Inspecting Results

Although quality is planned into a project, not inspected in, inspections are needed to prove the conformance to the requirements. An inspection can be done on the project as a whole, a portion of the project work, the project deliverable, or even an individual activity. Inspections are also known as:

■ Review
■ Product reviews
■ Audits
■ Walkthroughs

Creating a Control Chart

Ever feel your project is out of control? A control chart can prove it.

Control charts illustrate the performance of a project over time. They map the results of inspections against a chart as seen in Figure 8-3. Control charts are typically used in projects, or operations, where there are repetitive activities—such as manufacturing, a series of testing, or help desks.

FIGURE 8-3   Control charts illustrate the results of inspections.

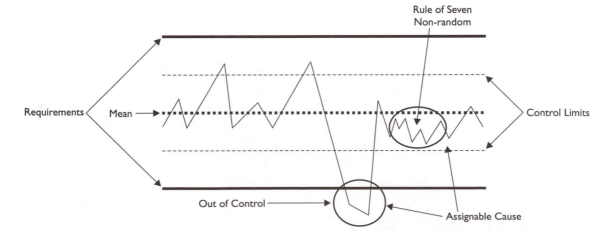

The outer limits of a control chart are set by the customer requirements. Within the customer requirements are the Upper Control Limits (UCL) and the Lower Control Limits (LCL). The UCL is typically set at +3 or +6 sigma, while the LCL is set at –3 or –6 sigma. Sigma results show the degree of correctness. Table 8-1 shows the four sigma values representing normal distribution. You'll need to know these for the PMP exam.

Value	Percent Correct
+/– 1 sigma	68.26 percent
+/– 2 sigma	95.46 percent
+/– 3 sigma	99.73 percent
+/– 6 sigma	99.99 percent

So what happened to sigma four and five? Nothing. They're still there; it's just the difference between three sigma at 99.73 and six sigma at 99.99 are so small that statisticians just jump onto six sigma. The mean in a control chart represents the expected result, while the sigma values represent the expected spread of results based on the inspection. A true six sigma allows only two defects per million opportunities and the percentage to represent that value is 99.99985%. For the exam, you can go with the 99.99%.

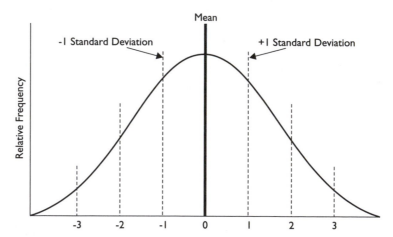

For example, if a manufacturer creates 1000 units per hour, and expects 50 units each hour to be defective, the mean would be 950 units. If the control limits were set at +/– three sigma, the results of testing would actually expect up to 953 correct units and down to 947 correct units.

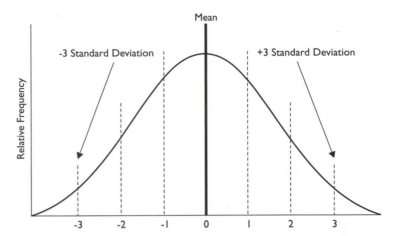

Over time, the results of testing are plotted in the control chart. Whenever a result of testing is plotted beyond the upper or lower control values, it is considered to be "out of control." When a value is out of control, there is a reason why—it's called an assignable cause. Something caused the results to change for better or for worse, and the result must be investigated to understand the why behind the occurrence.

Another assignable cause is "the Rule of Seven." The Rule of Seven states that whenever seven consecutive results are all on one side of the mean, this is an assignable cause. There has been some change that caused the results to shift to one side of the expected mean. Again, the cause must be investigated to determine why the change has happened.

While control charts are easily associated with recurring activities, like manufacturing, they can also be applied to project management. Consider the number of expected change requests, delays within a project, and other recurring activities. A control chart can plot out these activities to measure performance, positive and negative results, and track corrective actions.

on the job *Some project managers may believe that there should be no variance at all in the results of testing—they expect it to be 100 percent correct all the time. In some instances, this is valid; consider hospitals, military scenarios, and other situations dealing with life and death. When a project manager demands 100-percent perfection, the cost of quality issues needs to be revisited. What is the cost of obtaining perfection, versus the cost of obtaining 98 percent correctness?*

Creating Pareto Diagrams

A Pareto diagram is somewhat related to Pareto's Law: 80 percent of the problems come from 20 percent of the issues. This is also known as the *80/20 rule*. A Pareto diagram illustrates the problems by assigned cause from smallest to largest, as Figure 8-4 shows. The project team should first work on the largest problems and then move onto the smaller problems.

Completing a Statistical Sampling

Statistical sampling is a process of choosing a percentage of results at random. For example, a project creating a medical device may have 20 percent of all units randomly selected to check quality. This process must be completed on a consistent basis throughout the project, rather than on a sporadic schedule.

Statistical sampling can reduce the costs of quality control, but mixed results can follow if an adequate testing plan and schedule are not followed. The science of statistical sampling, and its requirements to be effective, is an involved process. There are many books, seminars, and professionals devoted to the process. For the PMP exam, know that statistical sampling uses a percentage of the results to test for quality. This process can reduce quality control cost.

Revisiting Flowcharting

Flowcharting uses charts to illustrate how the different parts of a system operate. Flow-charting is valuable in quality control because the process can be evaluated and tested to determine where in the process quality begins to break down. Corrective actions can then be applied to the system to ensure quality continues as planned—and as expected.

FIGURE 8-4

A Pareto diagram is a histogram that ranks the issues from largest to smallest.

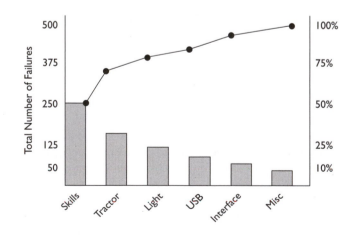

Applying Trend Analysis

Trend analysis is the science of taking past results to predict future performance. Sports announcers use trend analysis all the time: "The Cubs have never won in Saint Louis, on a Tuesday night, in the month of July, when the temperature at the top of the third inning is above 80 degrees."

The results of trend analysis allow the project manager to apply corrective action to intervene and prevent unacceptable outcomes. Trend analysis on a project requires adequate records to predict results and set current expectations. Trend analysis can monitor:

- **Technical performance**   Trend analysis can ask, "How many errors have been experienced by this point in the project schedule, and how many additional errors were encountered?"
- **Cost and schedule performance**   Trend analysis can ask, "How many activities were completed incorrectly, or came in late, or had significant cost variances?"

Results of Quality Control

Quality control should, first and foremost, result in quality improvement. The project manager and project team, based on the results of the tools and techniques to implement quality control, apply corrective actions to prevent unacceptable quality and improve the overall quality of the project management processes.

The corrective actions the project manager and the project team want to incorporate into the project may require change requests and management approval. The value and importance of the change should be evident so the improvement to quality is approved and folded into the project. In addition to quality improvement, there are other results of quality control:

- **Acceptance decisions**   Results of work are either accepted or rejected. Rejected items typically mean rework.
- **Rework**   Nonconformance to quality results in rework. Rework costs time and money and contributes to projects being late, over budget, or both. It is always more cost effective to do the work right the first time than to do it correct the second.

■ **Completed checklists**   If the project is using checklists to confirm the completion of work, then the completed checklists should become part of the project records. Some project managers require the project team member completing the checklist to initial the checklists as whole and complete.

■ **Process adjustments**   When results of inspections indicate quality is out of control then process adjustments may be needed to make immediate corrective actions or planned preventive actions to ensure quality improves. Process adjustments, depending on the nature of the adjustment, may qualify for a change request and be funneled through the Change Control System as part of integration management.

CERTIFICATION SUMMARY

What good is a project deliverable if it doesn't work, is unacceptable, or faulty? Project quality management ensures that the deliverables project teams create meet the expectations of the stakeholders. For your PMP examination, quality means delivering the project at the exact level of the design specifications and the project scope. No more, no less.

Quality and grade are two different things. Grade is the ranking assigned to different components that have the same functional purpose. For example, sheet metal may come in different grades based on what it is needed for. Another example is the grade of paper based on its thickness, ability to retain ink, and so on. Low quality is always a problem; low grade may not be.

Quality planning happens before project work begins—but also as work is completed. Quality planning can confirm the preexistence of quality—or the need for quality improvements. Quality is planned into a project, not inspected in. However, quality control uses inspections to prove the existence of quality within a project deliverable.

The cost of quality is concerned with the monies invested in the project to ascertain the expected level of quality. Examples of this cost include training, safety measures, and quality management activities. The cost of nonconformance centers on the monies lost by not completing the project work correctly the first time. In addition this fee includes the loss of sales, loss of customers, and downtime within the project.

Optimal quality is reached when the cost of the improvements equals the incremental costs to achieve quality. Marginal analysis is the study of when optimal quality is reached. The PMP candidate should know what marginal analysis is—and why management is concerned with it. Ideally, the cost of quality earns is earned back because the deliverables of the project are better and more profitable than if the quality of deliverables was lacking.

INSIDE THE EXAM

Quality, in project management, has many different meanings. For the PMP exam, you should know four key facts:

- Customer satisfaction is the conformance of the requirements and fitness for use.
- Quality is distinct from grade.
- Quality is the project team doing what was promised at the start of the project.
- Quality is concerned with prevention over inspection.

Don't get flustered over the difference between QC and QA. QC focuses on monitoring specific results of project work. QA focuses on monitoring overall performance. If it helps for the exam, think of QC being project-wide, and QA being organization-wide. Another aspect of QC is that the project team must be empowered to stop project work if quality is outside of the control limits set by the quality management plan.

The quality management plan spans all areas of project quality—not just the product the project is creating. The experience of the project as led by the project manager should be of quality as well. The relation between the project

deliverables and the project management quality is directly related.

Another area of quality is scheduling. A project manager must examine resources, how they are allocated, and pay attention to cost of quality for the assigned resources. One scheduling technique, just-in-time (JIT) scheduling demands higher quality. JIT does not order inventory, such as supplies and materials, until they are needed. This improves cash flow and reduces the cost of inventory not in use. However, a lack of quality in the project may cause defects. Because of the defects, the material in use is wasted and downtime occurs. Downtime occurs because there are no additional materials on hand and the project is waiting for new materials to arrive.

Finally, spend some time learning the values for the four sigmas in Table 8-2. You'll need them.

Value	Percent Correct
+/– 1 sigma	68.26 percent
+/– 2 sigma	95.46 percent
+/– 3 sigma	99.73 percent
+/– 6 sigma	99.99 percent

KEY TERMS

If you're serious about passing the PMP exams, memorize these terms and their definitions. For maximum value, create your own flashcards based on these definitions and review daily.

benchmarking	flowcharting	quality control
benefit/cost analysis	ISO 9000	quality management plan
checklists	operational definitions	quality policy
control charts	Pareto diagrams	statistical sampling
cost of nonconformance	process adjustments	trend analysis
cost of quality	quality assurance	quality control
design of experiments	quality audits	

TWO-MINUTE DRILL

Ensuring Project Quality

❑ The project manager is responsible for the overall quality management of the project and must set quality expectations based on the requirements of the customers and stakeholders.

❑ The project manager must integrate the quality control of the project with the quality assurance program of the performing organization.

❑ Quality is planned into a project, not inspected in.

Enforcing Project Quality

❑ The project team members (the people actually completing the project work) have the power and responsibility of the quality of the deliverables.

❑ The project team, as guided by the project manager and the quality management plan, should be empowered to stop the project work when preset, quality thresholds are exceeded.

❑ Quality planning is an iterative process. As quality concerns creep into the project the planning processes are revisted to ensure actions—preventive and corrective actions—are taken to ensure quality.

Implementing Quality Control

❑ Quality control monitors specific results within a project.

❑ Quality control is concerned that the results must satisfy relevant quality standards.

❑ Quality control can rely on root cause analysis used to eliminate unsatisfactory results.

❑ Quality control is completed through inspection.

Implementing Quality Assurance

❑ Quality assurance monitors overall results.

❑ Quality assurance may use a QA program to set quality standards.

❑ Quality assurance represents the implementation of the quality plan.

Relying on Quality Management

❑ Quality management is the process to ensure the project is completed with no deviations from the requirements. There are several quality management philosophies:

❑ **Total Quality Management (TQM)**   The organization strives for constant improvement for products and business practices.

❑ **Kaizen**   The organization applies small changes to products and processes to improve consistency, reduce costs, and provide overall quality improvements.

❑ **Marginal analysis**   The cost of the quality is not greater than the increased sales because of the level of quality implemented. Ideally, the revenue generated because of the quality improvements far exceeds the cost of the quality.

Evaluating Quality Costs

❑ The cost of quality is the amount of monies the performing organization must spend to satisfy the quality standards. This can include training, safety measures, additional activities implemented to prevent nonconformance.

❑ The cost of nonconformance to quality is the monies or events attributed to not satisfying the quality demands. These can include loss of business, downtime, wasted materials, rework, and cost and schedule variances.

❑ Optimal quality is reached when the cost of quality meets or exceeds the incremental cost to achieve quality.

Charting Quality Control

❑ **Fishbone diagram**   This is a cause-and-effect diagram that illustrates the factors which may be contributing to quality issues or problems. It is also known as an Ishikawa diagram.

❑ **Flow charts**   Flow charts demonstrate how a system works from start to finish, and illustrate how system components are integrated.

❑ **Pareto diagrams**   These histograms are related to Pareto's 80/20 rule, "80 percent of the problems come from 20 percent of the issues." The diagram charts the problems, categories, and frequency. The project team should first solve the larger problems and then move onto smaller issues.

❑ **Control Charts**   These charts plot out the results of inspections against a mean to examine performance against expected results. Upper and lower control limits are typically set to ± three or six sigma. Results that are beyond the control limit value are considered out of control. Out of control results have an assignable cause that requires investigation to determine why the result occurred. In addition, seven consecutive results on one side of the mean indicate an assignable cause and is known as the "Rule of Seven."

SELF TEST

I. Which of the following is responsible for the quality of the project deliverables?

   A. Project champion

   B. Project team

   C. Stakeholders

   D. Customers

2. What type of chart is this?

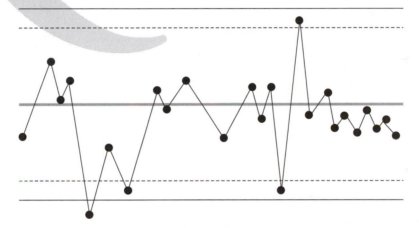

   A. Control

   B. Pareto

   C. Scatter

   D. Flow

3. You are the project manager for the BBB Project. Stacy, a project team member, is confused about what QA is. Which of the following best describes QA?

   A. QA is quality assurance for the overall project performance.

   B. QA is quality acceptance according to scope verification.

   C. QA is quality assurance for the project deliverable.

   D. QA is quality assurance for the project stakeholders.

4. You are the project manager for the Photo Scanning Project. This project is similar to another project you have completed. Your project is to electronically store thousands of historical photos for your city's historical society. Quality is paramount on this project. Management approaches you and asks why you have devoted so much of the project time for planning. Your response is which of the following?

A. This is a first-time, first-use project, so more time is needed for planning.

B. Planning for a project of this size, with this amount of quality, is mandatory.

C. Quality is planned into a project, not inspected in.

D. Quality audits are part of the planning time.

5. You are the project manager for the Floor Installation Project. Today, you plan to meet with your project team to ensure the project is completed with no deviations from the project requirements. This process is which of the following?

A. Quality planning

B. Quality management

C. Quality control

D. Quality assurance

6. You are the project manager for the ASE Project. This project must map to industry standards in order to be accepted by the customer. You and your team have studied the requirements and have created a plan to implement the deliverables with the appropriate level of quality. This process is called which of the following?

A. Quality planning

B. Quality management

C. Quality control

D. Quality assurance

7. Which of the following is an example of internal failure cost?

A. Rework

B. Quality audits

C. Random quality audits

D. Project team training

8. QC is typically a(n) _____ process.

A. Management

B. Project manager

C. Audit

D. Inspection

9. QA is typically a(n) _____ process.

   A. Management

   B. Project manager

   C. Audit

   D. Inspection

10. You are the project manager for a large manufacturer of wood furniture. Your new project is the Shop Table Project, which will be the creation and manufacturing of a new table for woodworkers to use in their wood shops. On this project you have elected to use JIT for scheduling. Which of the following is an advantage to using JIT?

    A. Requires materials to be readily available.

    B. Allows the project team to have control over the materials.

    C. Decreases the inventory investment.

    D. Allows for a broad range of deviation than other inventory solutions.

11. Your company has elected to use ISO 9000 standards. What is an attribute of ISO 9000?

    A. It ensures your company follows its own quality procedures.

    B. It ensures that your company will follow the set phases in each project from initiation to closure.

    C. It ensures that your company maps its processes to a proven process within the program.

    D. It ensures that QA and QC are integrated into the product or service your organization offers.

12. You are the project manager of the Halogen Installation Project. As this project gets underway, you receive notice from the program manager that the organization will be moving to Kaizen technologies as part of its quality management program. What are Kaizen technologies?

    A. Small improvements for small results

    B. Small improvements for all projects

    C. Small process and product improvements that are carried out on a continuous basis

    D. Small process improvements that are made to shorten the project duration

13. A fishbone diagram is the same as a(n) _____ chart.

    A. Ishikawa

    B. Pareto

    C. Flow

    D. Control

14. Management has asked you to define the correlation between quality and the project scope. Which of the following is the best answer?

    A. The project scope will include metrics for quality.

    B. Quality metrics will be applied to the project scope.

    C. Quality is the process of completing the scope to meet stated or implied needs.

    D. Quality is the process of evaluating the project scope to ensure quality exists.

15. Which of the following is most true about quality?

    A. It will cost more money to build quality into the project.

    B. It will cost less money to build quality into the project process.

    C. Quality is inspection driven.

    D. Quality is prevention driven.

16. _____ is a business philosophy to find methods to continuously improve products, services, and business practices.

    A. TQM

    B. ASQ

    C. QA

    D. QC

17. In quality management, which of the following is not an attribute of the cost of nonconformance?

    A. Loss of customers

    B. Downtime

    C. Safety measures

    D. Rework

18. You are the project manager for the KOY Project. This project requires quality that maps to federal guidelines. To ensure that you can meet these standards, you have elected to send the project team through training specific to the federal guidelines your project must adhere to. The costs of these classes can be assigned to which of the following?

    A. Cost of doing business

    B. Cost of quality

    C. Cost of adherence

    D. Cost of nonconformance

19. You are the project manager for the KOY Project. This project requires quality that maps to federal guidelines. During a quality audit, you discovered that a portion of the project work is faulty and must be done again. The requirement to do the work is an example of which of the following?

A. Cost of quality

B. Cost of adherence

C. Cost of nonconformance

D. Cost of doing business

20. Optimal quality is reached at what point?

A. When the stakeholder accepts the project deliverable.

B. When revenue from improvements equal the costs of conformance.

C. When revenue from improvement equals the incremental costs to achieve the quality.

D. When revenue from corrective actions equals the costs of the improvement.

21. You are the project manager of the JKL Project. The project is having some flaws in its production. Which analysis tool will allow you to determine the cause-and-effect of the production faults?

A. Flow chart

B. Pareto diagram

C. Ishikawa

D. Control chart

22. Linda is the project manager of a manufacturing project. She and her project team are using design of experiments to look for ways to improve quality. Which of the following best describes the method Linda and her team are using?

A. Design of experiments allows the project manager to move the relationship of activities to complete the project work with the best resources available.

B. Design of experiments allows the project manager to experiment with the project design to determine what variables are causing the flaws.

C. Design of experiments allows the project manager to experiment with variables to attempt to improve quality.

D. Design of experiments allows the project manager to experiment with the project design document to become more productive and provide higher quality.

23. You are the project manager of the Global Upgrade Project. Your project team consists of 75 project team members around the world. Each project team will be upgrading a piece of equipment in many different facilities. Which of the following could you implement to ensure the project team members are completing all of the steps in the install procedure with quality?

A. Checklists

B. WBS

C. PND

D. The WBS dictionary

24. Mark is the project manager of the PMH Project. Quality audits of the deliverables show there are several problems. Management has asked Mark to create a chart showing the distribution of problems and their frequencies. Management wants which of the following?

    A. Control chart
    B. Ishikawa chart
    C. Pareto diagram
    D. Flow chart

25. In the following graphic, what does the highlighted area represent?

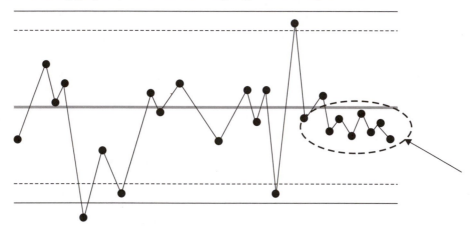

    A. Out of control data points
    B. In control data points
    C. Rule of seven
    D. Standard deviation

SELF TEST ANSWERS

1. ☑ **B.** The project team (the individuals completing the project work) is responsible for the quality of the project deliverables.
   ☒ **A** is incorrect; the project champion may review the work, but the responsibility to quality does not lie with this individual. **C** and **D** are also incorrect choices; the customer and other stakeholders are not responsible for the quality of the project.

2. ☑ **A.** The chart shown is a control chart.
   ☒ **B** is incorrect since a Pareto diagram maps categories of issues and their frequency. **C** is incorrect; a scatter chart compares common values across multiple categories. **D**, a flow chart, is incorrect also; flow charts illustrate how a process moves through a system and how the components are interrelated.

3. ☑ **A.** QA is concerned with overall project quality performance.
   ☒ **B, C,** and **D** are incorrect because they do not correctly explain quality assurance.

4. ☑ **C.** Of all the choices presented, this is the best answer. Quality is planned into the project and the planning requires time.
   ☒ **A** is incorrect because a project of this nature has been completed before. **B** is incorrect because there is not enough information provided to determine what the quality demands of the project are. **D** is incorrect because quality audits are not part of the planning processes.

5. ☑ **A.** Quality planning should be completed prior to the work beginning—and thereafter be revisited as needed.
   ☒ **B** is incorrect as Quality management is not an applicable answer to the scenario; **C** and **D** are incorrect, because QA and QC are part of quality management.

6. ☑ **A.** Quality planning is the process of creating a plan to meet the requirements of quality.
   ☒ Choices **B, C,** and **D** are incorrect because they do not explain the process in the questions scenario.

7. ☑ **A.** Internal failure cost is attributed to failure that results in rework. It is an example of the cost of nonconformance to quality.
   ☒ **B** and **C** are incorrect; quality audits are not a cost associated with nonconformance. **D** is incorrect because project team training is an example of the cost of conformance to quality.

8. ☑ **D.** QC requires an inspection of the work results. While quality is planned into a project, inspections ensure it exists.
   ☒ **A** is incorrect; QA is a managerial function. **B** is incorrect because another department, team member, or SME can complete QC. **C** is incorrect; an audit is too broad an answer for this question. Audits can be financial, schedule, or quality driven.

9. ☑ **A.** QA is typically a management process.

   ☒ **B** is incorrect because another department, team member, or SME can complete QC. **C** is incorrect because an audit is too broad of an answer for this question. Audits can be financial, schedule, or quality driven. **D** is wrong because QA is typically not an inspection process.

10. ☑ **C.** JIT, just-in-time scheduling, decreases the investment in inventory. However, mistakes with the materials can cause downtime if no additional materials are on hand.

    ☒ **A** is incorrect because materials are only available when they are needed. **B** is incorrect; the project team must use caution not to waste the materials. **D** is incorrect because JIT does not allow a broad range of deviation.

11. ☑ **A.** ISO 9000 is not a quality management system, but a system to ensure an organization follows its own quality procedures.

    ☒ **B, C,** and **D** are all incorrect. These choices do not correctly describe ISO 9000.

12. ☑ **C.** Kaizen technologies are small changes to processes and products on a steady, continuous basis to save costs and improve quality.

    ☒ **A** is incorrect; while Kaizen does implement small process changes, it does not aim for small results. **B** and **D** are also incorrect. Kaizen does not have to be implemented in all projects, though it often is. Kaizen is also not interested in necessarily reducing the project duration.

13. ☑ **A.** A fishbone diagram is the same as an Ishikawa diagram.

    ☒ **B, C,** and **D** are incorrect; these charts and diagrams accomplish goals other than the cause-and-effect of the Ishikawa.

14. ☑ **C.** Quality, in regard to the project scope, is about completing the work as promised.

    ☒ **A** is incorrect; the project scope will have requirements for acceptance, but may not have metrics for quality defined. **B** and **D** are also incorrect.

15. ☑ **D.** Quality is prevention driven. Quality wants to complete the work correctly the first time to prevent poor results, loss of time, and loss of funds.

    ☒ **A** and **B** are incorrect; there is no guarantee that a project will cost more or less depending on the amount of expected quality. Incidentally, lack of quality will likely cost more than quality planning because of the cost of nonconformance. **C** is incorrect because quality is planned into a project, not inspected in.

16. ☑ **A.** TQM, Total Quality Management, is a business philosophy to find methods to continuously improve.

    ☒ **B,** ASQ (American Society of Quality) is not a business philosophy. **C** and **D** are attributes of TQM, but are not correct answers for this question.

17. ☑ **C.** A safety measure is not an attribute of the cost of nonconformance, but rather a cost of adhering to quality.
☒ **A, B,** and **D** are incorrect choices; these are all attributes of the cost of nonconformance.

18. ☑ **B.** Training to meet the quality expectations are attributed to the cost of quality.
☒ **A, C,** and **D** are incorrect because these choices do not describe training as a cost of quality.

19. ☑ **C.** When project work results are faulty and must be done over, it is attributed to the cost of nonconformance to quality.
☒ **A, B,** and **D** are all incorrect; these values do not describe faulty work or the cost of nonconformance.

20. ☑ **C.** Marginal analysis provides that optimal quality is reached when the cost of the improvements equals the incremental costs to achieve the quality.
☒ **A, B,** and **D** are incorrect. These answers do not describe marginal analysis.

21. ☑ **C.** The key words "cause-and-effect" equate to the Ishikawa diagram.
☒ **A** is incorrect; a flow chart will show how a process moves through the system, but not the cause-and-effect of the problems involved. **B** is incorrect as well. A Pareto chart maps out the causes and frequency of problems. **D**, a control chart, plots out the results of sampling, but does not show the cause-and-effect of problems.

22. ☑ **C.** Of all the choices presented, C is the best. Design of experiments uses experiments and "what-if" scenarios to determine what variables are affecting quality.
☒ **A** is incorrect because design of experiments, in regard to quality, is not interested in changing the relationship of activities to complete project work. **B** and **D** are also incorrect because design of experiments will not be changing project design to determine where flaws exist or to become more productive.

23. ☑ **A.** Checklists are simple but effective quality management tools that the project manager can use to ensure the project team is completing the required work.
☒ **B, C,** and **D** are all incorrect. The WBS, PND, and WBS dictionary are not tools the project team can necessarily use to prove they've completed required work. Checklists are the best approach for this scenario.

24. ☑ **C.** Management wants Mark to create a Pareto diagram. Recall that a Pareto diagram maps out the causes of defects and illustrates their frequency.
☒ **A** is incorrect because a control chart does not identify the problems, only the relation of the results to the expected mean. **B** is incorrect because a cause-and-effect diagram does not map out the frequency of problems. **D** is also incorrect; flow charts show how a process moves through a system and how the components are related.

25. ☑ **C.** The highlighted area shows seven consecutive sampling results all on one side of the mean; this is known as the rule of seven and is an assignable cause.

☒ **A** is incorrect; these values are in control. **B** is correct, but it does not fully answer the question as choice **C** does. **D** is incorrect; standard deviation is a predicted measure of the variance from the expected mean of a sampling.

9

Introducing Project Human Resource Management

Project human resource management is multifaceted. It is the ability to lead, direct, and orchestrate the project team, the customers, project partners, contributors, and any other stakeholders to achieve the desired results for the project purpose.

Project managers cannot, and must not, do everything. They must rely on the project team to complete the project work. Have you ever worked on a project where the project manager wanted to do the work? Or the project manager assigned the mundane tasks to the project team and did the most important activities himself? Or the project manager completed the activities with the highest exposure? Not good. Project managers must delegate activities.

Project human resource management relies on the general management skills we discussed in Chapter 2:

- Leading
- Communicating
- Negotiating
- Problem solving
- Influencing

Project managers must find ways to motivate the project team to complete the work. There is a tendency, in many projects, for the project team to be very excited about the project at the start and then the excitement wanes as the project moves toward completion. The project manager must coach and mentor to develop the project team to ensure the excitement, willingness, and dedication to the project work continues.

Throughout the project the project manager will have to address project team retention, labor relations, performance appraisals, and, depending on the nature of the project work, health and safety issues. As most projects are new and temporary, so too are the relationships between the project team members and the project manager.

As the project progresses, the number of stakeholders in the project may change. The project manager and the project team will need to be aware of the coming flux of stakeholders and how this change may affect the dynamics of the project team and the project work. An approach to project human resources may work well in one phase of the project but not in another due to the stakeholders that have become involved.

Project human resource management may not be completely in the hands of the project manager. The performing organization's HR department may have control over the majority of the assignment and recruitment of the project team, but the project manager will need some knowledge as to the responsibility, power, and autonomy in order to comply with the organization's policies.

Preparing for Organizational Planning

Organizational planning is not planning to create an organization. Organizational planning is the process of mapping the project's roles, responsibilities, and reporting relationships to the appropriate people or groups of people. Organizational planning identifies the people involved with the project and determines what their role in the project is, whom they may report to—or receive a report from—and what their overall influence on the project work is.

Consider a project to create a community park. The project manager works for a commercial entity that will complete the project work. She identifies the people responsible for activities within her organization, the designers, engineers, installers, management, and so on. She will also have functional managers to coordinate employees' availability, financing to arrange procurement of resources needed for project completion, and senior management to report the status of the project work.

The project manager will also work and communicate with government officials for approval of the design, change requests, and overall schedule of the project. There'll be safety issues, landscaping questions, and other concerns that will come up as the project progresses.

Finally, the project manager will likely communicate with stakeholders that are not internal to her organization—for example, the people that live in the community and enjoy the park, and various government officials. These stakeholders will need to be involved in the planning and design of the park to ensure it satisfies the community's needs.

As you can see, organizational planning can involve both internal and external stakeholders. In most projects, organizational planning happens early in the project planning phase—but it should be reviewed and adjusted as the environment changes. Organizational planning is all about ensuring the project performs properly in the environment it is working in. Much of organizational planning focuses on communications—which we'll cover in the next chapter.

Identifying the Project Interfaces

Project interfaces are the people and groups the project manager and the project team will work with to complete the project. There are three types of interfaces:

- **Organizational interfaces**   These are the folks within the performing organization that the project team will work with to complete the project work. For example, a project to install a centralized, real-time database for customer orders and manufacturing will require the Sales, Finance, Manufacturing, and Information Technology organizational units to be involved. The different organizational units may all be involved throughout the project life, or their level of involvement may fluctuate depending on the project needs.

- **Technical interfaces** The technical interfaces describe the relationship between the project and the technical disciplines' input to the project. Consider a project to create a new building. The technical interfaces would include architects, mechanical engineers, structural engineers, and others. These interfaces would be involved throughout the project phases—and also between project phases for inspections, change requests, and so on.

- **Interpersonal Interfaces** Interpersonal interfaces describe the reporting relationship among the people working on the project. Depending on the nature of the project and the information to be shared, the communication can be informal, such as a hallway meeting, or formal, such as a variance report. We'll discuss formal and informal communications in the next module.

Identifying the Staffing Requirements

Every project needs people to complete the work. Staffing requirements are the identified roles needed on a project to complete the assigned work. For example, a project to install a new telephone system throughout a campus would require a menagerie of workers with varying skill sets: hardware and software gurus, telephony experts, electricians, installers, and others. The identified staff would be pulled from the resource pool. Any skills gaps would need to be addressed through staff acquisition, additional training, or procurement.

Identifying the Project Constraints

Constraints limit. When it comes to human resource constraints, the project manager is dealing with any factors that limit options for project completion. This is where creativity comes into play: the project manager must find a way to creatively acquire, schedule, or train the needed resources to complete the project. Common constraints include:

- **Organizational structure** Recall the organizational structures: functional, weak matrix, balanced matrix, strong matrix, and projectized? The project manager's authority in the organization is relevant to the organizational structure he is forced to work within.

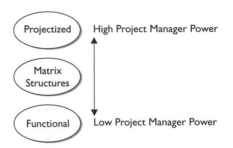

- ■ **Collective bargaining agreements**   The contractual agreements between employee groups, unions, or other labor organizations may serve as a constraint on the project. In these instances, there may be additional reporting relationships on the project status, work, and performance on project team members.

- ■ **Project Management Preferences**   If a project manager has had success with the organization and management of a project team in the past, the project manager will most likely want to re-create the success by following the same model. Current projects should emulate successful historical projects.

- ■ **Staffing**   Based on the competencies and talent of the project team, the assignments to activities are created. Project organization, scheduling, and workflow are often dependent on the abilities of the project team.

- ■ **Procurement**   When a particular qualification, skill, or specific person is requested as part of the project requirement, this requirement becomes a constraint on the project.

exam
ⓦatch
When a labor union or other employee group is identified as a constraint, a reporting relationship, or *other consideration of the project work, the union or group is considered a project stakeholder.*

Completing Organizational Planning

Organizational planning calls upon the project manager to consider the requirements of the project and the stakeholders involved—and how the nature of the project will require the project manager and the project team to interact with the stakeholders. In addition, the project manager has to consider the project team itself and how the team will be managed, led, and motivated to complete the project work according to plan.

The goal of organizational planning is to identify and plan for the constraints and opportunities brought about by the nature of the project work, the team's competence, and the demands of the performing organization and stakeholders. There are scores of books written on organizational planning, theory, and project team motivation. The goal of this conversation is to know the essentials to pass the PMP exam.

Relying on Templates

All projects are somewhat different, but some may resemble historical projects. The resemblance to historical projects allows the project manager to use proven plans as templates for current projects. Specifically, in light of organizational planning, the project manager can use the roles and responsibility matrixes and the reporting structure of historical projects as a model for the current project. As a heuristic, current projects should emulate successful historical projects.

Applying Human Resource Practices

The performing organization will likely have policies and procedures for the project manager to follow. The HR department should specify:

- Job responsibilities
- Reporting structures
- The project manager's role and autonomy
- Policies regarding project team member discipline
- The definition for customized organizational terms such as coach, mentor, or champion

Relating to Organizational Theories

There are many different organizational theories that a project manager can rely on to identify weakness and strengths, guide the project team, and move the project forward. The entire context of these theories is beyond the scope of this book; however, you should be familiar with several of these theories to pass the PMP exam.

Maslow's Hierarchy of Needs

According to Maslow, people work to take care of a hierarchy of needs. The pinnacle of their needs is self-actualization. People want to contribute, prove their work, and use their skills and ability. Figure 9-1 shows the pyramid of needs that all people try to ascend by fulfilling each layer one at a time.

FIGURE 9-1

Maslow says
people work for
self-actualization.

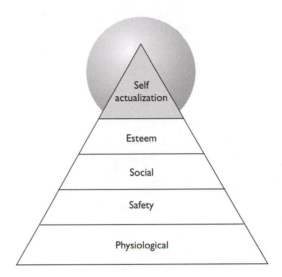

Maslow's five layers of needs, from the bottom-up, are

1. **Physiological**   The necessities to live: air, water, food, clothing, and shelter.
2. **Safety**   People need safety and security; this can include stability in life, work, and culture.
3. **Social**   People are social creatures and need love, approval, and friends.
4. **Esteem**   People strive for the respect, appreciation, and approval of others.
5. **Self-actualization**   At the pinnacle of needs, people seek personal growth, knowledge, and fulfillment.

Herzberg's Theory of Motivation

According to Frederick Herzberg, a psychologist and authority on the motivation of work, there are two catalysts for success with people:

1. **Hygiene agents**   These elements are the expectations all workers have: job security, a paycheck, clean and safe working conditions, a sense of belonging, civil working relationships, and other basic attributes associated with employment.
2. **Motivating agents**   These are the elements that motivate people to excel. They include responsibility, appreciation of work, recognition, the chance to excel, education, and other opportunities associated with work other than just financial rewards.

This theory says the presence of hygiene factors will not motivate people to perform, as these are expected attributes. However, the absence of these elements will demotivate performance. For people to excel, the presence of motivating factors must exist. Figure 9-2 illustrates Herzberg's Theory of Motivation.

McGregor's Theory of X and Y

McGregor's Theory states that management believes there are two types of workers, good and bad, as seen in Figure 9-3.

1. X is bad. These people need to be watched all the time, micromanaged, and distrusted. X people avoid work, responsibility, and have no ability to achieve.

2. Y is good. These people are self-led, motivated, and can accomplish new tasks proactively.

Ouchi's Theory Z

William Ouchi's Theory Z is based on the participative management style of the Japanese. This theory states that workers are motivated by a sense of commitment, opportunity, and advancement. Workers in an organization subscribing to Theory Z learn the business by moving up through the ranks of the company.

Ouchi's Theory Z also credits the idea of "lifetime employment." Workers will stay with one company until they retire because they are dedicated to the company that is in turn dedicated to them.

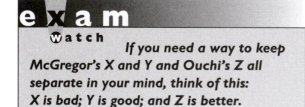

e x a m
w a t c h *If you need a way to keep* *McGregor's X and Y and Ouchi's Z all* *separate in your mind, think of this:* *X is bad; Y is good; and Z is better.*

Expectancy Theory

Expectancy Theory states that people will behave based on what they expect as a result of their behavior. In other words, people will work

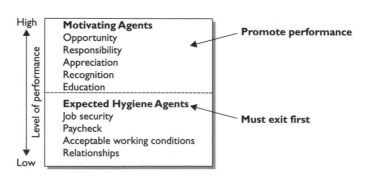

FIGURE 9-2

The absence of hygiene factors causes a worker's performance to suffer.

High

Level of performance

Low

Motivating Agents
Opportunity
Responsibility
Appreciation
Recognition
Education

Expected Hygiene Agents
Job security
Paycheck
Acceptable working conditions
Relationships

Promote performance

Must exit first

FIGURE 9-3

Management believes "X" people are bad and "Y" people are good.

X People

Micromanagement
No trust
Lazy
Avoid work

Y People

Self-led
Motivated
Capable

in relation to the expected reward of the work. If the attractiveness of the reward is desirable to the worker, they will work to receive the reward. In other words, people expect to be rewarded for their effort.

Completing Stakeholder Analysis

The project manager must make all efforts to identify all of the project stakeholders. Stakeholder analysis is the process of:

- Identifying the project stakeholders
- Identifying and documenting stakeholders' needs and concerns for the project
- Identifying stakeholders' ability to contribute to the project
- Prioritizing stakeholder demands for project completion
- Creating a communications methodology to gather and disperse information to the appropriate stakeholders when needed. (More on this in Chapter 10.)

Examining Organizational Planning Results

Organizational planning is part of the overall planning processes so it, too, is iterative. The outputs of organizational planning should be reviewed periodically throughout the project to ensure completeness and accuracy. Should events, people, or stakeholders change throughout the project, the following outputs of organizational planning should be updated to reflect the changes.

Creating the Role and Responsibility Assignments

There are slick definitions for roles and responsibility:

- **Role** Who does what
- **Responsibility** Who decides what

The assignment of the roles and responsibilities determines what actions the project manager, project team member, or individual contributor will have in the project. Roles and responsibilities generally support the project scope since this is the required work for the project.

An excellent tool that the project manager should create is the Responsibility Assignment Matrix (RAM). A RAM can be high-level—for example, mapping project groups to the high-level components of a WBS, such as architecture, network, or software creation. A RAM can also be detailed specific to the activities within the project work. Figure 9-4 is an example of a RAM.

Creating a Staffing Management Plan

The staffing management plan details how project team members will be brought onto the project and excused from the project. This subsidiary plan documents the process the project manager is expected to complete to bring new project team members aboard based on the conditions of the project.

For example, a project may require an application developer in the third phase of the project. The project manager may have to complete a job description of what the application developer will be responsible for, how their time will be used, and how long the role is needed on the project. HR or other functional managers may have to approve the request.

FIGURE 9-4   A Responsibility Assignment Matrix can map work to project team members.

WBS Component	Resource 1	Resource 2	Resource 3	Resource 4	Resource 5	Resource 6
Architectural	RS		R		A	
Foundation	A	R	I			
Framing	S		A		I	
Electrical	S			R		A
Interior	S	A			I	R

A = Accountable   R = Resource   I = Informed   S = Sign off

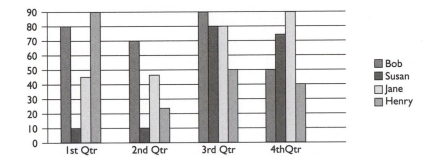

FIGURE 9-5

Resource histograms illustrate the demand for labor.

Management may also want to see a resource histogram, as Figure 9-5 illustrates, so they may plan employees' time and activities accordingly. Management may elect to hold off on the launch of a project based on the requirement for resources and the conflict with business cycles or other projects with higher priorities within the organization.

Each performing organization will likely have policies and procedures that should be documented, and followed, to bring resources onto the project team. In addition, the organization may have similar ways to excuse project team members from a project once their contribution has been completed.

The staffing management plan should

- Detail how project team members are brought onto and released from the project
- Account for employees' time on the project
- Use employees as needed, and when needed
- Remove or reduce worries about employment by communicating the expected need for resources

exam

watch *Scheduling unneeded resources is a waste of time and money. Only schedule resources on a project when they are needed. Functional Managers may want you, the project manager, to schedule resources on a project even though you don't need them. Not only is this outside of the staffing management plan it is a violation of the project management Professional Code of Professional Conduct.*

Creating an Organizational Chart

An organizational chart can help the project manager and the project team identify the reporting relationships among the project team, management, and other key stakeholders. Figure 9-6 is an example of an organizational chart, or org chart. The org chart can help the project manager identify what communication protocols are used in a large project. Org charts can also identify the relationship of team members and contributors in a smaller project.

An organizational breakdown structure (OBS) is also an organizational chart. This tool, however, identifies the organizational units or departments and what work packages they are responsible for within the project.

Documenting the Supporting Detail

The details influencing project decision should be documented. This supporting detail allows the project manager and management to reflect on why decisions were made. Supporting details may include:

- ■ **Organizational impact**   The project manager should identify the reasoning behind the decisions that were made. Specifically, if alternatives were identified,

FIGURE 9-6   Organizational charts identify reporting relationships within a project.

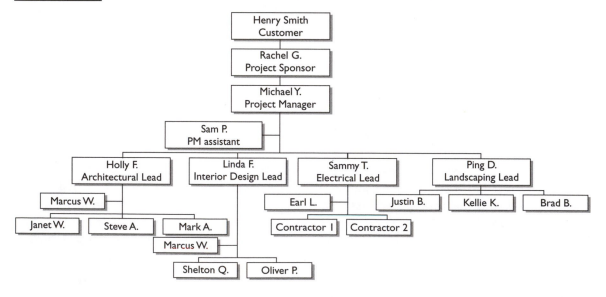

the project manager should explain why the alternatives were not selected in lieu of the plans that were created. This information can prove valuable later in the project if management needs to know the rationale behind the project manager's decisions.

- **Job descriptions**   These position descriptions define the job requirements, responsibilities, authority, and other details about the positions within the project team.

- **Training needs**   If the project team needs training in any area to complete the required work of the project scope, the project manager should identify and document the needs of the project team. Information on the type of training needed, the cost, modality, and reasoning why the training choice was selected should be included in this documentation.

Managing Staff Acquisitions

Have you ever managed a project where the resources you want on the project are not available? Or have you managed a project where the resources you've been assigned aren't the best resources to complete the project work? Staff acquisition is the process of getting the needed resources on the project team to complete the project work.

Staff acquisition focuses on working within the policies and procedures of the performing organization to obtain the needed resources to complete the project work. Negotiation, communication, and political savvy are key to getting the desired resources on the project team.

Referring to the Staffing Management Plan

The project manager will rely on the staffing management plan as an input to acquiring project team members. The staffing management plan details how project team members will be brought onto the project and excused from the project as conditions within the project demand. The staffing management plan is a subsidiary plan that documents the staffing requirements of the project.

Examining the Staffing Pool

In some organizations the project manager has little or no say on the project team assignments. No fun. In other organizations, project managers have the ability to recruit, or at least influence, the project team assignments. The project manager should ask questions about:

- **Experience** What is the experience of the project team member? Have they done similar work in the past—and have they done it well?
- **Interest level** Are the project team members interested in working on this project?
- **Characteristics** How will this individual team member work with other project team members?
- **Availability** Will the project team members desired for the project be available? Project managers should confer with functional managers on the availability of the potential team member.
- **Knowledge** What is the competency and proficiency of the available project team members?

Recruiting Project Team Members

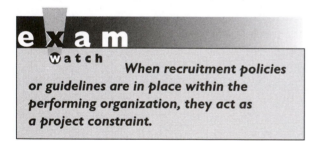

The project manager has to follow the rules of the organizations involved in the project. For example, an organization may forbid a project manager from approaching a worker directly to discuss their availability and desire to work on a project. The project manager may instead have to speak with the employee's functional manager to obtain the resource.

Acquiring the Needed Staff

A project needs a project team. Let me restate that. A project needs a *good, qualified, competent* project team. Their competency, experience, and availability will directly influence the success of the project. Armed with this notion, the project manager may rely on a few different tools and techniques to obtain the needed project team resources.

Negotiating for Resources

Most projects require the project manager to negotiate for resources. The project manager will likely have to negotiate with functional managers to obtain the needed resources to complete the project work. The functional managers and the project manager may struggle over an employee's time due to demands in ongoing operations, other projects, and effective utilization of resources. In other instances, functional managers may want to assign under-utilized resources on projects to account for their employee's time.

Project managers may also have to negotiate with other project managers to share needed resources among projects. Scheduling the needed resources between the project teams will need to be coordinated so both projects may complete successfully.

An organization's politics certainly come into play with staff acquisitions. Functional managers may want project managers to carry extra resources on the project in exchange for key personnel, added deliverables to the project, or other "favors" for the manager. In all instances, the project manager should follow the PMP Code of Professional Conduct. We'll discuss this infamous code of conduct in Chapter 13.

Working with Preassigned Staff

Project team members are often preassigned to a project for a number of reasons:

- Availability of the individual
- Promised as part of a competitive contract
- Required as part of the project charter of an internal project
- Opportunity for the staff member to complete on-the-job training

Whatever the reasoning behind the assignment of the staff to the project, the project manager should evaluate the project team for skills gaps, availability to complete the project work, and expectations of the project team members. The project manager must address any discrepancies between the requirements of the project work and the project team's ability to complete the work.

Procuring Staff

In some instances, the project manager may have no alternative but to procure the project team or individuals to complete the project work. Procurement will be discussed in detail in Chapter 12. In regard to project team procurement, reasons why the project manager can use this alternative include, but are not limited to, the following:

- The performing organization lacks the internal resources with the needed skills to complete the project work.
- The work is more cost effective to procure.
- The project team members are present within the organization, but they are not available to the current project.
- The project team members are present within the organization, but they cannot complete the needed work due to other project assignments.

Assembling the Project Team

Congratulations! The project team has been recruited or assigned to the project. With the project team assembled, the project manager can continue planning, assigning activities, and managing the project progression. Project team members can be assigned to the project on a full- or part-time basis depending on the project conditions.

Once the project team is built, a project team directory should be assembled. The project team directory should include:

- The project team members' names
- Phone numbers
- E-mail addresses
- Mailing addresses if non-collocated
- Contact information for key stakeholders
- Any other relevant contact information for each team member, such as photos, web addresses, and so on.

Developing the Project Team

Throughout the project, the project manager will have to work to develop the project team. The project manager may have to develop the ability of the individual team members so that they can complete their assignments. The project manager will also have to work to develop the project team as a whole so the team can work together to complete the project.

In matrix organizations, the project team members are accountable to the project manager and their functional managers. The development of the project team can prove challenging since the project team members may feel pulled between multiple bosses. The project manager must strive to involve and develop the project team members as individuals completing project work—and as team members completing the project objectives together.

Preparing to Develop the Project Team

The project manager will rely on several pieces of information to prepare for team development:

- **Staff assignments** The assignments of the project team members define the skills of the project team members, their need for development, and their ability to complete the project work as individuals, and as part of the collective team.

- **Project plan** The project plan defines the expectations of the project team, how the team will operate, and how the team will be expected to communicate, function, and perform.

- **Staffing management plan** Recall that the staffing management plan details how project team members will be brought onto the project and excused from the project.

- **Performance reports** As the project team completes work, performance reports will reflect on the quality, timeliness, and success of the project team. (Performance reports will be discussed in detail in Chapter 10.)

- **External Feedback** When things are not well with project team members, stakeholders are often happy to tell the project manager. In some instances, the project manager must query stakeholders and organizational interfaces on the performance of the project team members.

Leading Project Team Development

Due to the temporary and short-term nature of projects it can be tough for a group of strangers to come together, form relationships, and immediately create a successful project. Team development is the guidance, direction, and leadership the project manager offers to influence a project team.

The project managers are the power on the project team. While there may be some resistance of the project team to cooperate with the project manager, complete assigned duties, or participate as requested, the project team should realize the project manager is the project authority. There are five types of powers the project manager yields:

- **Expert** The authority of the project manager comes from experience with the technology the project focuses on.
- **Reward** The project manager has the authority to reward the project team.
- **Formal** The project manager has been assigned by senior management and is in charge of the project. Also known as positional power.
- **Coercive** The project manager has the authority to discipline the project team members. This is also known as "penalty power." When the team is afraid of the project manager, it's coercive.
- **Referent** The project team personally knows the project manager. Referent can also mean the project manager refers to the person who assigned him the position—for example, "The CEO assigned me to this position so we'll do it this way." This power can also mean the project team wants to work on the project or with the project manager due to the high priority and impact of the project.

Creating Team-Building Activities

Team-building activities are approaches to develop the team through facilitated events. Events can include:

- Team involvement during planning processes
- Defining rules for handling team disagreements
- Off-site activities
- Quick team-involvement activities
- Activities to improve interpersonal skills and form relationships

Dealing with Team Disagreements

In most projects, there will be instances when the project team, management, and other stakeholders disagree on the progress, decisions, and proposed solutions within the project. It's essential for the project manager to keep calm, lead, and direct the parties to a sensible solution that's best for the project. Here are seven reasons for conflict, in order of most common to least common:

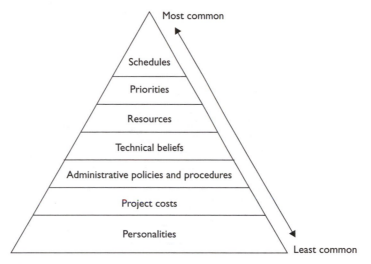

1. Schedules
2. Priorities
3. Resources
4. Technical beliefs
5. Administrative policies and procedures
6. Project costs
7. Personalities

So what's a project manager to do with all the potential for strife in a project? There are five different approaches to conflict resolution:

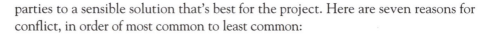

You can expect questions on these areas of conflict on the exam. Don't be duped into thinking personality conflicts are the biggest problem with conflict resolution; they are the least important.

■ **Problem solving** This approach confronts the problem head-on and is the preferred method of conflict resolution. You may see this approach as "confronting" rather than problem solving. Problem solving calls for additional research to find the best solution for the problem, and should be a win-win solution. It should be used if there is time to work through and resolve the issue. It also serves to build relationships and trust.

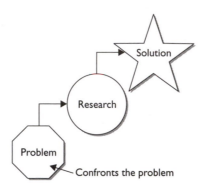

- **Forcing** The person with the power makes the decision. The decision made may not be the best decision for the project, but it's fast. As expected, this autocratic approach does little for team development and is a win-lose solution. Used when the stakes are high and time is of the essence, or if relationships are not important.

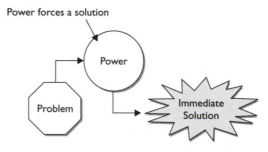

- **Compromising** This approach requires that both parties give up something. The decision made is a blend of both sides of the argument. Because neither party really wins, it is considered a lose-lose solution. The project manager can use this approach when the relationships are equal and no one can truly "win." This approach can also be used to avoid a fight.

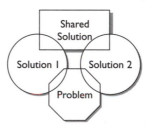

- **Smoothing** Smoothing "smoothes" out the conflict by minimizing the perceived size of the problem. It is a temporary solution but can calm team relations and boisterous discussions. Smoothing may be acceptable when time is of the essence or any of the proposed solutions will not currently settle the problem. This can be considered a lose-lose situation since no one really wins in the long-term. The project manager can use smoothing to emphasize areas of agreement between disagreeing stakeholders and thus minimize areas of conflict. It's used to maintain relationships, and when the issue is not critical.

- **Withdrawal**   This is the worst conflict resolution approach since one side of the argument walks away from the problem, usually in disgust. The conflict is not resolved and it is considered a yield-lose solution. The approach can be used, however, as a cooling off period, or when the issue is not critical.

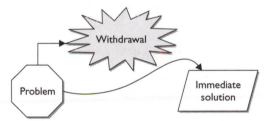

Relying on General Management Skills

A chunk of project management relies on general management skills. Specifically, the project manager relies on:

- **Leading**   Leading is the art of establishing direction, aligning people, and motivating the project team to complete the project work.

- **Communicating**   Good project managers are good communicators. Remember, half of communicating is listening.

- **Negotiating**   Project managers will likely negotiate for scope, cost, terms, assignment, and resources.

- **Problem solving**   Project managers must have the ability to confront and solve problems.

- **Influence**   Project managers use their influence to get things done.

Rewarding the Project Team

A reward and recognition system encourages, emphasizes, and promotes good performance and behavior by the project team. The reward and recognition system should be a formal, achievable approach for the project team to perform and be rewarded for their outstanding performance.

The relationship between the requirements for the reward and the power to achieve should not be limited. In other words, if the project manager is rewarded for completing a project by a given date, she needs the autonomy to schedule resources and make decisions so the goal is achievable.

The project team should be rewarded for good work and not for bad. For example, a project team should not be rewarded for completing a crucial assignment on schedule if the work is unacceptable because of quality issues.

Finally, the culture where the project is taking place should also be considered. It may be inappropriate to reward individual team members over an entire group, or vice versa. The project manager should be aware of the cultural differences and operate within the customs and practices of the environment to reward the project team without causing offense.

Dealing with Team Locales

Collocated teams are teams that work geographically close together to improve team dynamics and team relations. On large projects, it may be particularly valuable to bring all of the project team members together to a central location to work collectively on the project. A project headquarters or war room may be ideal.

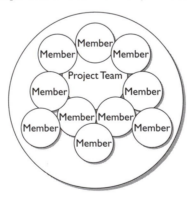

When collocation is not feasible, the project manager must make attempts to bring the project team together for team interaction, face-to-face meetings, and other avenues of communication to bolster relations.

Training the Project Team

The project team may require training to complete the project work, function as a project team, or participate in management skills such as finance or formal communications. Training can include:

- Formal education
- Classroom training
- On-the-job training
- Cross training (shadowing)

Examining the Results of Team Development

Team development is an ongoing process. Optimum team performance doesn't happen on the first day of the project, but hopefully it does well before the final day of the project. The primary goal of team development is to improve project team performance. Improvements can include:

- **Individuals**   Improvements to individual skill sets may allow the individual to complete their assigned work better, faster, or with more confidence.
- **Team**   Improvements to the project team may allow the team to perform with a focus on technical requirements, project work, and working together (in harmony) to complete the project work.
- **Individuals and team**   Improvements to either team members or the project team as a whole may lead to the better good of the project by finding better ways of completing the project work.

Another result of team development is the input to performance reviews of the project team members. Hopefully, all goes well and the project manager can report successful, willing, and cooperative team members. Honesty is paramount in reporting the performance of project team members.

INSIDE THE EXAM

Most project managers taking the PMP exam can rely on their practical experience to ace these questions. But as reinforcement, let's examine some key issues you should know going into the examination.

Project human resource management questions on the exam center around three big points:

- A role is who does what.
- A responsibility is who decides what.
- Project managers are responsible for the project. Team members fill roles on the project.

Because project managers are responsible for the success of the project, they have power to exert over the project team. Table 9-1 is a quick list of the powers that the project manager can have.

There are five organizational theories you may encounter on the exam:

- **Maslow's Hierarchy of Needs** People don't work for money, but for self-actualization.
- **Herzberg's Theory of Motivation** The presence of hygiene factors doesn't motivate people; the absence of hygiene

factors, however, hinders people's performance.

- **McGregor's Theory of X and Y** X people are lazy and do not want to work. Y people are self-led, motivated, and want to accomplish.
- **Ouchi's Theory Z** Workers and management cooperate for the good of the organization. Everyone wins!
- **Expectancy Theory** People expect to be rewarded for their effort.

Within projects there will likely be conflicts and disagreements among the project team and stakeholders. Conflicts typically stem from one of the following sources (in descending order):

1. Schedules
2. Priorities
3. Resources
4. Technical beliefs
5. Administrative policies and procedures
6. Project costs
7. Personalities

And to solve these conflicts? Table 9-2 lists various resolution methods.

TABLE 9-1	Power	Definition
The Powers of the Project Manager	Expert	The project manager is an expert with the technology the project focuses on.
	Reward	The project manager can reward the project team members.
	Coercive	The project manager can punish the project team members.
	Formal	The project manager is formally assigned to the role of the project manager.
	Referent	The project team knows the project manager. The project manager refers to the person that assigned them to the role of project manager.

CERTIFICATION SUMMARY

Project human resources management requires the project manager to lead and direct the project team, customers, and other stakeholders in unison to complete the project scope. Project human resources management requires working within the confines of the organizational policies. Project human resource management requires the ability to relate to the concerns and expectations of the stakeholders. And perhaps most importantly, it is tightly integrated with project communications management.

There are several human resource theories the PMP candidate should be familiar with to successfully pass the PMP examination. Here's a quick listing of these theories and their core beliefs:

- **Maslow's Hierarchy of Needs:** People work for self-actualization
- **Herzberg's Theory of Motivation:** Hygiene agents are expected by and can only demotivate if they are not present. Motivating agents provide opportunity to exceed, advance, and other rewards than just financial gains.

TABLE 9-2	Various Conflict Resolution Methods

Conflict Resolution	Quick Example
Problem solving (confronting)	Let's put our heads together, research the problem and find the best solution.
Forcing	Bob's got seniority here, so we'll go with his opinion on the solution.
Compromising	Let's take a little of both sides of the argument and create a blended solution.
Smoothing	Let's smooth this issue out. It's really not that big of a problem.
Withdrawal	I'm leaving. Do whatever solution works.

- **McGregor's Theory of X and Y:** This is a management theory that believes "X" people have to be micromanaged and distrusted. "Y" people are self-led and motivated.
- **Ouchi's Theory Z:** Workers are motivated by a sense of commitment, opportunity, and advancement. This theory centers on lifetime employment.
- **Expectancy Theory:** People behave based on what they expect as a result of their behavior.

Within a project there are roles and responsibilities. A role can be defined as "who does what," while a responsibility can be defined as "who decides what." A Responsibility Assignment Matrix (RAM) can map project work to specific project team members. This matrix clarifies which project team member is responsible for what actions within the project.

The RAM can help the project manager determine which resources are needed for what activities, but can also ensure that the adequate amount of resources are assigned to the project work. The project manager must work to ensure that extra resources are not assigned to project activities. It is wasteful to add unneeded resources to project work.

The Staffing Management Plan will dictate how resources are brought onto the project—and taken off of the project. This plan will serve as an input to staff acquisition. Should functional managers want to add unneeded team members the Staffing Management Plan can restrict the functional manager. The Staffing Management Plan works with the operational policies of the performing organization.

KEY TERMS

If you're serious about passing the PMP exams, memorize these terms and their definitions. For maximum value, create your own flashcards based on these definitions and review daily. You can find additional information on these terms in the project glossary.

coercive power	Herzberg's Theory of Motivation	referent power
collective bargaining agreements	Maslow's Hierarchy of Needs	resource histogram
compromising	McGregor's Theory of X and Y	responsibility
Expectancy Theory	Ouchi's Theory Z	reward power
expert power	problem solving	role
forcing	project interfaces	smoothing
formal power		Staffing management plan
		war room
		withdrawal

✓ TWO-MINUTE DRILL

Planning for Project Human Resource Management

❑ Project human resource management focuses on utilizing the people involved in the project in the most effective way. The people involved in the project are more than just the project team members, though they're the most obvious.

❑ The project manager can't forget to involve other stakeholders: customers, management, individual contributors, the project sponsor, and any other stakeholder unique to the project.

❑ Organizational planning calls on the project manager to identify the roles and responsibilities of the project and the reporting relationship within the organization.

❑ Reporting relationships can be internal, such as to management, or external, such as to a customer or community. The relationships and the procedure to communicate with these project interfaces must be documented.

Documenting Human Resources Management

❑ Because projects are often similar, the project manager can rely on templates to re-create the success of historical projects. Reporting structures, role and responsibility matrixes, and other human resource models can be replicated, and adjusted, between projects.

❑ The staffing management plan describes the process that the project manager must follow to bring resources onto a project, or to dismiss them from a project when the resources are no longer needed.

❑ The policies and procedures of the performing organization should be documented within the staffing management plan to ensure the guidelines are followed as management intends.

❑ The staffing management plan will also detail the policies of how the project manager can recruit project team members. The plan may also detail the procedure to procure resources for the project from vendors or consultants.

Involving the Project Stakeholders

❑ Throughout the project, the project manager must work with the project team to develop their ability to complete their project work, grow as a team, and focus on completing the project work accurately and on time.

❑ A reward and recognition system can help the project manager motivate the project team to perform as hoped.

❑ Special care to involve the project team must be given when the team is scattered geographically. The project manager can rely on face-to-face meetings, videoconferences, or teleconferences to promote non-collocated teams.

Developing the Project Team

❑ Ideally, the project is collocated and has access to a war room to refer to project information, research, schedules, and other project team members.

❑ The goal of team development is outstanding performance for the good of the project. Through training, the project team may increase their ability to work together and individually with a higher level of confidence, performance, and teamwork.

❑ The result of team development is project performance improvements. The improvements should be noted in an honest appraisal of the project team members' effort and contributions to the project.

SELF TEST

1. You are the project manager for the JHG Project. This project requires coordination with the Director of Manufacturing, Human Resources, the IT department, and the CIO. This is an example of what type of input to organizational planning?

   A. Organizational interfaces

   B. Technical interfaces

   C. Interpersonal interfaces

   D. Human resource coordination

2. Your project requires an electrician at month eight. This is an example of which of the following?

   A. Organizational interfaces

   B. Staffing requirements

   C. Contractor requirements

   D. Resource constraints

3. You are the project manager of the PUY Project. This project requires a chemical engineer for seven months of the project although there are no available chemical engineers within your department. This is an example of which of the following?

   A. Organizational interfaces

   B. Staffing requirements

   C. Contractor requirements

   D. Resource constraints

4. You are the project manager in an organization with a weak matrix. Who will have the authority on your project?

   A. The project manager

   B. The customer

   C. Functional management

   D. The team leader

5. You are the project manager for the LMG Project. Your project will have several human resource issues that must be coordinated and approved by the union. Which of the following statements is correct about this scenario?

   A. The union is considered a resource constraint.

   B. The union is considered a management constraint.

   C. The union is considered a project stakeholder.

   D. The union is considered a project team member.

6. You are the project manager of the PLY Project. This project is very similar to the ACT Project you have completed. What method can you do to expedite the process of organization planning?

    A. Use the project plan of the ACT Project on the PLY Project.
    B. Use the roles and responsibilities definitions of the ACT Project on the PLY Project.
    C. Use the project team structure of the ACT Project on the PLY Project.
    D. Use the project team of the ACT Project on the PLY Project.

7. In your organization, management is referred to as coaches. As a project manager, you are referred to as a project coach. A human resource document should be created to handle this scenario. What should it cover?

    A. How coaches are separate from managers.
    B. How coaches are the same as managers.
    C. How a coach is to complete his or her job.
    D. How the project team is to work for a coach.

8. Management has requested that you create a chart depicting all of the project resource needs and the associated activities. Management is looking for which type of chart?

    A. A roles chart
    B. A roles matrix
    C. A roles and responsibilities matrix
    D. A Gantt chart

9. Which of the following is an example of Theory X?

    A. Self-led project teams
    B. Micromanagement
    C. Team members able to work on their own accord
    D. EVM

10. You are the project manager of the PLN Project. The team members are somewhat "afraid" of you as project manager because they see you as management. They know that a negative review from you about their project work will impact their yearly bonus. This is an example of which of the following?

    A. Formal power
    B. Coercive power

C. Expert power

D. Referent power

11. You are the project manager of the MMB Project. The president of the company has spoken to the project team and told them the confidence and respect he has in you to lead the project to a successful completion. The project manager has what type of power on this project?

A. Formal power

B. Coercive power

C. Expert power

D. Halo power

12. Management has approached Tyler, one of your project team members. Tyler is a database administrator and developer, whose work is always on time, accurate, and of quality. He also has a reputation of being a "good guy" and is well liked. Because of this, management has decided to move Tyler into the role of a project manager for a new database administration project. This is an example of which of the following?

A. Management by exception

B. The halo effect

C. Management by objectives

D. McGregor's Theory of X and Y

13. Susan is the project manager for the PMG Project. She makes all decisions on the project team regardless of the project team objections. This is an example of which of the following management styles?

A. Autocratic

B. Democratic

C. Laissez faire

D. Exceptional

14. Which problem-solving technique is the best for most project management situations?

A. Confronting

B. Compromising

C. Forcing

D. Avoidance

15. Harold is a very outspoken project team member. All of the project team members respect Harold for his experience with the technology, but often things have to go in Harold's favor or things do not go well. During a discussion on a solution, a project team member waves her arms and says, "Fine, Harold, do it your way." This is an example of which of the following?

    A. A win-win solution
    B. A leave-lose solution
    C. A lose-lose solution
    D. A yield-lose solution

16. You are the project manager for the GBK Project. This project effects a line of business and the customer is anxious about the success of the project. Which of the following is likely not a top concern for the customer?

    A. Project priorities
    B. Schedule
    C. Cost
    D. Personality conflicts

17. Which theory believes that workers need to be involved with the management process?

    A. McGregor's Theory of X and Y
    B. Ouchi's Theory Z
    C. Herzberg's Theory of Motivation
    D. Expectancy Theory

18. _____ states that as long as workers are rewarded they will remain productive.

    A. McGregor's Theory of X and Y
    B. Ouchi's Theory Z
    C. Herzberg's Theory of Motivation
    D. Expectancy Theory

19. You are the project manager for Industrial Lights Project. You have been hired by your organization specifically because of your vast experience with the technology and with projects of this nature. The project is aware of your experience. You likely have what type of power on this project?

    A. Formal power
    B. Coercive power
    C. Expert power
    D. Referent power

20. You are the project manager for GHB Project. You have served as a project manager for your organization for the past ten years. Practically all of your projects come in on time and on budget. The project team has worked with you in the past and they consider you to be an expert project manager. They also like working with you. Given all of this, you likely have what type of power on this project?

    A. Formal power
    B. Coercive power
    C. Expert power
    D. Referent power

21. Which of the following is an example of coercive power?

    A. A project manager that has lunch with the project team every Thursday.
    B. A project manager that will openly punish any team member who is late with an activity.
    C. A project manager that has worked with the technology on the project for several years.
    D. A project manager that is friends with all of the project team members.

22. Charles is the project manager for the WAC Project. The customer and a project team member are in conflict over the level of quality needed on a sampling. Charles decides to split the difference between what the two stakeholders want. This is an example of which of the following?

    A. A win-win solution
    B. A win-lose solution
    C. A lose-lose solution
    D. A leave-lose solution

23. Mike is the project manager for a project with a very tight schedule. The project is running late and Mike feels that he does not have time to consider all the possible solutions that two team members are in disagreement over. Mike quickly decides to go with the team member with the largest amount of seniority. This is an example of which of the following?

    A. Problem solving
    B. Compromising
    C. Forcing
    D. Withdrawal

24. You are a project manager in a projectized organization. Your job as a project manager can be described best by which of the following?

    A. Full-time
    B. Part-time
    C. Expeditor
    D. Coordinator

25. What is the benefit of using a collocated team?
    A. The project team is dispersed so the team is self-led.
    B. The project team is dispersed so communication increases.
    C. The project team is in the same physical location so their ability to work as a team is enhanced.
    D. The project team is in the same physical location so project costs are greatly reduced.

SELF-TEST ANSWERS

1. ☑ **A.** The reporting interfaces for this project—the Directors of Manufacturing, Human Resources, and the IT department, as well as the CIO—are examples of the organizational interfaces.
   ☒ **B** is incorrect; technical interfaces are the technical gurus for the project, such as the engineers and designers. **C**, the interpersonal interfaces, is not the best choice since this relationship describes the different individuals working on the project. **D**, human resource coordination, is also incorrect.

2. ☑ **B.** Because the project requires the electrician, a project role, this is a staffing requirement.
   ☒ **A** is incorrect because it does not accurately describe the situation. **C** is incorrect; contractor requirements would specify the procurement issues, the minimum qualifications for the electrician, and so on. **D** is incorrect; a resource constraint, while a tempting choice, deals more with the availability of the resource or the requirement to use the resource.

3. ☑ **B.** The project needs the resource of the chemical engineer to be successful. When the project needs a resource, it is a staffing requirement.
   ☒ **A**, **C**, and **D** are all incorrect. This is not a situation describing an organizational interface or contractor requirements. Resource constraints might include a requirement to use a particular resource or that a resource must be available when certain project activities are happening.

4. ☑ **C.** In a Weak Matrix structure, functional management will have more authority than the project manager.
   ☒ **A**, **C**, and **D** are all incorrect since they do not have as much authority on a project in a weak matrix environment as functional management will have.

5. ☑ **C.** In this instance, the union is considered a project stakeholder since it has a vested interest in the project's outcome.
   ☒ **A** is incorrect because the union is not a resource constraint; they are interested in the project management methodology and the project human resource management. **B** is incorrect; the union is the counterweight to the management of the organization—not to the project itself. **D** is also incorrect; the union is not a project team member.

6. ☑ **B.** When projects are similar in nature, the project manager can use the roles and responsibilities definitions of the historical project to guide the current project.
   ☒ **A** is incorrect; the entire project plan of the ACT Project is not needed. Even the roles and responsibilities matrix of the historical project may not be an exact fit for the current project. **C** is incorrect; copying the project team structure is not the best choice of all the answers presented. **D** is also incorrect because using the same project team may not be feasible at all.

7. ☑ **C.** When project managers, or managers in general, are referred to as different terms, a job description is needed so the project manager can successfully complete the required obligations.
   ☒ **A** and **B** are incorrect choices. The project manager must know what the specific responsibilities, not the similarities and differences, between the current role and management. **D** is also incorrect; by the project manager knowing how to complete their job, the role of the project team should be evident.

8. ☑ **C.** Management is looking for a roles and responsibility matrix. This chart lists the roles and responsibilities, and depicts the intersection of the two.
   ☒ **A** and **B** are incorrect; management is looking for more than a listing of the roles and the associated responsibilities. **D** is not an acceptable answer for the scenario presented.

9. ☑ **B.** Theory X believes workers have an inherent dislike of work and will avoid it if possible. Micromanagement is a method, in regard to Theory X, to make certain workers complete their work.
   ☒ **A** and **C** are actually examples of McGregor's Theory Y. **D** is incorrect because EVM is not directly related to McGregor's Theory X and Y.

10. ☑ **B.** When the project team is afraid of the power the project manager yields, this is called coercive power.
   ☒ **A, C,** and **D** are incorrect since these describe assigned, referential, and technical power over the project.

11. ☑ **A.** The company president has assigned you to the position of the project manager, so you have formal power.
   ☒ **B** is incorrect because coercive power is the associated fear of the project manager. **C** is incorrect because expert power is derived from the project manager's experience with the technology being implemented. **D** is also incorrect; halo power is not a viable answer to the question.

12. ☑ **B.** The halo effect is the assumption that because the person is good at a technology they'd also be good at managing a project dealing with said technology.
   ☒ **A, C,** and **D** are all incorrect since these do not describe the halo effect.

13. ☑ **A.** Susan is an autocratic decision maker.
   ☒ **B** is incorrect because a democracy counts each project team member's opinion. **C** is incorrect; laissez faire allows the project team to make all the decisions. **D** is also incorrect; this is not exceptional project management.

14. ☑ **A.** Confronting is the best problem-solving technique since it meets the problem directly.
   ☒ **B** is incorrect; compromising requires both sides on an argument to give up something. **C** is incorrect; forcing requires the project manager to force a decision based on external inputs, such as seniority, experience, and so on. **D** is also incorrect; avoidance ignores the problem and does not solve it.

15. ☑ **D.** When Harold always has to win an argument and team members begin to give into Harold's demands simply to avoid the argument rather than to find an accurate solution, this is a yield-lose situation.

☒ **A** is incorrect since both parties do not win. **B** is incorrect since the project team member did not leave the conversation, but rather ended it. **C** is incorrect; a lose-lose is a compromise where both parties give up something.

16. ☑ **D.** Personality conflicts are likely a concern for the customer, but are not as important as project priorities, schedule, and cost. The customer hired your company to solve the technical issues.

☒ Choices **A**, **B**, and **C** are all incorrect since these are most likely the top issues for a company in a project of this magnitude.

17. ☑ **B.** Ouchi's Theory Z states that workers need to be involved with the management process.

☒ **A** is incorrect; McGregor's Theory of X and Y believes X workers don't want to work and need constant supervision; Z workers will work if the work is challenging, satisfying, and rewarding. **C** is incorrect; Herzberg's Theory of Motivation describes the type of people and what excites them to work. **D**, the Expectancy Theory, describes how people will work based on what they expect because of the work they do.

18. ☑ **D.** The Expectancy Theory describes how people will work based on what they expect because of the work they do. If people are rewarded because of the work they complete, and they like the reward (payment), they will continue to work.

☒ **A**, **B**, and **C** are all incorrect since these theories do not accurately describe the scenario presented.

19. ☑ **C.** You, the project manager, have expert power on this project because of your experience with the technology and with projects that are similar in nature.

☒ **A**, **B**, and **D** are all incorrect. These project management powers do not accurately describe the scenario. Formal power is appointed power. Coercive power describes fear of the project manager. Referent power describes power by association and personal knowledge.

20. ☑ **D.** This is referent power because the project team knows the project manager personally.

☒ **A** and **B** are incorrect choices; these do not describe the scenario. **C** is incorrect; expert power does not deal with the ability to lead and complete a project, but it focuses on being an expert with the technology that the project deals with.

21. ☑ **B.** Coercive power is the power a project manager yields over the project team. Coercive power is the formal authority a project manager has over the project team.

☒ **A** is incorrect; only referent power may come through lunch meetings. **C** is incorrect; experience is expert power. **D** is incorrect; interpersonal relationships are examples of referent power.

22. ☑ **C.** When both parties give up something, it is a compromise. A compromise is an example of a lose-lose solution.

    ☒ **A** is incorrect; win-win is accomplished through confrontation. **B** is incorrect; win-lose allows only one party to get what they want from the scenario. **D** is incorrect since a leave-lose solution is when one party walks away from the problem.

23. ☑ **C.** Forcing happens when the project manager makes a decision based on factors not relevant to the problem. Just because a team member has more seniority does not mean this individual is correct.

    ☒ **A, B,** and **D** are incorrect choices. Problem solving is not described in the scenario. **B,** compromising, happens when both parties agree to give up something. **D,** withdrawal, happens when a party leaves the argument.

24. ☑ **A.** project managers are typically assigned to a project on a full-time basis in a projectized organization.

    ☒ **B, C,** and **D** do not accurately describe the work schedule of a project manager in a projectized environment.

25. ☑ **C.** When a project team is collocated, all of the project team members are in the same physical location in order to increase their ability to work as a team.

    ☒ **A** and **B** are incorrect; collocated teams are not dispersed; non-collocated teams are dispersed. **D** is incorrect since a collocated team does not ensure that costs are reduced; in some situations, costs may be increased due to travel to bring all the team members together to complete the project.

10

Introducing Project Communications Management

W hat's the most important skill a project manager has? Communication. Project managers spend about ninety percent of their time communicating. Think about it: meetings, phone calls, memos, e-mails, reports, presentations, and the list goes on and on. Project managers spend the bulk of their day communicating news, ideas, and knowledge. A project manager is a communicator.

Project Communications Management centers on determining who needs what information and when—and then produces the plan to provide the needed information. Project Communications Management includes generating, collecting, disseminating, and storing communication. Successful projects require successful communication. Communication is the key link between people, ideas, and information.

Project Communications Management includes four processes, which may overlap each other and other knowledge areas. The four processes are:

- **Communication planning**   The project manager will need to identify the stakeholders and their communication needs and determine how to fulfill their requirements.

- **Information distribution**   The project manager will need to get the correct information on the correct schedule to the appropriate stakeholders.

- **Performance reporting**   The project manager will rely on EVM and other performance measurement to create status reports, measure performance, and forecast project conditions.

- **Administrative closure**   The project manager will need a routine of documentation, communication, and information distribution to close out a phase or project.

Communications Planning

Because project managers spend so much of their time invested in communications, it's essential for them to provide adequate planning for communication. Such planning focuses on who needs what information and when they need it. A project manager must identify the stakeholders' requirements for communication, determine what information is actually needed, and then plan to deliver the needed information on a preset schedule or based on project conditions.

Communications planning is typically completed early in the project. As part of this planning, the modality of the communications is documented. Some stakeholders may prefer a hard copy document rather than an e-mail. Later in the project these needs can change. Throughout the project, the needs of the stakeholders, the type of information requested, and the modality of the information should be reviewed for accuracy—and updated if needed.

Identifying Communication Requirements

Stakeholders will need different types of information depending on their interest in the project and the priority of the project. The project manager will need to complete an analysis of the identified stakeholders to determine what information they actually need—and how often the information is needed.

There is no value in expending resources on generating information, reports, and analyses for stakeholders who have no interest in the information. An accurate assessment of stakeholders' needs for information is required early in the project planning processes. As a rule of thumb, provide information when its presence contributes to success or when a lack of information can contribute to failure.

The project manager and the project team can identify the demand for communications on the basis of the following requirements:

- Project structure within the performing organization
- Stakeholder responsibility
- Departments and disciplines involved with the project work
- Number of individuals involved in the project and their locale
- Number and type of external communication needs (media, community, or customers)

On the PMP exam, and in the real world, the project manager will need to identify the number of communication channels within a project. Here's a magic formula to calculate the number of communication channels: $N(N-1)/2$, where N represents the number of identified stakeholders. For example, if a project has 10 stakeholders, the formula would read $10(10-1)/2$ for a total of 45 communication channels. Figure 10-1 illustrates the formula.

FIGURE 10-1

Communication channels must be identified.

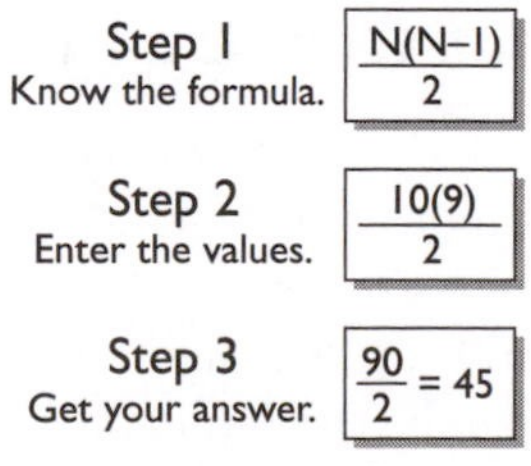

Step 1
Know the formula. $\dfrac{N(N-1)}{2}$

Step 2
Enter the values. $\dfrac{10(9)}{2}$

Step 3
Get your answer. $\dfrac{90}{2} = 45$

Exploring Communication Modalities

As part of the communications planning, the project manager should identify all of the required and approved methods of communicating. Some projects may be very sensitive and contain classified information that not all stakeholders are privy to; other projects may contain information that's open for anyone to explore. Whatever the case, the project manager should identify what requirements exist, if any, for the communication modalities.

Communication modalities can also include meetings, reports, memos, e-mails, and so on. The project manager should identify which are the preferred methods of communicating based on the conditions of the message to be communicated. Consider the following, which may have an effect on the communication plan:

- **Information schedule** Stakeholders, such as management and the project customer, may require regularly scheduled reports and updates. Should conditions within the project affect the project success, immediate communications may be expected.

- **Technology** Because of the demands of the project, there may be technology changes needed to fulfill the project request. For example, the project may require an internal web site that details project progress. If such a web site does not exist, then time and monies will need to be invested into this communication requirement.

- **Project staffing** The project manager should evaluate the abilities of the project team to determine if appropriate levels of competency exist to fulfill the communication requirements or if training will be required for the project team.

- **Project length** The length of the project can have an influence on the project technology. Advances in technology may replace a long-term project's communication model. A short-term project may not have the same technology requirements as a long-term project but could nevertheless benefit from the successful model a larger project uses.

Evaluating the Project Constraints and Assumptions

Every project has constraints and assumptions. Recall that constraints are any force that limits the project's options. A project constraint, such as contractual obligations, may require extensive communications. The requirements of the contract should be evaluated against the demands of the project staff to determine if extra resources will be needed to handle the communications.

Assumptions can also affect communications. Consider a project operating under the assumption that communications with management can happen only through e-mail. Management, however, expects the project manager to provide formal status reports and daily updates via memos and also needs staffing updates from each of the project team members. This false assumption can impose time demands the project manager had not expected.

Creating the Communications Plan

Based on stakeholder analysis, the project manager and the project team can determine what communications are needed. There's no advantage to supplying stakeholders with information that is not needed or desired. Time spent creating and delivering unneeded information is a waste of resources.

A Communications Management Plan can organize and document the process, types, and expectations of communications. It provides:

- A system to gather, organize, store, and disseminate appropriate information to the appropriate people. The system includes procedures for correcting and updating incorrect information that may have been distributed.

- Details on how needed information flows through the project to the correct individuals. The communication structure documents where the information will originate, to whom the information will be sent, and in what modality the information is acceptable.

- Specifics on how the information to be distributed should be organized, the level of expected detail for the types of communication, and the terminology expected within the communications.

- Schedules of when the various types of communication should occur. Some communication, such as status meetings, should happen on a regular schedule; other communications may be prompted by conditions within the project.

- Methods to retrieve information as needed.

- Instructions on how the Communications Management Plan can be updated as the project progresses.

Preparing for Information Distribution

Information distribution is the process of ensuring that the appropriate stakeholders get the appropriate information when and how they need it. Essentially, it's the implementation of the Communications Management Plan. The Communications Management Plan details how the information is to be created and dispersed—and also how the dispersed information is archived.

There are three elements that serve as inputs to information distribution:

- **Work results**   Work results, good or bad, serve as inputs to communication because they show progress (or lack of progress), quality issues, and other relevant information.

- **Communications Management Plan**   This plan serves as the guide on how to communicate on project issues within the performing organization.

- **Project plan**   The comprehensive project may have information, requirements, or described conditions that are integrated with communications.

Examining Communication Skills

Here's a news flash: communication skills are used to send and receive information. Sounds easy, right? If communication is so easy, then why are there so many problems on projects stemming from misunderstandings, miscommunications, failure to communicate, and similar communication failings.

Figure 10-2 demonstrates a few different communication models. All models, regardless of the technology involved, have a sender, a message, and a recipient. Depending on the communication model, several additional elements can be included. Here's a summary of all the different parts of communication models:

- **Sender**   The person or group sending the message to the receiver.

- **Encoder**   The device or technology that encodes the message to travel over the medium. For example, a telephone encodes the sender's voice to travel over the medium, the telephone wires.

- **Medium**   This is the path the message takes from the sender to the receiver. This is the modality in which the communication travels and typically refers to an electronic model, such as e-mail or telephone.

- **Decoder**   This is the inverse of the encoder. If a message is encoded, a decoder translates it back to usable format. For example, the sender's message is encoded to travel the telephone wires, and the receiver's phone system translates the message back to a usable format.

- **Receiver**   This is, of course, the recipient of the message.

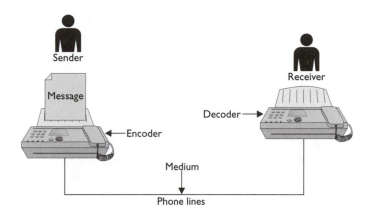

FIGURE 10-2

Sender models can vary based on the modality of the message.

Creating Successful Communications

The most common type of communication between a sender and a receiver is verbal communication. When verbal communications are involved, the project manager should remember that half of communication is listening. This means the project manager must confirm the receiver understands the message being sent. The confirmation of the sent message can be seen in the recipients body language, feedback, and verbal confirmation of the sent message. There are five terms that describe the process of communicating:

- **Paralingual** The pitch, tone, and inflections in the sender's voice affect the message being sent.

- **Feedback** The sender confirms the receiver understands the message by directly asking for a response, questions for clarification, or other confirmation of the sent message.

- **Active listening** The receiver confirms the message is being received through feedback, questions, prompts for clarity, and other signs of confirmation of the received message.

- **Effective listening** The receiver is involved in the listening experience by paying attention to visual clues from the speaker and paralingual characteristics and by asking relevant questions.

- **Nonverbal** Approximately 55 percent of communication is nonverbal. Facial expressions, hand gestures, and body language contribute to the message.

The words in a oral message actually only account for seven percent of the message. The tonality of the message accounts for 38 percent of the message. The remaining

55 percent of the message is body language. A classic example involves a person talking to a dog. If the person has a friendly voice and posture, the dog will likely be receptive. However, if the person has a mean voice and guarded posture, the dog may feel threatened and on guard. When project managers talk with stakeholders, they must be aware of their body language and posture—not just the words they are communicating.

The medium in communication can help or hinder the message. For example, when a project manager talks to a stakeholder in person, the stakeholder has the advantage not only of hearing the message and tone but also of seeing the body language. Take out body language in a conversation and the message is interpreted by just the words and tonality. Always be aware of the downsides of the various non-direct communication modalities: e-mail, reports, memos, and letters.

Creating a Communications Matrix

A communications matrix can help the project manager organize communication needs by identifying who needs what information and when. A communications matrix identifies all of the stakeholders and shows where communication originates and to whom it is intended. The following table shows a sample of a basic communications matrix.

	Project Manager	Project Sponsor	Project Office	Project Team	Functional Managers	Customers	Media	Government Agencies
Project Manager		X	X	X	X	X	X	X
Project Sponsor	X		X				X	
Project Office	X	X			X			
Project Team	X				X			X
Functional Managers	X	X		X				
Customers	X			X				
Media	X	X						
Government Agencies	X			X		X		

Creating Information Retrieval Systems

What good is information if no one can find it? An information retrieval system allows for fast and accurate access to project information. It can be a simple manual filing system, an advanced database of information storage, or a robust project management software suite. Whatever the approach, the information must be accessible, organized, and secure.

The project team, the project manager, the customer, and other stakeholders may need access to design specs, blueprints, plans, and other project information. A good information retrieval system is reliable and easy to navigate and is updated as new information becomes available.

Distributing Information

Throughout the project, the project manager, the project sponsor, the project team, and other stakeholders are going to need and supply information to one another. The methods for distributing information can vary—but the best modality is the one that's most appropriate to the information being conveyed. In other words, an e-mail may not be the correct format to share variance information on project costs.

Information can be distributed through the following as well as other methods, according to project demands and as technology provides:

- Project meetings
- Hard-copy documentation
- Databases
- Faxes
- E-mail
- Telephone calls
- Videoconferences
- A project web site

Examining the Results of Information Distribution

Information distribution results in the following:

- **Project records**   Project records are vital to the project team. Project records are the memos, correspondence, e-mails, and any other project-relevant information. It's important to secure and organize this information throughout the project for future reference. This information should be stored as part of the project archives.

■ **Project reports**   Reports are formal communications on project activities, status, and conditions. Management, customers, and policies within the performing organization may have differing requirements for when reports are required.

■ **Project presentations**   Presentations are useful in providing information to customers, management, the project team, and other stakeholders. The delivery and degree of formality of the presentation should be appropriate for the conditions and information being delivered within the project.

Reporting Project Performance

Throughout the project, customers and other stakeholders are going to need updates on the project performance. Performance reporting is the process of collecting, organizing, and disseminating information on how the project resources are being used to complete the project objectives. In other words, the people footing the bill and affected by the outcome of the project need some confirmation that things are going the way the project manager has promised.

Performance reporting covers more than just cost and schedule, though these are the most common concerns. Another huge concern is the influence of risks on the project success. The project manager and the project team must continue to monitor and evaluate risks, including pending risks and their impact on the project success.

Finally, another major issue with reporting is the level of quality. No one will praise the project manager and the project team for completing the project on time and on budget if the quality of the work is unacceptable. In fact, the project could be declared a failure and cancelled as a result of poor quality, or the project team would have to redo the work, business could be lost, or individuals could even harmed as a result of the poor quality of the project work.

Performance reporting involves six things:

■ **Status reports**   How's the project right now?

■ **Progress reports**   How complete is the project? How much more work remains?

■ **Forecasting**   Will this project end on schedule? Will the project be on budget? How much longer will this project take? And how much more money will this project need to finish?

■ **Scope**   How is the project meeting the project scope?

- **Quality**   What are the results of quality audit, testing, and analysis?
- **Risks**   What risks have come into the project and what has been their affect on the project?

Preparing for Performance Reporting

The project plan is one of the key inputs to performance reporting. The project plan contains the WBS, the project scope and requirements, and other documentation that can be used to measure project progress and performance.

Other inputs to performance reporting are the work results. Work results can be examined and measured for quality, time spent completing the work, and the monies required to complete the work results. The work results, as progress reports or completion of work results, can be measured against the estimates and expectations to reveal variances. The Communications Management Plan will detail how values are measured, for example EVM, and at what point variances call for communications to the appropriate stakeholders.

The last inputs to performance reporting are other project records, such as memos, product description, and other information relevant to the project. For example, a customer may request project status updates every quarter, regardless of where the project is in its timeline. Or a project may have multiple vendors whose contracts require differing levels and types of reporting from the project staff. This is a communication requirement that would be in the Communications Management Plan.

Reviewing Project Performance

The project manager will host performance review meetings to ascertain the progress and level of success the project team is having with the project work. Performance review meetings focus on the work that has been completed and how the work results are living up to the time and cost estimates. In addition, the project manager and the project team will evaluate the project scope to protect it from change and creep. The project manager and the project team will also examine quality and its affect on the project as a whole. Finally, the project manager must lead a discussion on pending or past risks and determine any new risks and overall risk likelihood and impact on the project's success.

Analyzing Project Variances

Performance review meetings are not the only tools the project manager uses to assess project performance. Prior to the performance reviews, or spurred by a performance review, the project manager needs to examine the time, scope, quality and cost variances within the project. The project manager will examine the estimates supplied for the time and cost of activities and compare it to the time and cost actually experienced.

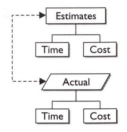

The goals of analyzing project variances are:

- Prevent future variances
- Determine the root cause of variances
- Determine if the variances are an anomaly or if the estimates were flawed
- Determine if the variances are within a predetermine acceptable range, such as negative ten percent or plus five percent
- Determine if the variances can be expected on future project work

In addition to examining the time and cost variances, which are the most common, the project manager must also examine any scope, resource, and quality variances. A change in the scope can skew time and cost predictions. A variance in resources, such as the expected performance by a given resource, can alter the project schedule and even the predicted costs of a project. Quality variances may result in rework, lost time, lost monies, and even rejection of the project product.

Completing Trend Analysis

Picture this: you're a project manager for a long-term project. You'd like to examine how performance has been for the past few years to predict how the upcoming performance will be expected. You're doing trend analysis. Trend analysis is an approach of studying trends within past performance to predict what upcoming experiences may be like. Trend analysis is great for long projects, analysis of team performance, and predicting future activities.

Using Earned Value Analysis

Remember Earned Value from Chapter 7? Earned Value, in case you were eager for Chapter 10 and flew past Chapter 7, is the basis of a common approach to performance measurement. It is a series of formulas that can reveal cost and time variances and can predict what may happen in the remaining portion of the project. Figure 10-3 provides a recap of earned value.

on the **Job**

EV is not the most common approach to performance measurement. It is, however, being widely used in government projects. More and more commercial projects are adapting the approach.

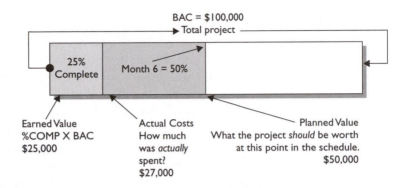

FIGURE 10-3

Earned Value
can show and
predict project
performance.

Variances

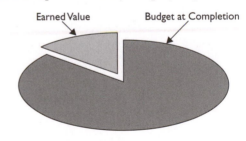

At the end of the project will there be a budget variance (VAR)? Any variance at the
end of the project is calculated by subtracting the Actual Costs (AC) of the project
work from the Budget at Completion (BAC). Throughout the project,
however, a variance is any result that is different from what planned or
expected.

Earned Value

Earned Value (EV) is the work that has been accomplished within the project plus the

authorized budget for the work that has
been accomplished. There are several
methods to calculate the EV of the project
work, but the most common method is
the percentage of the work completed
multiplied by the budget at completion
(BAC). For example, if a project has a
budget of $200,000 and ten percent of
the work is complete, the EV is $20,000.

Earned Value   Budget at Completion

Cost Variances

The Cost Variance (CV) is the difference between the Earned Value and the Actual
Costs (AC). For example, for a project that has a budget of $200,000 and has earned
or completed ten percent of the project value, the EV is $20,000.
However, due to some unforeseen incidents, the project manager had
to spend $25,000 to complete that $20,000 worth of work. The AC
of the project, at this point, is $25,000. The Cost Variance is $5,000.
The equation for Cost Variance is: $CV = EV - AC$.

Schedule Variances

A Schedule Variance (SV) is the value that represents the difference between where the project was planned to be at a point in time and where the project actually is. For example, consider a project with a budget of $200,000 that's expected to last two years. At the end of year one, the project team has planned the project to be 60 percent complete. The Planned Value (PV), then, for 60 percent completion equates to $120,000—the expected worth of the project work at the end of year one. At the end of year one, however, the project is only 40 percent complete. The EV at the end of year one is, therefore, $80,000. The difference between the PV and the EV is the SV: $40,000. The equation for Schedule Variance is: SV = EV–PV.

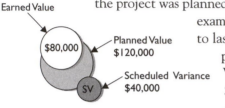

Earned Value $80,000
Planned Value $120,000
Scheduled Variance $40,000
SV

Cost Performance Index

The Cost Performance Index (CPI) shows the amount of work the project is completing per dollar spent on the project. In other words, a CPI of .93 means it is costing $1.00 for every 93 cent's worth of work. Or you could say the project is losing seven cents on every dollar spent on the project. In our example, the project has an EV of $20,000 and an AC of $25,000. The CPI for this project is .80. The closer the number is to 1, the better the project is doing. The equation for Cost Performance Index is: CPI = EV/AC.

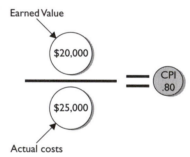

Earned Value $20,000
Actual costs $25,000
CPI .80

Schedule Performance Index

The Schedule Performance Index (SPI) is very similar to the CPI. The SPI, however, reveals how closely the project is on schedule. Again, the closer the quotient is to 1 the better. The formula is EV divided by the PV. In our example, the EV is $20,000, and let's say the PV, where the project is supposed to be, is calculated as $30,000. The SPI for this project is .67—way off target! The equation for Schedule Performance Index is: SPI = EV/PV.

Earned Value $20,000
Planned Value $30,000
SPI .67

Estimate at Completion

The Estimate at Completion (EAC) is a prediction of what the final project cost will be based on experiences in the project so far. There are several different formulas to calculate the EAC, all of which are included in Chapter 7. For

Here are a couple of index tips. EV comes first in any formula where it's used (those for CV, SV, CPI, and SPI). A variance is a subtraction problem; an index is a division problem. Also, pay close attention to the decimal point in the answer. A choice without the decimal is wrong; in other words "87" and ".87" are not the same.

now, and for the exam, here's the EAC formula you'll need to know: EAC = BAC/CPI. In our project, the BAC is $200,000. The CPI was calculated to be .80. The EAC for this project is $250,000.

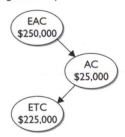

Estimate to Complete

The Estimate to Complete (ETC) shows how much more money will be needed to complete the project. It's a straightforward formula: EAC–AC. Our EAC was calculated to be $250,000, and let's say our AC is $25,000; our ETC would then be $225,000.

Variance at Completion

Whenever you talk about variances it's the difference between what was expected and what was experienced. The formula for the Variance at Completion (VAC) is VAC = BAC–EAC. In our example, the BAC was $200,000, and the EAC was $250,000, so the VAC is predicted to be $50,000.

EV and Communications

Based on the results of earned value analysis, a communication to management may be required. A common approach is through a method called a *bull's eye*. The bull's eye approach creates limits to what would be acceptable earned values. Any variances that exceed these limits automatically prompts a communication to management. Figure 10-4 is a sample bull's eye.

FIGURE 10-4

A bull's eye can determine when communication to management is required.

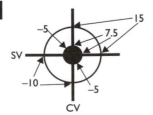

Here are five rules to remember the EVM formulas:

- Always start with EV.
- Variance means subtraction.
- Index means division.
- Less than 1 is bad in an index.
- Negative is bad in a variance.

The formulas for earned value analysis can be completed manually or through project management software. For the exam, you'll want to memorize these formulas. The table below is a summary of all the formulas and a sample, albeit goofy, mnemonic device.

Name	Formula	Sample Mnemonic Device
Variance	VAR=BAC–AC	Victor
Earned Value	EV=%complete X BAC	Eats
Cost Variance	CV=EV–AC	Carl's
Schedule Variance	SV=EV–PV	Sugar
Cost Performance Index	CPI=EV/AC	Corn
Schedule Performance Index	SPI=EV/PV	S (These three spell "SEE")
Estimate at Completion	EAC=BAC/CPI	E
Estimate to Complete	ETC=EAC–AC	E
Variance at Completion	VAC=BAC–EAC	Victor

Examining the Results of Performance Reporting

The goal of performance reporting is to share information regarding the project performance with the appropriate stakeholders. Of course, performance reporting is not something done only at the end of the project or after a project phase, but is rather done on a regular schedule, as detailed in the communication plan, or as project conditions warrant. Outputs of performance reporting include:

- **Performance reports**   These are the results and summation of the project performance analysis. The Communications Management Plan will detail the type of report needed based on the conditions within the project, the timing of the communication, and the demands of the project stakeholder.

- **Change requests**   Results of performance may prompt change requests to some area of the project. The change requests should flow into the change control system for consideration and approval or denial.

Performance reports and change requests are an input to the following Change Control Processes:

- Integrated Change Control
- Scope Change Control
- Schedule Change Control
- Cost Change Control

Completing Administrative Closure

The end of each project phase and the end of the project need administrative closure. Administrative closure is the documenting of the project results and the acceptance of the product by the customer or the project sponsor. Administrative closure is also needed should a project be terminated. Administrative closure includes the following:

- Documentation of the project work
- Confirmation that the product is in alignment with requirements and specifications
- Analysis of project success or failure
- Analysis of the effectiveness of the project management process
- Lesson Learned documentation

Administrative closure should happen at the end of each phase and at the end of the project. If the project manager waits too long to complete administrative closure, important information can be lost. The resource pool description should also be updated to reflect any new skills learned by the project team members as part of the project.

INSIDE THE EXAM

Communication is the most important skill a project manager can have. Project managers spend 90 percent of their time communicating. Since the project manager is expected to spend so much time communicating, you can bet the project manager needs a plan to determine what needs to be communicated, to whom, and when. The Communications Management Plan is the comprehensive plan the project manager and the project team rely on for all communication guidance.

The organizational structure affects the level of communications the project manager can expect. Matrix structures have to include the functional managers of the project team from the different units within the organization, whereas a functional organization does not have the same level of complexity in reporting.

The basic communication model consists of a sender, a message, and a receiver. When technology is involved, the project can become more complex: encoders, the medium, and decoders are included. Consider sending a fax: you are the sender and Jane is the recipient, and the message is the information on the page to be faxed. The encoder is your outgoing fax machine, and Jane's fax machine is the decoder. The telephone lines between the fax machines are the medium.

Management, customers, and other concerned stakeholders will be interested in the performance of the project. The project manager will need to meet their expectations on an established schedule or based on conditions within the project. One of the most common methods for showing performance is through earned value analysis.

Administrative closure happens at the end of each phase and at the end of the project. Administrative closure is the final documentation of the project; it includes the process of organizing, indexing, and archive all relevant project materials. The archived materials should show the project performance from start to formal acceptance that signals project closure.

Preparing for Administrative Closure

Any documentation used throughout the project phases that demonstrates project performance should be organized. The performance measurements set in the project plan should be included as part of these performance measurement documents. As the administrative closure happens, the project manager can refer to the original performance measurement goals and compare these to the experienced performance measurements. This comparison will reveal any variances and show overall project or phase performance.

In addition to the performance measurement documentation, the project manager will need all of the project plans, product specifications, technical documentation, drawings, and any other information relevant to the final product or the project or phase. These documents will allow the project manager, the customer, and the project sponsor to inspect the project product to confirm the deliverable of the phase is in alignment with what was planned for.

Completing Administrative Closure

Armed with the project information, the project manager can document, confirm, and close the project or phase. The end result of the project or phase includes the following:

- **Project archives** The sum of the documentation of the project should be organized, structured, and indexed for fast and accurate reference. In addition, any databases containing project information should be updated to reflect the completion of the project. A failure to update the databases and project archives can mislead future projects attempting to emulate the current project.

- **Procurement issues** Any time a project includes procurement issues, the contracts, purchase orders, invoices, warranties, and any other financial-related documentation should be indexed and archived for future reference.

- **Project closure** The project sponsor or the customer should confirm that the project has met all of the requirements of the project scope. When the requirements have been met, the project manager may have additional activities, as required by the performing organization. The project manager may need to complete any financial records, to sign-off of the project deliverable, and to complete employee evaluations and a final project summary for management.

- **Lessons Learned** As the project moves through its phases, the project manager and the project team should be completing the Lesson Learned for future reference. At the end of the project closure, the Lesson Learned documentation should be archived as well—for future reference.

Administrative closure uses the same tools and techniques as performance reporting, but takes a view of the entire project or phase.

CERTIFICATION SUMMARY

Communication is a project manager's most important skill. Project managers have to communicate with management, customers, the project team members, and the rest of the stakeholders involved with the project. The project manager's foundation is communication – without effective communication how will work get completed, progress reported, and information dispersed?

Communications planning centers on, "Who needs what information—and when do they need it?" Consider all of the different channels for communication on any project. That's many different possibilities for information to be lost, messages to be skewed, and progress hindered. The formula for calculating the communication channels is N(N–1)/2 where N represents the number of stakeholders. As a general rule, larger projects require more detail—and detail means more planning for communications.

The Communications Management Plan organizes and documents the communication processes, acceptable modalities for types of communication, and the stakeholder expectations for communication. The plan should detail how information is gathered, organized, accessed, and dispersed. The plan should also provide a schedule of expected communication based on a calendar schedule, such as project status meetings. Some communications are prompted by conditions within the project such as cost variances, schedule variances, or other performance related issues.

The communication model illustrates the flow of communication from the sender to receiver. The sender sends the message. The message is encoded by the encoder and travels over the medium. A decoder decodes the message for the receiver. This model is easy to remember if you apply the processes to a telephone call.

Within communicating there are five characteristics that affect the message:

- Paralingual: pitch, tone, and voice inflections
- Feedback: sender confirmation of the message by asking questions, for a response, or other confirmation signals
- Active listening: receiver confirms message receipt
- Effective listening: receiver offers confirmation of the message, such as nodding their head, asking questions, or other interactions.
- Nonverbal: facial expressions, hand gestures, and body language

KEY TERMS

To pass the PMP exams, you will need to memorize these terms and their definitions. For maximum value, create your own flashcards based on these definitions and review them daily. The definitions can be found within this chapter and in the glossary.

active listening	encoder	progress reports
administrative closure	Estimate at Completion	receiver
bull's eye	Estimate to Complete	Schedule Performance Index
Communications Management Plan	feedback	Schedule Variance
Cost Performance Index	forecasting	sender
Cost Variance	medium	status reports
decoder	N(N–1)/2	trend analysis
Earned Value	nonverbal	variance
effective listening	paralingual	Variance at Completion

✓ TWO-MINUTE DRILL

Planning for Communication

- ❏ Communication centers on who needs what and on when and how you are going to give it to them.
- ❏ Communication requirements are set by stakeholders.
- ❏ Communication planning is accomplished early in the planning processes.
- ❏ Communications are linked to the organizational structure of the performing organization.
- ❏ Constraints and assumptions can affect the communications planning.

Communications Management Plan

- ❏ Provides instructions on how to gather and disseminate project information.
- ❏ Provides instructions on the communications methods, such as hard copies, reports, and e-mail.
- ❏ Includes a schedule of expected communications, such as reports and meetings.
- ❏ Provides a method to access needed information between regularly scheduled communications.

Performance Reporting

- ❏ Status reporting provides current information on the project.
- ❏ Progress reporting provides information on what the team has accomplished—and may include information on what is yet to be accomplished.
- ❏ Forecasting provides information on how the remainder of the project or phase is expected to go.
- ❏ Variance analysis examines the reason why cost, schedule, scope, quality, and other factors may vary from what was planned.
- ❏ Trend analysis is the study of trends over time to reveal patterns and expectations of future results.
- ❏ Earned value analysis is a series of formulas that reveal and predict project performance.
- ❏ Change requests may stem from performance reports.

Administrative Closure

❏ Administrative closure is the formal documentation, organization, and archival aspects of a project or phase acceptance.

❏ Administrative closure should also happen when the project is terminated.

❏ The project archives include the complete index of all project records, documents, product specifications, and any relevant documents. The project archives will serve as historical information for future projects.

❏ The project team and the project manager complete the Lessons Learned documents throughout the project phases.

SELF TEST

1. Of the following, which one is not an example of formal communications?

A. Presentations to groups

B. Ad hoc conversations

C. Contractual agreements

D. Presentations to management

2. Of the following, which one is an example of informal communications?

A. Memos

B. Presentations to groups

C. Briefings

D. Speeches

3. You are the project manager for the LKH Project. Management has requested that you create a document detailing what information will be expected from stakeholders and to whom that information will be disseminated. Management is asking for which one of the following?

A. Roles and responsibilities matrix

B. Scope Management Plan

C. Communications Management Plan

D. Communications worksheet

4. Which one of the following will help you, the project manager, complete the needed Communications Management Plan by identifying the stakeholders and their communication needs?

A. Identification of all communication channels

B. Formal documentation of all communication channels

C. Formal documentation of all stakeholders

D. Communication matrix

5. You are the project manager for the JGI Project. You have 32 stakeholders on this project. How many communications channels do you have?

A. Depends on the number of project team members.

B. 496

C. 32

D. 1

6. You are the project manager for the KLN Project. You had 19 stakeholders on this project. You have added three team members to the project. How many more communication channels do you have now than before?

    A. 171

    B. 231

    C. 60

    D. 1

7. A memo has been sent to you, the project manager, project team members, and the project customers from the project sponsor. In this instance, who is the encoder?

    A. Project sponsor

    B. Project manager

    C. Project team members

    D. Project customers

8. Which one of the following can use EVM in its preparation for management?

    A. Status reports

    B. Trend reports

    C. Performance reports

    D. All of the above

9. What does the following figure mean?

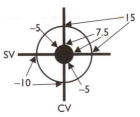

    A. It is a control chart to manage communications between the project manager and the project sponsor.

    B. It is a control chart to manageme communications between the project manager and Management.

    C. It is a variance chart to manage communications between the project manager and Management.

    D. It is a bull's eye to manage communications between the project manager and the Management.

10. Of the following, which term describes the pitch and tone of an individual's voice?

    A. Paralingual

    B. Feedback

    C. Effective listening

    D. Active listening

11. You are the project manager of the KMH Project. This project is slated to last eight years. You have just calculated EVM and have a CV of –$3500. What type of report is needed for management?

    A. Progress report
    B. Forecast report
    C. Exception report
    D. Trends report

12. In your Communications Management Plan, you have detailed administrative closure. At what point will administrative closure take place?

    A. When the project is archived
    B. At the completion of each phase
    C. Only when the project is complete or cancelled
    D. As management sees fit

13. You are the project manager for OOK Project. You will be hosting project meetings every week. Of the following, which one is not a valid rule for project meetings?

    A. Schedule recurring meetings as soon as possible
    B. Allow project meetings to last as long as needed
    C. Distribute meeting agendas prior to the meeting start
    D. Allow the project team to have input to the agenda

14. The three basic elements needed for communication in project management are

    A. Words, sentences, paragraphs
    B. Proper grammar, spelling, ideas
    C. Verbal, nonverbal, action
    D. Sender, receiver, message

15. Which one of the following is the method of analyzing project performance preferred in government projects?

    A. Communications management
    B. Management by walking around
    C. EVM
    D. Variance analysis

16. What percentage of a message is sent through nonverbal communications, such as facial expressions, hand gestures, and body language?

    A. Greater than 50 percent

B. 30 to 40 percent

C. 20 to 30 percent

D. 10 to 20 percent

17. Which one is not a filter for receivers of communication?

A. Culture

B. Conflict

C. Knowledge

D. Language

18. You are finalizing project completion. You will gather, generate, and disseminate project information. This is known as which one of the following?

A. Project closure

B. Project postmortem

C. Administrative closure

D. Operational transfer

19. Often in project management you will have to negotiate. Negotiations work best in which environment?

A. Caution and yielding

B. Sincerity, honesty, and extreme caution

C. Mutual respect and admiration

D. Mutual respect and cooperation

20. You are the project manager for the PMU Project. Your project has 13 members. You have been informed that next week your project will receive the seven additional members you requested. How many channels of communications will you have next week?

A. 1

B. 78

C. 190

D. 201

21. Which one of the following will result in the most productive results when negotiating?

A. Yielding

B. Forcing

C. Collaborating

D. Compromising

22. Which one of the following is an output from performance reporting?

   A. Trend analysis

   B. EVM

   C. Variance analysis

   D. Change requests

23. The process of sending information from the project manager to the project team is called which of the following:

   A. Functioning

   B. Matrixing

   C. Blended communications

   D. Transmitting

24. George is the project manager of the 7YH Project. In this project, George considers the relation between himself and the customer to be of utmost important. Which one of the following is a valid reason for George's belief in the importance of the relationship between the customer and himself?

   A. The customer will complete George's performance evaluation. A poor communication model between George and the customer will affect his project bonus.

   B. The customer is not familiar in project management. George must educate the customer on the process.

   C. The customer is always right.

   D. The communication between the customer and George can convey the project objectives more clearly than can the language in the project contract.

25. Which one of the following means that communications occur?

   A. The transfer of knowledge

   B. The outputting of knowledge

   C. The presence of knowledge

   D. The transmission of knowledge

SELF TEST ANSWERS

1. ☑ **B.** Ad hoc conversations, while often effective, are not examples of formal communications, as they are impromptu meetings.
   ☒ **A,** presentations to groups, is an example of formal communication. **C,** contractual agreements, are a type of formal communication. Finally, **D** is incorrect; presentations to management are formal.

2. ☑ **A.** Memos are examples of informal communication.
   ☒ Choices **B, C,** and **D** are incorrect, as presentations, briefings, and speeches are formal communication.

3. ☑ **C.** Management is requesting a Communications Management Plan, which details the requirements and expectations for communicating information among the project stakeholders.
   ☒ **A** is incorrect; a roles and responsibilities matrix depicts who does what and who makes what decisions. **B,** the Scope Management Plan, is also incorrect; this plan explains how changes to the scope may be allowed depending on the circumstances. **D** is not a valid choice for the question.

4. ☑ **D.** A communication matrix is an excellent tool to identify the stakeholders and their requirements for communication.
   ☒ **A, B,** and **C** are incorrect, as these choices do not fully answer the question. A communication matrix is the best tool to identify stakeholders' requirements for communication.

5. ☑ **B.** Using the formula $N(N-1)/2$, where N represents the number of stakeholders, there are 496 communication channels.
   ☒ Choices **A, C,** and **D** are incorrect; these values do not reflect the number of communication channels on the project.

6. ☑ **C.** This is a tough question, but typical of the PMP exam. The question asks how many more communication channels exist. You'll have to calculate the new value, which is 231, and then subtract the original value, which is 171, for a total of 60 new channels.
   ☒ **A.** is incorrect; 171 is the original number of communication channels. **B** is incorrect as this value reflects the new number of communication channels. **D** is not a valid choice.

7. ☑ **A.** The project sponsor is the source of the memo, as this is the sender of the message.
   ☒ **B, C,** and **D** are all recipients of the memo, not the sender, so they cannot be the source of the message.

8. ☑ **D.** Status, trend, and performance reports can all use EVM as an input.
   ☒ Choices **A, B,** and **C** are all incorrect, as EVM can be used in each of these reports.

9. ☑ **D.** The figure is called a communications bull's eye and is used to trigger communication needs to management when EVM results fall within the identified ranges.

☒   Choices **A, B,** and **C** are incorrect, as these choices do not accurately identify the illustration.

10. ☑ **A.** Paralingual is a term used to describe the pitch and tone of one's voice.
☒   **B,** feedback, is a request to confirm the information sent in the conversation. **C,** effective listening, is the ability to understand the message through what is said, facial expressions, gestures, tone and pitch, and son on. **D,** active listening, is the process of confirming what is understood and asking for clarification when needed.

11. ☑ **C.** An exception report is typically completed when variances exceed a given limit.
☒   **A** is incorrect; progress reports describe the progress of the project or phase. **B** is incorrect, as this is not a valid answer. **D,** trends report, is an analysis of project trends over time.

12. ☑ **B.** Administrative closure should take place at the completion of each phase.
☒   **A,** while tempting, is incorrect; administrative closure will need to be completed prior to archiving the project records. **C** is also incorrect; administrative closure does not take place only at project completion and cancellation; it can happen at the end of each project phase. **D** is not a valid choice.

13. ☑ **B.** Project meetings should have a set time limit.
☒   **A, B,** and **C** are incorrect answers because these are good attributes of project team meetings.

14. ☑ **D.** The three parts to communication are sender, receiver, and message.
☒   Choices **A, B,** and **C** are all incorrect choices.

15. ☑ **C.** EVM is all about analyzing project performance.
☒   **A.** communications management, focuses on managing communications, not performance. **B,** management by walking around, is an effective management style, but it does reflect project performance. **D,** variance analysis, focuses on the root causes of variances within the project, but not solely on the project performance.

16. ☑ **A.** Greater than 50 percent of a message is sent through nonverbal communications.
☒   Choices **B, C,** and **D** are incorrect.

17. ☑ **B** Conflict is not a filter of communication——it is a communication hindrance.
☒   Choices **A, C,** and **D** are incorrect choices; culture, knowledge, and language are filters for receivers.

18. ☑ **C.** Administrative closure is the process of generating, gathering, and disseminating project information.
☒   **A** and **B** are incorrect, as project closure and project postmortem involve more than just generating, gathering, and disseminating project information. **D,** operational transfer, is the process of moving the project deliverable into operations.

19. ☑ **D.** Mutual respect and cooperation is the environment needed for fair and balanced negotiations.

☒ **A,** caution and yielding, is not a good environment for negotiations. **B,** while tempting, is not the best choice. **C** is incorrect, as the people in negotiations don't necessarily need to admire one another.

20. ☑ **C.** The project currently has 13 team members and next week seven additional team members come aboard for a total of 20 team members. Using the formula N(N–1)/2 where N is the number of identified stakeholders the communication channels equal 190.

☒ **A, B,** and **D** are all incorrect choices.

21. ☑ **C.** Collaborating is the ideal method when negotiating. The goal of negotiations is to work together for the good of the project.

☒ **A,** yielding, is not working for the good of the project. **B,** forcing, exerts power over one party without properly negotiating. **D,** compromising, calls for both parties to give up something without necessarily working together for the good of the project.

22. ☑ **D.** Of all the choices, change requests is the only acceptable answer. Incidentally, there are two outputs of performance reporting: change requests and performance reports.

☒ **A.** Trend analysis is the study of project performance results to determine if the project is improving or failing. It is a tool used as part of performance reporting, but it is not an output of performance reporting. **B** and **C** are also tools used in performance reporting, but they are not an output of the process.

23. ☑ **D.** When information is sent, it is considered to be transmitted.

☒ **A, B,** and **C** are all incorrect choices.

24. ☑ **D.** George and the customer's relationship can allow clearer communication on the project objectives than what may be expressed in the project contract. The contract should take precedence on any issues, but direct contact is often the best way to achieve clear and concise communication.

☒ **A** is an incorrect choice as the focus is on personal gain rather than the good of the project. **B** is incorrect as the customer does not necessarily need to be educated on the project management process. **C** is incorrect; the customer is not always right——the contract will take precedence in any disagreements.

25. ☑ **A.** The transfer of knowledge is evidence that communication has occurred.

☒ **B** and **C** do not necessarily mean the knowledge has originated from the source and been transferred to the recipient. **D** is incorrect; messages are transmitted, but knowledge is transferred.

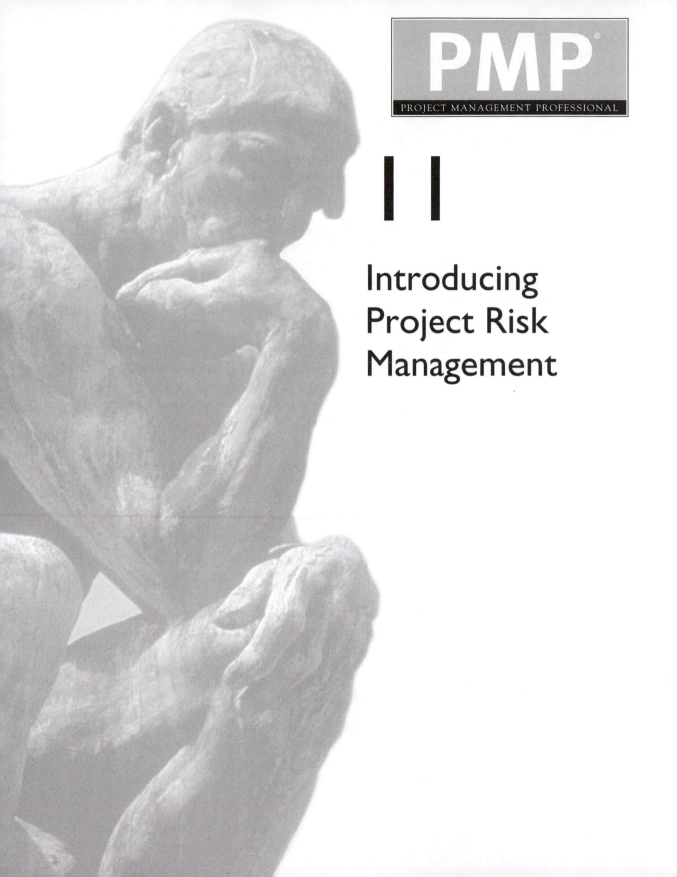

PMP
PROJECT MANAGEMENT PROFESSIONAL

11

Introducing Project Risk Management

Risk is everywhere. From driving a car to parachuting, risk is inherent in the activities we choose. Within a project, risks are unplanned events or conditions that can have a positive or negative effect on its success. Not all risks are bad, but almost all are seen as a threat.

The risks that activities bring are an exchange for the benefits we get from accepting that risk. If a person chooses to jump out of a perfectly good airplane for the thrill of the fall, the exhilaration of the parachute opening, and the view of earth rushing up, there is a risk that the chute may not open—a risk that thrill seekers are willing to accept.

Project managers, to some extent, are like these thrill seekers. Parachutists complete training, pack their chutes, check and double-check their equipment, and make certain there's an emergency chute for those "just-in-case" scenarios. Project managers—good project managers—have a similar approach.

Risks in a project, should they come to fruition, can mean total project failure, increased costs, and extended project duration among other things. Risk often has a negative connotation, but like the parachutist, the acceptance of the risk can also offer a reward. For the parachutist, the risk is certain death—but the reward is the thrill of the activity. For project managers, risk can mean failure, but the reward can mean a time or cost savings, as well as other benefits.

Risk management is the process in which the project manager and project team identify project risks, analyze and rank them, and determine what actions, if any, need to be taken to avert these threats. Associated with this process are the costs, time, and quality concerns of the project brought about by the solutions to those risks. In addition, the reactions to risks are analyzed for any secondary risks the solutions may have created.

In this chapter, we'll discuss risk management planning, risk identification, analysis, response planning, and the monitoring and control of the identified risks. For the PMP exam, you'll need a firm grasp on these concepts. You'll be taking a real risk if you don't know them well.

Planning for Risk Management

Risk management planning is about making decisions. The project manager, the project team, and other key stakeholders are involved to determine the risk management processes. The risk management process is in relation to the scope of the project, the priority of the project within the performing organization, and the impact of the project deliverables. In other words, a simple, low-impact project won't have the same level of risk planning as a high-priority, complex project.

Referring to the Project Charter

One of the first inputs to risk management is the project charter. The project charter, as you may recall, formally authorizes the project, and clearly identifies the project manager as the authority who will assign resources to the project. The charter is needed in risk management planning because it identifies the business need of the project and the overall product description.

Risks that can prevent the project from satisfying the business need of the project must be addressed. The product description must also be evaluated to determine what risks may be preventing the project work from obtaining the acceptable product description.

Relying on Risk Management Policies

Organizations often have a pre-defined approach to risk management. The policies can define the activities to initiate, plan, and respond to risk. The project manager must map the project risk management to these policies to conform to the organization's requirements. Within the confines of the risk management policy, the project manager must identify any component that can hinder the success of the project.

Considering Roles and Responsibilities

In many organizations, there are predefined roles and responsibilities that influence risk management planning, the decisions relevant to the risks, and the involvement of the project participants. These roles and responsibilities—and the policies associated with working with these individuals—should be identified and considered early in the project process to save time and frustration.

In addition, the project manager should have full knowledge of the power and autonomy he has on the project. For example, a project manager may want to create plans and reactions to the risks within a project, but the policies within the performing organization limit the amount of power the project manager has to make decisions regarding risk management. Knowledge of the limit of that power can help him work with management or customers to successfully alleviate risk.

Examining Stakeholder Tolerance

Depending on the project, the conditions, and the potential for loss or reward, stakeholders will have differing tolerances for risk. Stakeholders' risk tolerance may be known at the launch of the project, through written policy statements, or by their actions during the project.

Consider a project to install new medical equipment in a hospital: there's little room for acceptance of errors because life and death are on the line. No shortcuts or quick fixes are allowed. Now, consider a project to create a community garden. Not only are life and death not on the line in the garden project, but the acceptance of risk is different as well.

A person's willingness to accept risk is known as the utility function. The time and money costs required to eliminate the chance of failure is in proportion to the stakeholders' tolerance of risk on the project. The cost of assuring there are no threats must be balanced with the confidence that the project can be completed without extraordinary costs. Figure 11-1 demonstrates the utility function.

Using a Risk Management Plan Template

The performing organization may rely on templates for the risk management plan. The template can guide the project manager and the project team through the planning

FIGURE 11-1

The value of the project is relational to the cost of risk avoidance.

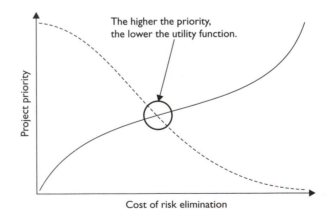

The higher the priority, the lower the utility function.

Project priority

Cost of risk elimination

processes, the risk identification, and the values that may trigger additional planning. Hopefully, the organization allows the template to be modified or appended based on the nature of the project. As most projects, however, resemble other historical projects, the template may need only minor changes to be adapted to the current project.

A risk management plan may grant the project manager decision-making abilities on risks below a certain threshold. Risks above a preset threshold will have to be escalated to management for determination of their cost and impact on the project success.

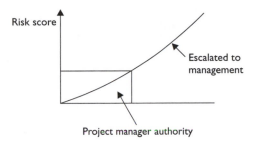

Revisiting the Work Breakdown Structure

The work breakdown structure (WBS) serves as an input to the risk management planning processes. The WBS is needed to help the project manager, and the project team identifies the components of the project and what risks may be unique to a particular area of the project versus a risk shared across the entire project.

For example, a project to create a new building has different components in the WBS: foundation, framing, interior, finishing, and so on. Within each parent component in the WBS there may be risk unique to only that category of deliverables. However, there may also be risks that should they come to fruition could affect the entire project's success. For example, a risk in the foundation could affect the entire structure later in the project life cycle. Figure 11-2 demonstrates how the WBS can contribute to risk management.

Creating the Risk Management Plan

Through planning meetings, the risk management plan is created. Risk management plan templates, performing organization policies, and the risk tolerance level of the stakeholders aid the creation of the risk management plan. Attendees should include:

- The project manager
- Project team leaders
- Key stakeholders

FIGURE 11-2

The WBS can
help identify risks
within the project.

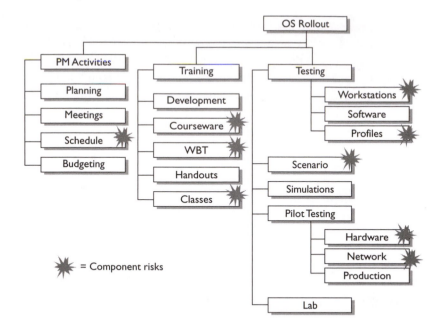

- Personnel specific to risk management
- Any other persons with authority or needed input to the risk management processes

Examining the Risk Management Plan

The risk management plan does not detail the planned responses to individual risks within the project—this is the purpose of the risk response plan. The risk management plan is responsible for determining:

- How risks will be identified
- How quantitative analysis will be completed
- How qualitative analysis will be completed
- How risk response planning will happen
- How risks will be monitored
- How ongoing risk management activities will happen throughout the project life cycle

Methodology

The methodology is concerned with how the risk management processes will take place. The methodology asks:

- What tools are available to use for risk management?
- What approaches are acceptable within the performing organization?
- What data sources can be accessed and used for risk management?
- What approach is best for the project type, the phase of the project, and which is most appropriate given the conditions of the project?
- How much flexibility is available for the project given the conditions, the timeframe, and the project budget?

Roles and Responsibilities

The roles and responsibilities identify the groups and individuals that will participate in the leadership and support for each of the risk management activities within the project plan. In some instances, risk management teams outside of the project team may have a more realistic, unbiased approach to the risk identification, impact, and overall risk management needs than the actual project team.

Budgeting

Based on the size, impact, and priority of the project, a budget may need to be established for the project's risk management activities. A project with high priority and no budget allotment for risk management activities may face uncertain times ahead. A realistic dollar amount is needed for risk management activities if the project is to be successful.

Scheduling

The risk management process needs a schedule to determine how often and when risk management activities should happen throughout the project. If risk management happens too late in the project, then the project could be delayed because of the time needed to identify, assess, and respond to the risks. A realistic schedule should be developed early in the project to accommodate risks, risk analysis, and risk reaction.

Risk Analysis Scoring

Prior to beginning quantitative and qualitative analysis, a clearly defined scoring system and interpretation of the scoring system must be in place. Altering the scoring process during risk analysis—or from analysis to analysis—can skew the seriousness of a risk, its impact, and the effect of the risk on the project. The project manager and the project team must have clearly defined scores that will be applied to the analysis to ensure consistency throughout the project.

Thresholds

Thresholds are preset factors to show when the project conditions cross an action or when a response is required. Like the risks analysis scoring, threshold determination will need to be determined as soon as possible within the project plan to avoid delays. The project team's ideal threshold may differ from the customer's. Establishing a preset value prior to the project implementation will save time, frustration, and additional costs and delays.

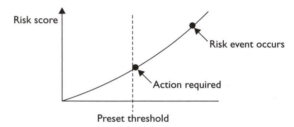

Reporting Formats

The reporting format requirements determine the type, detail, and requirements of the risk response plan. This plan is concerned with how the outputs of the risk management processes will be documented, analyzed, and communicated to management, customers, the project team, and other stakeholders.

Tracking

As risk management activities are induced, they will need to be documented. The documented actions and their results will support ongoing decisions within the current project (as well as future projects), and will serve as information for management, the project team, the customers, and other stakeholders. Should the performing organization choose to audit the risk management processes, the tracking of these activities is crucial. Based on the scope and impact of the project, the level of detail within the tracking and documentation of the risk management activities can vary.

Identifying Risks

After completing the risk management plan it's time to get to work identifying risks that can hinder the project's success. Risk identification is the process of identifying the risks and then documenting how their presence can affect the project. Risk identification is an iterative process and can be completed by the project manager, the project team, a risk management team, and even SMEs. In some instances, stakeholders and even people outside of the project can complete additional waves of risk identification.

Preparing for Risk Identification

The risk management plan is one of the key inputs to the risk identification process. It describes how the risks will be identified, requirements for risk analysis, and the overall management of the risk response process. The risk management plan does not include the actual responses to the risks, but rather the approach to the management of the process. In addition to the risk management plan, there are several other inputs to the risk identification process.

Relying on Project Planning

Effective risk identification requires an understanding of why the project exists. The people doing the risk identification have to understand the project's purpose in order to recognize risks that could affect the project. These risk identifiers should understand the customer's objectives, expectations, and intent.

Project planning outputs referenced here can include:

- The project charter
- The work breakdown structure
- Duration estimates
- The network diagram
- The project schedule
- Cost estimates
- The project budget
- Quality plans
- Resource requirements
- The resource management plan
- Procurement issues
- Communication requirements
- Assumptions
- Constraints

Creating Risk Categories

As risks are identified within the project, they should be categorized. Risk categories should be identified before risk identification begins—and should include common risks that are typical in the industry where the project is occurring. Risk categories help organize, rank, and isolate risks within the project. There are four major categories of risks:

- **Technical, quality, or performance risks** Technical risks are associated with new, unproven, or complex technology being used on the project. Changes to the technology during the project implementation can also be a risk. Quality risks are the levels set for expectations of impractical quality and performance. Changes to industry standards during the project can also be lumped into this category of risks.

- **Project management risks** These risks deal with faults in the management of the project: unsuccessful allocation of time, resources, and scheduling; unacceptable work results (low-quality work); and lousy project management as a whole.

- **Organizational risks** The performing organization can contribute to the project's risks through unreasonable cost, time, and scope expectations; poor project prioritization; inadequate funding or the disruption of funding; and the competition with other projects for internal resources.

- **External risks** These risks are outside of the project but directly affect it: legal issues, labor issues, a shift in project priorities, and weather. "Force majeure" risks can be scary and usually call for disaster recovery rather than project management. These are risks caused by earthquakes, tornados, floods, civil unrest, and other disasters.

Referring to Historical Information

Historical information is always an excellent source of information for risk identification. If the performing organization has done similar projects in the past, the historical information should be able to shed light on the risks identified early in the project, as well as risks identified throughout the project, and provide information in the final project reports. In addition to the documentation, stakeholders of the original project may have information to offer based on their experience within the project.

Historical information can also come from sources outside of the organization. The project manager should consider referencing commercial databases, articles, studies, and other readily available material relevant to the project work.

Identifying the Project Risks

Armed with the inputs to risk identification, the project manager and the project team are prepared to begin identifying risks. Risk identification should be a methodical, planned approach. Should risk identification move in several different directions at once then some risks may be overlooked. A systematic, scientific approach is best.

Reviewing Project Documents

One of the first steps the project team should take is to review the project documentation. The project plan, scope, and other project files should be reviewed. Constraints and assumptions should be reviewed, considered, and analyzed for risks. This structure review takes a very broad look at the project plan, the scope, and the activities defined within the project.

Brainstorming the Project

Brainstorming is likely the most common approach to risk identification. It's usually completed together as a project team to identify the risks within the project. The risks are identified in broad terms and posted, and then the risks' characteristics are detailed. The identified risks are categorized and will pass through qualitative and quantitative risk analysis later.

A multidisciplinary team, hosted by a project facilitator, can also complete brainstorming. This approach can include subject matter experts, project team members, customers, and other stakeholders to contribute to the risk identification process.

Using the Delphi Technique

The Delphi Technique is an anonymous method to query experts about foreseeable risks within a project, phase, or component of a project. The results of the survey are analyzed by a third party, organized, and then circulated to the experts. There can be several rounds of anonymous discussion with the Delphi Technique—without fear of backlash or offending other participants in the process.

The Delphi Technique is completely anonymous and the goal is to gain consensus on project risks within the project. The anonymous nature of the process ensures that no one expert's advice overtly influences the opinion of another participant.

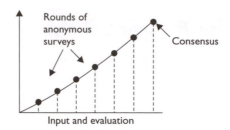

Identifying Risks Through Interviews

Interviewing subject-matter experts and project stakeholders is an excellent approach to identifying risks on the current project based on the interviewees' experience. The people responsible for risk identifications share the overall purpose of the project, the project's WBS, and likely the same assumptions as the interviewee.

The interviewee, through questions and discussion, shares his insight on what risks he perceives within the project. The goal of the process is to learn from the expert what risks may be hidden within the project, what risks this person has encountered on similar work, and what insight the person has into the project work.

Analyzing SWOT

SWOT means strengths, weaknesses, opportunities, and threats. SWOT analysis is the process of examining the project from each of the characteristic's point of view. For example, a technology project may identify SWOT as

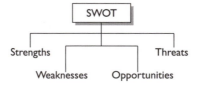

- ■ **Strengths**   The technology to be installed in the project has been installed by other large companies in our industry.
- ■ **Weaknesses**   We have never installed this technology before.
- ■ **Opportunities**   The new technology will allow us to reduce our cycle time for time-to-market on new products. Opportunities are things, conditions, or events that allow an organization to differentiate itself from competitors and improve its standing in the marketplace.
- ■ **Threats**   The time to complete the training and simulation may overlap with product updates, new versions, and external changes to our technology portfolio.

Using Checklists

If the current project is similar to projects completed in the past, using a checklist of risks is a good approach. The advantage of a checklist to identify risks is that it's a simple and direct approach to identify risks. The disadvantage of using a checklist for risk identification is that the participants may limit their risk identification to only the risk categories on the checklists. It's virtually impossible to create a complete and usable checklist of risks for most projects.

Checklists, if they are used, should be used as a guide—not as a complete and final list of risk identification. Risks that are not included on the checklists should be explored, documented, and planned for. Although checklists are an excellent tool, they often limit the project team in identifying all of the risks relevant to the current project.

Checklists are great for risk and quality management. At project closure, however, be certain to update the checklists for future projects. The current project will act as future historical information.

If checklists are used, then at project closure the checklist must be revisited to ensure the list is accurate and complete for future projects that may use the same checklists.

Examining the Assumptions

All projects have assumptions. Assumption analysis is the process of examining the assumptions to see what risks may stem from false assumptions. Examining assumptions is about finding the validity of the assumptions. For example, consider a project to install a new piece of software on every computer within an organization. The project team has made the assumption that all of the computers within the organization meet the minimum requirements to install the software. If this assumption were wrong, then cost increases and schedule delays would occur.

Examining the assumptions also requires a review of assumptions across the whole project for consistency. For example, consider a project with an assumption that a senior employee will be needed throughout the entire project work; the cost estimate, however, has been billed at the rate of a junior employee.

Utilizing Diagramming Techniques

There are several diagramming techniques that can be utilized by the project team to identify risks:

- **Ishikawa** These cause-and-effect diagrams are also called fishbone diagrams. These are great for root cause analysis of what factors are causing the risks within the project. The goal is to identify and treat the root of the problem, not the symptom.

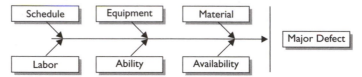

- ■ **Flow charts**   System or process flow charts show the relation between components and how the overall process works. These are useful for identifying risks between system components.

- ■ **Influence diagrams**   An influence diagram charts out a decision problem. It identifies all of the elements, variables, decisions, and objectives—and how each factor may influence another.

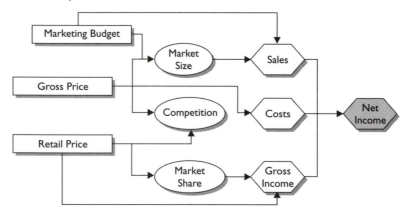

Examining the Results of Risk Identification

As the project progresses, and risk identification continues to happen, there are several outputs of risk identification:

- ■ **Risks**   Of course the most obvious output of risk identification is the risk that has been successfully identified. Recall that a risk is an uncertain event or condition that possesses the potential to have a positive or negative effect on the project's success.

- ■ **Triggers**   These are warning signs or symptoms that a risk has occurred or is about to occur. For example, should a vendor fail to complete their portion of the project as scheduled, the project completion may be delayed.

- ■ **Inputs to other processes**   Risk identification can contribute to other processes. For example, the WBS may not be sufficiently decomposed to allow risk identification to continue. Another example is that the current sequencing of activities has too many risks, so the rescheduling and sequencing of activities are needed. The reschedule and sequencing of activities will require risk identification to happen again.

Using Qualitative Risk Analysis

Qualitative risk "qualifies" the risks that have been identified in the project. Specifically, qualitative risk analysis examines and prioritizes the risks based on their probability of occurring and the impact on the project if the risks did occur. Qualitative risk analysis is a broad approach to ranking risks by priority, which then guides the risk reaction process.

The end result of qualitative risk analysis (once risks have been identified and prioritized) can lead to more in-depth quantitative risk analysis, or move directly into risk response planning.

---

exam
watch

When you think of "qualitative," think of qualifying. You are qualifying, or justifying, the seriousness of the risk for further analysis. Some PMP candidates like to remember that qualitative is a list. The "L" in qualitative and list ties the two together.

Preparing for Qualitative Risk Analysis

The risk management plan is the first input to qualitative risk analysis. The plan will dictate the process, the methodologies to be used, and the scoring model for identified risks. In addition to the risk management plan, the identified risks, obviously, will be needed to perform an analysis. These are the risks that will be scored and ranked based on their probability and impact. Figure 11-3 demonstrates all of the inputs to qualitative risk analysis.

The status of the project will also affect the process of qualitative risk analysis. Early in the project, there may be several risks that have not yet surfaced. Later in the project, new risks may become evident and need to pass through qualitative analysis. The status of the project is linked to the available time needed to analyze and study the risks. There may be more time early in the project, while a looming deadline near the project's end may create a sense of urgency to find a solution for the newly identified risks.

FIGURE 11-3

Many factors contribute to qualitative risk analysis.

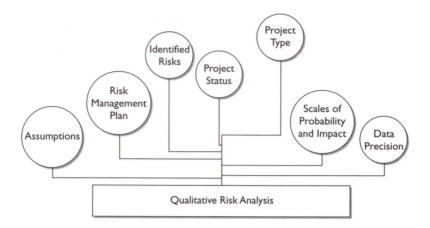

The project type also has some bearing in the process. A project that has never been done before, such as the installation of a new technology has more uncertainty than projects that have been done over and over within an organization. Recurring projects have historical information to rely on, while first-time projects have limited resources to build a risk hypothesis upon.

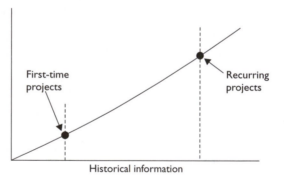

All risks are based upon some belief, proof, and data. The accuracy and source of the data must be evaluated to determine the level of confidence in the identified risks. A hunch that an element is a risk is not as reliable as measured statistics, historical information, or expert knowledge that an element is a risk. The data precision is in proportion to the reality of the risk.

Prior to the risk analysis, a pre-determined scale of probability and impact must be in place. There are multiple scales a project manager can elect to use, but generally these should be in alignment with the risk management plan. If the performing organization has a risk management model, the scale identified by the performing organization should be used. (We'll discuss the scale values in the next section.)

Finally, the assumptions used in the project must be revisited. During the risk identification process, the project team identified and documented the assumptions used within the project. These assumptions will be evaluated as risks to the project success.

Completing Qualitative Analysis

Not all risks are worth responding to while others demand attention. Qualitative analysis is a subjective approach to organizing and prioritizing risks. Through a methodical and logical approach, the identified risks are rated according to probability and potential impact.

The outcome of the ranking determines four things:

- It identifies the risks that require additional analysis through quantitative risk analysis.
- It identifies the risks that may proceed directly to risk response planning.
- It identifies risks that are not critical, project-stopping risks, but that still must be documented.
- It prioritizes risks.

Applying Probability and Impact

The project risks are rated according to their probability and impact. Risk probability is the likelihood that a risk event may happen, while risk impact is the consequence that the result of the event will have on the project objectives. Each risk is measured based on its likelihood and its impact. There are two approaches to ranking risks:

- Cardinal scales identify the probability and impact on a numerical value from .01 (very low) to 1.0 (certain).
- Ordinal scales identify and rank the risks as very high to very unlikely.

Creating a Probability-Impact Matrix

Each identified risk is fed into a probability-impact matrix, as seen in Figure 11-4. The matrix maps out the risk, its probability and possible impact. The risks with higher probability and impact are a more serious threat to the project objectives than the risks with lower impact and consequences. The risks that are threats to the project require quantitative analysis to determine the root of the risks, the methods to control the risks, and effective risk management. We'll discuss quantitative risk management later in this chapter.

FIGURE 11-4

A probability-
impact matrix
measures the
identified risks
within the
project.

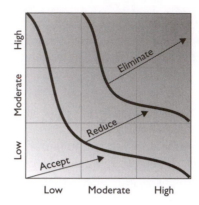

The project is best served when the probability scale and the impact scale are predefined prior to qualitative analysis. For example, the probability scale rates the likelihood of an individual risk happening and can be on a linear scale (.1, .3, .5, .7, .9) or the scale can be the ordinal scale. The scale, however, should be defined and agreed upon in the risk management plan. The impact scale, which measures the severity of the risk on the project's objectives, can also be ordinal or cardinal.

The value of identifying and assigning the scales to use prior to the process of qualitative analysis allows all risks to be ranked by the system and allows for future identified risks to be measured and ranked by the same system. A shift in risk rating methodologies mid-project can cause disagreements in the method of handling the project risks.

A probability-impact matrix, as seen in Figure 11-5, multiples the value for the risk probability by the risk impact for a total risk score. For example, an identified risk in a project is the possibility that the vendor may be late in delivering the hardware. The probability is rated at .9, but the impact of the risk on the project is rated at .10. The risk score is calculated by multiplying the probability times the impact—in this case, resulting in a score of .09.

The scores within the probability-impact matrix can be referenced against the performing organization's policies for risk reaction. Based on the risk score, the performing organization can place the risk in differing categories to guide risk reaction. There are three common categories based on risk score:

■ **Red condition**   High risk; these risks scores are high in impact and probability.

■ **Yellow condition**   These risks are somewhat high in impact and probability.

■ **Green condition**   Risks with a green label are generally fairly low in impact, probability, or both.

FIGURE 11-5

A probability-
impact matrix
scores the
identified risks.

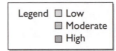

Risk Scores					
Probability					
0.9	0.05	0.09	0.18	0.36	0.72
0.7	0.04	0.07	0.14	0.28	0.56
0.5	0.03	0.05	0.10	0.20	0.40
0.3	0.02	0.03	0.06	0.12	0.24
0.1	0.01	0.01	0.02	0.04	0.08
	0.05	0.10	0.20	0.40	0.80
			Impact		

Legend ☐ Low
◩ Moderate
■ High

on the
job

Your organization may not have a classification of risks of red, yellow, and green. Your project risks should map to the methodology your organization uses to identify and classify project risks. If there is no classification of risks, take initiative and create one for your project. Be certain to document your classification for historical information and include this information in your Lessons Learned documentation.

Testing the Assumptions

False assumptions can ruin the project. A false assumption can wreck time, cost, and even the quality of a project deliverable. Assumptions, for this reason, are treated as risks and must be tested and weighed to truncate the possibility of an assumption turning against the project. Assumptions are weighed using two factors:

■ **Assumption stability**   How reliable is the information that led to this assumption?

■ **Assumption consequence**   What is the effect on the project if this assumption is false?

The answers to these two questions will help the project team be able to deliver the project with more confidence. Should an assumption prove to be false, the weight of the assumption consequence may be low to high—depending on the nature of the assumption.

Relying on Data Precision

One of the toughest parts of qualitative risk analysis is the biased, subjective nature of the process. A project manager and the project team must question the reliability and reality of the data that lead to the ranking of the risks. For example, Susan may have very high confidence in herself to work with a new, unproven technology. Based on this opinion, she petitions the probability of the work to be a very low score.

However, because she has no experience with the technology due to its newness, the probability of the risk of failure is actually very high. The biased opinion that Susan can complete the work with zero defects and problems is slightly skewed because she has never worked with the technology before. Obviously, a low-ranked score on a risk that should be ranked high can have detrimental effects on the project's success.

Data precision ranking takes into consideration the biased nature of the ranking, the accuracy of the data submitted, and the reliability of the nature submitted to examine the risk scores. Data precision ranking is concerned with:

- The level of understanding of the project risk
- The available data and information about the identified risk
- The quality of the data and information of the identified risk
- The reliability of the data about the identified risk

Examining the Results of Qualitative Risk Analysis

Qualitative risk analysis happens throughout the project. As new risks become evident and identified, the project manager should route the risks through the qualitative risk analysis process. The end results of qualitative risk analysis are:

- **Overall risk ranking of the project** The overall risk ranking of the project allows the project manager, management, customers, and other interested stakeholders to comprehend the risk, the nature of the risks, and the condition between the risk score and the likelihood of success for a project. The risk score can be compared to other projects to determine project selection, placement of talent to a project, prioritization, the creation of a benefit-cost ratio, or even the cancellation of a project because it is deemed too risky.

- **Prioritized risks** The risks in the project can be prioritized by their score, their rank of high, medium, or low, or by their WBS components. Risks can also be categorized by their urgency for an immediate response versus those risks that can wait for a response.

- **Identification of risks requiring additional analysis** The risks categorized as high will likely need additional analysis, such as quantitative analysis. Some risks may demand immediate risk management based on the nature of the risks and the status of the project.

■ **Trends in qualitative analysis**   As the project progresses and risk analysis is repeated, trends in the ranking and analysis of the risk may become apparent. These trends can allow the project manager and other risk experts to respond to the root cause and predicted trends to eliminate or respond to the risks within the project.

Preparing for Quantitative Risk Analysis

Quantitative risk analysis attempts to numerically assess the probability and impact of the identified risks. Quantitative risk analysis also creates an overall risk score for the project. This method is more in-depth than qualitative risk analysis and relies on several different tools to accomplish its goal.

Qualitative risk analysis typically precedes quantitative analysis. All or a portion of the identified risks in qualitative risk analysis can be examined in the quantitative analysis. The performing organization may have policies on the risk scores in qualitative analysis, which require the risks to advance to the quantitative analysis. The availability of time and budget may also be a factor in the determination of which risks should pass through quantitative analysis. Quantitative analysis is a more time-consuming process, and is therefore also more expensive. There are several goals of quantitative risk analysis:

■ To ascertain the likelihood of reaching project success

■ To ascertain the likelihood of reaching a particular project objective

■ To determine the risk exposure for the project

■ To determine the likely amount of the contingency reserve needed for the project

■ To determine the risks with the largest impact on the project

■ To determine realistic time, cost, and scope targets

Considering the Inputs for Quantitative Analysis

Based on the time and budget allotments for quantitative analysis, as defined in the risk management plan, the project manager can move into quantitative analysis. There are, however, seven inputs to quantitative risk analysis the project manager should rely on:

- **Risk management plan**   The risk management plan identifies the risk management methodology, the allotted budget for risk analysis, the schedule, and the risk scoring mechanics—among other attributes.

- **Identified risks**   The risks that have been identified and promoted to quantitative analysis are needed.

- **Prioritized risks**   The risks as ranked by weight, priority, or WBS component will need to be readily available. This information can offer significant information for the quantitative analysis of the risks, reveal trends among the risks, and show those risks that require the most attention.

- **List of risks marked for additional analysis**   Any risks with a high or moderate score need quantitative analysis. These risks require immediate attention since their presence can ensure detrimental effects on the project's success.

- **Historical information**   Similar projects will likely have similar risks. The history of how the risks were managed, mismanaged, or discovered during the project can provide crucial information regarding the current project. In addition, there may be historical information available through commercial databases or other sources.

- **Expert judgment**   Individuals, other project teams within the performing organizations, subject matter experts, or other consultants may provide valuable experience and insight into the identified risks.

- **Other planning outputs**   These include the cost and schedule estimates, documented logic of project decisions, scheduling information, and information on the technical attributes of the project.

Interviewing Stakeholders and Experts

Interviews with stakeholders and subject matter experts can be one of the first tools to quantify the identified risks. The interview can focus on worst-case, best-case, and most-likely scenarios if the goal of the quantitative analysis is to create a triangular distribution; most quantitative analysis, however, uses continuous probability distributions. Figure 11-6 shows five sample distributions: normal, triangular, uniform, beta, and lognormal.

FIGURE 11-6 Distributions illustrate the likelihood and impact of an event.

Normal

Lognormal

Beta

Triangular

Uniform

Continuous probability distribution is an examination of the probability of all possibilities within a given range. For each variable, the probability of a risk event, and the corresponding consequence for the event, may vary. In other words, dependent on whether the risk event occurs and how it happens, a reaction to the event may also occur. The distribution of the probabilities and impact include:

exam
watch   *Don't invest too much time*
on knowing these distribution types for the
exam. The questions on quantitative analysis
will focus on more accessible methods
than these in-depth, analytic approaches.

- Uniform
- Normal
- Triangular
- Beta
- Lognormal

Applying Sensitivity Analysis

Sensitivity analysis examines each project risk on its own merit. All other risks in the project are set at a baseline value. The individual risk then is examined to see how it may affect the success of the project. The goal of sensitivity analysis is to determine which individual risks have the greatest impact on the project's success and then to escalate the risk management processes on these risk events.

Using a Decision Tree

A decision tree is a method to determine which of two decisions is the best to make. For example, it can be used to determine buy-versus-build scenarios, lease-or-purchase equations, or whether to use in-house resources rather than outsourcing the project work. The decision tree model examines the cost and benefits of both decision outcomes and weighs the probability of success for each of the decisions.

The purpose of the decision tree is to make a decision, calculate the value of that decision, or to determine which decision costs the least. Follow Figure 11-7 through the various steps of the decision tree process.

FIGURE 11-7

Decision trees analyze the probability of events and calculate decision value.

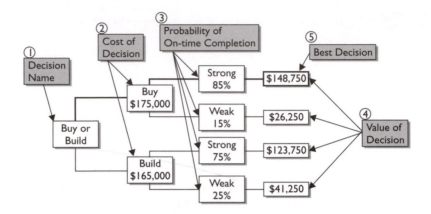

Completing a Decision Tree

As the project manager of the new GFB Project, you have to decide whether to create a new web application in-house or send the project out to a developer. The developer you would use (if you were to outsource the work) quotes the project cost at $175,000. Based on previous work with this company, you are 85 percent certain they will finish the work on time.

Your in-house development team quotes the cost of the work as $165,000. Again, based on previous experience with your in-house developers, you feel 75 percent certain they can complete the work on time. Now let's apply what we know to a decision tree:

■ Buy or build is simply the decision name.

■ The cost of the decision if you "buy" the work outside of your company is $175,000. If you build the software in-house, the cost of the decision is $165,000.

■ Based on your probability of completion by a given date, you apply the 85 percent certain to the "strong" finish for the buy branch of the tree. Because you're 85 percent certain, you're also 15 percent uncertain; this value is assigned to the "weak" value on the buy branch. You complete the same process for the build branch of the tree.

■ The value of the decision is the percentage of strong and weak applied to each branch of the tree.

■ The best decision is based solely on the largest value of all possible decisions.

Using a Project Simulation

Project simulations allow the project team to play "what-if" games without affecting any areas of production. The Monte Carlo technique is the most common simulation.

Monte Carlo got its name from Monte Carlo, Monaco (world-renowned for its slot machines, roulette wheels, and other games of pure chance). Monte Carlo, typically completed through a computer software program, completely simulates a project with values for all possible variables to predict the most likely model.

Examining the Results of Quantitative Risk Analysis

Quantitative risk analysis is completed throughout the project as risks are identified and passed through qualitative analysis, as project conditions change, or on a preset schedule. The end result of quantitative risk analysis include:

- **A prioritized list of risks** This list of quantified risks demonstrates those risks with the highest potential for endangering the project's success. This list includes the risks that have the greatest opportunity for the project. Each risk is identified with its probability and impact.

- **Probabilistic analysis** The risks within the project allow the project manager or other experts to predict the likelihood of the project success. The project may be altered by the response to certain risks; this response can increase cost and delay the project completion date.

- **Probability of costs and schedule objectives** Based on the identified risks, their impact, and probability of occurring, forecasts for the project schedule and the project costs are created. The more negative risks that occur within a project, the greater the chance of delays and increased costs.

- **Trends** As the project moves towards completion, quantitative risk analysis may be repeated over and over. In each round of analysis, trends in the identified risks may become visible. The trends in the risk can help the project team eliminate the root cause of the risk, reduce their probability, or control their impact.

Planning for Risk Response

Risk response planning is all about options and actions. It focuses on how to decrease the possibility of risks from adversely affecting the project's objectives, and on how to increase the likelihood of positive risks that can aid the project. Risk response planning assigns responsibilities to people and groups close to the risk event. Risks will increase or decrease based on the effectiveness of risk response planning.

INSIDE THE EXAM

Risk management planning is the process of determining how risk management will be handled. The stakeholder analysis will reveal their willingness to accept risk—which is also known as their utility function. The performing organization may have standard practices for risk management, risk management templates, or guidance from historical information.

There are two types of risk: business risk, which is gains or losses from a financial point of view; and pure risks, which only has a down side. Both types of risks must be assessed and managed.

Risk identification happens early on the project to allot time for risk response planning. Risk identification also happens throughout the project. The project manager, the project team, customers, and other stakeholders are involved in the process. There are several methods to risk identification, though interviews and the Delphi Technique are two of the most common approaches.

Qualitative analysis qualifies the list of risks in a matrix based on impact and probability. This subjective approach uses a common *very low, low, moderate, high,* and *very high* ranking. The risks can be prioritized based on their score.

After qualitative analysis, some risks may be sent through quantitative analysis. This approach attempts to quantify the risks with hard numbers, values, and data. Quantification of the risk can lead to time and cost contingencies for the project, priority of the risks, and an overall risk score. Monte Carlo simulations are typically associated with quantitative risk analysis.

There are four risk responses:

- **Avoidance** The project plan is altered to avoid the identified risk.
- **Mitigation** Effort is made to reduce the probability, impact, or both of an identified risk in the project before the risk event occurs.
- **Transference** The risk is assigned to a third party, usually for a fee. The risk still exists, but the responsibility is deflected to the third party.
- **Acceptance** The risks are seen as nominal so they are accepted. Risks, regardless of size, that have no other recourse may also be accepted.

As the project progresses, risk monitoring and control is implemented. Risks are monitored for signs that they may be coming to fruition. The project team and the project manager execute the risk response plan and document the results. Earned value analysis, which is typically used to measure project performance, can also be used to signal impending project risks.

The responses to identified risks must be in balance with the risk itself. The cost and time invested in a risk must be met with the gains from reducing the risk's impact and probability. In other words, a million-dollar solution for a hundred-dollar problem is unacceptable. The people or individuals that are assigned to the risk must have the authority to react to the project risk as planned. In most cases, there will be several risk responses that may be viable for the risk—the best choice for the identified risk must be documented, agreed upon, and then followed through should the risk come to fruition.

Preparing for Risk Response

To successfully prepare for risk response, the project manager, project team, and appropriate stakeholders will rely on several inputs—many of which stem from qualitative and quantitative risk analysis—such as:

- The risk management plan
- A list of prioritized risks
- Risk ranking
- A prioritized list of quantified risk
- A probabilistic analysis of the project
- The probability of the project meeting the cost and schedule goals
- The list of potential responses decided upon when risks were first identified
- Any risk owners that have been identified
- A listing of common cause risks to address multiple risks with an achievable solution
- Trends from qualitative and quantitative analysis

Creating Risk Responses

There are several tools and techniques that the project team can employ to respond to risks. Each risk should be evaluated to determine which category of risk response is most appropriate. When a category of risk response has been selected, the response must then be developed, refined, documented, and readied for use, if needed. In addition, secondary responses may be selected for each risk. The purpose of risk response planning is to bring the overall risk of the project down to an acceptable level. In addition, risk response planning must address any risks that are scored unacceptably high.

Avoidance   Transference   Mitigation   Acceptance

There are four categories of risk response as seen in Figure 11-8; each will be discussed in the following sections:

- Avoidance
- Transference
- Mitigation
- Acceptance

Avoiding the Risk

Avoidance is simply avoiding the risk. This can be accomplished many different ways and generally happens early in the project when any change will result in fewer consequences than later in the project plan. Examples of avoidance include:

You can remember the avoidance risk response by using the analogy of a lunch outing. If it's raining outside and you don't want to get wet, you can avoid the rain by staying indoors.

- Changing the project plan to eliminate the risk.
- Clarifying project requirements to avoid discrepancies.
- Hiring additional project team members that have experience with the technology that the project deals with.
- Using a proven methodology rather than a new approach

Transferring the Risk

Transference is the process of transferring the risk (and the ownership of the risk) to a third party. The risk doesn't disappear, it's just someone else's problem. Transference of a risk usually costs a premium for the third party to own and manage that risk. Common examples of risk transference include:

- Insurance
- Performance bonds
- Warrantees

- Guarantees
- Fixed-priced contracts

e x a m
w a t c h
You can remember the transference of a risk by using the same lunch outing analogy. If it's raining outside and you don't want to get wet at lunch, you can use transference by sending someone else out for lunch. Your co-worker may agree to go out in the rain if you'll pay for their lunch, too. Transferring a risk doesn't make the risk go away; the project still has the risk, but the ownership of the risk has been assigned to some other party.

Mitigating the Risk

Mitigating risks is an effort to reduce the probability and/or impact of an identified risk in the project. Mitigation is done—based on the logic—before the risk happens. The cost and time to reduce or eliminate the risks is more cost effective than repairing the damage caused by the risk. The risk event may still happen, but hopefully the cost and impact of the risk will both be very low.

Mitigation plans can be created so they are implemented should an identified risk cross a given threshold. For example, a manufacturing project may have a mitigation plan to reduce the number of units created per hour should the equipment's temperature cross a given threshold. The reduction is the number of units per hour that it may cost the project in time. Additionally, the cost of extra labor to run the equipment longer because the machine is now operating at a slower pace may be attributed to the project. However, should the equipment fail, the project would have to replace the equipment and be delayed for weeks while awaiting repairs.

Examples of mitigation include:

e x a m
w a t c h
Want to mitigate the risk of getting wet at lunch? Bring an umbrella. The rain is still falling, but you won't get soaked with an umbrella.

- Adding activities to the project to reduce the risk probability or impact
- Simplifying the processes within the project
- Completing more tests on the project work before implementation
- Developing prototypes, simulations, and limited releases

Accepting the Risks

Risk acceptance is the process of simply accepting the risks because no other action is feasible, or the risks are deemed to be of small probability, impact, or both and that a formal response is not warranted. Passive acceptance requires no action; the project team deals with the risks as they happen. Active acceptance entails developing a contingency plan should the risk occur.

A contingency plan is a predefined set of actions the project team will take should the risk event occur. A contingency plan has also been called "a worst-case scenario" plan. A similar plan, a fallback plan, instructs the project team on how to unravel the project work back to an acceptable point in the project. Both fallback plans and triggers or thresholds within the project conditions instigate the plans.

Most risk acceptance policies rely on a contingency allowance for the project. A contingency allowance is an amount of money the project will likely need in the contingency reserve based on the impact, probability, and expected monetary value of a risk event.

For example, Risk A has a 25 percent chance of happening and has a cost value of negative $2000. The probability times the impact equates to a negative $2000 expected monetary value (Ex$V). Another risk, Risk B, has a 40-percent chance of happening and has benefit value of $4000. The Ex$V for Risk B is $1600. If these were the only risks in the project, an ideal contingency reserve would be $400. This is calculated by adding the positive and negative risk values to predict the amount that the project is likely to be underfunded if the risks happen. Table 11-1 shows several risks and their Ex$V.

TABLE 11-1				
Contingency Reserve Calculations	**Risk**	**Probability**	**Impact: Cost Is Negative; Benefits Are Positive**	**Ex$V**
	A	20%	−$4000	−$800
	B	45%	$3000	$1350
	C	10%	$2100	$210
	D	65%	−$2500	−$1625
			Contingency Reserve Fund	$865

Examining the Results of Risk Response Planning

The major output of risk response planning is the risk response plan. This plan is also sometimes called the risk register since it includes all risks, their details, and the expected response for each. This plan describes the reaction to each identified risk and includes:

■ A description of the risk, what area of the project it may affect, the causes of the risk, and its impact on project objectives

■ The identities of the risk owners and their assigned responsibilities

■ The outputs of qualitative and quantitative analysis

■ A description of the response to each risk, such as avoidance, transference, mitigation, or acceptance

■ The actions necessary to implement the responses

■ The budget and schedule for risk responses

■ Both the contingency and fallback plans

Working with Residual Risks

The risk response plan also acknowledges any residual risks that may remain after planning, avoidance, transfer, or mitigation. Residual risks are typically minor and have been acknowledged and accepted. Management may elect to add both contingency costs and time to account for the residual risks within the project.

Accounting for Secondary Risks

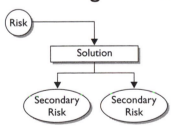

Secondary risks are risks that stem from risk responses. For example, transference may elect to hire a third party to manage an identified risk. A secondary risk caused by the solution is the failure of the third party to complete their assignment as scheduled. Secondary risks must be identified, analyzed, and planned for, just as any another identified risk.

Creating Contracts for Risk Response

When multiple entities are involved in a project, contractual agreements may be necessary to identify the responsible parties for identified risks. The contract may be needed for insurance purposes, customer acceptance, or acknowledgement of responsibilities between the entities completing the project. Transference is an example of contractual agreements for the responsibility of risks within a project.

Establishing a Contingency Reserve

Through risk response planning a contingency reserve should be established for time and cost values to respond to given risks should the risks come into play. Identifying the probability of a risk and multiplying the value by its cost impact can calculate a contingency reserve. For example, a risk has a 20 percent chance of happening. Should the risk occur, it would cost $4000 to correct. The contingency amount needed for this risk is 20 percent of the $4000, which is $800.

on the job

A contingency reserve may also be called a management reserve. Often, a management reserve deals with time while a contingency reserve deals with dollars. Some organizations lump time and money into the same reserve. You should know what nomenclature your organization uses—and what they anticipate the meaning of the reserves to be.

Justifying Risk Reduction

To reduce risk, additional time or monies are typically needed. The process and logic behind the strategies to reduce the risk should be evaluated to determine if the solution is worth the tradeoffs. For example, a risk may be eliminated by adding $7500 to a project's budget. However, the likelihood of the risk occurring is relatively low. Should the risk happen, it would cost, at a minimum, $8000 to correct and the project would be delayed by at least two weeks.

The cost of preventing the risk versus the cost of responding to it must be weighed and justified. If the risk is not eliminated with the $7500 cost, and the project moves forward as planned, it has, theoretically, saved $15,500 because the risk did not happen and the response to the risk did not need to happen.

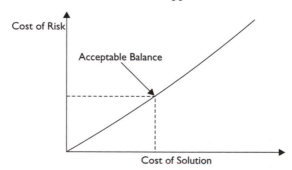

However, if the risk does happen, the project will lose at least $8000 and be delayed at least two weeks. The cost inherent in the project delay may be more expensive than the solution to the risk. The judgment of solving the risk to reduce the likelihood of delaying the project may be wiser than ignoring the risk and saving the cost by solving the risk problem.

Updating the Project Plan

The risk reactions, contingency plans, and fallback plans should all be documented and incorporated into the project plan—for example, updating the schedule, budget, and WBS to accommodate additional time, money, and activities for risk responses. The responses to the risks may change the original implementation of the project and should be updated to reflect the project plan and intent of the project team, management, and other stakeholders. A failure to update the project plan may cause risk reactions to be missed—and skew performance measurements.

Implementing Risk Monitoring and Control

Risks must be actively monitored and new risks must be responded to as they are discovered. Risk monitoring and control is the process of monitoring identified risks for signs that they may be occurring, controlling identified risks with the agreed responses, and looking for new risks that may creep into the project. Risk monitoring and control also is concerned with the documentation of the success or failure of risk response plans, and keeping records of metrics that signal risks are occurring, fading, or disappearing from the project.

Risk monitoring and control is an active process that requires participation from the project manager, the project team, key stakeholders, and, in particular, risk owners within the project. As the project progresses, risk conditions may change and require new responses, additional planning, or the implementation of a contingency plan.

There are several goals to risk monitoring and control:

- ■ To confirm risk responses are implemented as planned
- ■ To determine if risk responses are effective or if new responses are needed
- ■ To determine the validity of the project assumptions
- ■ To determine if risk exposure has changed, evolved, or declined due to trends in the project progression
- ■ To monitor risk triggers
- ■ To confirm policies and procedures happen as planned
- ■ To monitor the project for new risks

Preparing for Risk Monitoring and Control

Risk monitoring and control is an active process. There are several inputs the project team and the project manager must rely on to effectively monitor and control risks, such as:

- **The risk management plan**
- **The risk response plan**
- **Project communications**   The results of project work can inform the project manager and the project team of new and pending risks. In addition, project team members may create reports to monitor or document risks. These reports are known as issue logs, action-items, jeopardy warnings, and escalation notices.
- **New risk identification**   Throughout the project life cycle, new risks may surface that the project team and the project manager have not considered. These risks should be fed into the risk management process to identify valid responses.
- **Scope changes**   Change requests should be analyzed for their impact on the project—and for any risks in the change that could affect the project objectives, as well as any new risks the increased scope presents.

Completing Risk Monitoring and Control

Risk monitoring and risk control happens throughout the project. It is not a solitary activity that is completed once and never revisited. The project manager and the project team must actively monitor risks, respond with the agreed actions, and scan the horizon for risks that have not been addressed. Risk monitoring and control is a recurring activity that requires input from all project participants. There are several tools available to implement risk monitoring and control as the following sections discuss.

Completing Risk Response Audits

A risk response audit examines the planned risk response, how well the planned actions work, and the effectiveness of the risk owner in implementing the risk response. The audits happen throughout the project to measure the effectiveness of mitigating, transferring, and avoiding risks. The risk response audit should measure the effectiveness of the decision and its impact on time and cost.

Completing Periodic Risk Reviews

Project risk should be on the agenda at every project team meeting. The periodic risk review is a regularly scheduled discussion throughout the project to ascertain the level of foreseeable risks, the success of risk responses in the project to date, and a review of pending risks. Based on circumstances within the project, risk rankings and prioritization may fluctuate. Changes to the project scope, team, or conditions may require qualitative and quantitative analysis.

Using Earned Value Analysis

Earned value analysis measures project performance. When project performance is waning, the project is likely missing targeted costs and schedule goals. The results of earned value analysis can signal that risks are happening within the project—or that new risks may be developing.

For example, a schedule performance index (SPI) of .93 means the project is off schedule by seven percent. A risk based on this value could mean that the project team is having difficulty completing the project work as planned. Additional work will continue to be late, the project will finish late, and quality may suffer as the team attempts to rush to complete assigned tasks.

Measuring Technical Performance

Throughout the project, the project team's technical competence with the technology being used in the project should increase. The level of technical achievement should be in proportion to the expected level of technical performance within the project. If the project team is not performing at a level of expected technical expertise, the project may suffer additional risks due to the discrepancy. Technical performance can be measured by the success of completing activities throughout the project or through project phases.

Completing Additional Risk Planning

Most likely, new risks will become evident during the project implementation. The project team, project manager, and key stakeholders that discover the risks should communicate the risk. The risk must then be acknowledged, documented, analyzed, and planned for. The project team must be encouraged to communicate the discovery of new risks.

Often, project team members don't want to share discovered risks with the project manager because the presence of a risk can be seen as bad news. The project manager must stress to the project team members that identified risks should be communicated so the risks can be planned for through avoidance, mitigation, transference, or even acceptance.

Examining the Results of Risk Monitoring and Control

Risk monitoring and control helps the project become more successful. Risk monitoring and control measures the planned responses to risks—and creates reactions to unplanned risks. The outputs of risk monitoring and control also aim to help the project reach its objectives. There are six outputs of the process:

- **Workaround plans** Workarounds are documented in the project plan and the risk response plan. Workarounds are unplanned reactions to risks that were not identified or that were accepted.

- **Corrective actions** As risks come to fruition, corrective actions are needed to bypass the risk. The two types of corrective action are workarounds and contingency plans. Corrective actions are actions taken to bring the project back into compliance with the project plan.

- **Change requests** As workarounds and contingency plans are used, they require changes to the project plan. The changes to the project plan due to the risks are completed through integrated change control. The changes are documented, approved, and incorporated into the project plan.

- **Risk response plan updates** As risks occur, the responses to those risks should be documented and updated in the risk response plan. Should risk rankings change during the project, the change in ranking, the logic behind the change, and the results of the risk rank change should be documented in the risk response plan. For the risks that do not occur, the risks should be documented and considered closed in the risk response plan.

- **Risk database** A database of recognized risks, the planned response, and the outcome of the risk should be documented and recorded in an organization-wide risk database. This risk database can serve other project managers as historical information. Over time, the risk database can become a risk lessons learned program.

- **Checklist updates**   Checklists of identified risks will help future projects recognize and manage identified risks.

CERTIFICATION SUMMARY

PMP candidates will need a firm grasp on how to plan for, monitor, and control projects' risks. To effectively handle risks, the project manager will need to begin with risk management planning. A large, complex project will likely have more risks than a smaller project. In any situation, however, risks must be identified and planned for. The performing organization will often have risk management policies that dictate how the risk planning sessions are to be performed, and what level of risks call for additional planning.

Some stakeholders—and organizations—will be more tolerant to accept risks than others. A person's willingness to accept risk is called the *utility function*. A perfect example of the utility function is the stock market. Some people will only invest in solid, reliable stocks—but with little return on their investment. Other people will invest in startups, low-dollar stocks, and other high-risk companies—but will receive a higher yield if their investments pay off. The same is true with projects: some risks are worth taking while others are not. Risk planning and the utility function help the project manager determine which risks are acceptable.

As risks are identified the project manager can use the Delphi Technique to build consensus on which risks have the highest impact on the project. This anonymous approach allows participants to speak freely on the risks. Participants aren't hindered by the opinion of other stakeholders. The comments on the identified risks are distributed to all of the participants allowing participants to comment, concur, or dismiss opinions on the identified risks. Through rounds of discussion consensus on the risks are reached.

Qualitative risk analysis qualifies identified risks and creates a prioritization of the risks. Each risk is considered for its impact and likelihood of occurring. Once the risks have passed through qualitative risk analysis, quantitative risk analysis is needed. Quantitative risk analysis assesses the probability and impact of the risks and determines a risk score based on further analysis, discussion, expert judgment, simulations, and interviews with stakeholders.

KEY TERMS

If you're serious about passing the PMP exams, memorize these terms and their definitions. For maximum value, create your own flashcards based on these definitions and review daily. You can find additional information on these terms in the project glossary.

acceptance	mitigation	secondary risks
avoidance	qualitative risk analysis	sensitivity analysis
brainstorming	quantitative risk analysis	simulation
cause-and-effect diagrams	residual risks	system or process flowcharts
contingency reserve	risk	transference
decision tree analysis	risk categories	triggers
Delphi Technique, the	risk database	utility function
Ex$V	risk management plan	workarounds
influence diagram	risk owners	
interviewing	scales of probability and impact	

✓ # TWO-MINUTE DRILL

Planning for Risk Management

❑ Risk management planning is determining how the risk management activities within the project will take place. It is not the response or identification of risks, but the determination of how to manage project risks.

❑ Risk management planning is accomplished through planning meetings with the project team, management, customers, and other key stakeholders.

❑ Utility function is a person's willingness to accept risks

❑ The output of risk management planning is the risk management plan.

Managing Risk

❑ Risks are uncertain events that can affect a project's objectives for good or bad.

❑ Risks can be placed into four different categories: Technical, quality, or performance risks; project management risks; organizational risks; and external risks.

❑ Project files from published information and previous projects can serve as input to risk identification.

❑ The Delphi Technique allows participants to identify risk anonymously without fear of embarrassment. A survey allows results to be shared with all participants for comments on each other's anonymous input. Rounds of surveying and analysis can create consensus on the major project risks.

❑ Triggers are warning signs that a risk is about to happen or has happened.

Analyzing Identified Risks

❑ Risks are evaluated for their impact and likelihood.

❑ Risks can be ranked by ordinal ranking by using such indicators as very low, low, moderate, high, and very high.

❑ Risks can also be analyzed using a cardinal ranking system of numerical values that are assigned to each risk based on its impact and probability.

❑ An overall project risk ranking can be used to compare the current projects with other projects in the organization.

❏ The risks can be moved into quantitative analysis for further study.

❏ Risks are assigned numeric values. Such as: there is a 50 percent likelihood that the risk will occur, causing a $10,000 cost.

Risk Management Methods

❏ The Monte Carlo simulation can determine the likelihood of the project's success, predict the costs of a specific risk exposure, and identify realistic time, scope, and cost objectives. Interviews with stakeholders and subject matter experts are an excellent start for quantitative risk analysis.

❏ Decision trees help determine the cost, benefit, and value of multiple decisions. They are based on the cost of the decision and the probability of completing an objective.

Responding to Identified Risks

❏ Risk response planning focuses on reducing threats and increasing opportunities as a result of risks. Risk thresholds, defined in risk management planning, describe the acceptable level of risk within a company.

❏ Risk owners are the individuals or groups that are responsible for a risk response, and should participate in the risk response planning

❏ Risk avoidance changes the project plan to avoid the risk, as well as conditions that promote the risk, or it attempts to reduce the risk's impact on the project's success.

❏ Risk transference moves the risk consequence to a third party. The risk doesn't go away, just the responsibility of the risk. Though ultimately, the performing organization still retains the ultimate accountability and results of the risk event.

❏ Risk mitigation involves actions designed to reduce the likelihood of a risk occurring, reduce the impact of a risk on the project objectives, or both.

❏ Risk acceptance acknowledges the risk exists but the risk is not worthy of a more in-depth response, or a more in-depth response is not available for the risk.

❏ Residual risks are risks that remain after avoidance, transference, mitigation, and acceptance. Secondary risks are new risks that arise from a risk response.

Completing Iterative Risk Management

❏ Identified risks must be tracked, monitored for warning signs, and documented. The responses to the risks are monitored and documented as successful or less successful than expected.

❏ Issue logs, action-item lists, jeopardy warnings, and escalation notices are all types of communication reports the project team and risk owners must use to document and track identified risks.

❏ Risk response audits measure the success of the responses and the effectiveness of the cost, scope, and quality values gained or lost by the risk responses.

❏ Earned value analysis can measure project performance, but it can also predict and signal pending risks within the project.

As unexpected risks arise, the project team may elect to use workarounds to diminish the impact and probability of those risks. Workarounds, however, should be documented and incorporated into the project plan and risk response plan as they occur.

SELF TEST

1. Which of the following is not an input to risk management planning?

 A. The project charter

 B. Risk identification

 C. Defined roles and responsibilities

 D. WBS

2. Frances is the project manager of the LKJ Project. Which of the following techniques will she use to create the risk management plan?

 A. Risk tolerance

 B. Status meetings

 C. Planning meetings

 D. Variance meetings

3. Which of the following is the output of risk management planning?

 A. Roles and responsibilities

 B. Operational transfer issues

 C. Risk response plan

 D. Risk management plan

4. You are the project manager of the GHK Project. You and the manufacturer have agreed to substitute the type of plastic used in the product to a slightly thicker grade should there be more than a seven percent error in production. The thicker plastic will cost more and require the production to slow, but the errors should diminish. This is an example of which of the following?

 A. Threshold

 B. Tracking

 C. Budgeting

 D. JIT manufacturing

5. A person's willingness to tolerate risk is known as _____.

 A. The utility function

 B. Herzberg's Theory of Motivation

 C. Risk acceptance

 D. The risk-reward ratio

6. A risk trigger is also called which of the following?

   A. A warning sign

   B. A delay

   C. A cost increase

   D. An incremental advancement of risk

7. The customers of the project have requested additions to the project scope. The project manager brings notice that additional risk planning will need to be added to the project schedule. Why?

   A. The risk planning should always be the same amount of time as the activities required by the scope change.

   B. Risk planning should always occur whenever the scope is adjusted.

   C. Risk planning should only occur at the project manager's discretion.

   D. The project manager is incorrect; risk planning does not need to happen at every change in the project.

8. The risks of financial gain or loss are called _____.

   A. Business risks

   B. Financial risks

   C. Organizational risks

   D. Functional risks

9. _____ include(s) fire, theft, or injury, and offer(s) no chance for gain.

   A. Business risks

   B. Pure risks

   C. Risk acceptance

   D. Life risks

10. Complete this sentence: a risk is a(n)_____ occurrence that can affect the project for good or bad.

   A. Known

   B. Potential

   C. Uncertain

   D. Known unknown

11. When should risk identification happen?

   A. As early as possible in the initiation process

   B. As early as possible in the planning process

C. As early as possible in the controlling process

D. As early as possible in the execution process

12. You are the project manager of the KLJH Project. This project will last two years and has 30 stakeholders. How often should risk identification take place?

   A. Once at the beginning of the project

   B. Throughout the execution processes

   C. Throughout the project

   D. Once per project phase

13. Risk identification is considered to be _____. (Choose the best answer.)

   A. Iterative

   B. Self-led

   C. Mandatory

   D. Optional

14. You are the project manager for a project that will create a new and improved web site for your company. Currently, your company has over eight million users around the globe. You would like to poll experts within your organization with a simple, anonymous form asking for any foreseeable risks with the design, structure, and intent of the web site. With the collected information, subsequent anonymous polls are submitted to the group of experts. This is an example of _____.

   A. Risk identification

   B. A trigger

   C. An anonymous trigger

   D. The Delphi Technique

15. Which of the following describes SWOT?

   A. Analysis of strengths, weakness, options, and timing

   B. Analysis of strengths, weakness, opportunities, and threats

   C. An elite project team that comes in and fixes project risks and threats

   D. Ratings of 1 to 100

16. Which risk analysis provides the project manager with a risk ranking?

   A. Quantifiable

   B. Qualitative

   C. The utility function

   D. SWOT analysis

17. A table of risks, their probability, impact, and a number representing the overall risk score is called a _____.

   A. Risk table

   B. Risk matrix

   C. Quantitative matrix

   D. Qualitative matrix

18. You are presented with the following table:

Risk Event	Probability	Impact Cost/Benefit	Ex$V
1	.20	–4000	
2	.50	5000	
3	.45	–300	
4	.22	500	
5	.35	–4500	

What is the Ex$V for Risk Event 3?

   A. $135

   B. –$300

   C. $45

   D. –$135

19. You are presented with the following table:

Risk Event	Probability	Impact Cost/Benefit	Ex$V
1	.35	–4000	
2	.40	50000	
3	.45	–300000	
4	.30	50000	
5	.35	–45000	

Based on the preceding table, what is the amount needed for the contingency fund?

   A. Unknown with this information

   B. 249,000

   C. 117,150

   D. 15750

20. The water sanitation project manager has determined the risks associated with handling certain chemicals are too high. He has decided to allow someone else to complete this portion of the project, and so has outsourced the handling and installation of the chemicals and filter equipment to an experienced contractor. This is an example of which of the following?

    A. Avoidance
    B. Acceptance
    C. Mitigation
    D. Transference

21. A project manager and the project team are actively monitoring the pressure gauge on a piece of equipment. Sarah, the engineer, recommends a series of steps to be implemented should the pressure rise above 80 percent. The 80-percent mark represents what?

    A. An upper control limit
    B. The threshold
    C. Mitigation
    D. A workaround

22. You are presented with the following table:

Risk Event	Probability	Impact Cost/Benefit	Ex$V
1	.20	–4000	
2	.50	5000	
3	.45	–300	
4	.22	500	
5	.35	–4500	
6			

    Complete Risk 6 based on the following information: Marty is 60 percent certain that he can get the facility needed for $45,000, which is $7000 less than what was planned for.

    A. .60, 45,000, 27,000
    B. .60, 52,000, 31,200
    C. .60, 7,000, 4200
    D. .60, –7,000, –4200

23. How can a project manager determine whether it is better to make or buy a product?

    A. Decision Tree Analysis

    B. Fishbone model

    C. Ishikawa diagram

    D. ROI Analysis

24. Which of the following can determine multiple scenarios with risk and probability of impact?

    A. Decision trees

    B. Monte Carlo simulations

    C. Pareto charts

    D. Gantt charts

25. A project can have many risks with high-risk impact scores, but have an overall low risk score. How is this possible?

    A. The risk scores are graded on a bell curve.

    B. The probability of each risk is low.

    C. The impact of each risk is not accounted for until it comes to fruition.

    D. The risks are rated HML.

SELF TEST ANSWERS

1. ☑ **B.** Risk identification is not an input to risk management planning.

   ☒ **A**, **C**, and **D** are all incorrect. The project charter, defined roles and responsibilities, and the WBS are all inputs to risk management planning.

2. ☑ **C.** Planning meetings are used to create the risk management plan. The project manager, project team leaders, key stakeholders, and other individuals with the power to make decisions regarding risk management attend the meetings.

   ☒ Choices **A**, **B**, and **D** are incorrect as these choices do not fully answer the question.

3. ☑ **D.** The only output of risk management planning is the risk management plan.

   ☒ **A** is incorrect; roles and responsibilities are an input to the risk management planning process. **B**, operational transfer issues, may have associated risks, but they are not an output of the risk management planning process. **C**, the risk response plan, is not an output of risk management planning. It is an output of risk response planning.

4. ☑ **A.** An error value of seven percent represents the threshold the project is allowed to operate under. Should the number of errors increase beyond seven percent, the current plastic will be substituted.

   ☒ **B** is incorrect since tracking is the documentation of a process through a system or workflow, or the documentation of events through the process. **C**, budgeting, is incorrect. **D**, JIT manufacturing, is a scheduling approach to ordering the materials only when they are needed in order to keep inventory costs down.

5. ☑ **A.** The utility function describes a person's willingness to tolerate risk.

   ☒ **B**, is incorrect; Herzberg's Theory of Motivation is an HR theory that describes motivating agents for workers. **C** is also incorrect; risk acceptance describes the action of allowing a risk to exist because it is deemed low in impact, low in probability, or both. **D**, the risk-reward ratio, is incorrect. This describes the potential reward for taking a risk in the project.

6. ☑ **A.** Risk triggers can also be known as warning signs. Triggers signal that a risk is about to happen or has happened.

   ☒ **B**, **C**, and **D** are all incorrect, as these answers do not properly describer a risk trigger.

7. ☑ **B.** When the scope has been changed, the project manager should require risk planning to analyze the additions for risks to the project success.

   ☒ **A** is incorrect; the scope changes may not require the same amount of time as the activities needed to complete the project changes. **C** is incorrect because risk planning should not occur at the project manager's discretion, but instead should be based on evidence within the project and the policies adopted in the risk management plan. **D** is also incorrect; when changes are added to the project scope, risk planning should occur.

8. ☑   **A.** Business gains are directly tied to the risk of financial gains or loss.
    ☒   Choices **B, C,** and **D** are not relevant terms.

9. ☑   **B.** Pure risks are the risks that could threaten the safety of the individuals on the project.
    ☒   Choice **A** is incorrect because business risks affect the financial gains or loss of a project.
    C and **D** are incorrect since these terms are not relevant.

10. ☑   **C.** Risks are not planned, they are left to chance. The accommodation and the reaction to
    a risk can be planned, but the event itself is not planned. If risks could be planned, Las Vegas
    would be out of business.
    ☒   **A, B,** and **D** are all incorrect since these terms do not accurately complete the sentence.

11. ☑   **B.** Risk identification is a planning process and should happen as early as possible to allot
    adequate time for risk reaction planning.
    ☒   **A, C,** and **D** are all incorrect because risk identification does not happen as part of the
    initiation, controlling, or execution processes.

12. ☑   **C.** Risk identification happens throughout the project. Recall that planning is iterative;
    as the project moves towards completion, new risks may surface that call for identification and
    planned responses.
    ☒   **A** is incorrect; risk identification should happen throughout the project, not just at the
    beginning. **B** is incorrect because risk identification is part of planning. **D** is incorrect because
    the nature of the project phase may require and reveal more than one opportunity for risk
    identification.

13. ☑   **A.** Risk identification is an iterative process that should happen throughout the project life.
    ☒   **B** is incorrect since risk identification often requires intense analysis, team involvement,
    and experts to lead the process. **C** is incorrect; while risk identification may be considered
    mandatory, iterative is a better description because risk identification happens over and over.
    D is incorrect; risk identification is not optional.

14. ☑   **D.** An anonymous poll allowing experts to freely submit their opinion without fear of
    backlash is an example of the Delphi Technique.
    ☒   **A, B,** and **C** are incorrect; these choices do not accurately answer the question.

15. ☑   **B.** SWOT analysis is part of risk identification and examines the strengths, weakness,
    opportunities, and threats of the project to make certain all possibilities for risk identification
    are covered.
    ☒   **A** is incorrect because SWOT examines all four perspectives. **C** and **D** are incorrect because
    these ratings are part of quantitative-qualitative risk analysis.

16. ☑ **B.** The risk ranking is based on the *very high, high, medium, low,* and *very low* attributes of the identified risks.
    ☒ **A** is incorrect because it is not relevant to the questions. **C** is incorrect; utility function describes an organization's tolerance for risk. **D,** SWOT analysis, is part of risk identification.

17. ☑ **B.** A table of risks, their probability, and impact equate to a risk score in a risk matrix.
    ☒ **A** is incorrect since it does not fully answer the questions. **C** and **D** are incorrect because a risk matrix can be used in both quantitative and qualitative risk analysis.

18. ☑ **D.** Risk Event 3 has a probability of 45 percent and an impact cost of –$300, which equates to –$135.
    ☒ **A, B,** and **C** are all wrong because the values are incorrect answers for the formula.

19. ☑ **C.** The calculated amount for each of the risk events is shown in the following table:

Risk Event	Probability	Impact Cost/Benefit	Ex$V
1	0.35	–4000	–1400
2	0.4	50000	20000
3	0.45	–300000	–135000
4	0.3	50000	15000
5	0.35	–45000	–15750
			–117150

☒ **A, B,** and **D** are incorrect answers because they do not reflect the contingency amount needed for the project based on the preceding table.

20. ☑ **D.** Because the risk is not eliminated but transferred to someone else or another entity, it is considered transference.
    ☒ **A** is incorrect because the risk still exists, but it is handled by another entity. **B** is incorrect because the project manager has not accepted the risk, deciding instead to allow another entity to deal with it. **C** is incorrect; the risk has not been mitigated in the project.

21. ☑ **B.** The 80-percent mark is a threshold.
    ☒ **A** is incorrect; an upper control limit is a boundary for quality in a control chart. **C** is incorrect; mitigation is a planned response should a risk event happen. **D** is incorrect; a workaround is an action to bypass the risk event.

22. ☑ **C.** Marty is 60 percent certain he can save the project $7000. The $4200 represents the 60-percent certainty of the savings.

☒ **A, B,** and **D** are all incorrect since these values do not reflect the potential savings of the project.

23. ☑ **A.** A decision tree model can separate the pros and cons of buying versus building.

☒ **B** and **C** are incorrect; a fishbone diagram and an Ishikawa diagram show cause and effect. **D** is incorrect; ROI analysis does not answer the question as fully as a decision tree.

24. ☑ **B.** Monte Carlo simulations can reveal multiple scenarios and examine the risks and probability of impact.

☒ **A,** decision trees, help guide the decision making process. **C,** a Pareto chart, helps identify the leading problems in a situation. **D,** Gantt charts, compare the lengths of activities against a calendar in a bar chart format.

25. ☑ **B.** A risk can have a very high impact on the project, but inversely have an extremely low probability score.

☒ **A** is incorrect and not relevant to the scenario. **C** is not a true statement. **D** is also incorrect; a model using high, medium, low versus a numbering system would not alter the overall high or low risk score of the project.

12

Introducing Project Procurement Management

P rojects routinely require procurements. Projects need materials, equipment, consultants, training, and many other goods and services. Project procurement management is the process of purchasing the products necessary for meeting the needs of the project scope.

Procurement management involves planning, soliciting sources, choosing a source, administering the contract, and closing out the contract. Procurement management, as far as your PMP exam is considered, focuses on the practices from the buyer's point of view, not the seller's. The seller can be seen as a contractor, subcontractor, vendor, or supplier.

When buying anything from a vendor, the buyer needs a contract. A contract becomes a key input to many of the processes within the project. The contract, above anything else, specifies the rules and agreements for the project.

Here's a neat twist: when the seller is completing its obligations to supply a product, PMI treats those obligations as a project. In other words, if ABC Electricians were wiring a building for your company, ABC Electricians would be the performing organization completing its own project. Your company becomes the customer of their project—and is, of course, a stakeholder in their project.

In the scenarios described in this chapter, the seller will be outside of the performing organization. The buyer will be managing a project and procuring resources from a vendor. However, all of the details in this chapter can be applied to internal work orders, formal agreements, and contracts between organizational units within a single entity.

Planning for Procurement

Procurement planning is the process of identifying which part of the project should be procured from resources outside of the organization. Generally, procurement decisions are made early on in the planning processes. Procurement planning centers on four elements:

- Whether or not procurement is needed
- What to procure
- How much to procure
- When to procure

Referring to the Scope Statement

The project's scope statement serves as input to making procurement decisions. Because the project scope statement defines the project work, and only the required work, to complete the project, it also defines the limitations of the project. Knowing these limits of what the project includes can help the project manager, the contract specialists, or other procurement professional, determine what needs to be purchased and what does not.

Referring to the Product Description

The product description defines the details and requirements for acceptance of the project. This information also serves as valuable input to what needs to be procured— and to what does not. The product description defines what the end result of the project will be. When dealing with vendors to procure a portion of the project, the work to be procured must support the requirements of the project customer.

A statement of work (SOW) may define the work to be accomplished within the project, but it generally does not define the product description as a whole. However, when an entire project is to be procured from a vendor, the SOW and the product description become one and the same.

Relying on Procurement Resources

Often an organization will have resources for managing the procurement process, including contracting and negotiating on behalf of the project. If, however, the performing organization has no such resources for the project manager to rely upon, then it is up to the project manager to supply the procurement management resources, including capabilities for negotiating and for obtaining in a fiscally responsible way the right products or services for a fair price on behalf of the performing organization.

Evaluating the Market Conditions

Part of procurement management is to determine what sources are available to provide the needed products or services for the project. An evaluation of the marketplace is needed to determine what products and services are available and from whom and on what terms and conditions they are available.

While in most free market enterprise societies there are multiple vendors offering comparable products, there may be times when choices of vendors are limited. There are three specific terms to know for the PMP exam that you may encounter:

- **Sole source** Only one qualified seller exists in the marketplace.
- **Single source** The performing organization prefers to contract with a specific seller.
- **Oligopoly** There are very few sellers and the actions of one seller will have a direct effect on the other seller's prices and the overall market condition.

Evaluating Assumptions, Constraints, and Other Factors

The project assumptions and constraints can have direct influence on the procurement process. For example, a project with a time constraint to complete a project by a given deadline may be forced to procure additional laborers to complete portions of the project work in order to complete the project as scheduled

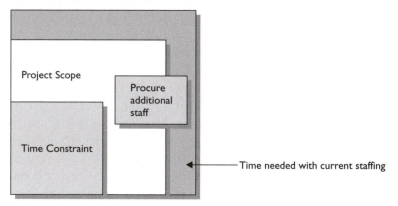

Assumptions can also affect procurement decisions. A false assumption that the installation of a piece of equipment was part of the quoted price could skew the project's budget. Assumptions, especially in procurement planning, must be eliminated if at all possible.

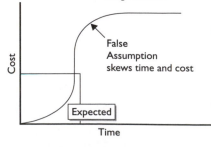

Other factors must also be considered to have effective procurement planning:

- Cost estimates
- Schedule estimates
- Quality management requirements

- Cash flow projections
- WBS components
- Risk management plans
- Staff acquisitions and development

Completing Procurement Planning

Procurement planning should be done early in the planning processes, with certain exceptions. As needs arise, as project conditions change, or as other circumstances demand, procurement planning may be required throughout the project. Whenever procurement planning happens early in the project, as preferred, or later in the project, as needed, a logical approach to securing the proper resources is necessitated.

Determining to Make or Buy

The decision to make or buy a product is a fundamental aspect of management. In some conditions it is more cost effective to buy—while in others it makes more sense to create an in-house solution. The make-or-buy analysis should be made in the initial scope definition to determine if the entire project should be completed in-house or procured. As the project evolves, additional make-or-buy decisions are needed.

The initial costs of the solution for the in-house or procured product must be considered, but so too must the ongoing expenses of the solutions. For example, a company may elect to lease a piece of equipment. The ongoing expenses of leasing the piece of equipment should be weighed against the expected ongoing expenses of purchasing the equipment and the monthly costs to maintain, insure, and manage the equipment.

For example, Figure 12-1 shows the mathematical approach to determining the whether it is better to create a software program in-house or buy one from a software company. The in-house solution will cost your company $25,000 to create your own software package and, based on historical information, another $2,500 per month to maintain the software.

The development company has a solution that will cost your company $17,000 to purchase, but the development company requires a maintenance plan for each software program installed, which will cost your company $2,700 per month. The difference between making the software and buying the software is $8,000. The difference between supporting the software the organization has made and allowing the external company to support their software is only $200 per month.

The $200 per month is divided into the difference between creating the software internally and buying the software—which is $8,000 divided by $200—40 months.

Make-or-buy formulas are common question topics on the PMP exam.

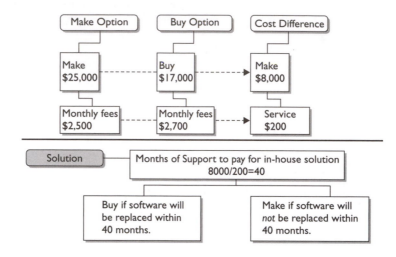

If the software is to be replaced within 40 months, the company should buy the software. If the software will not be replaced within 40 months, it should build the software.

There are multiple reasons why an organization may choose to make or buy. Here are some common examples or reasons for making and buying:

Reasons to Make	Reasons to Buy
Less costly	Less costly
Use in-house skills	In-house skills not available or don't exist
Control of work	Small volume of work
Control of intellectual property	More efficient
Learn new skills	Transfer risks
Available staff	Available vendor
Focus on core project work	Allows project team to focus on other work items

exam
watch
You may be presented with one or two questions on make versus buy. On the exam, as in the preceding example, you won't be confronted with tax benefits of make versus buy—though in your job as a project manager you may be. For the exam, focus on determining which is the most cost effective, fair solution.

Using Expert Judgment

Procurement planning can rely on expert judgment. It may be beneficial to rely on the wisdom of others—those in the performing organization or subject matter experts—to determine the need for procurement. Expert judgment for procurement management planning can come from the following:

- Units or individuals within the performing organization
- Consultants and subject matter experts
- Professional, trade, or technical associations
- Industry groups

Determining the Contract Type

There are multiple types of contracts when it comes to procurement. The project work, the market, and the nature of the purchase determines the contract type. Here are some general rules that PMP exam candidates, and project managers, should know:

- A contract is a formal agreement between the buyer and the seller. Contracts can be oral or written—though written is preferred.
- The United States backs all contracts through the court system.
- Contracts should clearly state all requirements for product acceptance.
- Any changes to the contract must be formally approved, controlled, and documented.
- A contract is not fulfilled until all of the requirements of the contract are met.
- Contracts can be used as a risk mitigation tool, as in transferring the risk. All contracts have some level of risk; depending on the contract type, the risk can be transferred to the seller. If a risk response strategy is to transfer, risks associated with procurement are considered secondary risks and must go through the risk management process.
- There are legal requirements governing contracts. In order for a contract to be valid, it must:
  - Contain an offer
  - Have been accepted
  - Provide for a consideration (payment)
  - Be for a legal purpose
  - Be executed by someone with capacity and authority
- The terms and conditions of the contract should define breaches, copyrights, intellectual rights, and *force majeure*.

Fixed-Price Contracts

Fixed-price contracts (also known as firm-fixed-price and lump-sum contracts) are agreements that define a total price for the product the seller is to provide. These contracts must clearly define the requirements the vendor is to provide. These contracts may also provide incentives for meeting or exceeding contract requirements—such as meeting deadlines—and require the seller to assume the risk of cost overruns, as Figure 12-2 demonstrates.

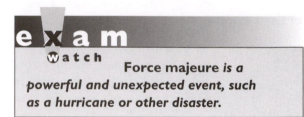

e x a m

ⓦatch Force majeure *is a powerful and unexpected event, such as a hurricane or other disaster.*

Cost-Reimbursable Contracts

These contract types pay the seller for the product. In the payment to the seller there is a profit margin—the difference between the actual costs of the product and the sales amount. The actual costs of the product fall into two categories:

- **Direct costs** costs incurred by the project in order for the project to exist. Examples include equipment needed to complete the project work, salaries of the project team, and other expenses tied directly to the project's existence.

- **Indirect costs** costs attributed to the cost of doing business. Examples include utilities, office space, and other overhead costs.

FIGURE 12-2

Fixed-Price Contracts transfer the risk to the seller.

T&M can be a high risk for buyer if contract does not include a "total not-to-exceed" clause, also called an NTE clause.

Time and
Materials
contracts must
be kept in check
or expenses can
skyrocket.

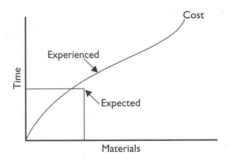

Cost-reimbursable contracts require the buyer to assume the risk of cost overruns. There are three types of cost-reimbursable contracts:

- Cost plus fixed fee
- Cost plus percentage of costs
- Cost plus incentive fee

Time and Materials Contracts

Time and Materials (T&M) contracts are sometimes called Unit Price contracts. They are ideal for instances when an organization contracts out a small projector for instances when smaller amounts of work within a larger project are to be completed by a vendor. T&M contracts, however, can grow dangerously out of control as more work is assigned to the seller. Figure 12-3 is an example of how T&M contracts can pose risk for the buyer.

Summary of Contract Types

On the PMP examination you can anticipate a few questions on contract types. Familiarize yourself with the following table:

Contract Type	Acronym	Attribute	Risk Issues
Cost Plus Fixed Fee	CPFF	Actual costs plus profit margin for seller	Cost overruns represent risk to the buyer.
Cost Plus Percentage of Cost	CPPC	Actual costs plus profit margin for seller.	Cost overruns represent risk to the buyer. This is the most dangerous contract type for the buyer.
Cost Plus Incentive Fee	CPIF	Actual costs plus profit margin for seller.	Cost overruns represent risk to the buyer.

Contract Type	Acronym	Attribute	Risk Issues
Fixed-Price	FP	Agreed price for contracted product. Can includes incentives for the seller.	Seller assumes risk.
Lump-Sum		Agreed price for contracted product. Can includes incentives for the seller.	Seller assumes risk.
Firm-Fixed-Price	FFP	Agreed price for contracted product.	Seller assumes risk.
Fixed Price Incentive Fee	FPIF	Agreed price for contracted product. Can includes incentives for the seller.	Seller assumes risk.
Time and Materials	T&M	Price assigned for the time and materials provided by the seller.	Contracts without "not-to-exceed" clauses can lead to cost overruns.
Unit-Price		Price assigned for a measurable unit of product or time. (For example, $130 for engineer's time on the project.)	Risk varies with the product. Time represents the biggest risk if the amount needed is not specified in the contract.

Examining the Results of Procurement Planning

Procurement planning is a process that should happen early in the planning processes. The outputs of procurement planning allow the project manager and the project team to proceed with confidence in the procuring of products and services needed to successfully complete the project. If it is determined early in the project that there is not a need for procurements then obviously the balance of the procurement processes is not necessary for the project.

Procurement Management Plan

This subsidiary project plan documents the decisions made in the procurement planning processes. It specifies how the remaining procurement activities will be managed. The plan details the following:

■ How vendors will be selected

- The type of contracts to be used

- The process of independent estimating

- The relationship between the project team and the procurement office within the performing organization (if one exists)

- The procurement forms, such as contracts, the project team is required to use

- How multiple vendors will be managed to supply their contracted product

- The coordination between sellers and the project team and among project activities, project reporting, scheduling, business operations, and other project concerns

Using the Statement of Work

In the Statement of Work (SOW), the seller fully describes the work to be completed and/or the product to be supplied. The SOW becomes part of the contract between the buyer and the seller. The SOW is typically created as part of the procurement planning process, and it allows the seller to determine if it can meet the written requirements of the SOW.

Particular industries have different assumptions about what constitutes an SOW. What one industry calls a SOW may be a Statement of Objectives (SOO) in another. A SOO is a document describing a problem to be solved by the seller.

Completing Solicitation Planning

Solicitation planning is the process of preparing to solicit sellers to provide products the project needs. It's a pretty straightforward business, as Figure 12-4 demonstrates. There are three inputs to solicitation planning:

- **Procurement Management Plan** This subsidiary plan sets out the methodologies and expectations of procurement within the performing organization.

- **Statement of Work** The SOW provides detailed information on what the seller will be providing for the performing organization. Recall that this document allows the seller to determine if it can provide the product and meet the requirements of the project team.

- **Other planning outputs** Other details within the project plan, such as the schedules, estimates, constraints, and assumptions, are referenced as their values may have direct influence on the solicitation process.

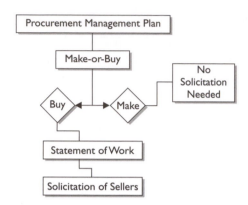

FIGURE 12-4

Solicitation
planning prepares
the performing
organization to
solicit products
from sellers.

Organizing Solicitation Materials

Solicitation planning relies on the outputs of procurement planning. The Procurement Management Plan will guide the process as the project team has planned, as the performing organization requires, or under the guidance of a procurement office within the performing organization.

There are two primary tools used for solicitation planning:

- **Standard form**   Within the performing organization, there may be many different standardized forms for contracts, descriptions of procurement items, bid documents, and other procurement-related documents.

- **Expert judgment**   Expert judgment may be needed to review and help the project manager select the best source for the procured product.

Examining the Results of Solicitation Planning

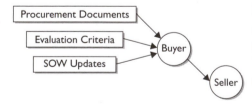

Solicitation planning guides the solicitation process. The outputs of solicitation planning help the project manager, the project team, and the sellers clearly communicate. The expectations between the buyer and seller are often not met because of a lack of solicitation planning.

Creating the Procurement Documents

One of the primary outputs of solicitation planning are the procurement documents. These documents guide the relationship between the buyer and seller. Communication between the buyer and the seller should always be specific as to the requirements and expectations of the seller. In initial communications, especially when requesting a price or proposal, the buyer should include the SOW, relevant specifications, and, if necessary, any non-disclosure agreements (NDA). Requests from buyers to sellers should be specific enough to give the seller a clear idea of what the buyer is requesting, but general enough to allow the seller to provide viable alternatives.

Here are some specific terms the project manager—and the PMP candidate— should be familiar with:

Document	Purpose
Bid	From seller to buyer. Price is the determining factor in the decision-making process.
Quotation	From seller to buyer. Price is the determining factor in the decision-making process.
Proposal	From seller to buyer. Other factors—such as skill sets, reputation, idea for the project solution—may be used in the decision-making process.
Invitation for Bid (IFB)	From buyer to seller. Requests the seller to provide a price for the procured product or service.
Request for Quote (RFQ)	From buyer to seller. Requests the seller to provide a price for the procured product or service.
Request for Proposal (RFP)	From buyer to seller. Requests the seller to provide a proposal to complete the procured work or to provide the procured product.

Creating Evaluation Criteria

Another output of solicitation planning is the evaluation criteria. The evaluation criteria is used to rate and score proposals from the sellers. In some instances, such as a bid or quote, the evaluation criterion is focused just on the price the seller offers. In other instances, such as a proposal, the evaluation criteria can be multiple values: experience, references, certifications, and more.

Updating the Statement of Work

The final outputs of solicitation planning are updates to the Statement of Work. As the project team creates the requirements from the sellers during invitations for bids, request for quotes, or request for proposals, they may discover other needed elements in the SOW. In addition, it is possible the bids, quotes, and proposals may offer alternatives the project team has not considered—and a new SOW is created.

Changes to the SOW should be updated, documented, and recorded to reflect the logic and reason behind the change.

INSIDE THE EXAM

Project Procurement Management begins with first determining which facets of the project can best be served through procurement. This decision really focuses on a make-or-buy analysis:

- Is it more cost effective to make or buy the product or service?

- Is it more time efficient to make or buy the product or service?

- Are the resources available within the organization to make the product or service?

If the decision has been made to buy the product or service, then a Statement of Work is needed to detail exactly what product or service the organization is buying. The SOW will be given to potential sellers, so they can prepare their offers in alignment with what is needed by the performing organization.

In order to find the potential sellers, the performing organization issues solicitations. Sellers can be found through a preferred vendor list, advertisements, industry directories, trade organizations, or other methods. The initial communication from the buyer to the seller is a request. Specifically, the seller issues one of the following documents:

- **Request for Proposals**   Used when there are multiple factors besides price to determine which seller is awarded the contract. The buyer is looking for a solution to a need.

- **Request for Quotations**   Used when the deciding factor is price.

- **Invitation for Bids**   Used when the deciding factor is price.

The seller can host a bidder conference to ensure that all sellers have equal opportunity to gain information about the procured work or service and that the information they do get is the same. After the seller conference, the selection process is based on several things:

- Procurement documents from the sellers

- Company policies and procedures

- Screening systems to sift out sellers that do not qualify for the work

- Weighting system to make an unbiased selection of a seller

Once the seller has been selected, the contract is created between the buyer and seller. This formal, preferably written, agreement between the buyer and seller will define all requirements of both the buyer and seller. The seller's requirements will specify how and when the work will be completed. The buyer's requirements will specify the terms and conditions the seller is expected to maintain. The contract may also include information on dispute resolution, how changes to the contract are to be made, and who are the authorities within the buyer's organization and the seller's organization

Contract administration is the process of ensuring that the seller meets the obligations and requirements specified in the contract. If changes arise in the project that affect the contract, there may be additional negotiation for payments based on the added or removed components of the procured work.

At the completion of the contract, the seller and buyer complete product verification, which is much like administrative closure, to confirm that the seller has met its obligations. Documentation of the procurement experience is created, so the information can be applied to other procurement activities on the current projects and to other projects within the organization.

Preparing for Solicitation

Once the solicitation planning has been completed, the actual process of solicitation can begin. Fortunately, the sellers, not the buyers, perform most of the activity in solicitations—usually at no additional cost to the project. The sellers are busy trying to win the business. There are two inputs to solicitations:

- *Procurement documents* are created in solicitation planning. These are the Invitations for Bid, Request for Proposal, and Request for Quote documents.

- *Qualified seller lists* are often maintained by performing organizations. These lists of qualified sellers (also preferred sellers or approved sellers) generally have contact information, history of past experience with the seller, and other pertinent information. In addition to the internal qualified seller list, there are many other resources to determine which sellers may qualify for the proposed work: Internet resources, industry directories, trade associations, and so on.

Completing Solicitation

Solicitation is the processing of inviting sellers to solicit the business of the performing organization. There are two primary tools needed to complete this process:

- **Bidder conferences**   A bidder conference, also called a contractor conference or vendor conference, is a meeting with prospective sellers to ensure that all sellers have a clear understanding of the product or service to be procured and are all on equal footing. Bidder conferences allow sellers to query the buyer on the details of the product to help ensure that the seller's proposal is adequate and appropriate for the proposed agreement. At this point of the process, all sellers are considered equal.

- ■ **Advertising**   In most circumstances, advertisements inviting bidders are expected. These advertisements can run in newspapers or trade journals specific to the industry of the organization. Some government agencies require advertisements inviting sellers to solicit the project work, attend a bidder conference, or present a proposal for the described work.

on the job   *A standard of procurement is that bids and quotes are looking for sellers to provide a price. Proposals are asking the sellers to provide solutions.*

Examining the Results of a Solicitation

The end result of a solicitation, as expected, is a collection of proposals, bids, and quotations. These documents indicate the sellers' ability and preparedness to complete the project work. The proposals should be in alignment with the stated expectations of the buyer, and they may be presented orally, electronically, or in hard copy format. Of course the relationship between the buyer and seller—and the type of information being shared—will determine which modality is the best choice of communication.

Determining Source Selection

Once the sellers have presented their proposals, bids, or quotes (depending on what the buyer requested of them), their documents are examined so that the project manager can select which sellers are the best choice for the project work. In many instances, price may be the predominant factor for choosing a particular seller—but not always. Other factors besides price may also be taken into consideration:

- ■ The cost of an item may not reflect the true cost to the performing organization if the item cannot be delivered in a timely manner. If a seller promises to have a product on site by a specific date and fails to do so, the project can be delayed, costing the organization thousands—or more—in losses.
- ■ Proposals can be separated into two categories: technical and commercial. The technical category describes the approach and methodology to complete the project work. The commercial category delves into the price to complete the

project work. An evaluation takes into consideration both categories in order to determine the best choice for the project.

■ Critical, high-priority projects may rely on multiple sellers to complete the project work. This redundancy can balance risk, cost, and opportunity among multiple vendors.

Preparing for Source Selection

Source selection weighs and evaluates the proposals, bids, and quotes for the procured portions of the project and then makes a determination as to which seller is the best for the project work. Source selection has three inputs to the decision-making process:

■ **Proposals**   The proposals, bids, and quotations provided by the sellers are key inputs. These are the documents the performing organization will evaluate to determine which seller is the best provider for the project.

■ **Evaluation criteria**   The evaluation criteria, such as referrals, samples of previous work, and references are considered. The evaluation criteria are evidence of the quality, depth, and experience of work the seller has performed in the past and, hopefully, is capable of performing on the current project. Evaluation criteria are developed in solicitation planning and applied in source selection.

■ **Organizational policies**   The performing organization likely has procurement policies and procedures the project manager is expected to follow in regard to source selection. The organizational policies should be known before starting the source selection process to avoid any discrepancies, conflicts of interest, or other breaches of the policies. For example, some organizations' procurement policies do not allow project managers to accept any gifts beyond $25 in value.

Completing the Source Selection Process

For the performing organization to finalize the process of source selection, there must first be eligible sellers. Assuming there are more than one seller that can satisfy the demands of the project, there are four tools and techniques the project manager can rely on:

■ **Contract negotiation**   The performing organization creates an offer, and the seller considers the offer. The contract negotiation process is an activity to create a fair price for the work the seller is to complete. The performing organization and the seller must be in agreement on the expectations, requirements, authorities, terms, technical and business management approaches, price—and any other pertinent factors covered within and by the contract—prior to signing the contract.

- **Weighting system**   A weighting system takes out the personal preferences of the decision-maker in the organization to ensure that the best seller is awarded the contract. A weighting system creates a matrix, as seen in Figure 12-5. Weights are assigned to the values of the proposals and each proposal is scored. Because the weights are determined before reviewing the proposals, the process is guaranteed to be free of personal preferences and bias. The seller with the highest score is awarded the contract.

- **Screening system**   A screening system is a method to remove sellers from consideration if they do not meet given conditions. For example, screening could require that sellers must be certified by a specific organization, have prior experience with the project technology, or meet other values. Sellers that don't meet the requirements are removed from the selection process and their proposals are not considered.

- **Independent estimates**   These estimates are often referred to as "should cost" estimates. These estimates are created by the performing organization, or outside experts, to predict what the cost of the procured product should be. If there is a significant difference between what the organization has predicted and what the sellers have proposed, either the Statement of Work was inadequate or the sellers have misunderstood the requirements.

Examining the Results of Source Selection

The one output of source selection is a contract between the buyer and the seller. A contract is a legally binding agreement between the buyer and seller in which the seller provides the described product and the seller pays for the product. Contracts are known by many names:

- Agreement
- Subcontract
- Purchase order
- Memorandum of understanding

Contracts have to be signed by a person with the power to authorize the requirements and payment specified in the contract. This role is called the delegation of procurement

FIGURE 12-5

Weighting systems remove personal preferences from the selection process.

Possible Score	20	20	15	10	10	5	20	100
Value	Experience	Certifications	Level IV Engineers	Security Clearance	Start Date	Waste Removal	Price	Total Score
ABC Constructions	15	20	7	10	10	5	12	79
Allen Builders	12	20	12	10	10	0	10	74
FRJ Construction	18	20	11	0	10	5	18	82
Howe & Who Construction	18	15	5	0	5	5	15	73
Martin & Martin	9	20	13	10	5	0	18	65
Ralph Engineers	15	8	8	0	10	5	17	73

exam watch

A letter of intent is not a contract, but a letter stating the buyer is intending to create a contractual relationship with the seller. Letters of intent are often used when there is an emergency procurement need and a contract is not available immediately.

authority. Whether this person is the project manager depends on the procurement policies of the performing organization.

In some organizations all contracts flow through centralized contracting. Centralized contracting requires all contracts for all projects to be approved through a central unit within the performing organization. Other organizations use a decentralized contracting approach, which assigns a contract administrator or contract officer to the project.

Performing Contract Administration

Contract administration is the process of ensuring that the seller lives up to the agreements in the contract. The project manager and the contract administrator must work together to make certain the seller meets its obligations. If the seller does not fulfill its contractual requirements, then legal remedies may ultimately be pursued.

Another aspect of contract administration, especially on larger projects with multiple sellers providing various products, is the coordination between the contractors. The project manager or contract officer schedules and confirms the performance of the sellers so that the deliverables, schedule, and performance of a contractor do not infringe or adversely affect the performance of another contractor.

Within the contract there must be the terms for payment. Typically the performance and progress of the contractor is directly linked to payments it receives. The project manager must track performance and quality to approve or decline payment as needed.

The contract should define the metrics for acceptance to avoid disagreements on performance.

Preparing for Contract Administration

The contract is needed as a guide for effective contract administration. The contract dictates the requirements and expectations of the seller and the buyer. The obligations of both parties should be in alignment with the contract; if not, disagreements, delays, and even work stoppage can ensue. In addition to the contract, there are three other inputs to contract administration:

- **Work results**   The seller's work results must be completed according to the requirements of the contract. As part of project plan execution, the seller must meet the quality standards of the performing organization and expected schedule of completion and stay within the anticipated costs and the specified range of variance.

- **Change requests**   Change requests can complicate contract administration. The performing organization's Change Control System has to mesh, somehow, with the seller's Change Control System. Changes to the project that affect the contracted work require changes to the contract, addendums to the contract, or a new contract for the additional or changed work. In some instances, the seller and the buyer may disagree about the cost of the changes. These differences may be labeled as claims, disputes, or appeals—they can ultimately can slow the project progress if they are not remedied.

- **Seller invoices**   Within the contract, the terms for payment are specified. The terms for payment may stipulate under what conditions the seller will provide an invoice for the work completed. In addition, the buyer may specify when and how the invoices are paid (for example, "Net 30 days from receipt of the invoice").

on the
Job   *If the seller's performance is unacceptable and a resolution to the problem cannot be found, the performing organization may elect to cancel the contract. This termination of the contract is also handled as a change request within the Change Control System.*

Completing Contract Administration

The actual process of completing contract administration relies heavily on communication between the project manager, the contract officer, and the seller. The communications plan may have considerations for how and when the communication between the buyer and seller should take place and what the purpose of the communication should be. There are three primary concerns, in addition to communication, within contract administration:

- **Contract change control system**   The contract change control system defines the procedures for how the contract may be changed. The process for changing the contract includes the forms, documented communications, tracking, conditions within the project, business, or marketplace that justify the needed the change, dispute resolution procedures, and the procedures for getting the changes approved within the performing organization. The system is part of Integrated Change Control.

- **Performance reporting**   Performance reporting is the communication between the project manager and management on how the seller is performing under the guidelines in the contract. Performance reporting is part of communications and should be documented within the Communications Management Plan.

- **Payment system**   Sellers like to be paid when they have completed their obligations. How the sellers are paid is controlled by the payment system, which includes interaction of the project manager and the Accounts Payable department. The performing organization may have strict guidelines for how payment requests are submitted and approved and how payments are completed. On larger projects, the project management team may have specific procedures for submitting the payment requests.

Reviewing the Results of Contract Administration

Contract administration calls for communication between the seller and buyer, the project manager and the vendor, and the stakeholders. There must be significant documentation of the agreement that both the buyer and the seller agree to before the procured work begins. Once the procured work, service, or product has been delivered from the seller to the buyer there must be agreement that the delivery is in alignment with the original agreement.

As part of contract administrations there are three outputs of contract administrations:

Correspondence

The performance of the contracted work, the contract obligations, and the procedures of the performing organization generate correspondence between the buyer and seller. The correspondence often takes the form of warnings, letters of discontent, and project performance reviews from the buyer to the seller. This correspondence can serve as documentation for legal action if disputes arise between the buyer and seller.

Contract Changes

Both approved and declined changes are documented as to their cost, time, and effect on the project and the procured work. Changes that are approved require updates to the project plan, subsidiary plans, and possibly to other project documentation.

Payment Requests

If the project is using an external payment system, there will be communication between the buyer and seller, and between the buyer and the external payment system. If the performing organization is handling its own payment processing, this output would simply be payments.

Performing Contract Closeout

Contract closeout is analogous to administrative closure. Its purpose is to confirm the obligations of the contract were met as expected. The project manager, the customer, key stakeholders, and, in some instances, the seller may complete product verification together to confirm that the contract has been completed.

Contract closeout can also be linked to administrative closure, because it is the process of confirming the work was completed. In instances when the contract was terminated, contract closeout is reviewed and is considered closed because of the termination. The project records should be updated to reflect the contract closeout and the acceptance of the work or product.

Reviewing Contract Documentation

To successfully close out a contract, the details of the contract may need to be reviewed. This review ensures that the product verification is complete and in accordance with the language and agreement in the contract. The review actually considers more than just the contract; the project manager should review and consider the following:

- Schedules of the procured work
- Contract change requests—approved and declined
- Documentation the seller has created and provided, if any
- Financial documents, invoices, payment records
- Results of contractual inspections

Auditing the Procurement Process

The successes and failures within the procurement process of the project are reviewed from procurement planning stage through contract administration. The intent of the audit is to learn from what worked and what did not work during the procurement processes. This knowledge can then be applied to other areas within the current project and to other projects within the performing organization.

Completing Contract Closeout

A contract file is a complete indexed set of records of the procurement process and is incorporated into the administrative closure process. These records include financial information as well as information on the performance and acceptance of the procured work.

Assuming the procured work is acceptable and meets the requirements of the contract, the contract can be closed. The formal closure of a project comes in a written notice from the contract officer to the seller. The notice informs the seller that its work is acceptable and that the contract is considered closed. The formal closure process may vary according to the size of the project. The requirements for contract closeout should be documented within the contract.

CERTIFICATION SUMMARY

Project procurement management allows a project to ascertain resources, materials, equipment, services, and other components needed to successfully complete the project. It is the process of finding sellers that can supply the needed products or services at a fair rate and meet the quality, time, and cost expectations of the project. The product description will help the project manager and the vendor determine what is the best solution for the procurement need.

One of the first activities the project manager and the project team complete together before procuring products is to determine the need to buy versus the ability to make the product. A decision tree can help the project manager determine which decision is most cost effective, reliable, and best for the project. A buy-versus-build analysis can compare the benefits of buying versus selling—including attributes other than just price and time.

Bidder conferences allow the bidders to meet with the project managers and other officials representing the seller to confirm the details of the Statement of Work. Recall that the Statement of Work is provided to all of the vendors that may be creating bids or proposals for the seller. The bidders' conference allows the bidders to obtain any additional information they may need to create a full and complete bid, quote, or proposal. It is part of the solicitation process and proceeds to source selection.

PMP candidates—and project managers—must be familiar with the different contract types and when to use each one. Here's a recap of the most common contract types:

- **Cost Plus Fixed Fee**   Details the fixed cost of the contract which includes a profit margin for the seller.
- **Cost Plus Percentage of Cost**   Has a price for the contracted product or service, but cost overruns are assigned to the buyer.
- **Cost Plus Incentive Fee**   The seller determines a price for the product or service—but includes an incentive reward for completing the procured work on time or ahead of schedule.
- **Fixed-Price**   A simple fixed price for the contract—but it can include an incentive for the seller to complete early, ahead of schedule, or other savings shared between the buyer and the seller.
- **Lump-Sum**   The contract has one price for all of the contracted work.
- **Time and Materials**   Price assigned for the time and materials provided by the seller.

KEY TERMS

To pass the PMP exams, you will need to memorize these terms and their definitions. For maximum value, create your flashcards based on these definitions and review them daily. The definitions can be found within this chapter and in the glossary.

Bid	Direct costs	Proposal
Bidder conferences	Evaluation criteria	Qualified seller list
Centralized contracting	Fixed-Price contracts	Quote
Contract	*Force majeure*	Request for Proposal
Contract administration	Indirect costs	Request for Quote
Contract change control system	Invitation for Bid	"Should cost" estimates
Contract closeout	Letter of Intent	Single source
Contract file	Make-or-buy analysis	Sole source
Cost-reimbursable contracts	Procurement	Statement of Work
Decentralized contracting	Procurement audits	Time and Materials
	Procurement Management Plan	

✓ TWO-MINUTE DRILL

Procurement Planning

- ❏ Procurement planning is determining which aspects of the project can best be fulfilled by procuring the specified products or services.
- ❏ The project scope serves as a key input, as this describes the work, and only the required work, needed to complete the project.
- ❏ A clearly defined product description is needed in order to successfully procure the product.
- ❏ Make-or-buy analysis calculates and predicts which is better: for the performing organization to make the product or to hire an entity outside of the organization to make the product.
- ❏ Some contracts can transfer the risk to the seller; other contract types require the buyer to retain the risk of cost overruns.

Solicitation Planning

- ❏ The Procurement Management Plan describes the procedures for procuring work or products.
- ❏ Bids and quotes are needed when the decision is made on price. Proposals are needed when decisions are based on other factors, such as experience, qualifications, and approaches to the project work.
- ❏ The buyer should provide the seller with a SOW, details on the type of response needed—such as a proposal, quote, or bid, and any information on contractual provisions, such as non-disclosure agreements or a copy of the model contract the buyer intends to use.

Solicitation

- ❏ Solicitation is requesting the potential sellers to provide bids, proposals, or quotes to complete the project work or supply the described product.
- ❏ An organization may retain a qualified seller list from which the project team is forced to select a vendor. In other instances, the project team can rely on trade associations, industry directories, and other resources to locate qualified sellers.
- ❏ Advertisements for the procured process in newspaper and trade publications can increase the list of sellers the buyer can choose from. Many government entities must publish procurement opportunities.

❑ Bidder conferences allow sellers to meet with the buyer to query the buyer on details of the procurement process. The goal of the bidder conference is to ensure that all prospective sellers have the same information and all of the needed information to complete an accurate bid or proposal.

Source Selection

❑ Samples of the sellers' previous, related products or services can serve as evaluation criteria.

❑ Contract negotiation focuses on finding a fair and reasonable price for both the buyer and the seller.

❑ Weighting systems are unbiased approaches to determine which seller has the best offer to complete the procured product or service.

❑ Screening Systems allow an organization to screen out sellers that do not qualify for the procured product or service.

❑ "Should cost" estimates are completed by the performing organization to determine if sellers completely understand the requirements of the project work.

Contract Administration

❑ Contract administration ensures the sellers are meeting their contractual obligations.

❑ Change requests may require updates to the contract between the buyer and the seller. Contract Change requests are part of the Integrated Change Control system.

❑ The project manager must document and report to the seller and management on how the seller is meeting its contract obligations.

Contract Closeout

❑ Contract closeout is similar to administrative closure.

❑ Contract documentation—such as the contract, schedules, relevant documentation, approved contract changes, performance reports, and other pertinent information—is needed to complete contract closeout.

❑ Procurement audits are intended to review, document, and share the successes and failures of the current project's procurement process. The information can be applied to other projects within the organization.

❑ A contract file is created and is included with the project records as part of the historical information of the current project.

SELF TEST

1. Which of the following may be used as a risk mitigation tool?
   A. Vendor proposal
   B. Contract
   C. Quotation
   D. Project requirements

2. A contract cannot have provisions for which one of the following?
   A. A deadline for the completion of the work
   B. Illegal activities
   C. Subcontracting the work
   D. Penalties and fines for disclosure of intellectual rights

3. You are the project manager for the 89A Project. You have created a contract for your customer. The contract must have what two things?
   A. Offer and consideration
   B. Signatures and the stamp of a notary public
   C. Value and worth of the procured item
   D. Start date and acceptance of start date

4. The product description of a project can help a project manager create procurement details. Which one of the following best describes this process?
   A. The product description defines the contracted work.
   B. The product description defines the requirements for the contract work.
   C. The product description defines the contracted work, which must support the requirements of the project customer.
   D. Both parties must have and retain their own copy of the product description.

5. Yolanda has outsourced a portion of the project to a vendor. The vendor has discovered some issues that will influence the cost and schedule of its portion of the project. How must the vendor update the agreement?
   A. As a new contract signed by Yolanda and the vendor.
   B. As a contract addendum signed by Yolanda and the vendor.
   C. As a memo and SOW signed by Yolanda and the vendor.
   D. Project Management contracts have clauses that allow vendors to adjust their work according to unknowns.

6. The United States backs all contracts through which of the following?
   A. Federal law
   B. State law
   C. Court system
   D. Lawyers

7. Terry is the project manager of the MVB Project. She needs to purchase a piece of equipment for her project. The Accounting department has informed Terry she needs a unilateral form of contract. Accounting is referring to which of the following?
   A. SOW
   B. Legal binding contract
   C. Purchase Order
   D. Invoice from the vendor

8. Bonnie is the project manager for the HGH Construction Project. She has contracted a portion of the project to the ABC Construction Company. Bonnie has offered a bonus to ABC if they complete their portion of the work by August 30. This is an example of which one of the following?
   A. Project requirement
   B. Project incentive
   C. Project goal
   D. Fixed-price contract

9. The purpose of a contract is to distribute between the buyer and seller a reasonable amount of which of the following:
   A. Responsibility
   B. Risk
   C. Reward
   D. Accountability

10. Privity is what?
    A. Relationship between the project manager and a known vendor
    B. Relationship between the project manager and an unknown vendor
    C. Contractual, confidential information between customer and vendor
    D. Professional information regarding the sale between customer and vendor

11. Sammy is the project manager of the DSA Project. He is considering proposals and contracts presented by vendors for a portion of the project work. Of the following, which contract is least dangerous to the DSA Project?

A. Cost plus fixed fee

B. Cost plus percentage of cost

C. Cost plus incentive fee

D. Fixed-price

12. In the following contract types, which one requires the seller to assume the risk of cost overruns?

A. Cost plus fixed fee

B. Cost plus incentive fee

C. Lump sum

D. Time and materials

13. Benji is the project manager of PLP Project. He has hired an independent contractor for a portion of the project work. The contractor is billing the project $120 per hour, plus materials. This is an example of which one of the following?

A. Cost plus fixed fee

B. Time and materials

C. Unit-price

D. Lump sum

14. Mary is the project manager of JHG Project. She has created a Statement of Work (SOW) for a vendor. For Mary's SOW to be a legal contract, what must be included?

A. Affidavit of agreement

B. Signatures of both parties agreeing to SOW

C. Signature of vendor

D. Signature of Mary

15. You are the project manager for a software development project for an accounting system that will operate over the Internet. Based on your research, you have discovered it will cost you $25,000 to write your own code. Once the code is written you estimate you'll spend $3,000 per month updating the software with client information, government regulations, and maintenance.

A vendor has proposed to write the code for your company and charge a fee based on the number of clients using the program every month. The vendor will charge you $5 per month per user of the web-based accounting system. You will have roughly 1,200 clients using the system per month. However, you'll need an in-house accountant to manage the time and billing of the system, so this will cost you an extra $1,200 per month.

How many months will you have to use the system before it is better to write your own code than to hire the vendor?

A. 3 months

B. 4 months

    C. 6 month

    D. 15 months

16. You are completing the closeout of a project to design a warehouse in Columbus, Ohio. The contract is a Cost Plus Incentive Fee contract. The target costs are $300,000, with a 10 percent target profit. However, the project came in at $275,000. The incentive split is 80/20. How much is the total contract cost??

    A. $300,000

    B. $275,000

    C. $310,000

    D. $330,000

17. A contract between an organization and a vendor may include a clause that penalizes the vendor if the project is late. The lateness of a project has a monetary penalty; penalty should be enforced or waived based on which one of the following?

    A. If the project manager could have anticipated the delay

    B. If the project manager knew the delay was likely

    C. Whether the delay was because of an unseen risk

    D. Who caused the delay and the reason why

18. A single source seller means what?

    A. There is only one qualified seller.

    B. There is only one seller the company wants to do business with.

    C. There is a seller that can provide all aspects of the project procurement needs.

    D. There is only one seller in the market.

19. Which one of the following is not a valid evaluation criterion for source selection?

    A. Age of the contact person at the seller

    B. Technical ability of the seller

    C. Contract requirements

    D. Price

20. Henry has sent the ABN Contracting Company a letter of intent. This means which one of the following?

    A. Henry intends to sue the ABN Contracting Company.

    B. Henry intends to buy from the ABN Contracting Company.

    C. Henry intends to bid on a job from the ABN Contracting Company.

    D. Henry intends to fire the ABN Contracting Company.

21. Martha is the project manager of the MNB Project. She wants a vendor to offer her one price to do all of the detailed work. Martha is looking for which type of document?

   A. RFP

   B. RFI

   C. Proposal

   D. IFB

22. Which one of the following is true about procurement documents?

   A. They offer no room for bidders to suggest changes.

   B. They ensure receipt of complete proposals.

   C. They inform the performing organization why the bid is being created.

   D. The project manager creates and selects the bid.

23. In what process group does source selection happen?

   A. Initiating

   B. Planning

   C. Executing

   D. Closing

24. You have an emergency on your project. You have hired a vendor that is to start work immediately. What contract is needed now?

   A. T&M

   B. Fixed fee

   C. Letter contract

   D. Incentive contract

25. You are the project manager for a seller. You are managing another company's project. Things have gone well on the project, and the work is nearly complete. There is still a significant amount of funds in the project budget. The buyer's representative approaches you and asks that you complete some optional requirements to use up the remaining budget. You should do which one of the following?

   A. Negotiate a change in the contract to take on the additional work.

   B. Complete a contract change for the additional work.

   C. Gain the approval of the project stakeholder for the requested work.

   D. Deny the change because it was not in the original contract.

SELF TEST ANSWERS

1. ☑ **B.** Contracts can be used as a risk mitigation tool. Procurement of risky activities is known as *transference*; the risk does not disappear, but the responsibility for the risk is transferred to the vendor.
   ☒ **A, C,** and **D** are all incorrect. A vendor proposal, a quotation, and project requirements do nothing to serve as a risk mitigation tool.

2. ☑ **B.** A contract cannot contain illegal activities.
   ☒ **A** is incorrect, as a contract can stipulate a deadline for the project work. **C** is incorrect; contracts can specify rules for subcontracting the work. **D** is also incorrect; a contract can assess a penalty and fines for disclosing intellectual rights and secret information.

3. ☑ **A.** Of all choices presented, **A** is the best choice. Contracts have an offer and a consideration.
   ☒ **B** is incorrect, as not all contracts demand signatures and notary public involvement. **C** is incorrect; a contract may not explicitly determine what the value and worth of the procured product or service is. **D** is also incorrect; a contract may specify a start date, but the acceptance of the start date is vague and not needed for all contracts.

4. ☑ **C.** The product description defines the details and requirements for acceptance of the project. This information also serves as a valuable input to the process of determining what needs to be procured. The product description defines what the end result of the project will be. When dealing with vendors to procure a portion of the project, the work to be procured must support the requirements of the project's customer.
   ☒ **A** is incorrect because the product description defines the product as a whole, not just the contracted work, which may be just a portion of the project. **B** is incorrect; the product description does not define the requirements for the contract work. **D** is also incorrect; the vendor likely will not have a copy of the product description..

5. ☑ **B** is the best answer of all the choices presented. Because the question is asking for the vendor to update the agreement, **B** is the best choice.
   ☒ **A,** while feasible, is not the best answer to the question. A new contract does not update the original agreement and may cause delays, as the contract may have to be resubmitted, re-approved, and so on. **C** and **D** are not viable answers.

6. ☑ **C.** All contracts in the United States are backed by the US court systems.
   ☒ **A, B,** and **D** are not correct answers.

7. ☑ **C.** A unilateral form of a contract is simply a purchase order.
   ☒ **A, B,** and **D** are all incorrect choices. A SOW is a statement of work. A legal binding contract does not fully answer the question. **D,** an invoice from the vendor, is not what the purchasing department is requesting.

8. ☑ **B.** A bonus to complete the work by August 30 is an incentive.
☒ **A** is incorrect, as the question does not specify August 30 as a deadline. **C** is incorrect, as "project goal" does not fully answer the question. **D** is incorrect because the contract details are not disclosed in this question.

9. ☑ **B.** A fair contract shares a reasonable amount of risk between the buyer and the seller.
☒ **A** is incorrect; a contract may transfer the majority of the responsibility to the vendor. **C** is incorrect; the reward is not an appropriate answer to the question. **D** is also incorrect; the accountability of the services contracted to the vendor is not shared between the buyer and the seller.

10. ☑ **C.** Privity is a confidential agreement between the buyer and seller.
☒ **A, B,** and **D** are incorrect choices, as these choices do not fully answer the question.

11. ☑ **D.** A Fixed-Price contract contains the least amount of risk for a project. The seller assumes all of the risk.
☒ **A, B, C** are incorrect, because these contract types carry the risk of cost overruns being assumed by the buyer.

12. ☑ **C.** A Lump Sum is a fixed fee to complete the contract; the seller absorbs any cost overruns.
☒ **A** and **B** are incorrect because these contracts require the seller to carry the risk of cost overruns. **D** is incorrect because Time and Materials contracts require the buyer to pay for cost overruns on the materials and the time invested in the project work.

13. ☑ **B.** The contractor's rate of $120 per hour plus the cost of the materials is an example of a Time and Materials contract.
☒ **A** is incorrect; a Cost Plus Fixed Fee charges the cost of the materials, plus a fixed fee, for the installation or work to complete the contract. **C** is incorrect; a Unit-Price has a set price for each unit installed on the project. **D** is also incorrect, as a Lump Sum does not break down the time and materials.

14. ☑ **B.** An SOW can be a contract if both parties agree to the SOW and sign the document as a contract.
☒ **A, C,** and **D** are incorrect. **A** is incorrect as it does not fully answer the question. **C** and **D** are incorrect; individuals with the authority from both parties need to sign the SOW.

15. ☑ **C.** The monies invested in the vendor's solution would have paid for your own code in six months. This is calculated by finding your cash outlay for the two solutions: $25,000 for your own code creation, and zero cash outlay for the vendor's solution. The monthly cost to maintain your own code is $3,000. The monthly cost of the vendor's solution is $7,200. Subtract your cost of $3,000 from the vendor's cost of $7,200 and this equals $4,200. Divide this number into the cash outlay of $25,000 to create your own code and you'll come up with 5.95 months. Of all the choices presented, **C**, six months, is the best choice.
☒ **A, B,** and **D** are all incorrect as they do not answer the question.

16. ☑ **C.** The total contract cost is $310,000. Here's how the answer is calculated: target cost is $300,000. The ten percent profit is $30,000. The finished cost was $275,000, a difference of $25,000 between the target and the actual. The contract calls for an 80/20 split if the contract comes in under budget. The formula reads finished costs + profit margin + (.20 X under budget amount).

    ☒ **A, B,** and **D** are all incorrect as these choices do not reflect the amount of the contract.

17. ☑ **D.** The party that caused the delay is typically the party responsible for the delay. It would not be acceptable for the project manager to willingly cause a delay and then penalize the contractor because the project was late.

    ☒ **A, B,** and **C** are all incorrect. **D** is the best answer as it answers the question fully.

18. ☑ **B.** A single source seller means there is only one seller the company wants to do business with.

    ☒ **A** describes a "sole source" seller. **C** is incorrect; there may be multiple sellers that can satisfy the project needs. **D** is also incorrect; just because there is only one seller in the market does not mean the seller can adequately and fully fill the project needs.

19. ☑ **A.** The age of the contact at the seller should not influence the source selection. The experience of the person doing the work, however, can.

    ☒ **B, C,** and **D** are all incorrect, as technical ability, objective requirements (such as qualifications and certifications), and price can be valid evaluation criteria.

20. ☑ **B.** Henry intends to buy from the ABN Contracting Company.

    ☒ **A, C,** and **D** are all incorrect; these choices do not adequately describe the purpose of the letter of intent.

21. ☑ **D.** An IFB is typically a request for a sealed document that lists the seller's firm price to complete the detailed work.

    ☒ **A** and **B,** Request for Proposal and Request for Information, are documents from the buyer to the seller requesting information on completing the work. **C,** a proposal, does not list the price to complete the work, but instead offers solutions to the buyer for completing the project needs.

22. ☑ **B.** Procurement documents detail the requirements for the work to ensure complete proposals from sellers.

    ☒ **A** is incorrect; procurement documents allow input from the seller to suggest alternative ways to complete the project work. **C** is incorrect; informing the performing organization on why the bid is being created is not the purpose of the procurement documents. **D** is not realistic.

23. ☑ **C.** Source selection happens during the Execution process group.

    ☒ **A, B,** and **D** are all incorrect, as these process groups do not include source selection.

24. ☑ **C.** For immediate work, a letter contract may suffice. The intent of the letter contract is to allow the vendor to get to work immediately to solve the project problem.

☒ Choices **A, B,** and **D** are all incorrect; these contracts may require additional time to create and approve. When time is of the essence, a letter contract is acceptable.

25. ☑ **C.** Any additional work is a change in the project scope. Changes to project scope should be approved by the mechanisms in the change control system. The stakeholder needs to approve the changes to the project scope.

☒ **A, B, and D** are not realistic expectations of the project. This questions border on the PMP Code of Professional Conduct. Typically, when a project scope has been fulfilled, the project work is done. The difference in this situation is that the additional tasks are optional requirements for the project scope.

13

PMP Code of Professional Conduct

T he PMP Code of Professional Conduct Is the authoritative guide on how the PMP should act as a professional, and how the PMP should behave with customers and the public in general. The PMP exam candidate will be tested on the knowledge of the PMP code of professional conduct.

The code, while only one page in length, covers a broad array of dos and don'ts for the PMP. Essentially, the PMP should always take the high road. There should be no room for misconceptions, errors in judgment, or actions that could be interpreted as conflicts of interest, shady, or just plain wrong.

Whenever the PMP is considering doing something that could be seen as wrong, just remember, "When in doubt, don't." The full PMP code of conduct is available through PMI's web site at: www.pmi.org/prod/groups/public/documents/info/pdc_pmpcodeofconductfile.asp

The PMP exam covers more than just the PMP code of professional conduct in regard to professional responsibility. Many of these topics have been covered in communications and human resources. The five areas of professional responsibility are:

- Ensuring integrity
- Contributing to the knowledge base
- Applying professional knowledge
- Balancing stakeholder interests
- Respecting differences

Responsibilities to the Profession

The PMP must adhere to a high set of principles, rules and policies. This includes the organizational rules and policies, the certification process, and the advancement of the profession. On the PMP exam, always choose the answer which best supports the PMP profession and the higher set of principles the PMP is expected to adhere to.

Complying with Rules and Policies

Honesty is expected in all areas regarding the PMP examination process, including Exam applications must be honest and reflect actual education and work experience.

- Test items, questions, answers and scenarios are not to be shared with other PMP candidates.

- PMP renewal information must reflect an honest assessment of education and experience.

- Continuing education information must be honest and accurate; continuing education reporting must reflect actual courses completed.

The PMP should report violations of the PMP code when clear and factual evidence exists of the code being violated. Based on the scenario, the reporting may be to PMI, to the performing organization's management, or to the proper law enforcement authorities.

The PMP must disclose to clients and customers scenarios where the PMP may be perceived as having an unfair advantage, a conflict of interest, or where they may profit from conditions within the project. Any appearances of impropriety must be avoided and disclosed.

Applying Honesty to the Profession

The PMP candidate is expected, at all times, to provide honesty in experience documentation, advertisement of skills, and performance of services. The PMP must, of course, adhere to and abide all applicable laws governing the project work. In addition, the ethical standards within the trade or industry should also be adhered to.

on the
job

Industry standards are recommendations for how the work and practice should be followed. Regulations are requirements for how the work and practice must be followed. A PMP must know the difference.

Advancing the Profession

The PMP must respect and recognize the intellectual work and property of others. The PMP can't claim others' work as his own. He must give credit where credit is due. Work, research, and development sources must be documented and acknowledged by the PMP relying on others' work.

Another method of advancing the PMP profession is to distribute the PMP code of professional conduct to other PMP candidates.

INSIDE THE EXAM

The PMP code of professional conduct, while only one page in length, implies many messages to the project management professional (PMP). The responsibility of the PMP centers on honesty and ethics. The PMP may often find themselves in scenarios where they can personally profit through the information within a project. For example, a PMP may discover a project is finishing ahead of schedule—but by finishing early, the PMP's contract will be closed and he'll lose income. The PMP must decide to finish the project early, or slow the project completion to gain personal income from the project scenario.

On the PMP exam, without breaking this very code, the PMP candidate will face many questions on professional conduct. Always, even if you disagree in theory with the outcome of the scenario, choose the moral high ground. The questions you'll face on the exam are extreme circumstances but they still test the knowledge of the PMP Code.

Part of the PMP code of professional conduct deals with customs and laws of foreign countries. The PMP must recognize these laws and customs and understand how to operate within them. The Sapir-Whorf Hypotheses believes an understanding of the local language, its implied meaning, and colloquialisms allows individuals to have a deeper understanding of the people, their values, and actions.

The PMP, when operating in countries other than their home country, should consider the practices and customs of the local country before reacting to conditions and scenarios. What may be considered a conflict of interest in one country, may be a common practice in another.

Culture shock is the initial disorientation a person first experiences when visiting a country other than his own. Ethnocentrism happens when individuals measure and compare a foreigner's actions against their own local culture. The locals typically believe their own culture is superior to the foreigner's culture.

Responsibilities to the Customer and to the Public

The PMP also has a responsibility to the customer of the project and the public. Projects that affect internal customers are expected to meet requirements, standards, and fulfill the business need of the performing organization. Essentially, the PMP is working for the customer.

Projects that serve a community and citizens have a responsibility that's somewhat tied to public service. The PMP is held accountable for the work completed for the public—and for the transactions, quality of work, and the ethics enforced in the project.

Enforcing Project Management Truth and Honesty

PMPs must represent themselves and their projects truthfully to the general public. This includes statements made in advertising, press releases, and in public forums. When project managers are involved in the creation of estimates truth is also expected. The PMP must provide accurate estimates on time, cost, services to be provided—and realistic outcomes of the project work.

When a project is assigned to the PMP, the project manager has the responsibility to meet the project scope as expected by the customer. PMPs work for the customer and must strive for customer satisfaction while fulfilling the project objectives. As part of the project implementation, the PMP must keep confidential information confidential. There is an obligation to the customer to maintain privacy, confidentiality, and non-disclosure of sensitive information.

Eliminating Inappropriate Actions

A PMP must avoid conflicts of interest and scenarios where conflicts of interest could seem apparent, opportunistic, or questionable to the customer or other stakeholders. In

When a project manager is completing a project for another company, the project manager must first conform to the policies of his organization. If his organization does not allow any gifts, then the project manager cannot accept any gifts from the client—even if the customs of the country allow it.

addition, the PMP must not accept any appropriate gifts, inappropriate payments, or any other compensation for favors, project management work, or influence of a project. The exception to this rule is when the laws or customs of the country where the project is being performed call for gifts to the project manager. However, the PMP should be aware of what gifts are acceptable and appropriate within the country where the project is taking place. Lavish gifts outside of the norm should be refused.

CERTIFICATION SUMMARY

The PMP Code of Professional Conduct and the professional conduct of a project manager accounts for 29 questions on the PMP examination. To answer these questions correctly the PMP candidate should always take the "ethical high road." The questions concerning ethics, conflict of interest, and personal gain are representative of the types of situations project managers can find themselves in on a regular basis. For the PMP exam—and in daily practice—follow the code of professional conduct and you'll do fine.

A project manager must follow the laws he is governed by. This means knowing the difference between optional standards and the required regulations. Next, the project manager must follow the policies of the organization he is employed by. This means any if the project manager's company has a policy against a certain condition—no matter how small or innocent it may seem—the policy must be followed first. Finally, the project manager must avoid conflict of interests and appearances of impropriety.

When a project manager is completing projects in another country the project manager must be respectful of the laws, people, culture, and values of the country the work is taking place in. Project managers must not succumb to ethnocentrism—the act of believing their own culture is better than anyone else's culture. The project manager must work to understand the culture, traditions, and expectations of the people he is working with in the foreign countries—while still complying with the policies of his organization.

KEY TERMS

To pass the PMP exams, you will need to memorize these terms and their definitions. For maximum value, create your own flashcards based on these definitions and review them daily. The definitions can be found within this chapter and in the glossary.

confidentiality	ethics	**PMP code of professional conduct**
conflict of interest	**inappropriate compensation**	

✓ TWO-MINUTE DRILL

Truthful Obligations of the PMP

❏ PMP candidates and professionals must provide accurate and truthful information in all aspects of PMP certification.

❏ PMP exam questions and scenarios should not be shared with other PMP candidates.

❏ Violations of the PMP code should be reported to the proper parties.

Ethical Obligations of the PMP

❏ PMPs must comply with all laws, regulations, and ethics in regard to project management practices.

❏ PMPs must acknowledge and recognize others' work, intellectual property, and development.

❏ PMPs must provide accurate and truthful information to the public and customers when estimating costs, services, and realistic outcomes of project work.

PMP Professional Code of Conduct In Practice

❏ PMPs must keep confidential information confidential.

❏ PMPs must avoid conflicts of interest and disclose any perceivable conflicts of interest.

❏ PMPs must not accept inappropriate compensation or gifts for their project management work.

SELF TEST

1. You are the project manager of the JKN Project. The project customer has requested that you inflate your cost estimates by 25 percent. He reports that his Management always reduces the cost of the estimates so this is the only method to get the monies needed to complete the project. Which of the following is the best response to this situation?

   A. Do as the customer asked to ensure the project requirements can be met by adding the increase as a contingency reserve.

   B. Do as the customer asked to ensure the project requirements can be met by adding the increase across each task.

   C. Do as the customer asked by creating an estimate for the customer's management and another for the actual project implementation.

   D. Complete an accurate estimate of the project. In addition, create a risk assessment on why the project budget would be inadequate.

2. You are the project manager for the BNH Project. This project takes place in a different county than where you are from. The project leader from this country presents a team of workers that are only from his family. You should do which one of the following?

   A. Reject the team leader's recommendations and assemble your own project team.

   B. Review the résumé and qualifications of the proposed project team before approving the team.

   C. Determine if the country's traditions include hiring from the immediate family before hiring from outside the family.

   D. Replace the project leader with an impartial project leader.

3. You are about to begin negotiations on a new project that is to take place in another country. Which of the following should be your guide on what business practices are allowed and discouraged?

   A. The project charter

   B. The project plan

   C. Company policies and procedures

   D. The PMP code of conduct

4. One of your project team members reports that he sold pieces of equipment because he needed the pay for his daughter's school tuition. He says he has paid back the money by working overtime without reporting the hours worked so that his theft remains private. What should you do?

   A. Fire the project team member.

   B. Report the team member to his manager.

   C. Suggest that the team member report his action to human resources.

D. Tell the team you're disappointed in what he did, and advise him not to do something like this again.

5. You are the project manager of the SUN Project. Your organization is a functional environment and you do not get along well with the functional manager leading the project. You are in disagreement with the manager on how the project should proceed, the timings of the activities, the suggested schedule, and the expected quality of the work. The manager has requested that you get to work on several of the activities on the critical path even though you and she have not solved the issues concerning the project. Which of the following should you do?

A. Go to senior management and voice your concerns.

B. Complete the activities as requested.

C. Ask to be taken off of the project.

D. Refuse to begin activities on the project until the issues are resolved.

6. PMI has contacted you regarding an ethics violation of a PMP candidate. The question is in regard to a friend that said he worked as project manager under your guidance. You know this is not true, but to save a friendship you avoid talking with PMI. This is a violation of which of the following?

A. The PMP code to cooperate on ethics violations investigations

B. The PMP code to report accurate information

C. The PMP code to report any PMP violations

D. Law concerning ethical practices

7. You are the project manager for the Log Cabin Project. One of your vendors is completing a large portion of the project. You have heard a rumor that the vendor is losing many of its workers due to labor issues. In light of this information, what should you do?

A. Stop work with the vendor until the labor issues are resolved.

B. Communicate with the vendor in regard to the rumor.

C. Look to secure another vendor to replace the current vendor.

D. Negotiate with the labor union to secure the workers on your project.

8. You are the project manager for the PMH Project. Three vendors have submitted cost estimates for the project. One of the estimates is significantly higher than similar project work in the past. In this scenario, you should do which of the following?

A. Ask the other vendors about the higher estimate from the third vendor.

B. Use the cost estimates from the historical information.

C. Take the high cost to the vendor to discuss the discrepancy before reviewing the issue with the other vendors.

D. Ask the vendor that supplied the high estimate for information on how the estimate was prepared.

Chapter 13:   PMP Code of Professional Conduct

9. You are the project manager of the LKH Project. This project must be completed within six months. The project is two months into the schedule and is starting to slip. As of now, the project is one week behind schedule. Based on your findings, you believe you can make some corrective actions and recover the lost time over the next month to get the project back on schedule for its completion date. Management, however, requires weekly status reports on cost and schedule. Which of the following should you do?

   A. Report that the project is one week behind schedule, but will finish on schedule based on cited corrective actions.

   B. Report that the project is on schedule and will finish on schedule.

   C. Report that the project is off schedule by a few days, but will finish on schedule.

   D. Report that the project is running late.

10. As a contracted project manager, you have been assigned a project with a budget of 1.5 million U.S. dollars. The project is scheduled to last seven months, but your most recent EVM report shows that the project will finish ahead of schedule by nearly six weeks. If this happens, you will lose $175,000 in billable time. What should you do?

   A. Bill for the entire 1.5 million dollars since this was the approved budget.

   B. Bill for the 1.5 million dollars by adding additional work at the end of the project.

   C. Report to the customer the project status and completion date.

   D. Report to the customer the project status and completion date and ask if they'd like to add any additional features to account for the monies not spent.

11. You are the project manager of the PMH Project. You have been contracted to design the placement of several pieces of manufacturing equipment. You have completed the project scope and are ready to pass the work over to the installer. The installer begins to schedule you to help with the installation of the manufacturing equipment. You should:

   A. Help the installer place the equipment according to the design documents.

   B. Help the installer place the equipment as the customer sees fits.

   C. Refuse to help the installer since the project scope has been completed.

   D. Help the installer place the equipment, but insist that the quality control be governed by your design specifications.

12. You are the project manager of the 12BA Project. You have completed the project according to the design documents and have met the project scope. The customer agrees that the design document requirements have been met; however, the customer is not pleased with the project deliverables and is demanding additional adjustments be made to complete the project. What is the best way to continue?

   A. Complete the work as the customer has requested.

   B. Complete the work at 1.5 times the billable rate.

    C. Do nothing. The project scope is completed.

    D. Do nothing. Management from the performing organization and the customer's organization will need to determine why the project failed before adding work.

13. You are the project manager of the AAA Project. Due to the nature of the project, much of the work will require overtime between Christmas and New Year's Day. Many of the project team members, however, have requested vacation during that week. What is the best way to continue?

    A. Refuse all vacation requests and require all team members to work.

    B. Only allow vacation requests for those team members who are not needed during that week.

    C. Divide tasks equally among the team members so each works the same amount of time.

    D. Allow team members to volunteer for the overtime work.

14. You are a project manager for your organization. Your project is to install several devices for one of your company's clients. The client has requested that you complete a few small tasks that are not in the project scope. To maintain the relationship with the client, you oblige her request and complete the work without informing your company. This is an example of:

    A. Effective expert judgment

    B. Failure to satisfy the scope of professional services

    C. Contract change control

    D. Integrated change control

15. You are completing a project for a customer in another country. One of the customs in this company is to honor the project manager of a successful project with a gift. Your company, however, does not allow project managers to accept gifts from any entity worth more than 50 dollars. At the completion of the project the customer presents to you, in a public ceremony, a new car. Which of the following should you do?

    A. Accept the car since it is a custom of the country; to refuse it would be an insult to your hosts.

    B. Refuse to accept the car, since it would result in a conflict with your organization to accept it.

    C. Accept the car and then return it, in private, to the customer.

    D. Accept the car and then donate the car to a charity in the customer's name.

16. You have a project team member who is sabotaging your project because he does not agree with it. Which of the following should you do?

    A. Fire the project team member.

    B. Present the problem to management.

    C. Present the problem to management with a solution to remove the team member from the project.

    D. Present the problem to management with a demand to fire the project team member.

17. You are the project manager of a project in Asia. You discover that the project leader has hired family members for several lucrative contracts on the project. What should you consider?

    A. Cultural issues

    B. Ethical issues

    C. Organizational issues

    D. Political issues

18. Of the following, which one achieves customer satisfaction?

    A. Completing the project requirements

    B. Maintaining the project cost

    C. Maintaining the project schedule

    D. Completing the project with the defined quality metrics

19. A PMP has been assigned to manage a project in a foreign country. The disorientation the PMP will likely experience as he gets acclimated to the country is known as:

    A. The Sapir-Whorf Hypotheses

    B. Time dimension

    C. Ethnocentrism

    D. Culture shock

20. You are the project manager for an information technology project. It has come to your attention that a technical problem has stopped the project work. How should the project manager proceed?

    A. Measure the project performance to date and account for the cost of the technical problem.

    B. Rebaseline the project performance to account for the technical problem.

    C. Work with the project team to develop alternative solutions to the technical problem.

    D. Outsource the technical problem to a vendor.

21. A PMP has been assigned to manage a project in a foreign country. What should be done to ensure that the project's success is not hindered by the fact that the project manager is working in a foreign country?

    A. Teach the project manager about the customs and laws of the foreign country.

    B. Find a project manager that is from that country.

    C. Assign the project manager a guide to the foreign country.

    D. Allow the project manager to travel home on weekends.

22. Your company does not allow project managers to accept gifts from vendors of any kind. A friend that you have known for years now works for a vendor that your company may be doing business with. Your friend from the vendor asks you to lunch to discuss an upcoming project and you accept. When the check arrives at the lunch table your friend insists on paying. You should:

    A. Allow the friend to buy because you've been friends for years.
    B. Allow the friend to buy because lunch isn't really a gift.
    C. Don't allow the friend to buy because your company does not allow any gifts from vendors.
    D. Insist that you purchase your friend's lunch and your friend buys yours.

23. You are a project manager on a construction project. Your project needs an experienced mason to repair and restore an old chimney that the customer wants to keep as part of the project. Your brother, as it happens, is an expert at restoring historical chimneys and you award the work to him. This is an example of:

    A. Networking
    B. A conflict of interest
    C. Poor procurement
    D. Acceptable practice, because your brother is an expert.

24. While studying for your PMP exam, you are invited to participate in a study group. At your first meeting another attendee announces that he has "real, live questions" from the PMP exam. What should you do?

    A. Examine the questions.
    B. Report the study group to PMI.
    C. Leave the study group.
    D. Ask where the person got the questions so you can report the testing center to PMI.

25. You are a project manager within an organization that completes technical projects for other entities. You have plans to leave your company within the next month to launch your own consulting business—which will compete with your current employer. Your company is currently working on a large proposal for a government contract that your new company could also benefit from. What should you do?

    A. Resign from your current job and bid against your employer to get the contract.
    B. Decline to participate due to a conflict of interest.
    C. Help your employer prepare the proposal.
    D. Inform your employer that you will be leaving their company within a month and it would be inappropriate for you to work on the current proposal.

SELF TEST ANSWERS

1. ☑ **D.** It would be inappropriate to bloat the project costs by 25 percent. A risk assessment describing how the project may fail if the budget is not accurate is most appropriate.
   ☒ **A, C,** and **D** are all incorrect since these choices are ethically wrong. The PMP should always provide honest estimates of the project work.

2. ☑ **C.** You should first confirm what the local practices and customs call for in regard to hiring family members before others.
   ☒ **A** and **D** are incorrect since they do not consider the qualifications of the project team leader and the project team. In addition, they do not take into account local customs. **B** is incorrect as well; although it does ponder the qualifications of the project team, it does not consider the local customs.

3. ☑ **C.** The company polices and procedures should guide the project manager and the decision he makes in the foreign country.
   ☒ **A** and **B** are incorrect since these documents are essential but usually do not reference allowed business practices. **D** is incorrect; while the PMP harbors crucial information, the company's policies and procedures are most specific to the project work and requirements.

4. ☑ **B.** This situation calls for the project team member to be reported to his manager for disciplinary action.
   ☒ **A** is inappropriate because the project manager may not have the authority to fire the project team member. **C** is inappropriate because the project manager must take action to bring the situation to management's attention. **D** is also inappropriate since there are no formal discipline actions taken to address the problem.

5. ☑ **B.** The project manager must respect the delegation of the Functional Manager.
   ☒ **A, C,** and **D** are all inappropriate actions since they do not complete the assigned work the functional manager has delegated to the project manager.

6. ☑ **A.** By avoiding the conversation with PMI in regard to the ethics violation of a friend, you are, yourself, violating the PMP Code to cooperate with PMI.
   ☒ **B, C,** and **D** are incorrect answers since they do not fully answer the question.

7. ☑ **B.** The project manager should confront the problem by talking with the vendor about the rumor.
   ☒ **A** is incorrect and would delay the project and possibly cause future problems. **C** is incorrect and may violate the contract between the buyer and seller. **D** is also incorrect—the agreement is between the vendor and the performing organization, not the labor union.

8. ☑ **D.** Most likely, the vendor did not understand the project work to be procured so the estimate is skewed. A clear statement of work is needed for the vendors to provide accurate estimates.

☒   **A, B,** and **C** are all inappropriate actions since they discuss another vendor's estimate. This information should be kept confidential between the buyer and seller. In some government projects, the winning bid may be required to be released.

9.   ☑   **A.** The project manager should report an honest assessment of the project with actions on how he plans to correct the problem.

☒   **B** is incorrect because it does not provide an honest answer to management. **C** is also incorrect because it does not provide an honest answer to management. **D** is incorrect because it does not provide a solution to the problem.

10.   ☑   **C.** Honest and accurate assessment of the project work is always required.

☒   **A** and **B** are incorrect because these actions do not reflect an honest assessment of the work. **D** is incorrect because it offers gold plating and recommends additional changes that were not part of the original project scope. In addition, because this is a contracted relationship, the additional work may not be covered within the original project contract and may result in legal issues.

11.   ☑   **C.** When the project scope is completed, the contract is fulfilled, the project is done. Any new work items should be sent through. In this instance, the contract change control system or a new contract should be created.

☒   **A, B,** and **D** are incorrect because these choices are outside of the scope and have not been covered in the contract.

12.   ☑   **C.** When the project scope has been completed, the project is completed. Any additional work, without a contract change or new contract, would be dishonest and would betray the customer or the project manager's company.

☒   **A** and **B** are both incorrect; additional work is not covered in the current contract. **D** is incorrect because the project did not fail—the deliverables met the requirements of the project scope and the design document.

13.   ☑   **D** is the best choice for this scenario because it allows the project team to be self-led and is sensitive to the needs of the project team.

☒   **A, B,** and **C** are all autocratic responses to the problem and while the results may seem fair, **D** is the best choice.

14.   ☑   **B.** When the project manager completes activities outside of the contract and does not inform the performing organization, it is essentially the same as stealing. The PMP must be held accountable for all the time invested in a project.

☒   **A** is incorrect; this is not expert judgment. **C** is incorrect because the contract has not been changed or attempted to be changed. **D** is also incorrect; the changes the project manager completed for the customer were not sent through any Change Control System, but were completed without documentation or reporting.

15. ☑ **B** is the best answer. Although this solution may seem extreme, it is the best answer because to accept the car in public would give the impression that the project manager has defied company policy. In addition, accepting the car would appear to be a conflict of interest for the project manager.

☒ **A, C,** and **D** are all incorrect. Accepting the car, even with the intention of returning it or donating it to charity, would be in conflict with the company's policies regarding the acceptance of gifts.

16. ☑ **C.** The project team member that is causing the problems should be presented to management with a solution to remove the project team member from the project. Remember, whenever the project manager must present a problem to management, he should also present a solution to the problem.

☒ **A** is incorrect because it likely is not the project manager's role to fire the project team member. **B** is incorrect because it does not address a solution for the problem. **D** is incorrect because the project manager's focus should be on the success of the project. By recommending that the project team member be removed from the project, the problem is solved from the project manager's point of view. Management, however, may come to the decision on their own accord to dismiss the individual from the company altogether. In addition, a recommendation from the project manager to fire someone may be outside the boundary of the human resource's procedure for employee termination.

17. ☑ **A.** The project manager should first determine what the country's customs and culture call for when hiring relatives. It may be a preferred practice in the country to work with qualified relatives first before hiring other individuals to complete the project work.

☒ **B, C,** and **D** are not the best choice in this scenario. They may be followed up by first examining the cultural issues within the country.

18. ☑ **A.** The largest factor when it comes to customer satisfaction is the ability to complete the project requirements.

☒ **B, C,** and **D** are incorrect because achieving these factors, while good, is not as complete as achieving the project requirements, which may include the cost, schedule, and quality expectations.

19. ☑ **D.** Culture shock is the typical disorientation a person feels when visiting a foreign country.

☒ **A** is incorrect; The Sapir-Whorf Hypotheses is a theory that believes an individual can understand a culture by understanding its language. **B** is incorrect; time dimension is the local culture's general practice for respecting time and punctuality. **C** is incorrect; ethnocentrism is the belief by a person that their own culture is the best and that all other cultures should be measured against it.

20. ☑ **C.** When problems arise that stop project tasks, the project manager should work with the team to uncover viable alternative solutions.
☒ **A** and **B** do nothing to find a solution to the problem, so they are incorrect. **D** is incorrect since the solution for the problem has not necessarily been addressed. The end result of **C**, to find an alternative solution, may be **D**, but outsourcing the problem to a vendor should not be the first choice in this scenario.

21. ☑ **A.** Training the project manager on the laws and customers of the foreign country is the best choice to ensure the project success is not jeopardized.
☒ **B, C,** and **D** may all work, but they are not the best option considering that the project manager has already been selected and needs to be educated about the foreign country's customs. **D** is incorrect because the travel option does not take into consideration the customs of the foreign country.

22. ☑ **C** is the best choice. Although you have been friends for years, the friend is now working with a vendor, and it would be inappropriate for the friend to purchase lunch. This would clearly be a violation of your company's policies because you and your friend are discussing an upcoming project.
☒ **A, B,** and **C** are all incorrect because you would be allowing your friend to purchase your lunch and this is against company policies.

23. ☑ **B.** This is a conflict of interest—or may appear to be a conflict of interest to others on the project. There are several things the project manager can do in this scenario: excuse himself from the decision because of the relationship with the brother, create a weighted scoring model and allow several vendors to participate, and others.
☒ **A, C,** and **D** are all incorrect, because these choices do not address the potential for the conflict of interest.

24. ☑ **C** is the best choice. You should not participate in the study group.
☒ **A** is incorrect as it clearly violates the PMP code of professional conduct. **B** and **D** are not good choices because there isn't any clear evidence that the questions, or claim, are genuine. The questions may have been purchased through a web site or other entity—not necessarily through a testing center.

25. ☑ **D.** Of the choices presented, this is the best answer. You should inform your employer of your intent to leave the organization and work on similar projects to avoid a conflict of interest.
☒ **A** is incorrect because you would have a conflict of interest, information gained about your current employer's proposal (such as price and methods), and other advantages that would be ethically wrong. **B** is incorrect because there is no rationale behind what the conflict of interest may be. **C** is incorrect because a conflict of interest exists by preparing the proposal for your future competition.

A

Critical Exam Information

Exam candidates want to pass their PMP exam on the first attempt. Why bother sitting for an exam if you know you're not prepared? In this appendix, you'll find the details that you must know to pass the exam. These facts won't be everything you need to know to pass the PMP exam—but you can bet you won't pass the exam if you do not know the critical information in this appendix.

Exam Test-Passing Tips

For starters, don't think of this process as preparing to take an exam, but think of it as "preparing to pass an exam." Anyone can prepare to take an exam: just show up. Preparing to take the PMP exam requires project management experience, diligence, and a commitment to study.

Days Before the Exam

In the days leading up to your scheduled exam, here are some basics you should do to prepare yourself for success:

- *Get some moderate exercise.* Find time to go for a jog, lift weights, take a swim, or do whatever workout routine works best for you.
- *Eat smart and healthy.* If you eat healthy food you'll feel good—and feel better about yourself. Be certain to drink plenty of water and don't overdo the caffeine.
- *Get your sleep.* A well-rested brain is a sharp brain. You don't want to sit for your exam feeling tired, sluggish, and worn-out.
- *Time your study sessions.* Don't overdo your study sessions—long, crash study sessions aren't that profitable. In addition, try to study at the same time every day at the time your exam is scheduled.

Practice the Testing Process

If you could take one page of notes into the exam what information would you like on this one page document? Of course you absolutely cannot take any notes or reference materials into the exam area. However, if you can create and memorize one sheet of notes, you absolutely may re-create this once you're seated in the exam area.

Practice creating a reference sheet so you can immediately, and legally, re-create this document once your exam has begun. You'll be supplied with several sheets of blank paper and a couple of pencils. Once your exam process begins, re-create your reference sheet. The following are key pieces of information you'd be wise to include on your reference sheet (you'll find all of this key information in this appendix):

- Activities within each process groups
- Estimating formulas
- Communication formula
- Normal distribution values
- Earned Value Management formulas
- Project management theories

Testing Tips

The questions on the PMP exam are fairly direct and not too verbose, but they may offer a few red herrings. For example, you may face questions that state, "All of the following are correct options expect for which one?" The question wants you to find the incorrect option, or the option that would not be appropriate for the scenario described. Be sure to understand what the question is asking for. It's easy to focus on the scenario presented in a question and then see a suitable option for that scenario in the answer. The trouble is, if the question is asking you to identify an option that is not suitable, then you just missed the question. Carefully read the question to understand what is expected for an answer.

Here's a tip that can work with many of the questions: identify what the question wants for an answer and then look for an option that doesn't belong with the other possible answers. In other words, find the answer that doesn't fit with the other three options. Find the "odd man out." Here's an example: EVM is used during the _____.

    A. Controlling phase

    B. Executing phase

    C. Closing phase

    D. Entire project

Notice how options A, B, and C are exclusive? If you choose A, the controlling phase, it implies that EVM is not used anywhere else in the project. The odd man out here is D, the entire project; it's considered the "odd" choice because it, by itself, is not an actual process group. Of course, this tip won't work with every question— but it's handy to keep in mind.

For some answer choices, it may seem like two of the four options are both possible correct answers. However, because you may only choose one answer, you must discern which answer is the best choice. Within the question, there will usually be some hint describing the progress of the project, the requirements of the stakeholders, or some other clue that can help you determine which answer is the best for the question.

Answer Every Question—Once

The PMP exam has 200 questions—you need to answer 137 questions correctly within four hours to pass. Do not leave any question blank—even if you don't know the answer to the question. A blank question is the same as a wrong answer. As you move through the exam and you find questions that stump you, use the "mark question" option in the exam software, choose an answer you suspect may be correct, and then move on. When you have answered all of the questions, you are given the option to review your marked answers.

Some questions in the exam may prompt your memory to come up with answers to questions you have marked for review. However, resist the temptation to review those questions you've already answered with confidence and haven't marked. More often than not, your first instinct is the correct choice. When you completed the exams at the end of each chapter, did you change correct answers to wrong answers? If you did in practice, you'll do it on the actual exam.

Use the Process of Elimination

When you're stumped on a question, use the process of elimination. For each question, there'll be four choices. On your scratch paper, write down "ABCD." If you can safely rule out "A," cross it out of the ABCD you've written on your paper. Now focus on which of the other answers won't work. If you determine that "C" won't work, cross it off your list. Now you've got a fifty-fifty chance of finding the correct choice.

If you cannot determine which answer is best, "B" or "D" in this instance, here's the best approach:

1. Choose an answer in the exam (no blank answers, remember?).

2. Mark the question in the exam software for later review.

3. Circle the "ABCD" on your scratch paper, jot any relevant notes, and then record the question number next to the notes.

4. During the review, or from a later question, you may realize which choice is the better of the two answers. Return to the question and confirm that the best answer is selected.

Everything You Must Know

As promised, this section covers all of the information you must know going into the exam. It's highly recommended that you create a method to recall this information. Here goes.

The 39 Project Management Processes

Table A-1 shows the 39 project management processes. The intersection of the Knowledge Area and each stage (Initiating, Planning, Executing, Controlling, and Closing) describes the activity that happens at that point in the project. For example, follow the Project Scope Management row and the Controlling column to find *Scope verification and change control.* –

Magic PMP Formulas

The following shows the major formulas you should know for the exam:

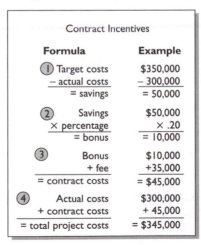

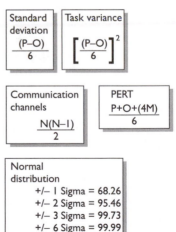

TABLE A-I The 39 Project Management Processes

Knowledge Area	Initiating	Planning	Executing	Controlling	Closing
Project Integration Management		Developing the project plan.	Project Plan Execution	Integrated Change Control	
Project Scope Management	Project Initiation	Creating and defining the project scope.		Scope verification and change control	
Project Time Management		Defining activities, their sequence and their estimated duration. Developing the project schedule.		Schedule control	
Project Cost Management		Determining the required resources, their estimated costs, and completing cost budgeting.		Enforcing cost control.	
Project Quality Management		Planning for quality.	Adhering to the performing organization's quality assurance requirements.	Enforcing quality control on the project.	
Project Human Resources Management		Completing organizational planning and staff acquisition	Ensuring team development.		
Project Communications Management		Creating the Communications Management Plan.	Distributing the required information to the appropriate parties.	Reporting on project performance.	
Project Risk Management		Completing risk management planning, risk identification, qualitative and quantitative risk analysis, and risk responses.		Monitoring and controlling risk.	
Project Procurement Management		Completing the procurement and solicitation planning.	Soliciting vendors to participate on the project. Completing source selection based on defined criterion, and then following-through with contract administration.		Completing the contract closeout.

Entry for Project Communications Management Closing: Completing administrative closure.

Earned Value Management Formulas

The following shows the EVM formulas you should know for the exam:

Earned Value Management formulas
VAR = BAC − AC
EV = %COMP × BAC
CV = EV − AC
SV = EV − PV
CPI = EV/AC
SPI = EV/PV
EAC = BAC/CPI
ETC = EAC − AC
VAC = BAC − EAC
TCPI = (BAC − EV) / EAC − AC

Older names:
BCWS = PV
BCWP = EV
ACWP = AC

Quick PMP Facts

This section has some quick facts you should be know at a glance. Hold on, this moves pretty fast.

Organizational Structures

Organizational structures are relevant to the project manager's authority. A project manager has authority from weakest to highest in the following order:

- Functional
- Weak matrix
- Balanced matrix
- Strong matrix
- Projectized

WBS Facts

The Work Breakdown Structure is the big picture of the project deliverables: it is not the activities that will create the project, but the components the project will create. The WBS helps the project team and the project manager create accurate cost and time estimates. The WBS also helps the project team and the project manager create an accurate activity list. The WBS is an input to five planning processes:

- Cost estimating
- Cost budgeting
- Resource planning
- Risk management planning
- Activity definition

Project Scope Facts

Projects are temporary endeavors to create a unique product. Projects are selected by one of two methods:

■ **Benefit measurement methods** These include scoring models, cost-benefit ratios, and economic models.

■ **Constrained optimization** These include mathematical models based on linear, integer, and dynamic programming. (This probably won't be on the PMP exam as a viable answer.)

The project scope defines all of the required work, and only the required work, to complete the project. Scope management is the process of ensuring that the project work is within scope and protecting the project from scope creep. The scope statement is the baseline for all future project decisions, as it justifies the business need of the project. There are two types of scope:

■ **Product scope** Defines the attributes of the product or service the project is creating

■ **Project scope** Defines the required work of the project to create the product

Scope verification is the process completed at the end of each phase and of each project to confirm that the project has met the requirements. It leads to formal acceptance of the project deliverable.

Project Time Facts

Time can be a project constraint. Effective time management is the scheduling and sequencing of activities in the best order to ensure that the project completes successfully and in a reasonable amount of time. These are some key terms for time management:

■ **Lag** Waiting between activities

■ **Lead** Activities come closer together and even overlap

■ **Free float** The amount of time an activity can be delayed without delaying the next scheduled activity's start date

■ **Total float** The amount of time an activity can be delayed without delaying the project's finish date

■ **Float** Sometimes called *slack*—a perfectly acceptable synonym

■ **Duration** May be abbreviated as "du". For example, du=8d means the duration is eight days.

There are three types of dependencies between activities:

- **Mandatory**   This hard logic requires a specific sequence between activities.
- **Discretionary**   This soft logic prefers a sequence between activities.
- **External**   Due to conditions outside of the project, such as those created by vendors, the sequence must happen in a given order.

Project Cost Facts

There are several methods of providing project estimates:

- **Bottom-up**   Project costs start at zero and each component in the WBS is estimated for costs and then the "grand total" is calculated. This is the longest method to complete, but provides the most accurate estimate.
- **Analogous**   Project costs are based on a similar project. This is a form of expert judgment, but it is also a top-down estimating approach so it less accurate than a bottom-up estimate.
- **Parametric Modeling**   Price is based on cost per unit; examples include cost per metric ton, cost per yard, cost per hour.

There are four types of costs attributed to a project:

- **Variable costs**   The costs are dependent on other variables. For example, the cost of a food-catered event depends on how many people register to attend the event.
- **Fixed costs**   The cost remains constant throughout the project. For example, a rented piece of equipment has the same fee each month even if it is used more in some months than others.
- **Direct costs**   The cost is directly attributed to an individual project and cannot be shared with other projects (for example, airfare to attend project meetings, hotel expenses, and leased equipment that is used only on the current project).
- **Indirect costs**   These are the cost of doing business; examples include rent, phone, and utilities.

Quality Management Facts

The cost of quality is the money spent investing in training; in meeting requirements for safety and other laws and regulations; and in taking steps to ensure quality acceptance. The cost of nonconformance is the cost associated with rework, downtime, lost sales, and waste of materials.

Some common quality management charts and methods include the following:

- *Ishikawa diagrams* (are also called *fishbone diagrams*) are used to find cause-and-effects that contribute to a problem.

- *Flow charts* show the relationship between components and the flow of a process through a system.

- *Pareto diagrams* identify project problems and their frequencies. These are based on the 80/20 Rule: 80 percent of project problems stem from 20 percent of the work.

- *Control charts* plot out the result of samplings to determine if projects are "in control" or "out of control."

- *Kaizen technologies* comprise approaches to make small improvements in an effort to reduce costs and achieve consistency.

- *Just-in-time* ordering reduces the cost of inventory but requires additional quality because materials would not be readily available if mistakes occur.

Human Resource Facts

There are several human resource theories the PMP candidate should be familiar with on the PMP Exam. They are the following:

- **Maslow's Hierarchy of Needs** There are five layers of needs for all humans: physiological, safety, social needs (such as love and friendship), self-esteem, and the crowning jewel, self-actualization.

- **Herzberg's Theory of Motivation** There are two catalysts for workers: hygiene agents and motivating agents.

  - **Hygiene agents** These do nothing to motivate, but their absence demotivates workers. Hygiene agents are the expectations all workers have: job security, a paycheck, clean and safe working conditions, a sense of belonging, civil working relationships, and other basic attributes associated with employment.

  - **Motivating agents** These are the elements that motivate people to excel. They include responsibility, appreciation of work, recognition, opportunity to excel, education, and other opportunities associated with work other than just financial rewards.

- **McGregory's Theory of X and Y** This theory states "X" people are lazy, don't want to work, and need to be micromanaged. "Y" people are self-led, motivated, and can accomplish things on their own.

- **Ouchi's Theory Z** This theory holds that the workers are motivated by a sense of commitment, opportunity, and advancement. Workers will work if they are challenged and motivated. Think participative management.

- **Expectancy Theory** People will behave based on what they expect as a result of their behavior. In other words, people will work in relation to the expected reward of the work.

Communication Facts

Communicating is the most important skill for the project manager. With that in mind, here are some key facts on communications:

- Communication channels formula: $N(N-1)/2$. N represents the number of stakeholders. For example, if you have 10 stakeholders the formula would read $10(10-1)/2$ for 45 communication channels. Pay special attention to questions wanting to know how many additional communication channels you have based on added stakeholders. For example, if you have 25 stakeholders on your project and have recently added 5 team members, how many additional communication channels do you now have? You'll have to calculate the original number of communication channels, $25(25-1)/2=300$; then calculate the new number with the added team members, $30(30-1)/2=435$; and finally, subtract the difference between the two: $435-300=135$, the number of additional communication channels.

- 55 percent of communication is nonverbal.

- Effective listening is the ability to watch the speaker's body language, interpret paralingual clues, and decipher facial expressions. Following the message, effective listening has the listener asking questions to achieve clarity and offering feedback.

- Active listening requires receivers of the message to offer clues, such as nodding the head to indicate they are listening. It also requires receivers to repeat the message, ask questions, and continue the discussion if clarification is needed.

- Communication can be hindered by trendy phrases, jargon, and extremely pessimistic comments. In addition, other communication barriers include noise, hostility, cultural differences, and technical interruptions.

Risk Management Facts

Risks are unplanned events that can have positive or negative effects on the projects. Most risks are seen as threats to the project success—but not all risks are bad. For example, there is a 20 percent probability that the project will realize a discount in shipping, which will save the project $15,000. If this risk happens the project will save money, if the risk doesn't happen the project will have to spend the $15,000. Risks should be identified as early as possible in the planning process. A person's willingness to accept risk is the Utility Function (also called the Utility Theory). The Delphi Technique can be used to build consensus on project risks.

The only output of the risk planning is the Risk Management Plan. There are two broad types of risks:

- **Business risk** The loss of time and finances (where a downside and upside exist).
- **Pure risk** The loss of life, injury, and theft (where only a downside exists).

Risks can be responded to in one of four methods:

- **Avoidance** Avoid the risk by planning a different technique to remove the risk from the project.
- **Mitigation** Reduce the probability or impact of the risk.
- **Acceptance** The risk's probability or impact may be small enough that the risk can be accepted.
- **Transference** The risk is not eliminated but the responsibility and ownership of the risk is transferred to another party (for example, through insurance).

Procurement Facts

A Statement of Work (SOW) is provided to the potential sellers so they can create accurate bids, quotes, and proposals for the buyer. A bidders' conference may be held so sellers can query the buyer on the product or service to be procured.

A contract is a formal agreement, preferably written, between a buyer and seller. On the PMP exam, procurement questions are usually from the buyer's point of view. All requirements the seller is to complete should be clearly written in the contract. Requirements of both parties must be met, or legal proceedings may follow. Contract types include the following:

- *Cost-reimbursable contracts* require the buyer to assume the risk of cost overruns.
- *Fixed-price contracts* require the seller to assume the risk of cost overruns.
- *Time-and-material contracts* are good for smaller assignments but can impose cost overrun risks to the buyer if the contract between the buyer and seller does not include a "not to exceed clause." This clause, commonly called an NTE clause, puts a cap on the maximum amount for the contract time and materials.
- A *purchase order* is a unilateral form of contract.
- A *letter of intent* is not a contract, but shows the intent of the buyer to purchase from a specific seller.

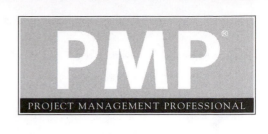

B

About the CD

T he CD-ROM included with this book comes complete with a full MasterExam, , the electronic version of the book, EZFlashCards study software, and a Microsoft Excel spreadsheet that illustrates important project management formulas. The software is easy to install on any Windows 98/NT/2000/XP computer and must be installed to access the MasterExam and flash card features. You may, however, browse both the electronic book and the Excel file directly from the CD without installation. To register for a second bonus MasterExam (another 250 study questions!), simply click the Online Training link on the Main Page and follow the directions to the free online registration.

System Requirements

Software requires Windows 98 or higher and Internet Explorer 5.0 or above and 20 MB of hard disk space for full installation. The electronic book requires Adobe Acrobat Reader. To access the Online Training from LearnKey you must have RealPlayer Basic 8 or Real1 Plugin, which will be automatically installed when you launch the Online Training site.

Installing and Running MasterExam

If your computer CD-ROM drive is configured to auto run, the CD-ROM will automatically start up upon inserting the disk. From the opening screen you may install MasterExam by pressing the *MasterExam* button. This will begin the installation process and create a program group named "LearnKey." To run MasterExam use START | PROGRAMS | LEARNKEY. If the auto run feature did not launch your CD, browse to the CD and Click on the "RunInstall" icon.

MasterExam

MasterExam provides you with a simulation of the PMP exam. You may take an open book exam, which provides the option of receiving hints, references, and answers; a closed book exam; or the timed MasterExam simulation.

When you launch MasterExam, a digital clock display will appear in the upper left-hand corner of your screen. The clock will continue to count down to zero unless you choose to end the exam before the time expires.

Electronic Book

The entire contents of the Study Guide are provided in PDF. Adobe's Acrobat Reader has been included on the CD.

Help

A help file is provided through the help button on the main menu page in the lower left hand corner. Individual help features are also available within the MasterExam application.

Removing Installation(s)

MasterExam installs to your hard drive. For best results for removal of programs use the START | PROGRAMS | LEARNKEY | UNINSTALL options to remove MasterExam.

If you desire to remove the Real Player use the Add/Remove Programs Icon from your Control Panel. You may also remove the LearnKey training program from this location.

Technical Support

For questions regarding the content of the electronic book, MasterExam, or CertCams, please visit www.osborne.com or e-mail customer.service@mcgraw-hill.com. For customers outside the 50 United States, e-mail: international_cs@mcgraw-hill.com.

LearnKey Technical Support

For technical problems with the software (installation, operation, removing installations), please visit www.learnkey.com or e-mail.

FlashCard Technical Support

For technical problems with the EZFlashCards software (installation, operation, removing installations), please visit or e-mail support@ezflashcards.com.

Glossary

Acceptance   This is a response to a risk event, generally made when the probability of the event and/or impact are small. It is used when mitigation, transference, or avoidance are not selected.

Active listening   This occurs when the receiver confirms the message is being received by feedback, questions, prompts for clarity, and other signs of having received the message.

Activity list   An output of activity definition that includes all of the activities to be performed within the project.

Activity on arrow   A network diagramming method where the arrows in the Arrow Diagramming Method network diagram represent the activities within the project.

Activity on node   A network diagramming method where the nodes in a project network diagram represent the activities.

Activity sequencing   A process for setting the order of activities within the project schedule.

Actual Costs (AC)   Used in earned value measurements; the actual cost of the work performed.

Administrative closure   The documenting of the project results and the acceptance of the product by the customer or the project sponsor. Administrative closure is also needed if a project is terminated.

Analogous estimating   This relies on historical information to predict estimates for current projects. Analogous estimating is also known as top-down estimating and is a form of expert judgment.

Application areas   These are the areas of business, industry, and trade about which the project manager may need special knowledge. Common application areas include legal issues, technical issues, engineering information, and manufacturing information.

Assumptions   Beliefs considered to be true, real or certain for the sake of planning.

Avoidance   This is one response to a risk event. The risk is avoided by planning a different technique to remove the risk from the project.

Benchmarking   A process of using prior projects within or external to the performing organization to compare and set quality standards for processes and results.

Benefit measurement methods   Used in comparing the value of one project against the value, or benefits, of another; often used in project selection models.

Benefit/cost analysis   The process of determining the pros and cons of any project, process, product, or activity.

Benefit/cost ratios   These models examine the cost-to-benefit ratio.

Bid   A document from the seller to the buyer. Used when price is the determining factor in the decision-making process.

Bidder conference (also called a contractor or vendor conference)
A meeting with prospective sellers to ensure all sellers have a clear understanding of the product or service to be procured. Bidder conferences allow sellers to query the buyer on the details of the product to help ensure that the proposal the seller creates is adequate and appropriate for the proposed agreement.

Bottom-up estimating   A technique where an estimate for each component in the WBS is developed and then totaled for an overall project budget. This is the longest method to complete, but it provides the most accurate estimate.

Brainstorming   The most common approach to risk identification; it is performed by a project team to identify the risks within the project. A multidisciplinary team, hosted by a project facilitator, can also perform brainstorming.

Budget at Completion (BAC)   The predicted budget for the project; what the project should cost when it is completed.

Bull's eye   Creates limits to the acceptable earned value metrics. Any variances within the preset values automatically prompt communication to management.

Cause-and-effect diagrams (also called Ishikawa diagrams and fishbone diagrams)   Used for root cause analysis of what factors are creating the risks within the project. The goal is to identify and treat the root of the problem, not the symptom.

Centralized contracting   All contracts for all projects need to be approved through a central contracting unit within the performing organization.

Change Control Board   A board that determines the validity and need of, and approves or denies, project change requests.

Change Control System   A system to formally accept, review, and act upon project change requests.

Chart of accounts   A coding system used by the performing organization's accounting system to account for the project work.

Checklists   A listing of activities that workers check to ensure the work has been completed consistently; used in quality control.

Closing   The period when a project or phase moves through formal acceptance to bring the project or phase to an orderly conclusion.

Coercive power   The type of power that comes with the authority to discipline the project team members. This is also known as "penalty power." Generally used to describe the power structure when the team is afraid of the project manager.

Collective bargaining agreements   These are contractual agreements initiated by employee groups, unions, or other labor organizations; they may act as a constraint on the project.

Communication channel formula   A formula to predict the number of communication channels within a project; the formula is $N(N-1)/2$, where N represents the number of stakeholders.

Communications Management Plan   A plan that documents and organizes the stakeholder needs for communication. This plan covers the communications system, its documentation, the flow of communication, modalities of communication, schedules for communications, information retrieval, and any other stakeholder requirements for communications.

Compromising   A conflict resolution method; this approach requires both parties to give up something. The decision ultimately made is a blend of both sides of the argument. Because neither party completely wins, it is considered a lose-lose solution.

Configuration management   Activities focusing on controlling the characteristics of a product or service. A documented process of controlling the features, attributes, and technical configuration of any product or service. Sometimes considered a rigorous change control system.

Constrained optimization methods   These are complex mathematical formulas and algorithms that are used to predict the success of projects, the variables within projects, and tendencies to move forward with selected project investments. Examples include linear programming, integer algorithms, and multi-objective programming.

Constraints   Any influence on the project that may limit the options of the project team in performing the project work.

Contingency reserve   A time or dollar amount allotted as a response to risk events that may occur within a project.

Contract   A legal, binding agreement, preferably written, between a buyer and seller detailing the requirements and obligations of both parties. Must include an offer, an acceptance, and a consideration.

Contract administration   The process of ensuring that the buyer and the seller both perform to the specifications within the contract.

Contract change control system   Defines the procedures for how contracts may be changed. Includes the paperwork, tracking, conditions, dispute resolution procedures, and the procedures for getting the changes approved within the performing organization.

Contract closeout   A process for confirming that the obligations of the contract were met as expected. The project manager, the customer, key stakeholder, and, in some instances, the seller complete the product verification together to confirm the contract has been completed.

Contract file   A complete indexed set of records of the procurement process incorporated into the administrative closure process. These records include financial information as well as information on the performance and acceptance of the procured work.

Control account plans   A control tool within the project that represents the integration of the project scope, the project schedule, and the budget. It allows management to measure the progress of a project.

Control charts   These illustrate the performance of a project over time. They map the results of inspections against a chart. Control charts are typically used in projects or operations that have repetitive activities such as manufacturing, test series, or help desk functions. Upper and lower control limits indicate if values are within control or out of control.

Controlling   The project is controlled and managed; the project manager controls the project scope and changes and monitors changes to the project budget, schedule, and scope by comparing plans to actual results and taking corrective action as necessary.

Core processes   These processes are common to all projects. The core processes are scope planning, scope definition, activity definition, resource planning, activity sequencing, activity duration estimation, cost estimating, risk management planning, schedule development, cost budgeting, and project plan development.

Cost baseline   This shows what the project is expected to spend. It's usually shown in an S-curve and allows the project manager and management to predict when the project will be spending monies and over what duration. The purpose of the cost baseline is to measure and predict project performance.

Cost budgeting   A process of assigning a cost to an individual work package. This process shows costs over time. The cost budget results in an S-Curve that becomes the cost baseline for the project.

Cost Change Control   This is part of the Integrated Change Control System and documents the procedures to request, approve, and incorporate changes to project costs.

Cost control   An active process to control causes of cost change, to document cost changes, and to monitor cost fluctuations within the project. When changes occur, the cost baseline must be updated.

Cost estimating   The process of calculating the costs, by category, of the identified resources to complete the project work.

Cost of conformance   The cost of completing the project work to satisfy the project scope and the expected level of quality. Examples include training, safety measures, and quality management activities.

Cost of nonconformance   The cost of completing the project work without meeting the quality standards. The biggest issue here is the money lost by having to redo the project work; it's always more cost-effective to do the work right the first time. Other nonconformance costs are loss of sales, loss of customers, downtime, and corrective actions to fix problems caused by the incorrect work.

Cost of quality   The cost of quality is the expense of all the activities within a project to meet quality objectives.

Cost Performance Index (CPI)   An index that measures how well the project is performing on cost: CPI=EV/AC.

Cost variance   The Cost Variance (CV) is the difference between the Earned Value(EV) and the Actual Costs (AC).

Cost-reimbursable contracts   A contract that pays the seller for the product. In the payment to the seller, there is a profit margin the difference between the actual costs of the product and the sales amount.

Critical Path Method (CPM)   The CPM is the most common approach to calculating when a project may finish. It uses a "forward" and "backward" path to reveal which activities are considered critical, and which contain float. If activities on the critical path are delayed, the project end date will be delayed.

Crashing   This is the addition of more resources to activities on the critical path in order to complete the project earlier. Crashing results in higher project costs.

Decision tree analysis   A type of analysis that determines which of two decisions is the best. The decision tree assists in calculating the value of the decision and determining which decision costs the least.

Decoder   This is a part of the communications model; it is the inverse of the encoder. If a message is encoded, a decoder translates it back to usable format.

Deliverable   The outcome of a project or project phase; a deliverable of a project can be a product or service.

Delphi technique   A method to query experts anonymously on foreseeable risks within the project, phase, or component of the project. The results of the survey are analyzed and organized and then circulated to the experts. There can be several rounds of anonymous discussions with the Delphi technique The goal is to gain consensus on project risks, and the anonymous nature of the process ensures that no one expert's advice overtly influences the opinion of another participant.

Design of experiments   This relies on statistical "what-if" scenarios to determine which variables within a project will result in the best outcome; it can also be used to eliminate a defect. The design of experiments approach is most often used on the product of the project, rather than the project itself

Direct costs   Costs incurred by the project in order for it to exist. Examples include equipment needed to complete the project work, salaries of the project team, and other expenses tied directly to the project's existence.

Discretionary dependencies   The preferred order of activities. Project managers should adhere to the order at their "discretion" and should document the logic behind the ordering. Discretionary dependencies have activities happen in a preferred order because of best practices, conditions unique to the project work, or external events. This is also known as soft logic.

Earned Value (EV)   The value of the work that has been completed and the budget for that work: EV=%Complete X BAC.

Earned value management   Earned value management integrates scope, schedule, and cost to give an objective, scalable point-in-time assessment of the project. EVM calculates the performance of the project and compares current performance against plan. EVM can also be a harbinger of things to come. Results early in the project can predict the likelihood of the project's success or failure.

Effective listening   The receiver is involved in the listening experience by paying attention to visual clues by the speaker and to paralingual intentions and by asking relevant questions.

Encoder   Part of the communications model; the device or technology that packages the message to travel over the medium.

Estimate at Completion (EAC)   A hypothesis of what the total cost of the project will be. Before the project begins, the project manager completes an estimate for the project deliverables based on the WBS. As the project progresses, there will likely be some variances between what the cost estimate was and what the actual cost is. The EAC is calculated to predict what the new estimate at completion will be.

Estimate to Complete (ETC)   Represents how much more money is needed to complete the project work: ETC=EAC-AC.

Estimating publications   Typically a commercial reference to help the project estimator confirm and predict the accuracy of estimates. If a project manager elects to use one of these commercial databases, the estimate should include a pointer to this document for future reference and verification.

Evaluation criteria   Used to rate and score proposals from sellers. In some instances, such as a bid or quote, the evaluation criterion is focused just on the price the seller offers. In other instances, such as a proposal, the evaluation criteria can be multiple values: experience, references, certifications, and more.

Executing   The project plans are carried out, or executed; the project manager coordinates people and other resources to complete the plan.

Expectancy theory   People will behave on the basis of what they expect as a result of their behavior. In other words, people will work in relation to the expected reward of the work.

Expert power   A type of power where the authority of the project manager comes from experience with the area that the project focuses on.

Facilitating processes   These processes support the project management core processes. They are done as needed throughout the project. The facilitating processes are quality planning, communications planning, organizational planning, staff acquisition, risk identification, qualitative risk analysis, quantitative risk analysis, risk response planning, procurement planning, and solicitation planning.

Fast Tracking   Doing activities in parallel that are normally done sequentially.

Feedback   A response, question for clarification, or other confirmation of having received a sent message.

Finish No Earlier Than (FNET)   This somewhat unusual constraint requires the activity to be in motion up until the predetermined date.

Finish No Later Than (FNLT)   This constraint requires the project or activity to finish by a predetermined date.

Finish-to-Finish   This relationship means Task A must complete before Task B can complete. Ideally, two tasks must finish at exactly the same time, but this is not always the case.

Finish-to-Start   This relationship means Task A must complete before Task B can begin. This is the most common relationship.

Fixed-price contracts   Fixed-Price Contracts are also known as Firm-Fixed-Price and Lump-Sum contracts. These contracts have a pre-set price that the vendor is obligated to perform the work or provide materials for the agreed price

Float   The amount of time a task can be delayed without delaying the project completion. Technically, there are three different types of float: *Free float* is the total time a single activity can be delayed without delaying the early start of any successor activities. *Total float* is the total time an activity can be delayed without delaying project completion. *Project float* is the total time the project can be delayed without passing the customer's expected completion date.

Flowchart   A chart that illustrates how the parts of a system occur in sequence.

Force majeure   A powerful and unexpected event, such as a hurricane or other disaster.

Forcing   A conflict resolution method where one person dominates or forces their point of view or solution to a conflict.

Forecasting   An educated estimate of how long the project will take to complete. Can also refer to how much the project may cost to complete.

Formal power   The type of power where the project manager has been assigned by senior management to be in charge of the project.

Fragnets (also called subnets)   Portions of a network diagram that branch off the project and are not on the critical path.

Free float   The total time a single activity can be delayed without delaying the early start of any successor activities.

Functional structure   An organizational structure that groups staff members according to their area of expertise (sales, marketing, construction, and so on). Functional structures require the project team members to report directly to the functional manager. In this type of structure, the project manager's authority and decision-making ability is less than the functional manager's.

Future value   A formula to calculate the future value of present money.

Graphical Evaluation and Review Technique (GERT)   Conditional advancement, branching, and looping of activities that is based on probabilistic estimates. Activities within GERT are dependent on the results of other upstream activities.

Hard logic   The logical relationship between activities based on the type of work. For example, the foundation of a house must be created before the frame of the house can be built. This is also known as mandatory dependency.

Herzberg's theory of motivation   Posits that there are two catalysts for workers: hygiene agents and motivating agents. Hygiene agents do nothing to motivate, but their absence de-motivates workers. Hygiene agents are the expectations all workers have: job security, paychecks clean and safe working conditions, a sense of belonging, civil working relationships, and other basic attributes associated with employment. Motivating agents are components such as reward, recognition, promotion, and other values that encourage individuals to succeed.

Historical information   Information the project may use from previous projects.

Indirect costs   Costs attributed to the cost of doing business. Examples include utilities, office space, and other overhead costs.

Influence diagram   An influence diagram charts out a decision problem. It identifies all of the elements, variables, decisions, and objectives and how each factor may influence another.

Initiating   This process group begins the project. The business needs are identified, and a product description is created. The project charter is written, and the project manager is selected.

Internal Rate of Return   The IRR is a complex formula to calculate when the present value of the cash inflow equals the original investment.

Interviewing   Interviewing subject matter experts and project stakeholders is an approach to identify risks on the current project based on the interviewees' experience.

Invitation for Bid   A document from the buyer to the seller. Requests the seller to provide a price for the procured product or service.

ISO 9000   An international standard that helps organizations follow their own quality procedures. ISO 9000 is not a quality system, but a method of following procedures created by an organization.

Kill point   The end of project phase where the project can be terminated on the basis of the experiences of the previous phase or the outcome of the project phase.

Lag   Positive time added to a task to move it away from the project start date; lag is adding time between activities.

Lead   Negative time added to a task to bring it closer to the project start date; lead is subtracting time between activities.

Lessons Learned   An ongoing documentation of things the project manager and project team have learned throughout the project. Lessons Learned are supplied to other project teams and project managers to apply to their ongoing projects. Lessons Learned are documented throughout the project, not just at the end of the project.

Letter of Intent   Expresses the intent of the buyer to procure products or services from the seller. Not the equivalent to a contract.

Make-or-buy analysis   Used in determining what part of the project scope to make and what part to purchase.

Management by projects   This approach characterizes organizations that manage their operations as projects. These project-centric entities could manage any level of their work as a project. These organizations apply general business skills to each project to determine their value, efficiency, and ultimately, return on investment.

Mandatory dependencies   This refers to the logical relationship between activities based on the type of work. For example, the foundation of a house must be created before the frame of the house can be built. This is also known as hard logic.

Maslow's hierarchy of needs   A theory that states that there are five layers of needs for all humans; physiological, safety, social, esteem, and the crowning jewel, self-actualization.

Matrix Structures   An organizational structure. There are three matrix structures: weak, balanced, and strong. The different structures are reflective of the project manager's authority in relation to the functional manager's authority.

McGregor's theory of X and Y   This theory states that "X" people are lazy, don't want to work, and need to be micromanaged. "Y" people are self-led, motivated, and strive to accomplish.

Medium   Part of the communications model; this is the path the message takes from the sender to the receiver. This is the modality in which the communication travels typically refers to an electronic model, such as e-mail or the telephone.

Mitigation   Reducing the probability or impact of a risk.

Monte Carlo Analysis   Predicts how scenarios may work out given any number of variables. The process doesn't actually create out a specific answer, but a range of possible answers. When Monte Carlo is applied to a schedule, it can present, for example, the optimistic completion date, the pessimistic completion date, and the most likely completion date for each activity in the project.

Net present value   NPV calculates the present value of monies returned on a project for each time period the project lasts.

Nonverbal communication   Approximately 55 percent of oral communication is non-verbal. Facial expressions, hand gestures, and body language contribute to the message.

Operational definitions   The quantifiable terms and values used to measure a process, activity, or work result. Operational definitions are also known as metrics.

Ouchi's Theory Z   This theory posits that workers are motivated by a sense of commitment, opportunity, and advancement. Workers will work if they are challenged and motivated.

Paralingual   The pitch, tone, and inflections in the sender's voice affect the message being sent.

Parametric modeling   A mathematical model based on known parameters to predict the cost of a project. The parameters in the model can vary based on the type of work being done. A parameter can be cost per cubic yard, cost per unit, and so on.

Pareto diagrams   A Pareto diagram is related to Pareto's Law: 80 percent of the problems come from 20 percent of the issues (this is also known as the "80/20 rule"). A Pareto diagram illustrates problems by assigned cause, from smallest to largest.

Planned Value (PV)   The worth of the work that should be completed by a specific time in the project schedule.

Planning   This process group is iterative. All planning throughout the project is handled within the planning process group.

PMBOK® Guide   Project Management Body of Knowledge, which includes all knowledge and practices within the endeavor of project management.

PMIS   Project management information system, which is typically a computer-program to assist in project management activities, recordkeeping, and forecasting.

Precedence Diagramming Method   The most common method of arranging the project work visually. The PDM puts the activities in boxes, called nodes, and connects the boxes with arrows. The arrows represent the relationship and the dependencies of the work packages.

Present value   A formula to calculate the present value of future money.

Problem solving   The ability to determine the best solution for a problem in a quick and efficient manner.

Process adjustments   When quality is lacking, process adjustments are needed for immediate corrective actions or for future preventive actions to ensure that quality improves. Process adjustments may qualify for a change request and be funneled through the Change Control System as part of integration management.

Process groups   The five process groups—initiating, planning, executing, controlling, and closing—comprise projects and project phases. These five process groups have sets of actions that move the project forward towards completion.

Procurement   The process of a seller soliciting, selecting, and paying for products or services from a buyer

Procurement audits   The successes and failures within the procurement process are reviewed from procurement planning through contract administration. The intent of the audit is to learn from what worked and what did not work during the procurement processes.

Procurement management plan   This subsidiary project plan documents the decisions made in the procurement planning processes. It specifies how the remaining procurement activities will be managed.

Product scope   The attributes and characteristics of the deliverables the project is creating.

Program Evaluation and Review Technique (PERT)   A scheduling tool that uses a weighted average formula to predict the length of activities and the project. Specifically, the PERT formula is (O+4ML+P)/6.

Programs   A collection of related projects working in alignment towards a common cause.

Progress reports   These provide current information on the project work completed to date.

Progressive elaboration   The process of providing or discovering greater levels of detail as the project moves toward completion.

Project   A temporary endeavor undertaken to create a unique product or service.

Project baselines   The accepted plans against which actual results are compared to identify variances.

Project calendar   A calendar that defines the working times for the project. For example, a project may require the project team to work nights and weekends so as not to disturb the ongoing operations of the organization during working hours. In addition, the project calendar accounts for holidays, working hours, and work shifts the project will cover.

Project charter   The charter authorizes the project, the project manager, and the required resources to complete the project work.

Project framework   The structure and fundamentals of project management. The project framework is composed of nine knowledge areas: project integration management, project scope management, project time management, project cost management, project quality management, project human resources management, project communications management, project risk management, project procurement management and five processes: initiating, planning, executing, controlling and close out.

Project integration management   The day-to-day actions of the project manager to ensure that all of the parts of the project work together. Composed of project plan development, project plan execution, and integrated change control.

Project life cycle   The duration of the project, composed of all the individual project phases within the project.

Project manager   The individual accountable for all aspects of a project.

Project phases   Projects are broken down into manageable sections. A project phase is the logical segmentation of the work to an identifiable point within the project. Phases can be viewed as completion of work to a specified date, the actual completion of work, or other milestone.

Project plan   The project plan is a collection of documents that is developed with the project team, stakeholders, and management. It is the guide to how the project should flow and how the project will be managed, and it reflects the values and priorities of and the conditions influencing the project.

Project portfolio management   A management process to select the projects that should be invested in. Specifically, it is the selection process based on the need, profitability, and affordability of the proposed projects.

Project scope   The work that has to be done in order to create the product. The project scope is concerned with the work—and only the required work—to complete the project.

Project scope management   Project scope management, according to the PMBOK, is "the processes to ensure that the project includes all of the work required, and only the work required, to complete the project successfully".

Project slack   The total time the project can be delayed without passing the customer's expected completion date.

Projectized structure   An organizational structure where the project manager has the greatest amount of authority. The project team is assigned to the project on a full-time basis. When the project is complete, the project team members move on to other assignments within the organization.

Proposal   A document from the seller to the buyer, responding to a Request for Proposal or other procurement documents.

Qualified seller list   The performing organization may have lists of qualified sellers, preferred sellers, or approved sellers. The qualified sellers list generally has contact information, history of past experience with the seller, and other pertinent information.

Qualitative risk analysis   An examination and prioritization of the risks based on their probability of occurring and the impact on the project if they do occur. Qualitative risk analysis guides the risk reaction process.

Quality Assurance   Overall performance is evaluated to ensure the project meets the relevant quality standards.

Quality audits   A quality audit is a process to confirm that the quality processes are performing correctly on the current project. The quality audit determines how to make things better for the project and other projects within the organization. Quality audits measure the project's ability to maintain the expected level of quality.

Quality Control   A process in which the work results are monitored to see if they meet relevant quality standards.

Quality Management Plan   This document describes how the project manager and the project team will fulfill the quality policy. In an ISO 9000 environment, the Quality Management Plan is referred to as the "project quality system."

Quality policy   The formal policy an organization follows to achieve a preset standard of quality. The quality policy of the organization may follow a formal approach, such as ISO 9000, Six Sigma, or Total Quality Management (TQM), or it may have its own direction and approach. The project team should either adapt the quality policy of the organization to guide the project implementation or create its own policy if one does not exist within the performing organization.

Quantitative estimating   Estimating on the basis of mathematical formulas to predict how long an activity will take or how much it will cost, using the quantities, units, or other metric of work to be completed.

Quantitative risk analysis   A numerical assessment of the probability and impact of the identified risks. Quantitative risk analysis also creates an overall risk score for the project.

Quote (or quotation)   A document from the seller to the buyer; used when price is the determining factor in the decision-making process.

Receiver   Part of the communications model: the recipient of the message.

Referent power   Power that is present when the project team is attracted to, or wants to work on the project or with, the project manager. Referent power also exists when the project manager references another, more powerful person, such as the CEO.

Request for Proposal   A document from the buyer to the seller that asks the seller to provide a proposal for completing the procured work or for providing the procured product.

Request for Quote   A document from the buyer to the seller asking the seller to provide a price for the procured product or service.

Residual risks   Risks that are left over after mitigation, transference, and avoidance. These are generally accepted risks. Management may elect to add contingency costs and time to account for the residual risks within the project.

Resource calendar   The resource calendar shows when resources, such as project team members, consultants, and SMEs, are available to work on the project. It takes into account vacations, other commitments within the organization, restrictions on contracted work, overtime issues, and so on.

Resource histogram   A bar chart reflecting when individual employees, groups, or communities are involved in a project. Often used by management to see when employees are most or least active in a project.

Resource leveling heuristics   A method to flatten the schedule when resources are over-allocated or allocated unevenly. Resource leveling can be applied in different methods to accomplish different goals. One of the most common methods is to ensure that workers are not overextended on activities.

Responsibility   Who decides what in a project.

Return on Investment (ROI)   The project's financial return in proportion to the amount of monies invested in the project.

Reward power   The project manager's authority to reward the project team.

Risk   An unplanned event that can have a positive or negative influence on the project success.

Risk categories   These help organize, rank, and isolate risks within the project.

Risk database   A database of recognized risks; the planned response and the outcome of the risk should be documented and recorded in an organization-wide risk database. The risk database can serve other project managers as historical information. Over time, the risk database can become a Risk Lessons Learned program.

Risk management plan   A subsidiary project plan for determining: how risks will be identified, how quantitative and qualitative analysis will be completed, how risk response planning will happen, how risks will be monitored, and how ongoing risk management activities will occur through the project lifecycle.

Risk owners   The individuals or groups responsible for a risk response.

Role   Who does what in a project.

Scales of probability and impact   Each risk is assessed according to its likelihood and its impact. There are two approaches to ranking risks: Cardinal scales identify the probability and impact by a numerical value, ranging from .01 as very low to 1.0 as certain. Ordinal scales identify and rank the risks descriptively as very high to very unlikely.

Schedule control   Part of Integrated Change Management, schedule control is concerned with three processes: the project manager confirms that any schedule changes are agreed upon; the project manager examines the work results, conditions, and conditions to know if the schedule has changed; and the project manager manages the actual change in the schedule.

Schedule Management Plan   A subsidiary plan of the overall project plan. It is used to control changes to the schedule. A formal Schedule Management Plan has procedures that control how changes to the project plan can be proposed, accounted for, and then implemented.

Schedule Performance Index (SPI)   This reveals the efficiency of work. The closer the quotient is to 1, the better: SPI=EV/PV

Schedule variance   The difference between the planned work and the earned work.

Scope statement   A document that describes the work, and only the required work, to meet the project objectives. The scope statement establishes a common vision among the project stakeholders to establish the point and purpose of the project work. It is used as a baseline against which all future project decisions are made to determine if proposed changes or work-results are aligned with expectations.

Scope verification   The process of the project customer accepting the project deliverables. Scope verification happens at the end of each project phase and at the end of the project. Scope verification is the process of ensuring the deliverables the project creates are in alignment with the project scope.

Scoring models (also called weighted scoring models)   These models use a common set of values for all of the projects up for selection. Each value has a weight assigned values of high importance have a high weight, while values of lesser importance have a lesser weight. The projects are measured against these values and assigned scores according to how well they match the predefined values. The projects with high scores take priority over projects will lesser scores.

Secondary risks   Risks that stem from risk responses. For example, the response of transference may call for hiring a third party to management an identified risk. A secondary risk caused by the solution is the failure of the third party to complete its assignment as scheduled. Secondary risks must be identified, analyzed, and planned for just as any identified risk.

Sender   Part of the communications model: the person or group delivering the message to the receiver.

Sensitivity analysis   This examines each project risk on its own merit to assess the impact on the project. All other risks in the project are set at a baseline value.

"Should cost" estimates (also known as independent estimates)
These estimates are created by the performing organization to predict what the cost of the procured product should be. If there is a significant difference between what the organization has predicted and what the sellers have proposed, either the Statement of Work was inadequate or the sellers have misunderstood the requirements.

Simulation   This allow the project team to play "what-if" games without affecting any areas of production.

Single source   A specific seller that the performing organization prefers to contract with.

Smoothing   A conflict resolution method that "smoothes" out the conflict by minimizing the perceived size of the problem. It is a temporary solution, but it can calm team relations and reduce boisterousness of discussions. Smoothing may be acceptable when time is of the essence or any of the proposed solutions would work.

Soft logic (also known as discretionary dependency)   The preferred order of activities. Project managers should use these relationships at their "discretion" and document the logic behind making soft logic decisions. Discretionary dependencies allow activities to happen in a preferred order because of best practices, conditions unique to the project work, or external events.

Sole source   The only qualified seller that exists in the marketplace.

Staffing management plan   This subsidiary plan documents how project team members will be brought onto the project and excused from the project.

Stakeholders   The individuals, groups, and communities that have a vested interest in the outcome of a project. Examples include the project manager, the project team, the project sponsor, customers, clients, vendors, and communities.

Start No Earlier Than (SNET)   This constraint requires that the project or activity not start earlier than the predetermined date.

Start No Later Than (SNLT)   This constraint requires that the activity begin by a predetermined date.

Start-to-Finish   This relationship requires that Task A start so that Task B may finish; it is unusual and is rarely used.

Start-to-Start   This relationship means Task A must start before Task B can start. This relationship allows both activities to happen in tandem.

Statement of Work (SOW)   This fully describes the work to be completed, the product to be supplied, or both. The SOW becomes part of the contract between the buyer and the seller. The SOW is typically created as part of the procurement planning process and is used by the seller to determine whether it can meet the project's requirements.

Statistical sampling   A process of choosing a percentage of results at random for inspection. Statistical sampling can reduce the costs of quality control.

Status reports   These provide current information on the project cost, budget, scope, and other relevant information.

Status review meetings   Regularly scheduled meetings to record the status of the project work. These commonly employed meetings provide a formal avenue for the project manager to query the team on the status of its work, record delays and slippage, and to forecast what work is about to begin.

Subnets (also called fragnets)   Portions of a network diagram that branch off the project and are not on the critical path.

Subproject   A subproject exists under a parent project but follows its own schedule to completion. Subprojects may be outsourced, assigned to other project managers, or managed by the parent project manager but with a different project team.

Supporting detail   Any information that support decisions, including logic employed and rationales, and the project plan as a whole. Supporting detail can include books, articles, web sites, vendor information, results of testing, historical information, and many others information sources.

System or process flowcharts   These show the relation between components and how the overall process works. They are useful for identifying risks between system components.

Time value of money   An economic model to predict what the future fiscal value may be based on current fiscal value. The time value of money can also reverse-engineer what predicted monies are worth in today's value.

Time-and-Materials   A contract type where the seller charges the buyer for the time and the materials for the work completed. T&M contracts should have a not-to-exceed clause (NTE) to contain costs.

Total slack   The total time an activity can be delayed without delaying project completion.

Top-down estimating   A technique that bases the current project's estimate on the total of a similar project. A percentage of the similar project's total cost may be added to or subtracted from the total, depending on the size of the current project.

Transference   A response to risks in which the responsibility and ownership of the risk is transferred to another party (for example, through insurance).

Trend analysis   Trend analysis is taking past results to predict future performance.

Triggers   Warning signs or symptoms that a risk has occurred or is about to occur (for example, a vendor failing to complete its portion of the project as scheduled).

Utility function   A person's willingness to accept risk.

Value added change   A change that positively impacts either the scope, schedule, or cost of a project without adversely impacting the other two aspects.

Variance   The difference between what was planned and what was experienced; typically used for costs and schedules.

Variance at Completion   The difference between the BAC and the EAC; its formula is VAC= BAC–EAC

War room   A centralized office or locale for the project manager and the project team to work on the project. It can house information on the project, including documentation and support materials. It allows the project team to work in close proximity.

Withdrawal   A conflict resolution method that is used when the issue is not important or the project manager is out-ranked. The project manager pushes the issue aside for later resolution. It can also be used as a method for cooling down. The conflict is not resolved, and it is considered a yield-lose solution.

Work Authorization System   A tool that can control the organization, sequence, and official authorization to begin a piece of the project work.

Work Breakdown Structure (WBS)   The WBS is a deliverable-orientated collection of project components. Work that isn't in the WBS isn't in the project. The point of the WBS is to organize and define the project scope.

Work Breakdown Structure dictionary   A reference tool to explain the WBS components, the nature of the work package, the assigned resources, and the time and billing estimates for each element.

Work Breakdown Structure template   A master WBS that is used in organizations as a starting point in defining the work for a particular project. This approach is recommended, as most projects in an organization are similar in the project lifecycles and the approach can be adapted to fit a given project.

Workarounds   Workarounds are unplanned responses to risks that were not identified or were accepted.

INDEX

E

F

G

INTERNATIONAL CONTACT INFORMATION

AUSTRALIA
McGraw-Hill Book Company
Australia Pty. Ltd.
TEL +61-2-9900-1800
FAX +61-2-9878-8881
http://www.mcgraw-hill.com.au
books-it_sydney@mcgraw-hill.com

CANADA
McGraw-Hill Ryerson Ltd.
TEL +905-430-5000
FAX +905-430-5020
http://www.mcgraw-hill.ca

**GREECE, MIDDLE EAST, & AFRICA
(Excluding South Africa)**
McGraw-Hill Hellas
TEL +30-210-6560-990
TEL +30-210-6560-993
TEL +30-210-6560-994
FAX +30-210-6545-525

MEXICO (Also serving Latin America)
McGraw-Hill Interamericana Editores
S.A. de C.V.
TEL +525-1500-5108
FAX +525-117-1589
http://www.mcgraw-hill.com.mx
carlos_ruiz@mcgraw-hill.com

SINGAPORE (Serving Asia)
McGraw-Hill Book Company
TEL +65-6863-1580
FAX +65-6862-3354
http://www.mcgraw-hill.com.sg
mghasia@mcgraw-hill.com

SOUTH AFRICA
McGraw-Hill South Africa
TEL +27-11-622-7512
FAX +27-11-622-9045
robyn_swanepoel@mcgraw-hill.com

SPAIN
McGraw-Hill/
Interamericana de España, S.A.U.
TEL +34-91-180-3000
FAX +34-91-372-8513
http://www.mcgraw-hill.es
professional@mcgraw-hill.es

**UNITED KINGDOM, NORTHERN,
EASTERN, & CENTRAL EUROPE**
McGraw-Hill Education Europe
TEL +44-1-628-502500
FAX +44-1-628-770224
http://www.mcgraw-hill.co.uk
emea_queries@mcgraw-hill.com

ALL OTHER INQUIRIES Contact:
McGraw-Hill/Osborne
TEL +1-510-420-7700
FAX +1-510-420-7703
http://www.osborne.com
omg_international@mcgraw-hill.com

Sound Off!

Visit us at **www.osborne.com/bookregistration** and let us know what you thought of this book. While you're online you'll have the opportunity to register for newsletters and special offers from McGraw-Hill/Osborne.

We want to hear from you!

Sneak Peek

Visit us today at **www.betabooks.com** and see what's coming from McGraw-Hill/Osborne tomorrow!

Based on the successful software paradigm, Bet@Books™ allows computing professionals to view partial and sometimes complete text versions of selected titles online. Bet@Books™ viewing is free, invites comments and feedback, and allows you to "test drive" books in progress on the subjects that interest you the most.